Beyond the Limits of Thought

Full autumn moon—
on the straw mat,
pine shadow.

KIKAKU (1661–1707)

Beyond the Limits of Thought

GRAHAM PRIEST

CLARENDON PRESS · OXFORD

OXFORD

UNIVERSITY PRESS

Great Clarendon Street, Oxford OX2 6DP

Oxford University Press is a department of the University of Oxford.
It furthers the University's objective of excellence in research, scholarship,
and education by publishing worldwide in

Oxford   New York

Auckland Bangkok Buenos Aires Cape Town Chennai
Dar es Salaam Delhi Hong Kong Istanbul Karachi Kolkata
Kuala Lumpur Madrid Melbourne Mexico City Mumbai Nairobi
São Paulo Shanghai Taipei Tokyo Toronto

Oxford is a registered trade mark of Oxford University Press
in the UK and in certain other countries

Published in the United States
By Oxford University Press Inc., New York

First edition published by Cambridge University Press 1995
First published by Oxford University Press 2002

British Library Cataloguing in Publication Data
Data available

Library of Congress Cataloging in Publication Data
Data available

ISBN 0-19-925405-2
ISBN 0-19-924421-9 (Pbk.)

10 9 8 7 6 5 4 3 2 1

Typeset by Keyword Typesetting Services Ltd,
Printed in Great Britain by
T.J. International Ltd.,
Padstow, Cornwall

空手道精神に捧げる

Karatedo seishin ni sasageru

Archytas, according to Euthydemus, put the question in this way: if I came to be at the edge, for example at the heaven of the fixed stars, could I stretch my hand or my stick outside, or not? That I should not stretch it out would be absurd, but if I do stretch it out, what is outside will be either body or place – (it will make no difference as we shall discover). Thus, Archytas will always go on in the same way to the fresh chosen limit, and will ask the same question. If it is always something different into which the stick is stretched, it will clearly be something infinite.

Simplicius, *Physics*

Woodcut of a fantastic depiction of the solar system, German School, 17th century.
Photo: Bridgeman Art Library/Private collection

Contents

Preface to the First Edition

This book had its origin in a series of seminars on the limits of thought at the University of Western Australia in 1988, given by Uwe Petersen and myself. For some years Uwe and I had been arguing the relative merits of Kant and Hegel, and we had both observed striking similarities between Kant's Antinomies and the paradoxes of self-reference. These themes were explored in the seminars. The result of the discussions was my paper 'The Limit of Thought – and Beyond' (*Mind* 100 (1991), 361–70). The present book is essentially a much expanded form of that paper.

In the next couple of years I realised that the issues involved have a much larger import than at first I had realised, indeed, that they stretch through the whole history of Western Philosophy. In 1990 I had a year's leave, and spent it investigating these matters and drafting the book. I am greatly indebted to Cambridge University for providing a most congenial and stimulating context for the research. I would like to thank Clare Hall for providing me with a Visiting Fellowship for the year; and I would particularly like to thank the Sub-Faculty of Philosophy, who not only provided me with ideal working conditions (a room in the Moral Sciences Library, somewhere to make tea, and office staff who were always friendly and helpful well beyond the call of duty), but also allowed me the opportunity of airing some of the material in a series of lectures in Michaelmas term. Many parts of the book have been served up to unsuspecting philosophers at numerous other universities in Britain, Australia, and North America.

Every philosopher is indebted to colleagues for help and criticism. In writing this book I am particularly so. I do not pretend to be an historian of philosophy, and on many occasions I have been grateful to colleagues for helping me understand historical material and preventing me from making blunders. I hope that those I have forgotten will forgive me if I list those whom I have not: James Allen, Myles Burnyeat, Stewart Candlish, Edward Craig, Jan Crosthwaite, Nick Denyer, Lawrence Goldstein, John Frow, Kevin Hart, Mark Lance, David Lewis, Uwe Petersen, Mark Sainsbury. I am also indebted to my colleagues in the Department of Philosophy at the University of Queensland, particularly Roger Lamb and Greg Restall, for many helpful discussions. To another of these, André Gallois, I owe a particular debt. On many occasions I have benefited from his unique ability to navigate his way through a philosophical thicket. Detailed comments on earlier drafts of the manuscript were given to me by Keith Hossack, Donald Baxter, and an anonymous reader. I have benefited greatly from these, and am very grateful for them. If I have still managed to get things wrong, it is no fault of the above.

Some parts of the book appear in print elsewhere. Part of chapter 4 occurs in 'Some Priorities of Berkeley', B. J. Copeland (ed.), *Logic and Reality: essays in pure and applied logic in memory of Arthur Prior*, Oxford University Press, 1994. Parts of chapters 9, 10, and 11 occur in 'The Structure of the Paradoxes of Self-Reference', *Mind* 103 (1994), 25–34. And part of chapter 14 occurs in 'Derrida and the Paradoxes of Self-Reference', *Australasian Journal of Philosophy* 72 (1994), 103–11. I am grateful to Jack Copeland, the editors of *Mind* and the *Australasian Journal of Philosophy*, and to Oxford University Press and the Australasian Association of Philosophy for permission to reprint. Last, but by no means least, I want to thank all the staff at Cambridge University Press who have been involved with the book. I have frequently benefited from their friendly and professional expertise.

Preface to the Second Edition

The first edition of *Beyond the Limits of Thought* was published in 1995, and has now been out of print for a couple of years. I am delighted to have the opportunity of bringing out a second edition. I would like to thank all the people who expressed their regret that the book was out of print. Most particularly, I would like to thank Peter Momtchiloff and Oxford University Press for taking on the second edition.

As I read through the first edition in preparing the second, I was surprised (and a little alarmed!) to see that there was virtually nothing in it that I wished to take back (though there are certainly places where I would that I had expressed myself a little differently). This has allowed the reproduction of the first edition pretty much intact. The only changes are typos and the odd factual mistake. I'm grateful to J. C. Beall and James Chase for finding many of the typos.

My ideas on the subject of the book have not ceased to develop, however. To reflect this, three new chapters have been appended to this edition. The first two are chapters which explore the limits phenomenon in significant philosophers not considered in the first edition, Heidegger and Nāgārjuna. Both chapters have been published (or at least accepted for publication) as papers elsewhere. The first appears in R. Gaskin (ed.), *Grammar in Early Twentieth Century Philosophy* (London: Routledge, 2001). The second, which was written jointly with Jay Garfield, is to appear in *Philosophy East and West*. I am grateful to Jay, Richard Gaskin, Routledge, and the Editor of *Philosophy East and West* for permission to republish. Jay I would like to thank especially, not only for teaching me so much about Indian philosophy, but also for his warmth and friendship since I met him only a few years ago. I have edited both papers slightly to make cross-references appropriate for the new context; but I have not changed anything else. Since the papers were written as stand-alone pieces, their inclusion here involves a little repetition; but not much. And sometimes it can even be useful to say the same thing in a different way.

The third additional chapter in this edition is completely new, and contains some thoughts that further extend the topic. Most of these are occasioned by reviews, critical notices, and discussion notes. There are many of these. Those of which I am aware of are: Bacon (1996), da Costa and Bueno (1996), Dale (1996), Dümont and Mau (1997), Grattan-Guinness (1998), Grim (1998), Kroon (2001), Marconi (1997), Mendelson (1997), Moore (1995), Restall

(1996), Smith (2000), Tennant (1998), Weir (1999), Williamson (1996), and Zalta (forthcoming). I would like to thank all these people for the thought and care that they have put into their reviews, and for the many kind remarks that they made about the book. I think that I failed to persuade a single one of them about the central claims of the book; still, I am not persuaded by many of their criticisms. I would be obsessive to comment on each review in detail, but the chapter takes up some of the more important points that they made. The chapter incorporates material from Priest (1998b) and (2000b). I am grateful to the Editor of *Mind* and to Oxford University Press for permission to reuse this material.

There were two things that I wanted to put in the first edition, but which it was not possible to put there. The first is a frontispiece. I am delighted that it has been possible to include it in this edition.

The second was a paragraph in the Preface, which was cut by Cambridge University Press, and which read as follows:

It is normal and correct for authors to thank those who have helped in the production of a work. It is not common for them to comment on hindrances; however, I want to do this. In the last five years the Australian Government's funding policy for universities and their research has been, in my opinion, little short of disastrous, especially in the humanities. Teaching and administrative loads have increased by an unprecedented factor. Not only have students suffered because of this, and library resources been cut back to a quite inadequate level, but those who have been unable to 'buy back' time in the form of research grants have had to squeeze their research into less and less time. Who pays the piper calls the tune: the majority of such money goes to people whose work is likely to produce short-term economic benefits, or something else on the Government's political agenda. (Naturally, philosophical projects are rarely of this kind.) This policy is not only short-sighted – since 'productive' research is ultimately dependent on more abstract research – it is oblivious to the fundamental human value of intellectual inquiry. While those of us who are aware of the situation remain silent, matters are unlikely to change.

I wish that I could say that the situation has changed for the better since 1995. Unfortunately, the reverse is the case. The petty agendas of the present Government have made matters several times worse. Fundamental damage is being done to the teaching and research of the humanities and the pure sciences in Australia. If government policies are not changed soon, the damage, in particular, to Australian philosophy will be virtually impossible to reverse.

I hope that if *Beyond the Limits of Thought* ever reaches a third edition, I will be able to say happier things about these matters.

Introduction

The way that can be spoken of is not the real way.

Lao Tzu, *Tao Te Ching*

Beyond the limit

1   The limits of thought

Finitude is a basic fact of human existence. Whether one treats this as a source of sorrow or of relief, it is without doubt that there are limits to whatever people want to do, be they limits of human endurance, resources, or of life itself. What these limits are, we can sometimes only speculate; but that they are there, we know. For example, we can only guess what the limit time for running a mile is; but we know that there is a limit, set by the velocity of light, if not by many more mundane things.

This book is about a certain kind of limit; not the limits of physical endeavours like running a mile, but the limits of the mind. I will call them limits of thought, though 'thought', here, should be understood in its objective, Fregean, sense, as concerning the contents of our intensional states, not our subjective consciousness.[1] One might also describe them as conceptual limits, since they concern the limits of our concepts. Whatever one calls them, by the end of the book I will have given a precise structural characterisation of the limits in question, in the shape of the Inclosure Schema. For the present, some examples will suffice to indicate what I have in mind: the limit of what can be expressed; the limit of what can be described or conceived; the limit of what can be known; the limit of iteration of some operation or other, the infinite in its mathematical sense.

Limits of this kind provide boundaries beyond which certain conceptual processes (describing, knowing, iterating, etc.) cannot go; a sort of conceptual *ne plus ultra*. The thesis of the book is that such limits are dialetheic; that is, that they are the subject, or locus, of true contradictions. The contradiction, in each case, is simply to the effect that the conceptual processes in question *do* cross these boundaries. Thus, the limits of thought are boundaries which cannot be crossed, but yet which are crossed.

In each of the cases, there is a totality (of all things expressible, describable, etc.) and an appropriate operation that generates an object that is both

---

[1] Peter Slezak has suggested to me that there may be an important connection between the phenomena that will concern us and subjective consciousness too. See Slezak (1983).

within and without the totality. I will call these situations *Closure* and *Transcendence*, respectively. In general, the arguments both for Closure and for Transcendence use some form of self-reference, a method that is both venerable and powerful.[2] Closure is usually established by reflecting on the conceptual practice in question. In a polemical context this can appear as an *ad hominem* argument. Arguments for Transcendence are of more varied kinds; often they involve applying a theory to itself. Some of them are more technical; a paradigm of these is diagonalisation, a technique familiar from the logical paradoxes. This construction is precisely a boundary-tearing heuristic which, given any boundary of a suitable kind, can be applied to violate it.

2   Dialetheism

That a contradiction might be true, or that dialetheism (the view that there are true contradictions) makes sense, may still be abhorrent, and even threatening, to many contemporary English-speaking philosophers. More likely than not, even the suggestion of it will be met with a look of blank incomprehension. How could a contradiction be true? After all, orthodox logic assures us that for every statement, α, only *one* of α and $\neg\alpha$ is true. The simple answer is that orthodox logic, however well entrenched, is just a *theory* of how logical particles, like negation, work; and there is no a priori guarantee that it is correct.[3]

Given two states of affairs, there are, in general, four possibilities: one but not the other holds, vice versa, both or neither. In particular, given the states of affairs α is *true* and α is *false*, there are, without begging any questions, those four possibilities. The standard logical theory just *assumes* that only two of them should be allowed for. Slightly more liberal views allow that a third may arise, the *neither* case. If nothing else, symmetry suggests that the fourth should be countenanced. Suppose, then, that we allow sentences to take as semantic values one of the corresponding four *subsets* of the set $\{true, false\}$. How do the truth (and falsity) conditions for, for example, negation and conjunction now work? Exactly as you would expect. $\neg\alpha$ is true iff α is false, and vice versa. Similarly, $\alpha \wedge \beta$ is true iff both conjuncts are true, and false if at least one conjunct is false. In parti-

---

[2] Arguably, it is more than that: it characterises philosophy itself. See Priest (1991a).

[3] Thus, when Quine ((1970), p. 81) complains that someone who maintains that a contradiction might be true just does not know what they are talking about, this is exactly analogous to a Newtonian physicist complaining that someone who holds that time might run at different rates in different frames of reference just does not know what they are talking about. For further discussion, see Priest (1987), ch. 14.

cular, if α is both true and false, so is $\neg\alpha$, and so is $\alpha \wedge \neg\alpha$. Hence, a contradiction can be true (if false as well).[4]

Since a logical theory of this kind is so easy to construct, it is worth asking *why* dialetheism should be so outrageous to the sensibility of modern philosophers. The answer is, I am afraid, sociological rather than rational. Until Aristotle, the idea that a contradiction might be true was a highly contested one.[5] Aristotle went to great lengths to argue against the idea in book 4 of the *Metaphysics*.[6] Because of Aristotle's magisterial authority in the Middle Ages, the subject became closed; and, unlike most other subjects on which Aristotle pronounced, was not substantially reopened subsequently – at least until recently. Few philosophers (with the notable exception of Hegel and some of his intellectual descendants) challenged Aristotle. And I know of no historical defence of the law of non-contradiction since Aristotle worth mentioning. Is this because Aristotle's arguments were conclusive? Hardly. Arguably, they do not work at all. But even if they were ultimately correct, they could not close debate on the issue: his major argument is so tortured that it is hard to tell what it is, and the others are little more than throw-away remarks.[7]

So what other arguments are there? Apart from an appeal to the received logical theory, which we have already seen simply to beg the question, the most common is that a contradiction cannot be true since contradictions entail everything, and not everything is true. This argument is no better than an appeal to the received semantics. Granted, not everything is true; but on the alternative semantics sketched above, as should be clear, the argument from $\alpha \wedge \neg\alpha$ to an arbitrary β need not preserve truth, and so is not valid.[8] More subtle arguments are to the effect that some crucial notion or other, for example, truth, validity, or rationality, requires consistency. I shall not take up these issues here. All that it is necessary to note is that these arguments, whatever they are, are neither obvious nor obviously correct. It is thus foolish to close one's mind to the possibility of dialetheism.

I certainly do not intend to imply that these arguments should not be discussed: they raise profound issues at the very heart of logic. I have discussed them in *In Contradiction* (1987), which contains a defence of dialethe-

---

[4] Semantics of this kind can easily be made rigorous. Details can be found in section 1 of the technical appendix to Part 3 of the book. There, I ignore the *neither* case, for reasons given in Priest (1987), 4.7.

[5] See, for example, Dancy (1975), ch. 3.

[6] In the same book, he argues against the possibility of a statement being neither true nor false, though in other places, for example, ch. 9 of *De Interpretatione*, he appears to show a good deal more sympathy with that idea.

[7] The arguments are described, analysed and rejected in Łukasiewicz (1971) and Dancy (1975).

[8] Similarly, the form of inference usually called the disjunctive syllogism (α, $\neg\alpha \vee \beta \vdash \beta$) is invalid. Let α be both true and false, and β just plain false. Then the premises of the syllogism are true (since a disjunction is true iff one disjunct is) but the conclusion is not.

ism, and to which I would refer readers for further details. In a sense, *In Contradiction* starts where Part 3 of this book leaves off: with dialetheism and the paradoxes of self-reference. Perhaps more importantly, the current investigations are an application of the main thesis of that book to one particular area, a more detailed investigation of one region of the transconsistent.

3   The history of limits

The relationship between the limits of thought and contradiction might be described as a vein that runs prominently through the history of Western philosophy – except that it is more like a major artery.[9] I have therefore chosen to structure this book as a series of case-studies on aspects of the thought of various historical philosophers.[10] If a philosopher does not appear in these pages I certainly do not intend to imply that the limits of thought do not play some role in their work. Historians of ideas soon learn – to their dismay – that their subject appears to be mathematically dense: between any two people who wrote on the matter there appears to be another. Thus, some selection must be made. I have chosen those philosophers who have made contributions to the matter, in the form of interesting ideas and arguments. Whether this interest is objective or merely subjective, I leave the reader to judge.

Although the material in the book is heavily historical, the book is not primarily an historical one. My interest throughout is in the substantial thesis concerning the dialetheic nature of limits of thought; the historical material is a vehicle for this. For this reason, and because I do not want the wood to be missed for the trees, I have not attempted discussions that an historian of philosophy might consider balanced. If I have tipped the scales in my favour, I ask that this be forgiven in the context. The fact that all of the interpretations fit neatly into a grander scheme says something in favour of each; and I hope that my interpretations of some of the philosophers involved are interesting in their own right.

4   The structure of the book

In Part 1 of the book, we will look at a number of pre-Kantian philosophers in whose work the limits of thought figure. Contradiction appears at various places in these works, though often below the surface. These philosophers

---

[9] I suspect that the same is true of Eastern philosophy too, though my knowledge of this is very limited.

[10] This requires a good deal of quoting. All italics in quotations are original unless otherwise specified. In accordance with Cambridge University Press house style, any ellipses at the beginning or end of a quotation have been omitted.

had intimations of the contradictory nature of the limits, and lay the ground for those who came later. Part 2 looks at the classic texts of Kant and Hegel. Between them, these two writers provide the first clean recognition (though in Kant's case, a rather grudging one) and theorisation of the situation. Their understanding was of an informal kind, however. A formal articulation of the structure involved was realised in subsequent discussions of the paradoxes of self-reference. Part 3 turns to this. In it, we will obtain a precise formal articulation of the phenomenon that concerns us. In Part 4 we turn to the philosophy of language. Many of the traditional problems of philosophy have found their modern formulations as problems about language; the one with which we are concerned is no different. In this part of the book, we will look at the realisation of the phenomenon in that area.

As will be evident, the case-studies we will cover in the book appear roughly in chronological order. One important thing that we will see as we go along is the emergence of a notable historical pattern. This may not be obvious in the initial parts of the book: it may appear that I am dealing with a number of disparate and unconnected phenomena. But, like the events in a detective story, they will all fall into place by the end. If the material strikes the reader as lacking unity at the start, I would just ask for a little patience.

It should be said straight away that most of the philosophers I discuss in the book would not have seen their work in terms of the pattern I have painted. Indeed, the thought that a contradiction might be true would have been anathema to most of them. However, a fuller understanding of philosophies, like that of people, can often be obtained in the light of what has been repressed. This is why an examination of the pertinent aspects of the work of these philosophers in the context of a self-conscious dialetheism is, I think, illuminating.

The most notable exception to the historical repression of contradiction is Hegel. He, above all philosophers, understood the dialetheic nature of the limits of thought, though his frustratingly obscure literary style may well cloak this fact from the casual reader (if any reader of Hegel could be described as casual). The chapter on Hegel is therefore the lynch-pin of the book. Like the vertex of a light cone, it focuses all the rays of thought that come before, as well as all those that come after.

5 . . . and the role of logic in it

Throughout the book I make use of the language of modern logic where this is appropriate. In the third part of the book, this is entirely unavoidable. Despite this, I hope that the book – or its main import, anyway – will be intelligible to people who know little logic. A first course should suffice. Even in the third part of the book I have tried to explain technical notions in such a way that they are intelligible to readers who are not logicians, provided only that they are prepared to take the material slowly. And the detailed arguments in this part of the book can usually be skipped without doing too much damage to the reader's understanding of the main points.

The logical notation I use throughout is entirely standard (or one of the standard ones[11]). Any non-standard notation is explained where it is introduced (though non-logicians might like to note that 'iff' is an abbreviation for 'if and only if'). A word should be said about the conditional, $\rightarrow$, however. I intend the issues in this book to be independent of theories of conditionality, in as far as this is possible. Hence I shall use the arrow as a generic conditional. Where the argument turns on some quite specific feature of the conditional, I shall usually comment on this fact.

The book, then, is a blend of logic and the history of philosophy. If it be an unusual blend, I trust it may still be a fruitful one. I hope that it gives all who read it a little of the pleasure it has given me to write it. Naturally, I would like to persuade the reader both that the limits of thought are dialetheic and that the application of this thesis illuminates the history of certain central aspects of philosophy. But even if the book does not do this, I hope that it will at least cause the reader to transcend the limits of their own thoughts, forcing them to go where no thought (or anyway, no thought of theirs) has gone before.

[11] Specifically, it is that of (for example) Bell and Machover (1977), sections 4, 5.

Part 1

The limits of thought in pre-Kantian philosophy

It would, I think, be enough to destroy any ... positive idea of the infinite to ask him that has it, whether he could add to it or no.

John Locke, *An Essay Concerning Human Understanding*

1 The limits of expression

Introduction

Four limits of thought in particular will concern us in the book: the limits of the expressible, the limits of the iterable (the mathematical infinite), the limits of cognition, and the limits of conception. There is, as we shall see in due course, a close connection between these things. However, no one before Kant perceived this clearly. In the first part of the book we will look at ways that these various limits arose in pre-Kantian philosophy. This will involve us in looking at a number of topics that may appear, initially, to have little to do with each other. As I said in the Introduction of the book, if this is so, patience will, I hope, be rewarded.

The first limit we will be concerned with here is the limit of the expressible, which is, perhaps, the most fundamental of the limits that will occupy us in the book. One might suppose, for a number of reasons, that features of the (non-linguistic) world are such as to transcend the ability of language to express them. If this is indeed so, then attempts to say what these are, are liable to end up in contradiction. For in saying what those features are, one is liable to say the unsayable.

In this chapter we will look at three reasons for supposing there to be features of the world that transcend language. Good candidates for features of the world that are liable to fall into this category are ones that might be thought to constitute ultimate reality, in some sense; for example, fundamental matter or God. We will look at an account of each of these two things that places it in the category of the inexpressible: Aristotle's account of prime matter, and Cusanus' account of God. First, however, we will start with a much more radical reason for the existence of the inexpressible; one that, if it were correct, would show that the whole of reality is like this: Cratylus' view of the flux of meaning.

1.1 The flux

Cratylus was a philosopher of the fifth century BC, a rough contemporary of Socrates, and a follower of the philosopher Heraclitus. Heraclitus held, famously, that everything is in a state of change or flux.[1] What, exactly, he meant by this is somewhat moot, but we may distinguish a weaker and a stronger interpretation. For something to be in a state of change it is arguably necessary and sufficient for it to be in the process of losing *some* of its properties. The weaker interpretation is simply that everything is changing in this sense. A much stronger interpretation is that everything is losing *all* of its properties. After all, if everything is changing, then the fact that x is P is changing. Whatever the historical Heraclitus held (and there is no particular reason to suppose that he held the strong form of the doctrine[2]), Cratylus himself held the strong form.

The weak form of the doctrine is a very plausible one, at least if we restrict ourselves to the material world. Given that there are two things in the cosmos that are in motion with respect to each other (which seems beyond doubt), then it follows that everything is in motion with respect to at least one thing. Hence, everything is changing its position with respect to something, and so is changing one of its properties. The stronger form appears less plausible. Australia, for example, is in the Southern hemisphere; it was yesterday, and will be tomorrow. Here, then, is a property of Australia that is not changing. Of course, Australia is in a process of continental drift, and this may have taken it into the Southern hemisphere, and may one day take it out. But this is hardly to say that this property is changing now. There is a possible reply here, however. If we are thinking not in terms of days and weeks, but in terms of geological epochs, then it becomes much more natural to say that Australia's being in the Southern hemisphere is now (in this epoch) changing. Thus, with more generous time spans, the stronger thesis becomes more plausible.

In due course the question of whether the meanings of words and sentences are changing will arise. Whilst it can hardly be maintained that the meanings of words change overnight, it certainly does seem to be true that they are changing, provided we concern ourselves with a sufficiently generous time span. Over hundreds of years most words change their usages and hence their meanings. Meanings, too, are therefore subject to the stronger version of Heraclitus' thesis.

1.2   Plato against Cratylus

Cratylus' strong version of the doctrine of flux was attacked by Plato. This is primarily in the *Theaetetus*, 181b–183c. The relevant part of the argument goes

---

[1] See Barnes (1979), ch. 4.
[2] Ibid., p. 69.

as follows (182c4–d10).[3] Socrates is Plato's mouthpiece and Theodorus has the unenviable task of defending Cratylus:

SOCRATES. . . . you say that all things change and flow, don't you?
THEODORUS. Yes.
SOCRATES. With both the kinds of change we distinguished; both moving and altering?
THEODORUS. Yes, certainly, they must be, if they're to be completely changing.
SOCRATES. Well now, if things were only moving, and not undergoing alteration, we'd be able to say, surely, that the moving things flow qualified in such-and-such ways. Isn't that right?
THEODORUS. Yes.
SOCRATES. Whereas since not even this stays constant, that the flowing thing flows white [say], but it changes, so that there's a flux of that very thing, whiteness, and change to another colour, in order not to be convicted of staying constant in that respect — since that's so, can it ever be possible to refer to any colour in such a way as to be speaking of it rightly?
THEODORUS. How could it be, Socrates? Indeed, how could it be possible to do so with any other thing of that kind, if it's always slipping away while one was speaking; as it must be, given that it's in flux?

Note the phrase 'the flowing thing flows white' in Socrates' last speech; we will return to this. The above argument is embedded in a discussion of perception. The dialogue then goes on to illustrate the point by applying it to this.

SOCRATES. And what shall we say about perception of any given kind, for instance that of seeing or hearing? Shall we say it ever stays constant in just that guise, namely, seeing or hearing?
THEODORUS. No, we mustn't, if everything changes.
SOCRATES. So we shouldn't speak of anything as a case of seeing, any more than as not a case of seeing, or as any other perception any more than as not that perception; at any rate, we shouldn't do so if everything is changing in every way.
THEODORUS. No.

Now, how this argument is to be interpreted depends on the interpretation of the phrase 'the flowing thing flows white' and, crucially, what its subject refers to. A natural way of taking this (in virtue of what Socrates says in his previous speech) is as referring to the moving thing. But another possible way (in virtue of the reference to whiteness itself in the next phrase) is to take it as referring to whiteness itself, or what it is to be white.

Suppose we interpret it in the first way, then the force of the argument is simply that if everything is in a state of flux it is impossible to say anything true. It is not just that by the time we have enunciated something, say that an object is white, the state of affairs it describes will have changed. Rather, as the illustration concerning perception makes clear, the point is that since the object

<hr />

[3] The translation is taken from McDowell (1973).

is in a constant state of change it is neither determinately white nor determinately not white. The claim that it is white is not, therefore, true.

An argument of this kind is used in the *Cratylus* itself (439c7–440a4) against the view that the Platonic forms, in particular, are in a state of flux:[4]

SOCRATES. . . . Consider, my worthy Cratylus, a question about which I often dream. Shall we assert that there is any absolute beauty, or good, or any other absolute existence, or not?

CRATYLUS. I think there is, Socrates.

SOCRATES. Then let us consider the absolute, not whether a particular face, or something of that sort, is beautiful, or whether all these things are in flux. Is not, in our opinion, absolute beauty always such as it is?

CRATYLUS. That is inevitable.

SOCRATES. Can we, then, if it is always passing away, correctly say that it is this, then it is that, or must it inevitably in the instant while we are speaking, become something else and pass away and no longer be what it is?

CRATYLUS. That is inevitable.

SOCRATES. How, then, can that which is never in the same state be anything? For if it is ever in the same state, then obviously at that time it is not changing; and if it is always in the same state, and is always the same, how can it ever change or move without relinquishing its own form.

CRATYLUS. It cannot do so at all.

SOCRATES. No, nor can it be known by anyone. For at the moment when he who seeks to know it approaches, it becomes something else and different, so that its nature and state can no longer be known; and surely there is no knowledge which knows that which is in no state.

CRATYLUS. It is as you say.

The argument is not terribly convincing. Its flaw is in moving from a premise of the form that a thing is changing states, to the conclusion that it is not determinately in any state. This is invalid: Australia, though it may, in a sense, be changing from being in the Southern hemisphere, is still determinately in it. Even if we make the change as fast as possible, the point remains. Suppose that a car accelerates from rest with a velocity, v, given by the equation $v=t$, where t is time (and both v and t are measured in suitable units). Then at $t=1$ its velocity is instantaneously 1. Although it is changing, it does not follow that the velocity is not determinately 1 at that instant.

Possibly, Plato would have argued as follows. If something is in a state for only an instant, then, since the instant has no duration, the thing is in a state for no time, and hence not in that state. However, we now have (arguably) a better understanding of the relationship between points and continua than did Plato, and from this perspective we can see that the subsidiary argument is itself fallacious since it confuses time with duration: a state of affairs can hold at an instant whilst that instant itself has no duration.

---

[4] The translation is from Fowler (1970), pp. 187f.

1.3   The stability of meaning

The second, and rather different, interpretation of the argument in the *Theaetetus* emerges if we interpret the ambiguous phrase as referring to whiteness itself, that is, the meaning of the predicate 'white'. (After all, if everything is changing, then so is this.) If the meaning of 'white' is constantly changing then there is no way that we can say that something is white: when we have said it our words will mean something different.[5] Hence it would seem to follow that on Cratylus' view nothing can be expressed.

I do not want to enter into the dispute concerning the correct way to interpret the argument here.[6] However, this interpretation does at least make the exchange a few lines later a bit more intelligible (183a4–b8):

SOCRATES. . . . what has . . . become clear is, apparently, that if all things do change, then every answer, whatever it's about, is equally correct: both that things are so and that they're not so, or if you like, both that things come to be so and that they come to be not so, so as not to bring those people to a standstill by what we say.

THEODORUS. You're right.

SOCRATES. Yes, Theodorus, except that I said 'so' and 'not so'. One oughtn't even to use the word 'so', because what's so wouldn't any longer be changing; and, again, one oughtn't to use 'not so', because that isn't a change either. No, those who state that theory must establish some other language, because as things are they haven't got expressions for their hypothesis: unless perhaps 'not even so', said in an indefinite sense, might suit them best.

THEODORUS. Yes, that would certainly be a more appropriate idiom.

On this interpretation the argument is to establish that nothing can be expressed. In particular, then, Cratylus' own view is inexpressible. *Prima facie*, this need not involve him in contradiction. After all, if he is prepared to live in silence, then he can just accept this view. And there is some evidence that the historical Cratylus took the force of this argument. For, as Aristotle reports (*Metaphysics*, 1010a 7–15), Cratylus was ultimately reduced to silence:[7]

Again, seeing that the whole of nature is in motion, and that nothing is true of what is changing, [some] supposed that it is not possible to speak truly of what is changing in absolutely all respects. For from this belief flowed the most extreme opinion of those I have mentioned – that of those who say they 'Heraclitize', and such as was held by Cratylus, who in the end thought one should say nothing and only moved a finger, and

---

[5] McDowell (1973), p. 181, puts the argument in a slightly different way. According to him, if whiteness itself is always changing then we cannot identify it to predicate it of something. I think this is less plausible: from the fact that something is constantly changing it does not follow that we cannot identify it. People change all the time, but are normally reidentifiable.

[6] Cornford (1935), pp. 98–9, and McDowell (1973), p. 183, argue for the second interpretation; Crombie (1963), pp. 27–33, and Bostock (1988), pp. 99–110, disagree.

[7] The translation is from Barnes (1979), p. 68.

reproached Heraclitus for saying that you cannot step into the same river twice – for he himself thought that you could not do so even once.

If, however, Cratylus does express his views, as, presumably, he did, if he expressed views about stepping into rivers, then he does seem to be in a contradictory position. And even if he does not say anything, there still seems to be a contradiction implicit in his position. For, after all, even to come to the conclusion that one cannot speak, it is necessary to express this thought to oneself, and how can one do this if there is no language (not even a language of thought!) in which this can be expressed?

We meet here the inexpressible, and the contradiction to which it leads, for the first time. By applying Cratylus' theory to itself it follows that it is not in the domain of the expressible (Transcendence); but he does succeed in expressing it, at least to himself (Closure).

Let us scrutinise the argument to inexpressibility again, however. We saw in 1.1 that the extreme Heraclitean view that everything (including the meanings of words) is in a state of flux is plausible if, but only if, we take a sufficiently generous time scale. Now if the meanings of Cratylus' words change very suddenly, say, before a hearer can hear and understand them, then I think it fair enough to say that he cannot express his views. But words change their meanings only over relatively long periods of time, in which case Cratylus can certainly express his views to a localised audience (though maybe not in an eternal – though therefore irrelevant – way). Thus, the argument to Transcendence fails. Despite this, the affair raises the important question of what happens if and when meanings may be indeterminate, which will be of central concern to us later in the book.

1.4   Aristotle on substance and change

Let us now turn to our second topic: prime matter as this notion appears in Aristotle. Or the traditional interpretation of this; for it should be said straight away that the question of whether Aristotle held there to be prime matter is a contentious one. That he did, is certainly the traditional view. Some notable modern scholars have attacked the claim;[8] and other equally notable scholars have defended the traditional view.[9] It seems to me that Aristotle does hold the view that there is prime matter, though exactly what he is prepared to claim may be different in different places.[10] However, I have no intention of entering the exegetical debate here. My interest is in the notion of prime matter itself,

[8] For example, King (1956); Charlton (1970), appendix.
[9] For example, Solmson (1958), Robinson (1974), Guthrie (1981), pp. 226–31; see p. 228, fn. 3 of this for other references to the discussion.
[10] See Dancy (1978).

and so in the way that the Aristotelian pronouncements have traditionally been understood.

The (eco)logical niche for a notion of prime matter is generated in Aristotle by the interaction of two things: a theory of substance and a theory of change. Let us start with the former. This is explained in *Metaphysics*, 7 (notably the first few chapters). For Aristotle, the world is made up of substances, such as people, tables, bones. These can be referred to by the subjects of sentences. Substances have properties (or accidents in Aristotle's terminology). These are referred to by the predicates of the corresponding sentences. Thus, for example, consider the sentence 'Mrs Thatcher is in Downing St'.[11] 'Mrs Thatcher' refers to a certain substance, viz., Mrs T. 'is in Downing St', refers to a property of this substance, viz., being in Downing St.

Substances themselves are a fusion of two aspects, which Aristotle calls form (or essence) and matter. Form is the more important of these; the form of a substance tells you what it *is*, as opposed to merely giving one of its properties. Thus, for example, Mrs T. *is* a person, but is merely to be found in Downing St; personhood is of her essence. The matter of a substance is that in which form is realised. We will come back to this in a moment.

Now to change: This is discussed in *Physics* 1 (particularly 1.7) and *On Generation and Corruption* (particularly 2.1). In these places Aristotle distinguishes between two sorts of change. The first, alteration (coming to be *something*), is the simplest. In this, a substance remains the same, but at least one of its properties changes. So, for example, when Mrs T. goes shopping she is no longer in Downing St. This change is an alteration. The second kind of change is coming to be (*simpliciter*). In this sort of change a substance itself comes into, or goes out of, existence. Suppose, for example, Mrs Thatcher dies. Then her essence (personhood) ceases to be, but something remains, viz., the flesh and bones which previously had constituted her. It is therefore natural to identify this with the matter of Mrs T. Previously it had had the form of personhood. Now it bears a different form, viz., that of corpsehood. But now note that this flesh and bones is just a substance; and being a person, or a corpse, are just different accidents of it at different times. In a change of the second type, then, a substance disappears because a substance of a lower type loses an accident that was the form of the higher substance.

1.5 Prime matter

The more fundamental substance, flesh and bones, can itself be the subject of a change of the second kind; for example, when it decomposes into its elements. Hence, the story must be repeated again: this substance is itself a fusion of

---

[11] The trouble with using contemporary examples is that time passes. Still, better an example that is out of date than one that is both out of date and hackneyed.

Table 1

	Substance	(Matter	Form)	Sample Property
Level 3	Mrs T.	flesh and bones	personhood	being in Downing St.
Level 2	flesh and bones	chemical elements	human tissue	being a person
Level 1	chemical elements	X	wet, dry, etc.	being human tissue
Level 0	X	–	–	being wet, dry, etc.

form and matter; the matter is a lower-level substance (certain chemical elements) and the form is one of its properties (being flesh and blood). Thus we have a hierarchy of substances.[12] In Aristotle, the hierarchy, in a simplified form, is as depicted in Table 1, where the chemical elements, note, are Aristotle's (earth, air, fire, and water); and can change into one another in a change of the second kind.

Note that the matter at level n+1 is the same as the substance at level n, and the form at level n+1 is a property of the substance at level n. Hence, the same thing can be both matter (*qua* the bearer of form) at one level and substance (*qua* the possessor of properties) at another. This principle connects the two levels. Let us therefore call it the *Linkage Principle*.

Now, at last, we come to prime matter. This is just the matter at level 1, that is, the substance at level 0. (I have marked it with an X in Table 1. For here lies, as we shall see, the unknown.) It will be useful to separate two distinct claims about the nature of prime matter.

The first is that prime matter (considered as the substance at level 0) is the ultimate bearer of all properties. This is so since properties are hereditary downwards. Thus, all the properties of Mrs T. (for example, being in Downing St) are properties of the substance which composes her (flesh and bones). And the properties of this flesh and bones (being in Downing St, being constituted as a person) are properties of the substances composing them (the elements); and so on. Let us call this:

Thesis 1: Prime matter is the ultimate subject.

As Aristotle puts it (*Metaphysics*, 1028b35[13]), prime matter is:

that of which other things are predicated, whilst it itself is not predicated of anything else.

---

[12] See Guthrie (1981), p. 227; Dancy (1978), p. 404.
[13] All quotations from Aristotle in this chapter are taken from Barnes (1984).

The second claim is that prime matter, residing on the lowest level, is not itself enformed matter of a lower level (which is why Table 1 has blanks there). It therefore has no form, only accidents. Let us call this:

Thesis 2: Prime matter has no essence.

As Aristotle puts it (*Metaphysics*, 1029a24–25), prime matter is:

of itself neither a particular thing nor of a particular quantity nor otherwise positively characterised; nor yet negatively, for negations also will belong to it only by accident.

Or, as the medievals put it, prime matter is 'pure possibility'. It can be anything; but is, in itself, nothing.

1.6   The problem with prime matter

Theses 1 and 2 are the heart of the traditional theory of prime matter. Yet they are the heart of a notion that is distinctly problematic. As we saw, to say what a substance *is* (as opposed to citing some of its properties) is to give its form or essence. Thus, since the substance X has no form, one cannot say what it is. No sentence of the form 'X is . . . ' (where this is an attempt to give an essence) is true. This observation was not lost on Aristotle. 'Matter', Aristotle says, 'is unknowable in itself' (*Metaphysics*, 1036a7). And here Aristotle is clearly talking of prime matter, since there is nothing unknowable about higher-level matter – such as flesh and bones.

The elusiveness of prime matter dogged the notion throughout Antiquity and the Middle Ages, causing debates about its nature, as well as attempts to dispose of the notion.[14] However, the notion survived happily into the eighteenth century, and is, arguably, Locke's notion of substance. He, too, drew the same conclusion (*Essay*, I, 4, 18):

we have no . . . clear Idea [of substance] at all, and therefore signify nothing by the word substance, but only an uncertain supposition of we know not what, i.e. of something whereof we have no particular distinct positive idea, which we take to be the substratum, or support of those ideas we do know.

Which triggered perhaps the most scathing attack of all on the notion; that by Berkeley.[15]

This tradition concerning the unknowability of prime matter does not get to the heart of the problem, however. Prime matter is unknowable, it is true. But it is impossible to know what it is precisely because it is impossible to say what it is: by Thesis 2, it has no form. Prime matter is, therefore, precisely something beyond the limit of the expressible (Transcendence). But we can quite

---

[14] See, for example, Sorabji (1988), chs. 1–4.
[15] See *Principles of Human Knowledge*, sections 16, 17.

happily give its essence; we have already done so in describing it (Closure). What makes something prime matter, as opposed to some other kind of substance, is exactly that it is the bearer of all properties, whilst it itself has no essence, as Theses 1 and 2 have it. (Its essence, to put it bluntly, is to be essenceless.) Thus prime matter exhibits the typical contradiction at the limit of the expressible, though Aristotle, as far as I know, never observed this.

1.7   Subject and form

In virtue of this, it behooves us to consider whether there are any good reasons for supposing there to be prime matter. When I say this, I do not mean something that fits into Table 1 as it stands. Physics has long since outdated this, both by changing the elements and by adding further levels of determinate substances below them, such as atoms and sub-atomic particles. In this sense, prime matter is just an outdated bit of physics, as Dancy ((1978), p. 391) says. Rather, I mean whether there is something satisfying Theses 1 and 2; perhaps something on the bottom level of a modern table of substances. Surprisingly, Aristotle gives no explicit argument for the existence of prime matter; it is, perhaps, a natural assumption, given his theories of matter and change; but is not entailed by them as we shall see.

Let us start with the question of whether there must be something satisfying Thesis 1, an ultimate subject. This would certainly be true if the regress of substances does terminate. Is there any reason to suppose it does? Guthrie ((1981), p. 227) suggests that, for Aristotle, the regress had to terminate because of his 'horror of the infinite regress'. As an interpretation of Aristotle, this has great plausibility. As we will see in the next chapter, Aristotle held that there could not be a completed infinity; and if the regress of substances continued to infinity they would all be present in the top level substance, and so the infinity would be a completed one. Hence, the regress cannot go on indefinitely. Though this is a plausible interpretation of Aristotle, as an argument that the regress terminates it is not a very good one. For as we shall also see in the next chapter, the arguments against a completed infinity cannot be made good.

A rather different argument for the existence of an ultimate subject (though not, I think, an Aristotelian one) is as follows. Consider, for example, me and all my properties: being tall, having a moustache, practising karate-do, etc. What makes all these *my* properties. What constitutes their unity? A natural answer is that all the properties belong to the same thing, viz., me. Similarly, given any body, there is an ultimate subject which bears all the properties of that object, and so constitutes their unity: the object itself.

Notice that this argument for the existence of an ultimate subject does not imply that the regress terminates. The regress might go round in a loop at some stage, matter at one level being a substance at a *higher* level! In this case, all the substances in the loop would be ultimate subjects. Indeed, the loop might be very small, a single substance looping back on itself, so that it itself is its own matter. However, the argument is a plausible one, and so gets us at least as far as Thesis 1.

Let us turn to Thesis 2. Is there any reason to suppose that the ultimate subject is formless? If the regress goes round in a loop then, as we have just noted, there are ultimate subjects; and, since they are not bottom, they have form. The quick answer, therefore, is 'no'. But, even supposing the ultimate subject to be the substance of level 0, the answer is still 'no'. We can hold the theory of substance *and* the theory of change *and* the bottoming out of the regress. We simply insist that the level 0 substance *does* have both a form and a matter. The Linkage Principle simply does not apply at the bottom level (though we can still accept it for higher levels). The form and matter of the level 0 substance cannot be thought of as inherited from below; they are *sui generis*. In this way the whole of the Aristotelian schema is preserved by adding a couple of new entries to Table 1: viz., a matter and form on the bottom line (which are, in any case, really required by the theory of substance). Thesis 1 specifies exactly the form: it is to be the bearer of all properties. It makes no sense to ask what the matter is, since one can ask only what *substances* are; and this matter is not a substance. Of course, if the level 0 substance could cease to be, and we are to preserve the theory of change, the matter would have to be a lower level substance. It just follows that it cannot cease to be. (But this is ruled out for Aristotle anyway: if prime matter could cease to be it would lose its form; but it hasn't got one, so it cannot cease to be.)

Are there any other arguments for the claim that the level 0 substance has no essence? In *Metaphysics* 7.3, Aristotle gives a thought experiment as to how we can arrive at prime matter (in thought, not in practice, since matter and its form are not physically separable). We simply take a body and strip off all its properties: colour, weight, 'length, breadth and depth'; what is left when all these have been removed is the prime matter. Now if this is intended as an argument that the level 0 substance has no essence then it begs the question. For to assume that the form gets stripped off in the process is exactly to assume that it is a property; but on the present scheme the essence is not a property – of anything.

In part of the *Timaeus* Plato presents the notion of a receptacle of qualities, χωρα, which in some ways is similar to Aristotle's notion of prime matter.[16] Moreover, Plato uses an argument to try to establish that the receptacle has no intrinsic properties; it cannot have them since, otherwise, it would 'obtrude them and receive the other qualities badly'. However good this argument is for

---

[16] For references and discussion, see Sorabji (1988), pp. 32ff. Charlton ((1970), appendix) argues that the traditional notion of prime matter owes more to this passage in the *Timaeus* than to Aristotle.

Plato, it will not help Thesis 2. For there is no reason to suppose that the form of the level 0 substance is incompatible with any properties. Indeed, since its form is exactly to be the bearer of all properties, its form is clearly compatible with the possession of any property whatever.

There is, as far as I can see, no other argument for the conclusion that the bottom level substance has no form. Hence the arguments for the existence of prime matter (both as a bottom level and as formless) fail. Though Aristotle had witnessed the possibility of the limit of the expressible, he had not demonstrated its existence.

1.8   Cusanus on God

So let us move on to another candidate for something beyond the limits of the expressible: God. Many have been tempted by the thought that God is ineffable, and so transcends anything that can be said about Her.[17] There are strong elements of this in the Neoplatonist tradition of negative theology. But nowhere do we find the idea more graphically expressed than in the fifteenth-century German philosopher, Nicholas of Cusa.

Cusanus defines God simply as the Maximum, where 'we speak of a thing being the greatest or maximum when nothing greater than it can exist' (*Of Learned Ignorance*, I, 2[18]). God, then, is a species of the infinite. Moreover, according to Cusanus, because God is infinite, there can be no way that we can comprehend Him. As he puts it (*Of Learned Ignorance*, I, 4):

There can be nothing greater in existence than the simple, absolute maximum; and since it is greater than our powers of comprehension – for it is infinite truth – our knowledge of it can never mean that we comprehend it.

This may seem a bit swift. Why does the incomprehensibility of something follow from its infinitude? Essentially, it is because, according to Cusanus, our categories are finite; and no finite category can 'fit' an infinite object. If this is right, then God is not only beyond comprehension, but facts about God are beyond expression. For any way of expressing such facts would require us to subsume God under some category or other. Hence, facts about God are beyond expression (Transcendence).

This does not stop Cusanus expressing (and presumably comprehending) various facts about God, however. He is quite explicit in attributing properties required by dogma, such as the Trinity (*Of Learned Ignorance*, I, 17). But even if piety did not force him into this contradiction, logic itself would. For Cusanus' description of God must characterise It, or he would not be talking

---

[17] All pronouns are wrong.
[18] Quotations are taken from Heron (1954).

about the thing in question. Moreover, even to claim that God is incomprehensible is to express a certain fact about God. Hence we have Closure.[19]

There are various ways one might try to defuse this contradiction,[20] but I will not pursue them here; for neither does Cusanus. He has the courage of his logical convictions and accepts this contradiction about God as true. In fact, he gets rather carried away with the situation and insists that *all* contradictions are true of God – which does not follow at all, as any paraconsistent logician could have told him – (*Of Learned Ignorance*, I, 4):

in no way do they [distinctions] exist in the absolute maximum. The absolute maximum ... is all things, and whilst being all, is none of them; in other words, it is at once the maximum and minimum of being.

Cusanus, then, unlike Aristotle, not only perceives the contradictions at the limits of the expressible, but endorses them.

1.9   Objects and categories

Having seen this, we should go back and scrutinise Cusanus' argument more carefully. Cusanus argues that God cannot be (truly) described, because God, being infinite, can fall under no finite category. But why does this follow? Cusanus explains (*Of Learned Ignorance*, I, 3):

A finite intellect ... cannot ... reach the absolute truth of things. Being by nature indivisible, truth excludes 'more' or 'less', so that nothing but truth itself can be the exact measure of truth: for instance that which is not a circle cannot be the measure of a circle, for the nature of a circle is one and indivisible. In consequence, our intellect, which is not the true, never grasps the truth with such precision that it could not be comprehended with an infinitely greater comprehension.

We see that Cusanus is operating with a 'mirror' conception of categorisation. An adequate category must share the relevant properties with the object categorised, just as an adequate image must share the relevant properties with the object it images.

How acceptable this conception of categorisation was in the fifteenth century, I am not competent to judge. But clearly, from a modern   perspective, it has no plausibility. Categories hardly ever share crucial properties with the objects categorised. The category of redness is not red; the notion of foreignness is not foreign; the notion of length is not long. And, for good measure, the notion of a circle is not circular either. Hence, there is no reason to suppose

---

[19] Interestingly in this context, Stace (1961) claims that when mystics are forced into uttering something contradictory because of their ineffable insights, this is precisely because those contradictions are true.

[20] We will discuss one when we come across Anselm in a later chapter. Some others are discussed in Alston (1956).

that a category adequate to characterise the infinite must be infinite; and with this observation Cusanus' argument collapses.

I know of no other arguments to the effect that the categories of our language cannot correctly characterise God which I find persuasive.[21] And hence I conclude that Cusanus' position is without support. Though Cusanus had recognised the contradictory nature of things beyond the expressible, he, too, had failed to establish that there are such things.

Conclusion

In this chapter we have looked at three Pre-Kantian philosophers whose views led them to the conclusion that there were things beyond the expressible, and so into the contradiction typical of the limits of thought – though only one (Cusanus) recognised and endorsed the contradiction. As we have seen, the arguments of the three to the conclusion that there are things beyond the expressible, cannot be defended. However, similar arguments of later philosophers are not so easily disarmed. For the present, though, let us leave the limits of the expressible and move on to the second of the limits that will concern us. Cusanus, as we saw, was forced into contradiction because of features of an infinitude. In the next chapter, we will look at infinity itself.

---

[21] Though we will meet another argument to the effect that finite categories cannot characterise infinite objects when we come to Hegel.

2 The limits of iteration

Introduction

In this chapter we will meet a second limit of thought. This arises when there is some operation that is applied over and over again as far as possible. I will call this, for obvious reasons, the limit of the iterable: the most notable case of this is the mathematical (ordinal) infinite.

For reasons that I will not speculate on here, the mathematical infinite has exercised a primitive fascination for people from earliest times; it is at the heart of issues in philosophy, mathematics and even theology. Despite this fact – or perhaps its cause – the notion is a deeply paradoxical one. For various reasons that we will come to in due course, it has seemed to people that though there be no greater than the infinite; yet there be a greater. This is, in fact, the leitmotif of the book.

In virtue of this paradox, the notion of the mathematical infinite has often been considered problematic. It is commonly claimed that these problems were cleared up in the nineteenth century, by the writings of Dedekind, Cantor, and others. For example, Russell:[1]

For over two thousand years the human intellect was baffled by the problem [of infinity] ...
A long line of philosophers, from Zeno to M. Bergman, have based much of their metaphysics upon the supposed impossibility of infinite collections ... The definitive solution to the difficulties is due ... to Georg Cantor.

The claim, however, is wrong. The works of these nineteenth-century mathematicians produced a great advance in our understanding of the infinite; the transfinite is one of the most beautiful mathematical discoveries. But they did not remove the fundamental paradox of the mathematical infinite; they merely relocated it (though the relocation was sufficient to hide it for a while). But this is to get ahead of the story.

The most sophisticated early account of the infinite is undoubtedly Aristotle's. It was he who brought together the various problems concerning the infinite raised by the thought of the pre-Socratics, and tried to give a

---

[1] (1926), pp. 164, 169; see Moore (1990), p. 110.

theory which could cope with them. In the first part of the chapter we will look at Aristotle on the infinite: we will see that he perceived contradiction at the limit of the iterable, and sought to avoid it. Further substantial developments would have to wait some 2,000 years; but the contradiction at the limit of the iterable can be glimpsed again before that in a rather unexpected place: Leibniz on the cosmological argument for the existence of God. In the second part of the chapter we will look at this.

2.1   Generated infinities

Before we start, however, let me explain some useful terminology. Suppose that we have an operator that applies to objects of a certain kind. When applied to an object of that kind it may produce nothing, or it may produce an object of the same kind. I will call such an operator a *generator* since, by applying the operator again and again, we can generate a sequence of objects. Whatever results by iterating applications of the operator as often as possible in this way I will call a *limit of iteration*.

There is no reason, in general, to suppose that the application of a generator always produces a novel object (or even an object at all); but, if it does, I will call it an *infinity generator*, since iterated applications produce an infinity of objects. In this case I will call the limit of iteration a *generated infinity*. A paradigm example of an infinity generator is adding one. Other examples might be: taking half of an object, or forming the thought of an object. A paradigm example of a generated infinity is ω, i.e., $\{0, 1, 2, 3...\}$, obtained from 0, by applying the generator $1+x$ indefinitely.[2] Generated infinities are the limits of iteration that will be our primary concern.

2.2   ... in Aristotle

Let us now turn to Aristotle. What was his theory of the infinite? It can be summed up very simply: the infinite does not exist. Aristotle's account of infinity is given in his *Physics*, mainly in the last three sections of Book 3. There, he explains that although there clearly are infinity generators, and these can be applied indefinitely, there are no such things as the limits these generate. In his words (*Physics*, 3.7, 206a26–206b16):[3]

The infinite exhibits itself in many ways – in time, in the generations of man, and in the divisions of magnitudes. For generally the infinite has this mode of existence: one

---

[2] Note that, since an infinity generator must produce an object different from everything obtained so far, it is better to conceptualise it as an operator on a *collection* of objects of the appropriate kind. Thus, instead of the operator $1+x$, it is better to think of the operator $1 + \max(X)$, where X is a finite set of numbers. However, we will ignore this subtlety for the present.

[3] Quotations from Aristotle in this chapter are taken from Barnes (1984).

thing is always being taken after another, and each thing that is taken is always finite, but always different. Again, 'being' is spoken of in several ways, so that we must not regard the infinite as a 'this', such as a man or a horse, but must suppose it to exist in the sense in which we speak of the day or the games as existing – things whose being has not come to them like that of a substance, but consists in a process of coming to be or passing away, finite, yet always different ... The infinite, then, exists in no other way, but in this way it does exist, potentially or by reduction.

It is common to distinguish between two notions of the infinite: the potential and the actual (or completed).[4] Loosely, the potential infinite is some indefinitely extensible operation; the actual infinite is the state produced when the operation has been performed more than a finite number of times. Aristotle, as he says, is describing the potential infinite, whilst what I have called the infinite is the actual infinite. The 'actual/potential' terminology is not terribly happy. The potential infinite is neither potential nor infinite. It is not potential, at least in the way that most things are potential in Aristotle; for it (as opposed to parts of it) can never come into being. And it is not infinite, since at any stage it is finite. (The sense of actuality in which the actual infinite is actual, might also be thought to be moot.) However, the terminology is now too well entrenched to change easily; so I will use it. Aristotle is saying, then, that there are only potential infinities; there are no (actual) infinities.

2.3   Time

Let us now turn to the question of whether Aristotle's view, that there are no completed infinities, can be maintained. Aristotle considers some arguments to the effect that there are actual infinities in *Physics* 3.4, 203b16–26, and answers them very briefly at 5.8, 208a5–25. By and large, the arguments do not establish their conclusions. They point to the existence of various infinity generators, and just assume that there must be a corresponding infinity. Aristotle has to do little more than point out that this does not follow.

Employing arguments from modern set theory, it is easy to conclude that infinities exist. Consider ω, for example. This is certainly an actual infinity (when it is being considered as a unity, as it is, for example, when it is thought of as a member of some other collection). But though hitting Aristotle with transfinite set theory certainly provides a technical knock out, it is not really within the Queensberry Rules. More interesting is whether Aristotle can maintain his position in his own terms. As we shall see, he cannot.

The most persuasive way of arguing against Aristotle is provided by finding an infinitude that is instantiated in some process in time. If that process then comes to a conclusion, the infinity must be completed, and so the limit must

---

[4] Or as the medievals put it, the syncategorematic and categorematic infinite. See Moore (1990), ch. 3.

exist. The clearest such processes that instantiate infinities are motion and time itself.

Let us take time first. Time past and time future both instantiate infinity generators (one day before; one day after) – assuming a Newtonian view of time, anyway. Moreover, in the case of time past the process, and so the infinity, is completed by the present. Aristotle actually considers this argument briefly and replies that 'time . . . [is] infinite; but the parts that are taken do not persist' (*Physics*, 3.8, 208a20). In other words, time past is not actually infinite since not all of its parts exist (at any one time). This objection is rather disingenuous. For a totality to have a size it is not necessary for all its members to coexist temporally, as Aristotle sometimes realises. For example, one can quite sensibly inquire how many people have been born since Aristotle's death. Hence, to point out that past times do not all exist together is an *ignoratio*: the set of all past times can still be a completed infinity in the sense required.

Lear ((1979–80), p. 207) suggests a way out for Aristotle. He notes that the fact that after every heartbeat in my childhood there was another, does not imply that there was an infinite number of heartbeats in my childhood. Time may be like that. This suggestion does not, however, appear very plausible. The reason that 'the next heartbeat in my childhood' is not an infinity generator (unlike 'next heartbeat' would be – if I were to live forever) is that the term 'childhood' is vague: being a child gradually fades out; and it is for this reason that it is impossible to pick out the last heartbeat. 'Prior time', or 'prior time in the past' does not seem at all similar. 'Past' is not a vague term. It is not the case that as we go further and further back things become less and less past until they are not past at all! Whenever it is there, the past is 100 per cent there.

The only plausible way out of the conclusion that time past is (actually) infinite, seems to me to be to deny that time past is potentially infinite, that is, that it is Newtonian. One might do this if, for example, one took the General Theory of Relativity to imply that both time and the material cosmos started together at the Big Bang. The geometry of time would then be highly non-Euclidean. Whether or not this move is possible, I leave for modern physicists to argue out; it is not a move that is open to Aristotle. Once you admit that time past is potentially infinite (as Aristotle does), it follows that it is actually infinite.

2.4 Motion

The second way in which an infinity can be instantiated in an actual and terminated process concerns motion. This can be seen, as might be expected, with the help of one of Zeno's arguments.

Consider a body (which we might identify for present purposes with the point which is its centre of mass) which moves from A (say 0) to B (say 1).

Consider the sequence of spatial points in the motion 0, 1/2, 3/4, 7/8 ... each point (save the first) halving the distance between the previous point and 1. The generator that takes us from one point to the next is clearly an infinity generator. Alternatively, and equivalently, so is the function that takes us from each half to the next: [0, 1/2], [1/2, 3/4], [3/4, 7/8] ... Moreover, the infinity is completed by the time that the body arrives at B.

Aristotle discusses this paradox of Zeno and, naturally, does not accept the conclusion. His solution is to deny that the points (or halves) in question exist. As we shall see, Aristotle regards it as absurd to suppose that the continuum is composed of points. In particular, a point is simply a division of the continuum into two parts, produced by a body at rest. Hence, if the motion of the body is continuous there are no (actual) points between A and B and no corresponding halves. As Aristotle puts it (*Physics* 8.8, 263a23–30):

In the act of dividing the continuous distance into two halves one point is treated as two, since we make it a beginning and end [of different halves] ... But if divisions are made in this way, neither the distance nor the motion will be continuous; for motion if it is to be continuous must relate to what is continuous; and though what is continuous contains an infinite number of potential halves, they are not actual halves. If ... [the body] makes the halves actual ... [it will not have] a continuous but an intermittent motion.

One might wonder why a body has to be at rest to actualise a point. But putting this aside, this avoidance of completed infinity comes close to being self-defeating. For Aristotle concedes, apparently without realising it, that there is an infinite number of *potential* halves. He goes on to say (263b3–5):

to the question whether it is possible to pass through an infinite number of units either of time or of distance we must reply that in a sense it is and in a sense it is not. If the units are actual, it is not possible; if they are potential, it is possible.

It would seem, then, that there is a completed infinity of possible points between A and B. Nor is this admission about possible points an aberration on Aristotle's part. For, as we shall see, Aristotle is committed to the view that any stretch of continuum can be bisected, and hence there must be a potential infinity of potential points between A and B. This infinity is completed by the time the body arrives at B.[5]

A second objection against Aristotle is as follows. We can accommodate Aristotle's theory of points and still show that there is a completed infinity of actual points (or halves). Suppose that the body moving from A to B travels as follows: it moves to the halfway point in 1/4 second; it then rests for 1/4 second; it then moves half of the rest of the way in 1/8 second; it then rests for

---

[5] Sorabji (1983), p. 213, notes the unfortunate admission but thinks that Aristotle can get out of trouble by insisting that the infinitude of potential points is itself a potential infinite. He cannot, since the infinitude is completed.

1/8 second; and so on. (Thus, if the body starts at $t=0$, it is moving between times of the form $1 - 1/2^n$ and $1 - 1/2^n + 1/2^{n+2}$ ($n \geq 0$), and is at rest at other times.) The body stops at each of the Zenonian points, and so realises them; but it still arrives at B after one second. We have, therefore an infinity generator of actual points.[6]

2.5   The continuum

As we have just seen, Aristotle cannot avoid accepting the existence of actual infinities. It is therefore time to look at his reasons against the existence of the actual infinite. Aristotle gives a number of arguments against the existence of the infinite. Many of these (especially in *Physics* 3.5) are against the existence of physical infinities, and depend on his physical theories of place and motion. But he also has some arguments that are more abstract, and less vulnerable to the demise of his physical theories. I will discuss two of these which attempt to show, in effect, that the actual infinite involves contradictions.

The first argument derives from another of Zeno's arguments,[7] and concerns the nature of the continuum. If infinite limits exist then a body may be divided 'through and through', but (*On Generation and Corruption*, 1.2, 316a15–16):

to suppose that a body (i.e. a magnitude) is divisible through and through, and that this division is possible, involves a difficulty. What will there be in the body which escapes the division?

To see what Aristotle has in mind, take some finite stretch of continuum (say [0,1]); divide it in half, i.e. remove its mid-point from the set of points (note that the division here is a conceptual one; Aristotle is not talking about the application of hacksaws); divide the halves in half; and so on. The operation of dividing each remaining piece in half is an infinity generator. Now take this to the limit. What is the result? A set of somethings; but what is each something?

A magnitude [i.e. something with positive length]? No: that is impossible, since then there will be something not divided, whereas *ex hypothesi* the body was divisible *through and through*. But if it be admitted that neither a body nor a magnitude will remain, and yet division is to take place, the body will *either* consist of points (and its constituents will be without magnitude) *or* it will be absolutely nothing. If the latter, then it might both come to be out of nothing and exist as a composite of nothing; and thus presumably the whole body will be nothing but an appearance. But if it consists of points, it will not possess magnitude. For when points were in contact and coincided to

---

[6] A similar example is given in Bostock (1973–4), though this will not quite do since the body stops only instantaneously at each point, and Aristotle requires an object to stop for a period if it is to define a point. See Sorabji (1983), p. 324.

[7] See Vlastos (1967).

form a single magnitude, they did not make the whole any bigger (since, when the body was divided into two or more parts, the whole was not a bit smaller or bigger than it was before the division); hence, even if all the points be put together they will not make any magnitude.[8]

We have a three-way fork. Either (i) what is left has length, or (ii) it does not; in the second case (iia) it is either nothing or (iib) it is a lengthless point. The case (i) is contradictory since all positive lengths have been divided (after n divisions all undivided pieces have length $1/2^n$, which can be made as small as we please). The case (iia) is contradictory since an amalgam of nothings is nothing; the case (iib) is contradictory since a collection of dimensionless points cannot have positive dimension.

With a little rearranging we can put this argument as follows. Let us call the things that result from division through and through *atoms*; and let the totality of all things that can be (conceptually) divided be D. Now, first, an atom cannot be a member of D (Transcendence), since it is obtained by dividing through and through and so cannot be further divided. But an atom must have magnitude, since a magnitude cannot be composed of non-magnitudes. Hence an atom can be divided, i.e., it is a member of D (Closure). According to this argument, atoms, one kind of limit of the iterable, instantiate contradictions typical of the limits of thought.

So much for the argument. Does it work? History has not been kind to the argument, as anyone with a basic knowledge of measure-theory will know.[9] We can accept the impossibility of the first two of Aristotle's horns: atoms (that is, points) have no length; and something cannot be a collection of nothings. But the third fails: a length *can* be made up of points, that is, things with no length. Aristotle is quite right that if you delete a single point from a set, you do not decrease its length; and conversely, if you add a single point to a set of points you do not increase its length. But it does not follow that you cannot increase the length of a set by adding points to it. It is tempting to suppose that this follows by a simple sorites argument, which is, presumably, what motivated Aristotle's thought.[10] And, indeed, adding points one at a time will never increase the length.[11] To increase the length you need to add a non-denumerable number, more than can be added 'one at a time'. Aristotle, of course, did not have the benefits of modern point-set theory; and without these his argument is a compelling one. Yet it fails, none the less. What is left in the limit generated by iterated halving of [0,1] is the set of points not of the form $m/2^n$ $(0 < m < 2^n)$. And this has length 1!

---

[8] *On Generation and Corruption*, 1.2, 316a24–34.

[9] See, for example, the first few chapters of Halmos (1950).

[10] See, for example, *Physics* 6.1, where Aristotle is clearly considering the possibility of adding point by point.

[11] Even in the limit in normal, i.e. countably additive, measures.

2.6 Infinite parts

The second of Aristotle's arguments attempting to show that the completed infinite is contradictory is more obscure, being little more than a throw-away remark; but it is potentially more important. Discussing Anaxagoras' cosmology, he says (*Physics* 1.4, 188a2–5):

in each of his infinite bodies there would be already present infinite flesh and blood and brain – having distinct existence, however, from one another, and no less real than the infinite bodies, and each infinite: which is contrary to reason.

Aristotle clearly regards it as contradictory to suppose that an infinite whole (and *a fortiori*, presumably, a finite whole) could have infinite parts. He does not, however, explain why. Ross, in his commentary, suggests ((1936), p. 486) that this is because 'bodies existing side by side necessarily bound each other, and are therefore not infinite'. Perhaps this is right, though it strikes me as implausible since it is pretty obvious that an infinity can be bounded, at least on one side (consider $\{x; x \geq 0\}$).

More plausible reasons as to why parts cannot be infinite are, I think, those expounded by subsequent Aristotelians. Those given by Philoponus, the sixth-century AD Alexandrian philosopher, will illustrate the point.[12] Philoponus turned Aristotle's account of infinity against his own view of the eternity of the world. Had the world been eternal then the total number of years before 1991, say, would be (actually, and not just potentially) infinite. But, equally, the years before 1990 would be actually infinite. Hence we would have an infinitude with an infinite part. And what is supposed to be absurd about this is that there could be something bigger than an infinitude.

But why should there not be something larger than infinity? If you define infinity to be that greater than which there cannot be, then of course it is absurd; but this is not the notion of infinity that Aristotle and his followers are working with. The absurdity is, I suggest, the clash with the idea codified as the Euclidean axiom that the whole must be greater than its (proper) parts (*Elements*, Book 1, Common Notion 5). Thus, a part cannot be the same size as the whole, viz., infinite.[13]

It might be suggested that this begs an important question. Why, after all, can there not be infinities of different sizes? That there cannot be, is axiomatic in Aristotelian and early medieval thinking.[14] But even if we grant that there could be, this is irrelevant to the present case, since the years before 1991 and

---

[12] For a review of these see Todd (1980). For further discussion see Sorabji (1983), ch. 14.

[13] Another *reductio* used by Philoponus goes as follows. If the number of years, that is, the number of Januaries, before 1990 is infinite then the number of months before 1990 must be infinite also; and, since there are twelve months to the year, this infinity must be twelve times the size of the first. Again, we have something (the set of months) being the same size as a proper subset (the set of Januaries).

[14] See Murdoch (1982), p. 569.

1990 can be paired one-to-one in a now standard way. The function that maps each year to its predecessor is such a correlation. (I do not know who first observed this sort of correlation; it was certainly known to the medievals.) Hence, by the natural criterion of sameness of size, there are exactly as many years before 1990 as there are before 1991.

As with the continuum argument, with a little reworking, this argument can be put into the form typical of a contradiction at the limit of thought. Take some completed infinity (say, the years up to 1990), c, and let C be the class of things the same size as c. Now take any novel object (say 1991) and add this to c. The new collection is bigger than c, by the Euclidean Axiom, and so not in C (Transcendence); but it is infinite and hence the same size as c (or is the same size as c by the pairing argument), and so is in C (Closure).

Now, and to return to Aristotle, if this was the thought that lay, probably half-formed, behind his remark about Anaxagoras, history has shown it not to be correct. The story is familiar to anyone with a first course in set-theory, and so needs no long telling. One needs to distinguish between one set being a subset of another and one set having a smaller cardinality that another.[15] Once one makes this distinction it can then be shown that a proper subset of a set *can* have the same cardinal size as the whole, and so the Euclidean Axiom fails (though it is true for finite totalities – from which the original intuition of its correctness was, presumably, drawn). Indeed, it is exactly its failure which became, for Bolzano, Dedekind, and Cantor, the mark of an infinitude. The argument to Transcendence therefore fails.

We have now looked at two of Aristotle's arguments aimed at showing that a completed infinite produces contradictions. Of the two, the second, being the more general, is historically more important. In a nutshell, the contradiction it diagnoses is that any finite addition to an infinite magnitude does not increase its size, though by the Euclidean Axiom, it must. In the Middle Ages this problem became known as the 'annihilation of number' (since the infinite size annihilates any finite addend) or the problem of 'unequal infinities'.[16] As we have seen, advances in mathematics, particularly in the nineteenth century, enabled both contradictions to be resolved. But the framework in which this could be done, the general theory of sets, provided new and much more powerful arguments for paradoxes of the actual infinite. The resolutions had dealt only with symptoms, not with causes. What these arguments are we will see in detail in a later part of the book, but we can get a glimpse of them in

---

[15] Possibly the first person to make this distinction was Gregory of Rimini (see Murdoch (1968)), though the earliest definitive statement is by Bolzano in 1851 (see sections 19–23 of Bolzano (1950)).

[16] See Dauben (1979), p. 122. For more detailed discussions of the treatments of both arguments in the Middle Ages see Kretzmann (1982); Moore (1990), ch. 3; Murdoch (1981), (1982).

another pre-Kantian philosopher: Leibniz. To set the scene, I will start by considering Aquinas' cosmological argument.

2.7   Aquinas' cosmological argument

In the *Summa Theologica* Aquinas gave five arguments for the existence of God. Of these, the first three are variations on a certain theme, which is Aristotle's argument for a prime mover in *Physics* 8.5, and goes as follows: starting from some event in the world, a regress is constructed, which, it is then claimed, must terminate. The regresses concern motion, cause, and necessary condition. Aquinas' second argument, concerning (efficient) causation, will demonstrate the structure nicely. As he puts it (Hick (1964), pp. 83–4):

In the world of sensible things we find there is an order of efficient causes. There is no case known (neither is it, indeed, possible) in which a thing is found to be the efficient cause of itself; for so it would be prior to itself, which is impossible. Now in efficient causes it is not possible to go on to infinity, because in all efficient causes following in order, the first is the cause of the intermediate cause, and the intermediate is the cause of the ultimate cause, whether the intermediate cause be several, or one only. Now to take away the cause is to take away the effect. Therefore, if there be no first cause amongst efficient causes, there will be no ultimate, nor any intermediate, cause. But if in efficient causes it is possible to go on to infinity, there will be no first efficient cause, neither will there be an ultimate effect, nor any intermediate efficient causes; all of which is plainly false. Therefore it is necessary to admit a first efficient cause, to which everyone gives the name of God.

Now, the last clause, identifying the first cause with God, is a complete *non-sequitur*; but our interest lies in the argument used to establish the existence of a first cause as such. This concerns the generator 'cause of' as applied to events or states of affairs. (The distinction is of no importance here; I will use 'event' and 'state of affairs' interchangeably.) To apply it we do not need to assume that the cause of something is unique. We need only suppose that the generator picks out one of the pertinent causes. Given any event, say the death of Hegel, we can apply the generator. If we succeed in producing an event, a cause of Hegel's death, this must be a different event, since no event can cause itself (as Aquinas points out). There is, however, according to Aquinas, no guarantee that the generator is an infinity generator. The event may have *no* cause. The point of the argument is exactly to establish the existence of such an event.

Does it succeed? In discussing this, it is important to note that when Aquinas appeals to the notion of cause here, he does not have in mind the notion of cause that would first come to the mind of a modern reader, viz., an event temporally *prior to* the event it brings about (such as smoking causing lung cancer). Rather, he means an event (or state of affairs) *simultaneous with* the event in question such that the relation of causal dependence between them is, none the less, asymmetric. (So that when he uses the word 'prior' he is referring to causal, not temporal, priority.[17]) Standard examples are: the motion of the pen is causally dependent on the motion of my fingers; the motion of my fingers is dependent on the firing of nerve cells in my hand, and so on. The medievals called the first kind of cause *per accidens*, and the second kind of cause *per se*. The distinguishing feature of a *per se* cause is that (unlike causes *per accidens*) if the effect exists, the cause must exist too, since it is (now) bringing it about. It is not that Aquinas thinks that causation *per accidens* is not a legitimate notion of causation (he does); it is just that it is not the notion that is in use here.

Now to the causal regress: Aquinas could have argued, as did Philoponus, that if the regress were infinite, then since its first member (i.e., the final result in causal terms) has actually occurred, the infinity would be a completed infinity, which is impossible for Aristotelian reasons. But Aquinas did not argue in this way. He thought that there was nothing logically impossible about a completed infinite regress as such. For example, Aquinas thinks it quite *possible* that regresses generated by *per accidens* causation might go on for ever. They do not: there was a first event. But this can be established only by revelation, not by logic.[18] And he was quite right in this; there is nothing contradictory about Annie having been engendered by Betty, who was engendered by Cathy, who was ... and so on *ad infinitum*.

If, then, the argument is to work, it must be because of some special feature of causation *per se*. Unfortunately, the reasoning that Aquinas uses in the above quotation is quite fallacious. Aquinas notes that if there is a first cause then, if this were 'taken away' no effects would occur either, i.e., *if there were no first cause nothing would happen*. He then points out that if there were an infinite regress there would be no first cause, and applies the italicised conditional just established to conclude that there would be no effect. But this is quite illicit; for the conditional is itself established on the assumption that there is a first cause, and is therefore not available if the regress is infinite.

An infinite regress of *per se* causes is quite possible, as the following hypothetical but quite consistent situation shows. Suppose that we have a linear continuum with suitable coordinates. For every natural number, n, there is an object, a_n, at the point whose coordinate is n. Each a_n is in one of two states: active and passive. a_n is in an active state iff it is affected by a_{n+1}. If a_0 is active it goes red; if it is passive it goes blue. For $n>0$, if a_n is in a passive state it does nothing; if it is in an active state it affects a_{n-1} (instantaneously). Now, there are only two possible states for the system: a_0 red, or a_0 blue. Consider the first of these. For $n>0$ a_n affects a_{n-1}; but it can do so only

[17] See, for example, Copleston (1961), pp. 117ff.; Hick (1970), pp. 41ff.; Kenny (1969), pp. 41f.

[18] See Hick (1970), p. 41, for discussion and references.

because it is in an active state; and it is this because it is affected by a_{n+1}. We have here an infinite regress of causes *per se*. Hence, Aquinas' argument fails.

2.8   Leibniz' repair

This flaw in the argument was obvious to many of Aquinas' successors. Some tried to patch it, most notably, Leibniz. Leibniz does not try to find some reason for ruling out the infinite regress; his strategy is to accept the regress (or at least its possibility), but to argue that the existence of God still follows. For example, in 'On the Ultimate Origin of Things', Leibniz observes, with an analogy, that even if there is a regress it makes sense to ask why *it* should have occurred (Latta (1898), pp. 338f.):

Let us suppose that a book of the elements of geometry existed from all eternity and that in succession one copy of it was made from another, it is evident that although we can account for the present book by the book from which it was copied, nevertheless, going back through as many books as we like, we could never reach a complete reason for it, because we can always ask why such books have at all time existed, that is to say, why books at all, and why written in this way. What is true of books is also true of the different states of the world; for, in spite of certain laws of change, the succeeding state is, in some sort, a copy of that which precedes it. Therefore, to whatever earlier state you go back, you never find in it the complete reason of things, that is to say, the reason why there exists any world and why this world rather than some other.

He then goes on to provide the answer to this question:

You may indeed suppose the world eternal; but as you suppose only a succession of states, in none of which do you find the sufficient reason, and as even any number of worlds does not in the least help you to account for them, it is evident that the reason must be sought elsewhere ... From this it is manifest that even if by supposing the eternity of the world, we cannot escape the ultimate extramundane reason of things, that is to say, God.

Four things are clear from these quotations. From the first, it is clear that Leibniz has in mind a temporal regress rather than Aquinas' simultaneous regress. Next, Leibniz prefers talk of reasons to talk of causes; and there is good reason for this. He is in the process of demonstrating that there can be a cause for the cosmos. This cause must therefore be 'outside' the cosmos, and so not in time. 'Reason' may therefore be a better word. None the less, for this chapter I will continue to use 'cause' for any explanatory state, in or out of time. Third, the second quotation shows that Leibniz is invoking the Principle of Sufficient Reason (PSR). What this is, exactly, I will return to, but a traditional way of stating it is as follows: for every contingent state of affairs (i.e. state that could (have) be(en) otherwise), there is a reason why it is as it is.

The fourth, and final, thing is the most important for our purposes: Leibniz observes that we may ask for a cause of the whole sequence of Aquinas' causes, even though this is infinite. In our language: the generator 'cause of' can be applied to the infinity it generates, which is, in modern jargon, an ω-sequence (that is, a sequence isomorphic to the natural numbers). In other words, Leibniz countenances applications of such an operator to an infinite sequence. Well, he countenances one such application anyway; he just assumes that the application of the operator to the ω-sequence will give God. But this is far too swift. First, there is no reason to suppose that the reason for the ω-sequence is extramundane. For if the events in the sequence occur in Zenonian fashion, for example, at times t, t − 1/2, t − 3/4, etc., the cause of the sequence might be some quite mundane event at t − 1. But even if the sequence of events extends back through all time, and so its reason cannot be a state in time, it does not follow that the state is a divine existence; it does not even follow that it is a necessary state of affairs. For the cause may itself be contingent, and so have its own cause.

Leibniz would, I am sure, have replied to this point as follows. If the cause is contingent, then we can simply apply the operator again, and so keep going. Eventually, we must come to a point where the operator is no longer applicable, and so the cause in question is not contingent. This reply countenances the possibility of infinitude after infinitude. Leibniz was not averse to such a bold idea however, as is clear from the following passage (*Monadology*, sections 36, 37[19]):

There is an infinity of present and past forms and motions which go to make up the efficient cause of my present writing; and there is an infinity of minute tendencies of my soul, which go to make its final cause [i.e. purpose].
And as all the *detail* again involves other prior or more detailed contingent things, each of which still needs a similar analysis to yield its reason, we are no further forward: and the sufficient or final reason must be outside the sequence or *series* of particular contingent things, however infinite this series may be.

Does Leibniz' strategy work? Let us spell it out a little more carefully. Consider the sequence generated by repeated applications of the operator 'cause of', as far as possible. That is, whenever we have an event we generate its cause (if it has one); and whenever we have an unbounded sequence of causes, we generate its cause (if it has one); and we do this as far as possible.[20] Call the sequence generated σ, and let the *limit of* σ be either its last member, if it has one, or σ itself if it does not. Now note that the operator cannot be applied to the limit of σ to generate a new cause. For if it could, σ would not be the result of applying the operator as many times as possible. Hence, since

---

[19] Latta (1898), pp. 237f. The idea that there are infinitudes of different sizes also plays an important role in his version of the calculus. See Robinson (1966), pp. 261–4.

[20] Leibniz could not have spelled out what this means exactly, but we know that it means a transfinite sequence indexed by ordinals. At limit ordinals the operator produces the cause of the whole preceding sequence.

the PSR fails to generate a new state, the limit of σ must be necessary rather than contingent. If the limit of σ is σ itself then, since it is necessary, it must have some necessary member; for as Leibniz, in effect, observes in the second quotation above, if all the members of σ are contingent, σ is contingent. It follows, therefore, whatever the limit of σ is, that σ contains some necessary member. We have therefore established the existence of a necessary cause.[21] So the strategy does work.

Whether the necessary cause is the last member of the sequence σ (and so the first cause) depends on what line we take on whether necessary states of affairs may themselves have causes. If we rule that they do not, then the necessary cause must be the last member of the sequence, and so the Ultimate Cause. It should be noted, however, that even with this ruling, we are a long way from establishing the existence of God, for at least two reasons. The first is that the necessary cause has not been shown to be unique. If we had started with a different initial event, or let the operator 'cause of' pick out different causes, we would have obtained another sequence; and there is no guarantee that its necessary state would be the same. Secondly, even if it were, there is no reason to believe – so far, anyway – that it has any other divine properties (such as omnipotence, omniscience, etc.). It must be extramundane since it is not contingent; but the fact that it is out of this world does not make it God.

2.9   The principle of sufficient reason

I should say, lest there be some misunderstanding, that I do not think that the argument of the previous section proves the existence of a necessary state of affairs that causes other members in its sequence. The problem, as traditional wisdom has it, is with the PSR.[22] Whilst it is certainly true that most of the things we normally come across have causes, I see no reason to suppose that more unusual things must have causes. If a certain understanding of quantum physics is right, then it would appear that many unusual things (in the sense that they are not met with in normal experience) have no cause: the decay of a particular radio-active atom, and similar quantum transitions, seem to be completely spontaneous. Moreover, to the extent that the purpose of the argument is to establish a cause of the cosmos, a premise to the effect that every contingent state has a cause would clearly seem to beg the question.

However, while we are on the subject of the PSR, let us return to its formulation. According to the version I gave, every contingent state of affairs

---

[21] A similar argument can be found in Meyer (1987).
[22] See, for example, Hick (1970), p. 51; Mackie (1982), ch. 5.

has a reason. But Leibniz sometimes formulates the Principle rather differently, to the effect that *every* state of affairs has a reason. For example:[23]

The fundamental principle of reasoning is *that there is nothing without a reason*; or, to explain the matter more distinctly that there is no truth for which a reason does not subsist.

Naturally, since I think that the weaker version of the PSR is false, I think this stronger version is false too; but let us re-run the argument of the last section for a first cause, using this version of the PSR. For a novel phenomenon then emerges. Consider the sequence generated by repeated applications of the generator 'cause of', and let this be σ, as before. (It can have no last member now.) By the PSR, we can apply the operator to this to produce a reason for σ. Assuming that nothing can be a reason for itself,[24] this reason cannot be a member of σ (Transcendence). But the cause of σ is exactly one of the things generated by applying the operator in the prescribed fashion. Hence it is in σ (Closure); and hence we have a contradiction at the limit of the iterable.

Conclusion

Leibniz did not, as far as I know, make the above observation. Had he done so, he would have been before his time – by at least a century, if not two. But it serves to bring out the full significance (in the present context) of Leibniz' observation that it may be possible to apply infinity generators to an infinite totality, and so foreshadows future developments. We will pursue these in due course. However, let us leave the limit of the iterable for the moment, and move on to the third of the limits of thought that will concern us: the limit of cognition.

---

[23] Section 1 of *Metaphysical Consequences of the Principle of Reason*, p. 172 of Parkinson (1973). See also sections 32–6 of the *Monadology*.

[24] Natural as this principle is, I am not sure that Leibniz subscribed to it. Contingent truths certainly cannot explain themselves; but maybe necessary ones can, though Leibniz frequently gives distinct reasons for necessary truths. (See for example, the passages referred to in the previous footnote.) I think that the best position for Leibniz is that necessary truths are explained by the fact that they are necessary – a different fact.

3 The limits of cognition

Introduction

So far, we have met two limits of thought: the limit of expression and the limit of iteration (the mathematical infinite). In this chapter we will meet a third: the limit of cognition. As we shall see, this, too, takes us to the verge of contradictions of the characteristic kind.

Cognition concerns relationships that arise between agents and the world that they cognise. Specifically, it concerns the relationships between thought, or language, and the states these (successfully, one hopes) relate to; between representations and the things represented. Typical such relationships, and the ones that will be our primary concern, are knowledge, truth, and rational belief.

We have already met various problematic claims to the effect that certain things transcend our cognition: states in flux (1.3), prime matter (1.6) and God (1.8). But, as might be expected, the situation is thrown into sharpest relief by any doctrine to the effect that there are very definite limits to cognition. Perhaps no doctrine of this kind is more extreme than one according to which there is no objective knowledge of the world at all. A number of views of this kind arose in pre-Kantian philosophy. In this chapter we will look at a couple of them. One way in which the doctrine can arise is in virtue of the claim that there is no objective truth at all (and hence no objective knowledge). This is relativism, and is one of the topics we will look at, mainly through the views of Protagoras. A second way that it can arise is in virtue of the claim that, though there may be objective truths, no evidence can establish what these are. This is skepticism, and is the other topic we will look at, mainly through the writings of Sextus Empiricus.

The contradictions at the limit of cognition that we will look at are all generated in a uniform way. We start with some thesis of the following form, which, for want of a better name, I will call the *Cognition Schema*:

$$\forall x(x \in \Sigma \to Cx)$$

where the quantifiers range over statements, and C is some cognitive predicate ('is (un)known, (un)true', etc.). We then instantiate the quantifiers in the Schema with (a name for) the Schema, or its negation, itself. To what effect, we will see, in due course. With these preliminary remarks out of the way, let us turn to the first of the topics: skepticism.

3.1 Varieties of skepticism

Skepticism flourished in certain periods in Ancient Greece; and most arguments for skepticism derive from arguments used by the Greek skeptics. Hence it is appropriate to approach the topic through them. There were, in fact, two skeptical traditions in Ancient Greece.[1] The earlier one derives from Pyrrho, and is therefore usually called Pyrrhonism. The other developed in the Academy, and its most distinguished adherent was Carneades. (We will see the major difference in a moment.) The most notable skeptic of the period was the last: the second century AD philosopher Sextus Empiricus. Sextus was a Pyrrhonian, but he also spoke at length about his predecessors, including Carneades. Moreover, since he is the only Greek skeptic whose works have survived, we are largely dependent on him for an account not only of Pyrrhonism, but also of Academic skepticism. Hence we will approach the topic of skepticism largely through his writings.

There are many quite distinct forms of skepticism.[2] They can all be stated by forms of the Cognition Schema. What distinguishes them is simply how they instantiate Σ and C. Depending on the form, the set Σ may comprise propositions about God, the future, noumena or any number of other things. In the case of Greek skepticism, Σ was the class of statements about how things are, as opposed to how they appear to be. Typical members of Σ are the claims: 'The wine is sweet', 'It is day', and so on; typical non-members of Σ are the corresponding: 'This wine appears to me to be sweet', 'It seems to me that it is day', and so on. Greek skeptics claimed that statements of appearances are epistemically unproblematic (since the evidence for them is right before our eyes, as it were); but statements about how things actually are, are not. As Sextus puts it (*Outlines of Pyrrhonism*, I, 22):[3]

That we adhere to appearances is plain from what we say about the [epistemological] Criterion ... The Criterion ... is, we say, the appearance, giving this name to what is virtually the sense-presentation. For since this lies in feeling and involuntary affection, it is not open to question. Consequently, no one, I suppose, disputes that the underlying object has this or that appearance; the point in dispute is whether the object is in reality such as it appears to be.

The question of the condition C is slightly more complex. It is always the negation of some positive epistemological notion, P; but there are a number of

---

[1] For an excellent discussion of the two, see Stough (1969).
[2] On the history of the various forms of skepticism, see Popkin (1967).
[3] All quotations from Sextus are taken from Bury (1933).

these. Positive epistemological notions come in a continuum. At the weakest end is something like *it is rationally more probable than not*; at the strongest end is the attitude *it is rationally certain*. I will use the phrase 'rational acceptability' for an attitude at the weakest end of the spectrum. I am aware that such terminology is contentious (and in particular, that one might want a good deal more than the minimal end of the scale for real rational acceptability); but in the present context the definition is just meant to be stipulative.

Even more contentious is where knowledge appears on the scale. Many people think that it is to be applied only to the maximal extreme, since anything less than rational certitude cannot be knowledge. Fallibilists about knowledge, on the other hand, are prepared to use the term for the top end of the scale, not just its top point. Fallibilists about knowledge have to add an extra condition for knowledge, however. For a necessary condition for knowledge is truth. Rational certitude, presumably, implies this; anything less does not. Thus, fallibilists must say that something is known only if it is both at the high end of the scale, and is true. Fortunately we do not need to discuss these issues further for our purposes.[4]

Now, what epistemological attitude is appropriate in a statement of Greek skepticism? In the skepticism of Carneades, and, more generally, Academic skepticism, the attitude was (rational) certitude. Hence their skepticism was to the effect that one cannot be certain about how things are (as opposed to appear), though one may have rational reasons for thinking one view better than another. Sextus, on the other hand, and more generally the Pyrrhonians, formulated their skepticism in terms of rational acceptability. Hence their skepticism was of a much more extreme kind, to the effect that there is *no rational reason of any kind* to prefer any claim about how things are to any other; or, in the phrase Sextus uses, 'no more (this than that)' where (*Outlines of Pyrrhonism*, I, 190):

this indicates our feeling, whereby we come to end in equipoise because of the equipollence of the opposed objects [*sc.* propositions]; and by 'equipollence' we mean equality in respect of what seems probable to us, and by 'opposed' we mean in general conflicting, and by 'equipoise' a refusal of assent to either alternative.

The state of equipoise is usually called *epoche*.

3.2   Sextus' argument for skepticism

Sextus compiled and polished all the arguments used for skepticism in both the streams of Greek skepticism. Many of the arguments are *ad hominem*, against various non-skeptics, and, in particular, the Stoics. However, the

---

[4] For an introduction to the enormous literature see, for example, Pollock (1986) or Lehrer (1990).

corner-stone of his skepticism was a very general argument based on the Tropes of Aenesidemus.

The Tropes are all arguments to the effect that the way things appear is dependent on such things as the sense-organs of the perceiver, other subjective factors, the context of perception, and so on. As a corollary, it follows that the same thing can be perceived in quite different, even contradictory, ways by different perceivers, or the same perceiver at different times. An object, for example, appears large when you are close to it, and small when you are far away. These arguments have largely been absorbed into Western philosophy, and are not now contentious.

What Sextus makes of them is, however, contentious. Sextus argues that because the world (i.e., what is the case) is perceived as different by different observers, one can never infer that the world is so-and-so from the mere fact that it appears so-and-so. What is needed, in addition, is some criterion to distinguish those appearances that are veridical from those that are not (*Outlines of Pyrrhonism*, I, 114):

For he who prefers one impression to another, or one 'circumstance' to another, does so either uncritically or without proof or critically and with proof; but [if he were to do it uncritically] ... he would be discredited. [So] ... if he is to pass judgment on the impressions he must certainly judge them by some criterion.

But now we have a problem. For we have reason to believe that the results of applying the criterion are correct only if we have reason to believe that the criterion itself is correct. And the criterion is not itself a statement of appearances; hence, if it is justified it must have some rationale or proof; and now the question arises as to what justification we have for believing that proof to be correct. Clearly, to appeal to the criterion at this point would be to beg the question (*Outlines of Pyrrhonism*, I, 117):

in this way both the criterion and the proof are involved in the circular process of reasoning, and thereby both are found to be untrustworthy; for since each of them is dependent on the credibility of the other, the one is lacking in credibility just as much as the other.

The only other possibility is that we must be able to give another proof of the correctness of this proof. But the question now arises as to the justification of this proof. Clearly, we are embarked on a regress; and if the regress is not to be terminated illicitly by appealing to the very criterion we were supposed to be justifying, it must go to infinity. But then it is vicious. For then there is no way that we could ever establish that the criterion, or any proof in the series, is correct (*Outlines of Pyrrhonism*, I, 122f.):

if he [who is trying to justify the criterion] asserts that the proof is true he will be asked for a proof of its truth, and again, for a proof of this latter proof, since it also must be true, and so on *ad infinitum*. But to produce proofs to infinity is impossible; so that neither by the use of proofs will he be able to prefer one sense-impression to another.

Thus, there is no way of justifying the claim that one set of appearances, as opposed to another, is a better indication of how things are. And hence there is no reasonable belief about how things are, as opposed to appear.

3.3   Analysis of the argument

Sextus' argument is an intriguing one. It has a major flaw, however. It assumes that our beliefs about how things are, are all obtained from our beliefs about how things appear to be, by applying some filter which lets through only the veridical perceptions. This assumption he took over from the Stoics; and its empiricism cannot be sustained. It can do no justice to our beliefs concerning, for example, mathematics or theoretical science.

However, this observation does not go to the heart of the matter, since there clearly are beliefs about the world that we have, and that we have in pretty much the way that Sextus supposes – at least in a 'rational reconstruction' of the process. For example, I believe that there is a flag on the pole of the building opposite that in which I write; and I believe this because I can see it out of the window. But even in this case Sextus' argument fails: I do have good (though by no means infallible) reason to suppose that there is a flag.

The flaw in Sextus' argument is, I take it, the claim that in order to have reasonable grounds for my belief I need some criterion which vouchsafes my perceptions. This is to misunderstand the relationship between experience and reason. Experience is always a reason for believing that the world is in such and such a way. It is a defeasible reason, and may be defeated by other things. The defeaters may be many and varied. We may know them in advance; for example, I may be aware that my perception at such distances is not reliable. Alternatively, we may learn them afterwards; for example, I may learn that the appearance of a flag is produced by a cunning hologram. If and when the defeaters arise, the experience ceases to be reasonable ground for the belief. But even though the evidence is defeasible, it is evidence, none the less, without further justification.[5]

The situation may be clarified by thinking of it in terms of non-monotonic logic.[6] Non-monotonic inferences are inferences of the form:

   α; there is no reason to suppose otherwise – so β

---

[5] The most eminent exponent of this kind of line was probably Thomas Reid. See his *Essays on the Intellectual Powers of Man*, for example, Essay II, ch. 22. A more modern exponent is Pollock. See Pollock (1986), ch. 2.

[6] For an introduction to non-monotonic logic, see ch. 6 of Genesereth and Nilsson (1987).

In the case in question, α is of the form 'It appears to be the case that β'. Further information, γ, may turn up which does give us reason to suppose otherwise (that is, is a defeater). Hence, although we may have $\alpha \vdash \beta$, we do not necessarily have $\alpha \wedge \gamma \vdash \beta$ – which is the mark of a non-monotonic logic.

To illustrate the situation further, suppose that a hitherto unknown painting is discovered. In style and age it is a typical Rembrandt; it also bears what appears to be Rembrandt's signature. The painting appears to be a Rembrandt; and, no defeaters being known, we infer that it is a Rembrandt. But now suppose that a stroke-for-stroke identical picture turns up, and it is clear that at least one is a forgery, but that there is no indication as to which it is. Then this information provides a defeater for the former inference. Notice that the mere *possibility* of the existence of the *doppelgänger* is not a defeater; but its actuality is. In a similar way, the Trope arguments of Sextus certainly establish that given any perception it is possible for things to appear different to another, or to oneself at a different time, but this is not sufficient to defeat the inference.

One objection to this kind of account is given by Lehrer ((1990), pp. 64f.), who argues that for the inference from 'It appears that β' to β to work (even non-monotonically), there must be some suppressed premises. For example, to infer that there is a flag on the mast of the building opposite, I must have information concerning what flags are like, etc. Thus, 'It appears that β' can never on its own justify β. (And the extra premises are not themselves state-ments of appearance; so the regress looms.) This, I think, misplaces the rela-tionship of the role that the extra information plays with respect to the inference. The information is not required as a premise for the argument. (A young child, for example, might not even be able to articulate the informa-tion, but still makes the inference.) Rather, the information is that in virtue of which the inference is reasonable. In exactly the same way, the fact that a deductive argument is valid is not itself a premise of the argument; it is the fact in virtue of which the argument is reasonable (as was wittily exposed by Lewis Carroll (1895)). If the inference *is* reasonable then its sole premise gives a reason for the conclusion. *Why* the inference is reasonable is a different ques-tion, and not one that needs to be answered before we know the premise to be a reason (any more than we must have a theory as to why *modus ponens* is valid before α and 'If α then β' provide a reason for β). Hence the regress is not generated.

It is worth noting that Sextus' argument does establish Carneades' form of skepticism, at least for certain kinds of claims. Just because the inference to how things are is non-monotonic, it is possible that a defeater may turn up, and so that we may have to retract our conclusion. It is not, therefore, certain. Put differently, if one takes the inference: it appears to be the case that α; hence it is certain that α; to be itself a non-monotonic inference, then the mere pos-sibility of alternative perceptions, and all that this may entail, *is* a defeater for this inference. Hence it is never valid. Posterity has, in fact, strengthened this version of the skeptical argument. For we now have a much better understanding of the theory-dependence, and consequent fallibility, of observation; but I shall not pursue this matter here.[7]

This is hardly a comprehensive discussion of the topic. However, it at least indicates where, I take it, the argument for Sextus' form of skepticism fails; which is sufficient for the present.

3.4   Skepticism and self-reference

Let us set the failure of Sextus' argument aside for the moment; suppose that it worked. The following situation would then arise. A skeptical claim is an instance of the Cognition Schema of the form $\forall x(x \in \Sigma \to \neg Px)$ where Σ is some class of claims, in our case, claims that the world is such-and-such (as opposed to appears to be such-and-such); and P is a positive epistemological attitude. Equivalently, let Π be the set of all statements that are P, then skepticism is the view that $\forall x(x \in \Sigma \to x \notin \Pi)$. Call this claim φ, and take angle brackets to be a name-forming operator; so that $\langle \varphi \rangle$, is the name of φ. Applying skepticism to itself, we obtain: $\langle \varphi \rangle \in \Sigma \to \langle \varphi \rangle \notin \Pi$. Next, observe that φ is not itself a statement concerning appearances, i.e., $\langle \varphi \rangle \in \Sigma$. It follows that $\langle \varphi \rangle \notin \Pi$, (Transcendence). In Sextus' case P is rational acceptability. Hence we have demonstrated that Sextus' skepticism is not rationally acceptable.

But, by supposition, Sextus' arguments provide cogent reasons for supposing that φ *is* rationally acceptable, i.e., that $\langle \varphi \rangle \in \Pi$ (Closure). Moreover, Sextus would seem to be committed to this fact. After all, he spends several hundred pages giving reasons for skepticism. If he does not suppose that he is demonstrating that skepticism is rationally acceptable, what on earth does he think he is doing? We would therefore seem to have a contradiction of the kind characteristic of the limits of thought.[8]

Sextus was aware of this. What was his response? He denied that the arguments show that skepticism is rationally acceptable (that is, the argument to Closure). He claimed that the arguments have rational force until they are deployed. At this point, however, they cease to have force, since they 'destroy themselves'. He put it as follows (*Against the Logicians*, II, 480–1):

---

[7] For a brief discussion and references, see, for example, ch. 3 of Chalmers (1976).

[8] Notice that the contradiction does not arise for Carneades and similar skeptics, who take P to be certitude. The result of applying their skepticism to itself is the claim that skepticism is not certain. The argument to Closure fails, however. For them, the skeptical arguments simply show that their skepticism is rationally acceptable. They do not show that it is certain, for the conclusions are only as good as the premises, and these are not certain.

there are many things which produce the same effect on themselves as they produce on other things. Just as, for example, fire after consuming the fuel destroys also itself, and like as purgatives after driving the fluids out of the body expel themselves as well, so too the argument . . . can cancel itself also. And again, just as it is not impossible for the man who ascends to a high place to overturn the ladder with his foot after the ascent, so also it is not unlikely that the Sceptic after he has arrived at the demonstration of his thesis by means of the argument . . . as it were a step ladder, should then abolish this very argument.

Sextus, then, tried to avoid the contradiction by explicitly bringing time into the issue. Before the force of the arguments is felt, they have force; after, they do not. This solution is not satisfactory. If he were talking about the persuasive content of the arguments – a purely psychological matter – then things could be as the metaphor of the ladder suggests; so that they are persuasive until they are seen to be self-undercutting, by which time their work is done. And Sextus does often talk of the arguments as therapeutic, advanced purely to have the desired psychological effect. But this reply is an *ignoratio*. For we were not talking about the persuasive power of the arguments, but about their rational force; and this is not a time-dependent matter. If Sextus' arguments worked then they would show that skepticism is rationally acceptable, contrary to his committed position that they are not.

A much better line for him to take would be simply to accept the logic of his own conclusion: that the arguments he uses have no rational force. Nor need this be as embarrassing as it at first appears. For he can quite consistently maintain that the arguments are all intended *ad hominem* against someone who does not accept skepticism. Against such people, who accept the premises of the arguments, the arguments must have rational force. Against people, such as skeptics, who do not accept the premises, they have no force. This line is advocated, successfully, by the modern-day Pyrrhonian, Feyerabend. In *Against Method* (1975), Feyerabend uses all kinds of arguments in support of a skeptical position; but he stresses that the arguments are *ad hominem*.[9]

Sextus is not out of the woods yet, however. Even if he does not think that his arguments show skepticism to be rationally acceptable, he still maintains skepticism. And how can one maintain something that one does not hold to be rationally acceptable? To assert something involves taking on the commitment to support it with rational grounds for supposing it to be (objectively) true if challenged; if one refuses to do this, it voids the act of its social significance. To put it bluntly, such a person can legitimately be ignored. (The point is well argued in Brandom (1983).) By maintaining skepticism Sextus is therefore committed to the view that it is rationally defensible.

---

[9] See section 1 of Feyerabend (1977). Similar comments are also made by Hume about skeptical arguments in the last paragraph of the *Treatise*, I, 4, 2.

Sextus is well aware of this difficulty, too. His solution is simple; he denies that he maintains skepticism. He neither asserts nor denies it. In the state of *epoche* the skeptic neither asserts nor denies anything (*Outlines of Pyrrhonism, I*, 192):

Non-assertion ... is avoidance of assertion in the general sense in which it includes both affirmation and negation, so that non-assertion is a mental condition of ours because of which we refuse either to affirm or to deny anything.

Unfortunately Sextus now appears to be asserting something else (to the effect that he is not asserting anything); and this is equally contradictory. Sextus could maintain that he is not really asserting this either. But this would be (a) equally contradictory; and (b) disingenuous. For, in making this utterance, Sextus does intend us thereby to believe that he asserts nothing; and this is exactly what assertion amounts to.[10] Hence, Sextus' attempts to avoid the contradiction at the limit of cognition work only by generating a contradiction at the limit of the expressible. His claim that he is not asserting anything is, by his own view, not something he is asserting (Transcendence). But he *is* asserting it (Closure). We have here, for the first time, a phenomenon that will become familiar: the attempt to avoid the contradiction at one limit of thought forces one into a contradiction at another.

3.5   Protagorean relativism

We have not finished with Sextus yet. However, let us leave him for the moment, and turn to the second reason one might have for denying the existence of objective knowledge: that there is no objective truth. The most famous proponent of this view was also the most famous of the Sophists, Protagoras. Unfortunately, his book, *Truth*, has not survived, and so we have to rely on secondary sources for our knowledge of his views. Of these, the major one is Plato's dialogue the *Theaetetus*. How accurate a portrayal of Protagoras' views this is, may be a contentious issue.[11] I do not want to enter the debate here. By 'Protagoras' I shall just mean the Protagoras of the *Theaetetus*. If this person is simply a construction of Plato, this does not matter: it is the ideas themselves in which we will be interested.

The topic of the *Theaetetus* is exactly the nature of knowledge, though it wanders far and wide through the issue. (In the first part of chapter 1 we already saw part of one of the labyrinths through which the discussion wends: the flux.) As usual, the dialogue stands up, and, in the person of Socrates, knocks down, a number of different definitions. A major definition discussed is to the effect that knowledge is perception (mooted at 151e1–4). What 'percep-

---

[10]   See Priest (1987), 4.6.
[11]   Though it is commonly held to be reasonably accurate. See Kerford (1967).

tion' means here is an important question. Sometimes, as we shall see, it means simply sense perception; at other times it is interpreted as appearance in general. In particular, it is almost immediately interpreted this way, when the definition is said to be identical with Protagoras' famous dictum with which *Truth* is reputed to have started (152a2–4):[12]

a man is the measure of all things: of those which are, that they are, and of those which are not, that they are not.

Protagoras' relativism about knowledge is a simple consequence of his relativism about truth. This is made clear in the dialogue, when Protagoras' view is glossed immediately (152a6–8) as:

everything is, for me, the way it appears to me, and is, for you, the way it appears to you.

We will next be concerned with the arguments put forward for and against this view. It is important, at the start, to note that the concept of truth employed here is a relativist one, in the sense that the truth of any claim is relative to a cognitive agent (true for x). Protagoras need not claim that there is no objective (agent independent) notion of truth (truth *simpliciter*). All that he needs to claim is that nothing satisfies such a notion.

3.6   The argument for relativism

The argument for the relativity of truth in the *Theaetetus* comes in two parts. The first (152b f.) points, in effect, to the phenomena to be codified later in the Tropes of Aenesidemus: how things appear to be varies from person to person. This in itself does not get us very far. Unless 'is true (for me)' merely means 'appears to me to be so' – in which case Protagoras' view is a rather uninteresting tautology – we still need something that takes us from how things appear (to me) to how things are (for me). This is provided by an argument for the infallibility of appearances. It is a long argument which starts around 153d8 and culminates around 160c8 with the sentence 'so my perception is true for me – because it's always of the being that's mine'.

The argument depends on an unusual account of sensory perception. For present purposes, the main features of it are as follows. In perception, the perceiver and the world combine to produce a unique object, the thing perceived. This is unique to the pair producing it and, crucially, private to the perceiver. Hence, there can be no question of the perceiver being wrong about it.

I will not give a detailed account of the argument. This is unnecessary here. The question at issue is whether the argument succeeds in establishing

---

[12] Quotations from the *Theaetetus* are taken from McDowell (1973).

Protagorean relativism; and the answer is that it does not, for several reasons. First, the passage in question presents little more than an exposition of the theory of perception: no real reason is given as to why we should accept it. Secondly, it is a rather dubious theory anyway since it divorces the contents of perceptual claims from the world that (partly) produces them. Thirdly, the inference from the claim that the object of perception is private to the conclusion that the perceiver cannot be wrong about it is fallacious. (A hallucination is a private object, but the fact that I hallucinate a person coming through the door does not imply that a hallucination *is* coming through the door.)[13] Finally, and crucially, the argument establishes, at best, the infallibility of how things appear in the case of *sensory perception*. The *Theaetetus* is reasonably liberal about what might be counted as a case of sense perception ('seeings, hearings, smellings, feelings of cold, feelings of heat ... pleasures, pains, desires, fears' 156b4–6). But it is clear that the object of perception is constructed as a direct result of an immediate input from the world.[14] Hence it can hardly establish the veridicality of how things appear in the general sense, as when one says it appears to Protagoras that his doctrine is true, to use an example of a kind that will become crucial in a moment.

3.7 Socrates' attack

As we have seen, the argument for Protagorean relativism in the *Theaetetus* fails. Let us set this aside for the present and turn to Socrates' attack on the doctrine. Socrates has three major arguments against the doctrine. Only one of these will concern us here, that at 169d3–171d8.[15] Socrates observes that if someone, x, believes Protagoras' doctrine, they must agree that no one ever makes a false judgment. This, in itself, is said to be incredible (170c9), though Protagoras would not have conceded this. (No person makes a judgment that is

---

[13] And arguably, the privacy of the object even renders the claim of correctness senseless. The object is rather like Wittgenstein's beetle in a box (*Philosophical Investigations*, section 293).

[14] See McDowell (1973), pp. 137f. McDowell suggests (p. 118), and I think plausibly, that the official sense of perception at issue here is non-propositional altogether.

[15] The second (161c) is a very swift *ad hominem* argument to the effect that Protagoras' view is human chauvinist. The third is launched immediately afterwards, and is to the effect that if whatever anyone believes is true to them, then all views are equally good, and so there is no such thing as wisdom (which Protagoras professes to teach). After an interlude, Protagoras (in the person of Socrates) replies (166d f.) that wisdom has nothing to do with truth; the wise person is, essentially, one whose views are most effective in producing happiness. Again, after an interlude, Socrates objects to this reply (177c ff.), essentially, that whether or not a person's views are conducive to producing the effect aimed at is an objective matter, and not one in which each person's view is equally valid. The patient's view of whether they have recovered, for example, is more valid than the doctor's. I am dubious that this argument works, if Protagoras is prepared to stick to his guns and insist that judgments about efficacy are relative, too (which he may do, it seems to me, with just as much plausibility as with judgments about other matters).

false *for themself*; but they may make a judgment that is false *for x*.) The main argument comes when the observation is applied to Protagoras' view itself (171a5–c7):

SOCRATES. [The observation] involves this very subtle implication. Protagoras agrees that everyone has in his judgments the things which are. In doing that, he's surely conceding that the opinion of those who make opposing judgments about his own opinion – that is, their opinion that what he thinks is false – is true.

THEODORUS. Certainly.

SOCRATES. So if he admits their opinion is true – that is, the opinion of those who believe that what he thinks is false – he would be conceding that his own opinion is false?

THEODORUS. Certainly.

SOCRATES. But the others don't concede that what they think is false?

THEODORUS. No.

SOCRATES. And Protagoras, again, admits that judgments of theirs are true, too, according to what he has written.

THEODORUS. Evidently.

SOCRATES. So his theory will be disputed by everyone, beginning with Protagoras himself; or rather, Protagoras himself will agree that it's wrong. When he concedes that someone who contradicts him is making a true judgment, he will himself be conceding that a dog, or an ordinary man, isn't the measure of so much as one thing that he hasn't come to know. Isn't that so?

THEODORUS. Yes.

SOCRATES. Well then, since it's disputed by everyone, it would seem that Protagoras' *Truth* isn't true for anyone: not for anyone else and not for Protagoras himself.

The argument is an attempt to establish that Protagoras' view is true for no one, including himself (whilst the same is not true of the views of his opponents). The key part of it is that where Socrates attempts to show that Protagoras' views are false by his own lights.

The argument is a very simple one, and proceeds as follows. Let a be any opponent of Protagoras, let Σ be the set of claims maintained by a, and let T be 'is true'. Then according to Socrates, Protagoras is committed to:

$$\forall x(x \in \Sigma \rightarrow Tx) \tag{1}$$

Call this φ. Then since $\neg\varphi$ is in Σ, we have that $T\langle\neg\varphi\rangle$; and so Protagoras is committed to the view that his own doctrine is false. Unfortunately, there is a simple error in the argument. Protagoras is not committed to (1). What he is committed to is:

$$\forall x(x \in \Sigma \rightarrow T_a x)$$

where T_a is the relative truth predicate, 'true for a'. The argument shows that Protagoras is committed to $T_a\langle\neg\varphi\rangle$. But this is benign enough, and without some way of moving from here to $T\langle\neg\varphi\rangle$, or at least $T_p\langle\neg\varphi\rangle$ (where p is Protagoras), the argument collapses.

Denyer ((1991), pp. 99–100) tries to repair the argument by suggesting that for statements like Protagoras', truth and truth for a person come to the same thing, so that we can simply ignore the relativisation. He points out that if one takes an indexical claim, such as 'I am hot', this can be true for one person (for example, Adam) but not another (for example, Eve). But if the indexicality is resolved, as in 'Adam is hot', it no longer makes sense to suppose that the truth value of the statement can vary from person to person. Now, for Protagoras, statements *are* indexicals in a certain sense. But the problem with Denyer's repair is that, for Protagoras, the qualifier 'is true for x' takes an indexical and produces *another* indexical. Consider the claim 'there are true logical contradictions'. This is true for Priest, but false for Aristotle. Now consider the claim: 'That there are true logical contradictions is true for Marx.' Is this true? Well, it is true for Priest, but not, for example, for Acton.[16] People can and do disagree over what was true for Marx.[17]

3.8   Nothing is true

Unfortunately (for Protagoras), his self-referential worries are not over. For Protagorean relativism is committed to the claim that nothing is (objectively) true, i.e., the instance of the Cognition Schema $\forall x(x \in \Sigma \rightarrow \neg Tx)$, where Σ is the set of all statements and T is a non-relative truth predicate. Let this sentence be φ. Then, by the usual argument, it follows that $\neg T\langle\varphi\rangle$. Hence, Protagoras' own views are not true (Transcendence). But Protagoras has given arguments for his view. If these arguments worked, they would establish that φ is true (Closure).

Sextus faces a similar problem. And it will be illuminating to compare the two. He, too, maintains that nothing is true (*Outlines of Pyrrhonism*, II, 88):

the true things are either apparent only, or non-evident only, or in part non-evident and in part apparent; but none of these alternatives is true, as we shall show; therefore nothing is true.

His reasons are, however, rather different from those of Protagoras. Sextus maintains a verificationist account of truth. In particular, he takes verification to be a necessary condition for truth.[18] He never, as far as I am aware, argues for this, or even spells the matter out clearly. The fact, though, is at its most obvious when he argues that nothing is true, immediately after the passage just

---

[16]   See Priest (1989b), section 1.
[17]   This argument assumes that 'true for x' is an iterable operator. But even Denyer argues that this is the sensible line for Protagoras to take ((1991), p. 94).
[18]   See Stough (1969), pp. 140 ff.

quoted. For when we look at the arguments Sextus uses in support of this claim we meet the familiar circularity and regress arguments of 3.2, which are really about verification.

These also make it clear that when Sextus says that *nothing* is true, he is talking about claims as to how things *are*, not how they appear. Despite this, the self-referential problem is the same, since φ is just such a claim. Sextus never discusses the contradiction, as far as I know, but what he would have said about it is obvious enough. He would simply have maintained that he does not assert that nothing is true, φ, for the reasons we examined in 3.4. As we saw there, this move generates contradictions of its own. The important point here, however, is that Protagoras cannot make even this move to extract himself from contradiction. His assertions and arguments are direct and not in the least *ad hominem*.

In defence of Protagoras, it might be suggested that the arguments advanced by him are intended to establish only that φ is true *for Protagoras* and not true *simpliciter*. But this line cannot be sustained. As I argued in 3.4, asserting is a social activity, and to assert something is precisely to take on the commitment that the thing asserted is objectively correct.[19] Assertion (and *a fortiori* giving reasons), therefore presupposes a commitment to the objective correctness of what is asserted. As Passmore puts it:

to engage in discourse at all [Protagoras] has to assert that something is the case. It is not just that he is pretending to have a certain social role, that of teacher or 'wise man', which he is not entitled to claim ... The matter cuts deeper: it is presupposed in all discourse that some propositions are true, that there is a difference between being the case and not being the case, and to deny this in discourse is already to presuppose the existence of the difference.[20]

3.9   Cognition and paradox

We have seen that both Sextus and Protagoras fall into contradiction at the limits of cognition. This is academic at the moment, however; for these contradictions are predicated on the assumptions that Sextus' arguments for skepticism, and Protagoras' arguments for relativism, work. And as we have seen, they do not. But this is not the end of the matter.

Let φ be any instance of the Cognition Schema, $\forall x(x \in \Sigma \rightarrow x \notin \Pi)$, where Π is the set of all statements defined by some cognitive predicate, P, that entails (objective) truth (such as knowledge or truth itself), and where Σ is any

---

[19] In fact, objective truth is precisely the aim of assertion. See Priest (1987), 4.5.

[20] Passmore (1970), pp. 67–8. The fact that there is a difference between truth and untruth does not, note, entail that nothing is both.

set that contains φ (for example, the set of all statements). Now consider the following deduction.

Suppose $\langle\varphi\rangle \in \Pi$

then φ since being P entails being true

i.e. $\forall x(x \in \Sigma \rightarrow x \notin \Pi)$

so $\langle\varphi\rangle \in \Sigma \rightarrow \langle\varphi\rangle \notin \Pi$

But $\langle\varphi\rangle \in \Sigma$

Hence $\langle\varphi\rangle \notin \Pi$

Thus, $\langle\varphi\rangle \in \Pi$ entails $\langle\varphi\rangle \notin \Pi$; it follows (by the Law of Excluded Middle or *reductio*) that $\langle\varphi\rangle \notin \Pi$. Thus, we have established, on no assumptions, that φ is not P. This would not trouble Sextus (when P is knowledge), or Protagoras (when P is truth). But note that if P is truth then it follows that φ is false, i.e., $\neg\forall x(x \in \Sigma \rightarrow x \notin \Pi)$; and thus, arguably, that $\exists x(x \in \Sigma \wedge x \in \Pi)$. But this x cannot be φ itself (since φ is not true), so there must be something else in Σ. This is paradoxical since, as far as the logic of the argument goes, apart from containing φ, Σ was quite arbitrary. Yet we have a proof that there must be something else in it.[21]

We can make this explicit by taking Σ to be, by definition, the set whose only member is φ, i.e., $\forall x(x \in \Sigma \leftrightarrow x = \langle\varphi\rangle)$ (*). (This is not quite as straightforward as it may seem since φ was originally defined in terms of Σ, so the definition is circular. However, the problem can be cleaned up by techniques of self-reference.[22]) As before, we have a proof that $\langle\varphi\rangle \notin \Pi$ (Transcendence). But now we can establish Closure as follows:

$\langle\varphi\rangle \notin \Pi$

so $\forall x(x = \langle\varphi\rangle \rightarrow x \notin \Pi)$[23]

but $\forall x(x \in \Sigma \leftrightarrow x = \langle\varphi\rangle)$ (*)

so $\forall x(x \in \Sigma \rightarrow x \notin \Pi)$ by transitivity of $\rightarrow$

i.e. φ

Hence $\langle\varphi\rangle \in \Pi$ since Π is the set of truths. We therefore have a contradiction of the characteristic kind. In fact, the contradiction is a rather familiar one. The

---

[21] This paradox is spelled out very nicely by Prior (1961). For a further discussion, see Priest (1991b).

[22] For example, let 'Σ' be some new name, and let φ be the sentence $\forall x(x = \langle\varphi\rangle \rightarrow x \notin \Pi)$. We now stipulate that 'Σ' refers to $\{\varphi\}$. See Kripke (1975), p. 693.

[23] Those who think that $\rightarrow$ is relevant will have to take it to be an enthymematic implication at this point, as in Meyer (1973), p. 172.

statement φ says of all the things in Σ, and consequently just of itself, that it is not true. It is therefore just the Liar paradox, a paradox whose credentials are as ancient as those of skepticism, if not as those of relativism.[24] Moreover, in the case of the present construction, if P is knowledge we have Closure too, since the above argument *establishes* φ as true, and so φ is known. This is the Knower paradox of Kaplan and Montague.[25]

Conclusion

We have seen that Sextus' and Protagoras' views generate contradictions of the kind typical of the limits of cognition. These contradictions depend, ultimately, on their arguments for skepticism and relativism, which, as we saw, do not work. But we have also seen that in the vicinity of these contradictions there are others that are produced by applying instances of the Cognition Schema to itself, and that depend on no such arguments. Neither Sextus nor Protagoras observed these contradictions. And what they would have made of them had they done so, I will not speculate. Future generations made a good deal of them, as we shall see in due course. At any rate, they show the contradictions at the limit of cognition. In the next chapter we move from cognition to conception.

[24] See, for example, the references to the paradox in Kneale and Kneale (1962).

[25] See Kaplan and Montague (1960). Strictly speaking, for the argument to Closure to work in this case, we need not just (*), but that (*) is known to be true. But, since (*) is true by definition, this is unproblematic.

4   The limits of conception

Introduction

In this chapter we will discuss the last of the four limits that will concern us in the book: the limit of conception. It is common enough to suppose that there are things beyond conception; but *prima facie* at least, it is difficult to do so without conceiving them in some sense. Hence the contradiction at the limit of conception. We will see this phenomenon arising in two pre-Kantian philosophers. The first is Anselm, whose concern is God. The second is Berkeley, whose concern is quite different: idealism. Despite the difference, we will see that Anselm and Berkeley are tied together by more than just contradiction. They also share certain views about how objects may be characterised. Specifically, they both subscribe to the view that if an object is characterised as the (or a) thing with such and such properties, then it must have those properties. If we let δ be some description operator (so that $\delta x\varphi(x)$ may be read as 'a/the thing with property φ'), then they both subscribe to the schema:

$$\varphi(\delta x\varphi(x))$$

Following Routley (1980), I will call this the *Characterisation Principle*, 'CP' for short. As we shall see, the CP is not, in general, correct. Despite this, the contradiction at the limit of conception shines through the work of these two philosophers.

4.1   Anselm's ontological argument

In 1.8 and 1.9 we met Cusanus and his views on God. Cusanus held that God is ineffable; but, as we saw there, the reason for this is precisely that God is beyond categorisation, and so conception. We will start this chapter with Anselm of Canterbury, the eleventh-century philosopher and theologian, in whom this idea is worked out in much more careful detail.

Anselm of Canterbury is now remembered mainly for his version of the Ontological Argument for the existence of God. In chapter 2 of his *Proslogion* he defines God to be a being greater than which cannot be conceived. His argument for the existence of such a being (curiously enough, addressed to God in person) is then given in the following famous passage:[1]

Is there, then, no such nature as You, for the Fool has said in his heart that God does not exist? But surely when this very Fool hears the words 'something nothing greater than which can be thought', he understands what he hears. And what he understands is in his understanding, even if he does not understand [judge] it to exist . . . But surely that than which a greater cannot be thought cannot be only in the understanding. For if it were only in the understanding, it could be thought to exist in reality – which is greater [than existing only in the understanding]. Therefore, if that than which a greater cannot be thought existed only in the understanding, then that than which a greater *cannot* be thought would be that than which a greater *can* be thought! But surely this conclusion is impossible. Hence, without doubt, something than which a greater cannot be thought exists both in the understanding and in reality.

Anselm's argument is by *reductio* and can be summarised thus. No being greater than God can be conceived to exist. But suppose that God does not exist. Then a being just like God except that he existed would be greater; hence a being greater than God could be conceived. Contradiction.

Anselm's argument raises many ticklish issues. An obvious and contentious one is how we should understand the crucial Neo-platonist premise that a being like God except that it exists, would be greater.[2] Another, is why we should suppose this to be true. Fortunately, we can pass over these issues here.[3] The reason is that it is clear that the argument also assumes the CP. At the first step, God (which is defined to be a being greater than which cannot be conceived) is assumed to be such that a greater being cannot be conceived. (Moreover, the being which, by definition, is like God except that it exists is assumed to exist, since it is greater.)[4] As we shall see in a moment, given the CP there is a version of the Ontological Argument which dispenses with all the other machinery.

4.2   The inconceivability of God

Before we see this, however, let us look at a less well known chapter of the *Proslogion*, chapter 15. In this short chapter Anselm says:

[1] Quotations from the *Proslogion* are taken from Hopkins and Richardson (1974).

[2] My own shot is as follows. Let τx be 'x is conceived'. Then God (g) may be defined as $\delta x \neg \exists y (\tau y \wedge y > x)$. (Quantifiers, note, are not existentially loaded.) Let $\varphi(x)$ be the second-order condition $Ex \wedge \forall P(P \neq E \rightarrow (Px \leftrightarrow Pg))$, where E is existence. Then the claim is $\forall x (\neg Eg \wedge \varphi(x) \rightarrow x > g)$.

[3] For a discussion of a number of issues involved in the argument, see Campbell (1976).

[4] In the notation of fn. 2, applying the CP to g and $\delta x \varphi(x)$, and throwing in the principle $\tau \delta x \varphi(x)$ gives the desired contradiction.

Therefore, O Lord, not only are You that than which a greater cannot be thought, but You are also something greater than can be thought. For since something of this kind can be thought [viz., something which is greater than can be thought], if You were not this being then something greater than You could be thought – a consequence which is impossible.

What, exactly, the structure of Anselm's argument is, is less than obvious. However, again, it is clear that it depends on the CP, since it relies on the claim that nothing greater than God can be thought – and, for good measure, it requires that the thing that is greater than can be thought *is* greater than can be thought. It is also clear that the argument assumes that God can be thought of, or else there is no reason for supposing that something greater than anything that can be thought of is greater than God.[5]

Leaving the cogency of the argument aside for the moment, it is clear that Anselm is caught in a contradiction characteristic of a limit of thought. The argument shows that God is not in the set of things that can be conceived (Transcendence). Yet Anselm obviously is conceiving God in putting forward the argument (Closure).

Anselm is, in general, aware of the contradiction involved in saying anything about the inconceivable. In chapter 65 of the *Monologion* he tries to defuse the problem by insisting that our concepts do not apply to God literally, but only by analogy (*per aliud*). This solution cannot be sustained. For in the claim that God is inconceivable 'inconceivable' must have its literal sense, or the whole force of the claim is lost. God must therefore be literally conceivable, if only as the inconceivable. In any case, the move will not remove this particular

---

[5] The best I can make of the argument is as follows. It requires us to take God, g, to be $\delta x \neg \exists y (\tau y \wedge y > x \wedge y \neq x)$. Then if g^* is $\delta x \forall y (\tau y \to x > y)$, two applications of the CP give:

$$\neg \exists y (\tau y \wedge y > g \wedge y \neq g) \tag{1}$$
$$\forall y (\tau y \to g^* > y) \tag{2}$$

The logic of the argument also requires the following:

$$\tau g \tag{3}$$
$$\tau g^* \tag{4}$$

Now suppose that $g \neq g^*$.

	$\tau g \to g^* > g$	by (2)
so	$g^* > g$	by (3)
Hence	$\tau g^* \wedge g^* > g \wedge g^* \neq g$	by (4)
so	$\exists y (\tau y \wedge y > g \wedge y \neq g)$	

contradicting (1). Hence by *reductio* $g = g^*$. And so:

$$\forall y (\tau y \to g > y) \qquad \text{by (2)}$$

The main problem with this reconstruction is that the clause $y \neq x$ seems to be redundant in the definition of g since it is entailed by the clause $y > x$. But if we delete it, the supposition $g \neq g^*$ is redundant and so does not get discharged in the *reductio*. The only solution I can offer is that Anselm does not take $y > x$ to entail $y \neq x$. After all, (2) and (4) entail that $g^* > g^*$, and presumably it is not the case that $g^* \neq g^*$.

problem. As I have just observed, the logic of the argument itself requires that 'God is conceivable' is true (in exactly the same sense that conceivability is used in the conclusion), so the argument itself locks Anselm into this claim.

4.3   The characterisation principle

As we have seen, Anselm ends in a contradiction at the limit of thought, but he does so by assuming the CP: that an object characterised as an, or the, object satisfying certain properties does indeed have those properties. This certainly looks like a logical truth; and, if it is, we can prove the existence of God very simply. The conditions taken to characterise God are normally called the perfections (omniscience, omnipotence, etc.). Let Px be a predicate expressing the conjunction of these. Let Ex be the predicate 'x exists', if it is not one of the conjuncts already. (It is usually taken to be so.) Now consider the condition 'Px ∧ Ex'. By the CP, a (the) thing satisfying these properties satisfies these properties. Something, therefore, satisfies these properties. Hence there is some existing thing satisfying P, i.e., God exists.[6]

The trouble with this argument is that, as far as its logic goes, the property P is absolutely arbitrary. We could therefore prove the existence of every thing, possible and impossible (after all, Px does not have to be consistent) – which is slightly too much. The problem is, actually, even worse than this. If the CP were correct, we could establish an arbitrary sentence, ψ, by applying the CP to the condition x = x ∧ ψ. The CP, then, is not a logical truth. I think that it appears so plausible because the claim that a (the) thing that is P is P is easily confused with the claim that everything that is P is P, which *is* a logical truth.

It is usually reckoned that the Ontological Argument was destroyed by Kant (*Critique of Pure Reason*, A598=B626 ff.), who argued that existence is not a predicate. There is, as a matter of fact, no problem about a syntactic existence predicate. In orthodox logic the formula ∃yy = x is such a thing. What Kant actually says is that existence is not a *determining* predicate. On a reasonably generous reading of the *Critique* this can be interpreted as the view that existence is not a predicate that can be used in a valid instance of the CP, as versions of the Ontological Argument require.

Leaving Kant aside, there certainly are instances of the CP that are true: the highest mountain in the world, for example, is, undoubtedly, the highest mountain in the world. However, the essential point remains: the CP cannot be assumed in general. And until the instances of it that are used in Anselm's arguments are legitimised (which no one has ever succeeded in doing), this is sufficient to sink the arguments of *Proslogion* 2 and 15. Anselm, then, did not

---

[6] This is essentially Descartes' version of the Ontological Argument in the 5th *Meditation*.

succeed in establishing the contradiction at the limit of conception. The matter is different when we turn to Berkeley.

4.4   Berkeley's master argument for idealism

The context of Berkeley's concerns is idealism. Idealisms come in many kinds. Berkeley's idealism was of a very strong kind, to the effect that nothing which is not itself a mind exists, unless it is before a mind in some sense: perceived, conceived, let us just say thought. As he puts it in the *Principles of Human Knowledge*, section 6:

all the choir of heaven and the furniture of the earth, in a word, all those bodies which compose the mighty frame of the world, have not any substance without a mind ... their being is to be perceived or known.

As is clear from the last sentence of this quotation, Berkeley held a much stronger view: that all things (except, possibly, minds themselves) are *essentially* thought. It is not just that there *is* nothing that is not thought; there *could be* nothing. Important as it is in Berkeley's philosophy, this stronger view need not concern us here. Hence, slightly inaccurately, I will call the claim that everything is thought of, 'Berkeley's Thesis'.

Berkeley advanced a number of arguments for his Thesis. Most of these are direct arguments depending on various empiricist assumptions, and have been well hammered in the literature.[7] He has one argument of a different kind, however; one on which, he says, he is prepared to rest everything. This will be the only one that will concern us here. It is given about three quarters of the way through the first of the *Three Dialogues Between Hylas and Philonous*.[8] Philonous is Berkeley's mouthpiece, Hylas the unlucky stooge. I enumerate for future reference:

i.   PHILONOUS. I am content to put the whole upon this issue. If you can conceive it possible for any mixture or combination of qualities, or any sensible object whatever to exist without the mind, then I will grant that it actually be so.
ii.   HYLAS. If it come to that, the point will soon be decided. What more easy than to conceive of a tree or house existing by itself, independent of, and unperceived by any mind whatever. I do at this present time conceive them existing after this manner.
iii. PHILONOUS. How say you, Hylas, can you see a thing that is at the same time unseen?
iv.   HYLAS. No, that were a contradiction.
v.   PHILONOUS. Is it not as great a contradiction to talk of *conceiving* a thing which is *unconceived*?

---

[7] See, for example, Tipton (1974), Pitcher (1977), Dancy (1987).
[8] And also in section 23 of the *Principles of Human Knowledge*.

vi.   HYLAS. It is.

vii.   PHILONOUS. The tree or house therefore which you think of, is conceived by you?

viii.   HYLAS. How should it be otherwise?

ix.   PHILONOUS. And what is conceived is surely in the mind?

x.   HYLAS. Without question, that which is conceived is in the mind.

xi.   PHILONOUS. How then came you to say, you conceived a house or a tree existing independent and out of all minds whatever?

xii.   HYLAS. That was I own an oversight.

The most difficult problem concerning this argument is to know what, exactly, it is. The fact that it is given informally, and in dialogue form at that, makes this a very sensitive issue. Because of this and the fact that several commentators have taken the argument to be little more than a sophism, I will formalise it. This will help to see what, if anything, is wrong with it; and just as importantly, what is not.

4.5   Analysis, stage I

There are a couple of preliminary issues that we can get sorted out straight away. Berkeley normally talks of conceiving, but sometimes talks of perceiving (ii). Although there is a world of difference between these two notions, Berkeley, because of his theory of perception, which is not relevant here, runs them together. As we shall see, nothing in the argument hangs on this and we shall do no injustice if we ignore this distinction.[9]

More troublesome is the fact that Berkeley slides between a predicative use of 'conceives' – *conceive y* (v, ix, x), *think of y* (vii), *y is in the mind* (i, ix, x) – and a propositional use – *conceive of y as being F* (ii, xi), *conceive it possible for y to be F* (i). Now, whatever connection there is between these two uses, we certainly cannot start by assuming one. I shall write the predicate as τ and the propositional operator as T. These may be read canonically as 'is conceived' and 'it is conceived that', respectively. (I put both of these in the passive, since, although it is Hylas who is doing the conceiving, the particular agent in question is irrelevant to the argument.) In this notation, Berkeley's Thesis is the negation of:

$$\exists x \neg \tau x \tag{0}$$

Notice that in the propositional use Berkeley sometimes talks of conceiving x to be F (ii, xi), and sometimes of conceiving it *possible* for x to be F (i). But the 'possible' is really doing no real work here, as is witnessed by the fact that the modality occurs but once in the argument. Berkeley, like many people, thinks

---

[9] In particular, there is no sophistic slide between the two notions, *contra* Wisdom (1953), pp. 8f., and Thomson (1956).

of 'conceive to be possible' as simply equivalent to 'conceive'. Clearly, conceiving a state of affairs to be possible entails conceiving that state of affairs.
Berkeley thinks the converse also holds: note that Hylas tries to demonstrate
that something can be conceived to be possible (i) by conceiving it (ii).
Philonous does not complain.

Now, what is the argument supposed to prove? What is at issue is, as stated
by Philonous (i), whether one can conceive that there is something that is not
conceived. Hylas claims that he does conceive such a thing (ii):

$$T\exists x\neg\tau x \tag{1}$$

showing that one can $(\varphi \to \Diamond\varphi)$. Philonous applies a *reductio* to (1) to show
that he does not, and so (by the modal inference of Necessitation), cannot.

The conclusion of the *reductio*, $\neg T\exists x\neg\tau x$, is not Berkeley's Thesis. Rather,
it is a statement to the effect that the negation of Berkeley's Thesis is not
thought (and since there is a logical demonstration of this fact, cannot be
thought). Though this may not be proof of the Thesis, it is clearly a substantial
victory for Berkeley if he can show that his opponents cannot even conceive
their own thesis (or conceive it to be possible if Berkeley is right about the
identification).

Next, how is the reduction supposed to proceed? Philonous thinks that (1) is
true since it follows from the fact that he can think of some object, c (a tree or
house, but its nature is not important), existing unconceived (ii):

$$T\neg\tau c \tag{2}$$

Whether or not this is so, notice that the *reductio* that Philonous performs is on
(2), not (1). Here is the first puzzle, then. Even if (2) implies (1), it is clear that
(1) does not imply (2); how, then, is the *reductio* supposed to work?

Let us leave this for the time being and ask what the contradiction is, to
which (2) is supposed to lead. It is 'conceiving a thing that is unconceived' (v).
We may reasonably understand this as $\exists x(\tau x \wedge \neg\tau x)$, where this is clearly
meant to follow from:

$$\tau c \wedge \neg\tau c \tag{3}$$

Now how is (3) supposed to follow from (2)? The first conjunct is supposed to
follow from the fact that Hylas is doing the conceiving (vii–x). In particular, to
conceive c as being something is, *ipso facto*, to conceive of c. Let us call this the
Conception Schema:

$$T\varphi(c) \to \tau c \tag{4}$$

How is the second conjunct of (3) supposed to follow? On this the text is silent.
Hylas just assumes it, and there seems no reason why it should follow from (2).
It would appear that if Hylas had had his wits about him he should just have
said: look Phil, I know that I conceived that c was unconceived; but that

doesn't imply that c *is* unconceived, any more than my conceiving the moon to be blue implies that it *is* blue. Here, then, we have the second puzzle: where does the second conjunct of (3) come from?[10]

Let us take stock. The argument so far looks as follows, with ? indicating the lacunae. I put the argument in an informal natural deduction form (essentially in the style of Prawitz (1965)). The bar over a premise indicates that it is an axiom, not an assumption, and so not a candidate for being discharged.

$$
\begin{array}{c}
\dfrac{T\exists x\neg\tau x}{?}
\end{array}
$$

$$
\dfrac{\dfrac{T\neg\tau c \qquad \overline{T\neg\tau c \,\rightarrow\, \tau c}}{\tau c} \qquad \dfrac{?}{\neg\tau c}}{\dfrac{\tau c \,\wedge\, \neg\tau c}{\exists x(\tau x \,\wedge\, \neg\tau x)}}
$$

4.6 Analysis, stage II

How are the gaps in the argument to be filled in?[11] The key is to go back and consider the object, c, which the reasoning is supposed to show to be inconsistent. As we noted, the exact nature of this is unimportant; all that is important is that it is some particular object which is not being conceived. Now reasoning about an arbitrarily chosen object of a certain kind is very familiar to logicians. Its cleanest formalisation uses an indefinite description operator, ε. About how, exactly, this should behave we need not go into in detail.[12] All we need to assume is that if there are any objects satisfying $\varphi(x)$ then '$\varepsilon x\varphi(x)$' refers to one of them (maybe picked out officially by a choice-function). Such semantics will clearly verify Hilbert's (first) ε-axiom (a restricted version of the CP):

$$\exists x\varphi(x) \,\rightarrow\, \varphi(\varepsilon x\varphi(x))$$

Given this, we can now simply identify c with $\varepsilon x\neg\tau x$. What then happens to the two lacunae in the argument that we noted? One appears to be filled easily. The conjunct $\neg\tau c$ is now just $\neg\tau\varepsilon x\neg\tau x$: an arbitrarily chosen thing that is not conceived, is not conceived. This is just an instance of the CP and looked so

[10] Pitcher (1977), pp. 113ff., and Tipton (1974), pp. 174f., argue that Berkeley confuses the properties of the conception with properties of the thing conceived, and so, in effect, fault the argument at this point. There is a sense in which this is right; but, as we shall see, it is not the end of the matter.
[11] An answer different from the one I shall give is provided in Prior (1955). This is discussed and rejected in Priest (1994a).
[12] For the orthodox Hilbertian account, see Leisenring (1969). For a slightly different account, see Priest (1979b).

much like a logical truth (at least until Kant) that it is natural that Berkeley would not have felt constrained to comment further on the matter; which explains the silence in the text.

What of the other? The gap between (1) and (2) is closed if we assume that T 'prefixes' logical consequence, i.e., that:

$$\text{if } \vdash \alpha \rightarrow \beta \text{ then } \vdash T\alpha \rightarrow T\beta$$

In words: if α entails β then, that α is conceived entails that β is conceived. Taking $\varphi(x)$ in the ε-axiom to be $\neg\tau x$ gives:

$$\exists x \neg\tau x \rightarrow \neg\tau c$$

And prefixing T then gives exactly what is required.

The Prefixing Principle is a standard one in logics for epistemic operators similar to T (such as 'it is believed that' and 'it is known that'). It must be admitted that it involves a clear idealisation of the agent doing the conceiving (believing, etc.). In particular, they must be thought of as 'following through' all the logical consequences of their conceptions (beliefs, etc.). But this seems quite harmless in the present context precisely because Philonous is clearly taking Hylas through these consequences – or the relevant ones anyway. Alternatively, one might simply reinterpret τ as 'is conceivable', and similarly for T. Prefixing is then perfectly acceptable. Of course, the exact force of the argument is then changed. I will return to this in a moment.

As we see, given the acceptability of the Prefixing Principle, both gaps in the argument are filled. It then goes as follows:

$$
\cfrac{
  T\exists x\neg\tau x \qquad
  \cfrac{\exists x\neg\tau x \rightarrow \neg\tau c}{T\exists x\neg\tau x \rightarrow T\neg\tau c}
}{
  \cfrac{
    \cfrac{T\neg\tau c \qquad T\neg\tau c \rightarrow \tau c}{\tau c} \qquad \neg\tau c
  }{\tau c \wedge \neg\tau c}
}
$$

(The last, existentially quantified, line of the original formalisation is now redundant, and so dropped.) This is the most plausible reconstruction of Berkeley's argument that I am aware of.

Unfortunately, it is still not certifiably sound. As we noted, it depends on the CP; and we have already seen that this cannot be assumed in general. This raises the question of the conditions under which the CP does hold. There is an interesting historical story to be told here involving Leibniz, Kant, Meinong, Russell, and others, but this is not the place to tell it. We need assume no more than we have done already, in the shape of Hilbert's ε-axiom: if there is an x satisfying $\varphi(x)$ then $\varphi(\varepsilon x \varphi(x))$ is true. Thus, $\neg\tau c$ ($\neg\tau\varepsilon x\neg\tau x$) can be validly inferred from $\exists x\neg\tau x$; and hence the following modification of Berkeley's argument is a valid deduction of a contradiction.

$$\frac{\quad}{\exists x\neg\tau x \to \neg\tau c}$$

$$\frac{T\exists x\neg\tau x \quad T\exists x\neg\tau x \to T\neg\tau c}{T\neg\tau c} \qquad\qquad \frac{}{\quad}$$

$$\frac{T\neg\tau c \to \tau c \qquad \exists x\neg\tau x \quad \exists x\neg\tau x \to \neg\tau c}{}$$

$$\frac{\tau c \qquad\qquad\qquad \neg\tau c}{\tau c \wedge \neg\tau c}$$

Moreover, the extra premise, $\exists x\neg\tau x$, is exactly the denial of Berkeley's Thesis. The argument therefore works; that there are unconceived things, and that this itself is conceived, together entail a contradiction.

One of the benefits of formalising the argument is establishing that it is formally valid. Hence, the argument is valid however the predicate τ and the sentence operator T are interpreted, provided only that the interpretations validate the pertinent principles: the Conception Schema and Prefixing. In particular, we can interpret T as 'it is conceiv*able* that' and τ as 'is conceiv*able*'. The argument then is just as good (indeed, possibly better, as I just noted). I will call this reinterpretation of the argument the *modal interpretation*.

4.7   Berkeley's response

Berkeley's argument (or at least, its repaired form) demonstrates that a contradiction follows from the claim that something is not conceived (and that this itself is conceived). Berkeley's response was to wield a *reductio* and conclude that everything is conceived (no surprise, since the whole point of the argument was to demonstrate idealism).

The response is inadequate, however, for two reasons. The first is that this conclusion is quite unacceptable, even on Berkeley's own terms. As I have just noted, it is perfectly legitimate to reinterpret the argument in certain ways. There are numerous such reinterpretations whose conclusions would have been quite unacceptable to Berkeley. For example, one can interpret τ as 'is conceived of *now*', 'is conceived of *by me*', 'was conceived of by Berkeley on his 42nd birthday', etc. (with corresponding changes in the interpretation of T). None of this would have been acceptable to Berkeley, as many commentators have noted.[13] For example, Berkeley is quite clear that things may exist unconceived by me, since God conceives them: God himself must exist independently of my conception.

The second reason is that, whatever Berkeley thought, there are very good reasons for supposing the assumptions of the reduction to be true. I will address this question first; then I will turn to its relevance.

The premises of the argument concern conception. The first thing we need to do here is clarify this notion. In particular, is it extensional, i.e., do we have

---

[13] Armstrong (1965), p. 10; Pitcher (1977), pp. 112f.; Tipton (1974), p. 161.

$x = y \rightarrow (\tau x \leftrightarrow \tau y)$? Suppose, for example, that you conceive of George Eliot. George Eliot was Marian Evans. Have you conceived of Marian Evans? In a sense you have not; in a sense you have, but you may not know this. Now the argument involves quantification into the scope of τ, in the form of the ε-operator; and the sense of quantification into intensional contexts is notoriously problematic. Quantification into intensional contexts must have sense (since we often operate with it informally), and maybe the premises with τ understood intensionally are true. But until we have a clearer understanding of what this sense is, we will do best to interpret conception in its extensional sense here. It is worth noting that even those who hold that conceiving is mainly (primarily, normally) intensional cannot deny that there is an extensional sense, namely, conception-under-some-description-or-other. And just as we can (and I will) interpret 'conceive' extensionally, we can (and I will) interpret 'conceivable' extensionally (conceivable-under-some-description-or-other).

Now, one premise of the argument is: it is conceived that there is something that is unconceived; or, on the modal interpretation: it is conceivable that there is something inconceivable. Both of these are unproblematically true since I, for one, conceive such things. Even to suppose them as the first step of a *reductio* requires one to conceive them (they do not even have to be possible).

The other premise of the argument is: there is something that is unconceived; or, in the modal interpretation: there is something that is inconceivable. The first of these is, again, unproblematically true. It is obviously difficult to give an example of something that is unconceived (difficult, though not impossible as we have seen!); but we know that there are (and were) things going on on planets in galaxies far away in space and time that no sentient being will ever think of. These are unconceived things. Moreover, in my life I have only a finite number of thoughts, and so will conceive of only a finite number of things; and so will everyone else. The number of things conceived (even by the human race) is therefore finite. Since there is an infinite number of things (numbers, points in space, etc.), most of them will not be conceived.

The claim that there are some things that are inconceivable is less clearly true. It is pretty clear that a medieval monk could not conceive of a computer programmer, a Hilbert Space or a black hole, at least under those descriptions: he did not have the concepts available. And presumably, in exactly the same way, there are things of which we can not now conceive, but of which future generations will be able to. But recall that conceivability is extensional here; and it does not follow from this that these things are not conceivable by us under any description. The premise is, none the less, true. If something is conceivable there must be some way of singling it out before the mind. Such singling out may involve direct perception (acquaintance) or may be purely by description. Now consider, for example, a point in space. Continua being dense, there is no way that any particular point can be picked out by our finite perception; and, since there is an uncountable number of points but only a countable number of descriptions in our language,[14] there is no way that every point can be picked out by a description. The matter is even clearer with uncountable totalities of mathematical entities, like the ordinals, where perception is not even on the cards. There are not enough names to go around for every ordinal. But even if there were, we have no way of singling out most ordinals to pin names on them.[15]

Having established the truth of the premises, let us turn to the relevance of this fact. This is that a *reductio* is illegitimate in the context of the argument. If the premises of the argument are true, so is the conclusion; but if the contradiction entailed by certain assumptions is true, this entailment cannot be used to reduce those assumptions to absurdity. How, exactly, one cashes out this insight depends on a variety of factors, such as the exact details of the semantics of descriptions and of the underlying logic, but the situation is essentially as follows. Let the conjunction of the negation of Berkeley's Thesis and the conceivability of this be α. Let β be the conjunction of the other premises of the argument, namely, the instances of the ε-axiom and the Conception Schema employed. $\alpha \wedge \beta$ entails a contradiction. If entailment contraposes, we can get from this to $\neg(\alpha \wedge \beta)$. But even if we can get here, the argument from this and β to $\neg\alpha$ is an instance of the disjunctive syllogism; and this fails in dialetheic contexts of the kind we are in.[16]

There is a way that Berkeley – or at least, Berkeley fortified by Hilbert's theory of ε-terms – could have short-circuited the *reductio* to obtain his conclusion.[17] In Hilbert's ε-calculus the inference from $\varphi(\varepsilon x\neg\varphi(x))$ to $\forall x\varphi(x)$ is valid; this is just the contraposed form of the ε-axiom. In particular, therefore, the inference from τc to $\forall x\tau x$ is valid. Now, take the fragment of the repaired argument up to τc, and stick this inference onto the end. We get:

$$\frac{\dfrac{\dfrac{\dfrac{T\exists x\neg\tau x \qquad \dfrac{\exists x\neg\tau x \rightarrow \neg\tau c}{T\exists x\neg\tau x \rightarrow T\neg\tau c}}{T\neg\tau c} \qquad T\neg\tau c \rightarrow \tau c}{\tau c}}{\forall x\tau x}}{}$$

Thus, Berkeley might have traded in his *reductio* proof for a direct, or at least, *ad hominem* argument. 'Look Hylas', he might have made Philonous say, 'you agree that you do conceive that something exists unconceived. Well, it follows from this that everything is conceived!'

---

[14] See ch. 8 if you are not familiar with the terms 'countable' and 'uncountable'.
[15] For some further relevant discussion, see ch. 5 of Nagel (1986).
[16] See the Introduction to the book, fn. 8.
[17] As both John Bacon and Vladimir Smirnov pointed out to me.

Neat as this argument is, it fails. The reason is that though the ε-axiom contraposes in non-dialetheic semantics, it does not do so in dialetheic semantics. To see why, suppose that some things are φ and only φ, some things are $\neg\varphi$ and only $\neg\varphi$, and some things are both. It follows that $\forall x\varphi(x)$ is just plain false (since the universal quantifier acts like an infinitary conjunction). '$\varepsilon x\neg\varphi(x)$', we are agreed, denotes one of the things that satisfies $\neg\varphi$, but if it also satisfies φ then $\varphi(\varepsilon x\neg\varphi(x))$ is true (and false too; but at least true). Hence the contraposed ε-axiom fails to be truth-preserving.[18]

4.8   Some objections

As we have now seen, Berkeley's response to the argument was incorrect. In the process we have seen that premises that are true entail a contradiction, which is also, therefore, true. But with an argument as subtle as the one in question, it is natural that many will still be suspicious of its soundness. Let us consider a few suspicions.

One possible objection is as follows: ε-terms cannot be combined with quantification into intensional contexts, such as T, or trouble ensues. For example, by prefixing the ε-axiom, we get: $T\exists x\varphi(x) \rightarrow T\varphi(\varepsilon x\varphi(x))$. Hence, by Existential Generalisation we get $T\exists x\varphi(x) \rightarrow \exists xT\varphi(x)$, which is false. (I can be thinking that something is φ without thinking of some particular thing that it is φ.) In general, the way out of this difficulty is to make the scope of ε-terms explicit (as in Fitting (1972)). However, neither the problem nor the solution is of importance here; for, as a simple inspection will show, the repaired Berkeleyan argument makes no use of quantification into T-contexts. T may be understood purely *de dicto* (or, equivalently in this context, the ε-terms can all be taken to have narrow scope); and with such a reading its use is completely unproblematic.

A second objection[19] is that when T is understood *de dicto* the Conception Schema fails. If one is thinking *de dicto* that Paris is the capital of France, one is not necessarily thinking of *Paris* at all. This raises further questions concerning the notion of conceiving that is supposed to be working here. I am happy to agree that there are certainly legitimate conceptions of conception for which the Schema fails. For example, in one sense of conception it might be necessary to be acquainted with a thing, in some fairly strong sense, to be said to conceive it. The *de dicto* Conception Schema obviously fails for this sense. However, there is a weaker, and perfectly legitimate (extensional) notion of conception for which the Schema it true. To conceive of something in this

---

[18] This can be turned into a formal counter-model in the semantics of the appendix to Part 3. I leave the details as an exercise.

[19] Put to me independently by Thomas Forster, Mark Lance, and David Lewis.

sense it is necessary only to bring before the mind and understand a noun-phrase (or other representation) which, as a matter of fact, refers to (or represents) the object in question. If I conceive that c is φ and 'c' refers to something (which it certainly does if 'c' is '$\varepsilon x\neg\tau x$' and $\exists x\neg\tau x$) then I am conceiving of the thing in this sense (whether or not I am acquainted with it or know anything else of it).

A final, and desperate, objection might be to reject the whole notion of indefinite descriptions as referring phrases. A person might do this on the ground that all indefinite articles in English are to be handled using the existential quantifier (which is demonstrably false[20]) or on some other more plausible view. Naturally, the onus is on such a person to produce an account of the semantics of indefinite descriptions – and show that it does not satisfy one of the principles of the argument. But, in a sense, this move would be beside the point. For indefinite descriptions are inessential to the argument. It could be run equally using definite descriptions. For example, given the infinitude of ordinals, they cannot all be conceived of. Yet one can simply run the argument with the phrase '*the* least ordinal not conceived of'. The result is effectively the same. If this reminds the reader of certain logical paradoxes, their thoughts are not wide of the mark. We will return to this in a later chapter.

The objections I have been considering are to the original interpretation of the argument; but parallel objections could be made to the modal interpretation. The replies, too, would be parallel. Furthermore, in reply to the second objection one should note that, given standard modal principles, the logical truth of the Conception Schema for 'conceive' entails the Conception Schema for 'conceivable': for given that $\Box\,(T\varphi(c) \to \tau(c))$, $\Diamond T\varphi(c) \to \Diamond\tau(c)$ follows.

4.9 Berkeley's paradox

As we have now seen, Berkeley's *reductio*, despite his attempts to defuse its conclusion, establishes a contradiction. In fact, as should be clear, it is a contradiction typical of a limit of thought. As one half of the (repaired) argument demonstrates, c ($\varepsilon x\neg\tau x$) is not in the class of conceived (conceivable) things (Transcendence); but, as the other half shows, it *is* in the class of conceived (conceivable) things (Closure).

We can even cut through much of the detail of the argument. Take the (repaired) argument and knock off everything up to the proof of τc. What remains is then:

---

[20] For example, if x is a non-empty set of non-empty sets the following is a choice set on x in ZF {y; for some z in x, y is a (selected) member of z} (see Leisenring (1969), pp. 105ff.). It is well known that in general choice sets cannot be demonstrated to exist in ZF if only the usual quantifiers are available.

$$\frac{\exists x \neg \tau x \quad \exists x \neg \tau x \to \neg \tau c}{\tau c \qquad \qquad \neg \tau c}$$
$$\overline{\tau c \land \neg \tau c}$$

Let us call this the *Core Argument*. The Core is an argument to a contradiction from the negation of Berkeley's Thesis together with the extra premise, τc. It does not employ the Conception Schema, Prefixing, or even the operator T. Moreover, the extra premise is true, or at least can be made true. One *can* conceive of an object that is not conceived (inconceivable), in the appropriate sense; I do, and so can you.

Of the two interpretations of this argument (the original and the modal), it is, arguably, the modal interpretation that is the more fundamental. For the truth of the conclusion of the original interpretation is a merely contingent affair, depending as it does on the fact that someone is actually doing the conceiving; whilst the truth of the conclusion on the modal interpretation depends on no similar assumptions. At any rate, in future chapters I will call the modal interpretation of the Core Argument *Berkeley's Paradox*.[21]

Conclusion

With these baptisms, the first part of the book ends. The string of pre-Kantian intimations that limits of thought may be contradictory comes to a climax in Berkeley's argument (the first pre-Kantian argument we have met that succeeds in establishing a contradiction at the limits of thought – though we have glimpsed later ones). Berkeley's idealism prevented him from realising the contradiction; but idealism is no escape, as we have seen. In the next part of the book, we turn to the two philosophers in whose work the contradictory nature of the limits of thought was recognised and theorised for the first time: Kant and Hegel.

---

[21] In (1992) Slater comments on what is, in effect, Berkeley's Paradox. In as far as I understand them, his comments come to the following. Berkeley's Thesis is true, but innocuous, when properly understood; and hence the argument can be interpreted as a *reductio*. Slater gives an independent argument for the Thesis, and attempts to show why it is innocuous. The independent argument is, essentially, the last one we looked at the end of 4.7, and as we saw there, it fails. (Slater gives an argument of sorts for the contraposability of the ε-axiom, but this simply begs the question.) The Thesis is supposed to be innocuous since a certain description ('a thing not denoted by this term') refers to everything. Now, this is just not possible according to the standard semantics of ε-terms that I have been operating with. So even if Slater has some non-standard semantics in mind, this is beside the point. Slater does sketch an independent argument for the claim that the term in question refers to everything, but this, too, depends on contraposing the ε-axiom.

Part 2

The limits of thought in Kant and Hegel

We say: but that isn't how it is! – it *is* like that though! and all we can do is keep repeating these antitheses.

Ludwig Wittgenstein, *Culture and Value*

5 Noumena and the categories

Introduction

In the first part of the book we found limits of thought appearing at various sites in philosophy. We also found numerous intimations that they could be contradictory, in the form of arguments produced by various philosophers. None of these philosophers, with the exception of Cusanus, was happy to accept that they were dealing with a literally contradictory object; and even Cusanus had little theoretical understanding of the situation in which he found himself. This state of affairs changed radically in the eighteenth century, however, with the work of Kant and Hegel. In these philosophers, for the first time, we arrive at a general recognition of the contradictory nature of the limits of thought, together with a theorisation of how and why this occurs. In this part of the book we will review the relevant work of these two philosophers, starting with Kant.

We have met four limits of thought: the limit of conception, the limit of expression, the limit of cognition, and the limit of iteration (the generated infinite). By and large, these limits arose in quite different contexts, and had little to do with each other. When we turn to Kant we find all these limits occurring. The first three arise in connection with Kant's views on the Categories; the last in connection with his account of the Antinomies. Moreover, in Kant these limits are not at all independent, but interact in an important way, as we shall see. In this chapter I will deal with the first topic (the Categories), saving the second (the Antinomies) till the next. Due to the interaction of the various notions, however, neither chapter stands completely on its own.

The principal text we will be concerned with is the *Critique of Pure Reason* (to which all citations refer, unless otherwise stated[1]). The aim of this text is to chart the logical geography of the most general features of thought and, as its name suggests, spell out their limits. Unsurprisingly, then, it is forced to confront the contradictions inherent in the limits of thought. Interpreting the *Critique* is a very sensitive issue, however. This is so partly because of

---

[1] All quotations from the *Critique* in this chapter and the next are taken from Kemp Smith (1933).

the abstract and jargonated way in which Kant expresses himself. More importantly, it is because it is a text composed over some ten years, during which
time his views changed. The interpreter's nightmare is exacerbated by the fact
that Kant made major changes to the second edition of the *Critique*; and, to
make matters worse, published a short and 'popular'! version, between the two
editions, *Prolegomena to any Future Metaphysics*.

The result is a set of documents that contain numerous internal contradictions, not of the kind that we are looking at – which are due to the fact that
the subject involved is inherently contradictory – but which are due simply to
the patchwork of their construction. (All of this is meticulously documented in
Kemp Smith (1923).) Thus, though what I shall say seems to me to be a
correct interpretation of the considered Kant, it would be foolish to deny
the possibility of other interpretations; and to take on other commentators
here would certainly result in obscuring the wood for the trees, so I shall
not attempt it. If I am right, Kant should get the credit for being the first
person to note that contradictions of the kind we are discussing are, in some
sense, inherent in the limits of thought. If I am wrong, the credit merely goes
to someone else.

5.1   Phenomena and noumena

The crucial distinction for both this chapter and the next is Kant's distinction
between phenomena and noumena. Phenomena are, essentially, those things
that are perceivable via the senses. I use 'thing' in a fairly loose way here, to
include objects such as buildings, countries, and stars; and events such as the
extinction of the dinosaurs, plane journeys, and the death of Hegel. Noumena,
or at least what we can say about them, are more problematic, as we shall see.
However, essentially, those things are noumena which are not phenomena. To
the extent that they can be 'brought before the mind' at all, they can be
conceived, but not perceived. Some examples of noumena that Kant cites
are: God, the cosmos, and the soul.[2] Further examples we will come to in a
moment.

The distinction between phenomena and noumena makes perfectly good
sense for a non-Kantian, as much as for a Kantian. And all can agree that
phenomena are in space and time (or just time in the case of internal sensations). Many would argue, however, that not all things in (space and) time are
phenomena. For there are many physical entities, including those that are
responsible for our perceptions (such as photons and electromagnetic radiation), which are not themselves perceivable.

---

[2] See the *Prolegomena*, section 45.

It is therefore important to note that Kant has a somewhat idiosyncratic view about what sorts of things phenomena are. For Kant thinks that objects in themselves cannot be perceived, or *intuited* in his jargon; what are perceived are our mental representations of such objects. He calls this view 'Transcendental Idealism'. As he explains it (A109):

Appearances are the sole objects which can be given to us immediately, and that in them which relates immediately to the object is called intuition. But these appearances are not things in themselves; they are only representations, which in turn have their object – an object which cannot itself be intuited by us, and which may, therefore, be named the non-empirical, that is, transcendental object = x.

The phenomena or representations perceived are a result of something contributed by the things in themselves (in some sense which we will need to come back to), but also of the a priori structure our mind employs to constitute the representations (intuitions). In particular, space and time are not features of things themselves, but are the most important such structures. For Kant, a horse is a spatio-temporal representation of an object; but what the representation is a representation of (which the rest of us might call a horse) is neither perceived nor in space and time.

It follows that for Kant all things in space and time are phenomena, as well as the converse. So when Kant talks about the objects, or things in themselves as he puts it, which occasion our representations, he is talking about noumena. Theoretical entities, such as photons and electromagnetic radiation, to the extent that Kant could make sense of such notions at all (which does not seem very great) are phenomena.

5.2 The categories of judgment

Noumena are precisely, it will turn out, contradictory objects beyond conception, of the kind that we have already met in the last chapter. However, this will not be at all clear at the moment. For noumena are, by definition, objects beyond perception, not conception. And Kant, as we have just seen, carefully distinguishes between the two, as Berkeley does not (4.5). Moreover, as Kant notes (B310), there is nothing contradictory about the notion of a noumenon as such. The contradiction arises because of Kant's views concerning the Categories; so let us turn to these.

Categories are concepts of a certain kind. Kant calls them 'pure', meaning that they have no empirical content (unlike, for example, the concept *horse*). The precise details are not too important, but how they are obtained is. Kant abstracts them from what he took to be the logical forms of judgments, or statements as we might now put it. In the neo-Aristotelian logic he endorsed, every judgment has a quality, quantity, relation, and modality. And it may have

Table 2

	Logical Form	Category
Quantity	Singular	Unity
	Paricular	Plurality
	Universal	Totality
Quality	Affirmative	Reality
	Negative	Negation
	Infinitive	Limitation
Relation	Categorical	Substance
	Hypothetical	Cause
	Disjunctive	Community
Modality	Problematic	Possibility
	Assertoric	Existence
	Apodictic	Necessity

each of these in one of three ways. Corresponding to each of these ways is a Category; these can be displayed as in Table 2.[3]

To illustrate: consider, for example, the judgment 'Some capitalists may not be compassionate.' This has particular quantity, negative quality, categorical relation, and problematic modality. It thus deploys the Categories of plurality, negation, substance, and possibility. Or again, the statement 'If a piece of metal is heated then, necessarily, it expands' has universal quantity, affirmative quality, hypothetical relation, and apodictic modality. It thus deploys the Categories of totality, reality, cause, and necessity.

The exact details of the taxonomy do not now withstand much thought. A judgment such as 'all capitalists are exploiters or some workers are exploited' is both particular and universal; the judgment 'Oswald killed Kennedy' is categorical, but clearly causal; and so on. But the underlying weakness here is in no small measure due to the inadequacy of the theory of logical form in traditional logic. It would be an interesting exercise to draw up a similar table of Categories based on a modern notion of logical form (one which, for example, gave a distinctive form to agentives), but I shall not attempt this here. The only points we need to note are that the Categories are abstracted from the logical forms of judgments, and, crucially, that each judgment

[3] I take the table from the *Prolegomena*, section 21, except that I have reversed the order of the three quantities, following Bennett (1966), p. 77. Quotations from the *Prolegomena* are all from Beck (1950). It is perhaps stretching the point a little to say that the category of modality is a matter of logical form in the modern sense, for Kant takes this to be semantic rather than syntactic. See A74=B100 ff. I will ignore this subtlety.

deploys one or more such Category, as Kant himself remarks in the following corollary (A245=B302):

[The Categories] cannot themselves be defined. The logical functions of judgments in
general, unity and plurality, assertion and denial, subject and predicate, cannot be
defined without perpetrating a circle, since the definition itself must be a judgment,
and so must already contain these functions.

It is worth noting that in the *Prolegomena*, sections 18ff., Kant distinguishes
between objective and subjective judgments, only the former of which deploy
the Categories. This, however, is an aberration in Kant's thought, and, by the
second edition of the *Critique*, subjective judgments have become mere asso-
ciations of ideas.[4]

5.3   The applicability of the categories

Having sorted out the Categories, the next, and crucial, point to note is Kant's
view that they can be (meaningfully) applied only to phenomena. As Kant puts
it in the *Prolegomena* (section 30):

even if the pure concepts of the understanding are thought to go beyond objects of
experience to things in themselves (*noumena*), they have no meaning whatever.

Kant comes back to this point again and again in the *Critique* (for example,
A95, B147, A139=B178, A239=B298). His arguments for it are somewhat
weak, however.

As far as I can see, there are three. The first, and major one, concerns the
so-called Transcendental Deduction of the Categories. Kant faces the problem
of what grounds we have for supposing that the Categories can be applied to
anything, or, in more modern jargon, how we can be sure that our language
applies to reality. Whilst more modern philosophers might try to argue this in
terms of some feature of the nature of language, its use or evolution, Kant
seeks the solution in the nature of consciousness.

We do not need to follow the argument through all its tortuous turns;
essentially, it runs as follows. It is a feature of each individual consciousness
that it has a unity. (The perceptions of the depression of the keys on which I
type and of the keys' clicking belong to one consciousness.) How is this
possible? It is possible, according to Kant, because the objects of consciousness
themselves have a unity. (The depression of the keys and the sound of the
clicks form part of the one thing: my typing.) How is this unity possible? The
answer, again according to Kant, is that it is precisely my judgments deploying
the Categories that unify these disparate things. (The depression of the keys
causes the clicking sound.) Thus, the applicability of the Categories is guar-

[4] See Kemp Smith (1923), pp. 288f.

anteed by, ultimately, the unity of my consciousness. It follows that the Categories are mental features that are – like space and time – constitutive of my perceptions, mental representations. And thus that they apply just to phenomena. As Kant sums it up (A111):

The a priori conditions of a possible experience in general are at the same time conditions of the possibility of objects of experience. Now, I maintain that the Categories, above cited, are nothing but the conditions of thought in a possible experience just as space and time are the conditions of intuitions for that same experience. They are fundamental concepts by which we think objects in general for experiences, and have therefore a priori objective validity. This is exactly what we desired to prove.

For present purposes we need not discuss the part of Kant's argument to the effect that it is the Categories that make the unity of my consciousness possible. For, even if that is right, the final stage of the argument is a patent *non-sequitur*. From the fact that the Categories just are a certain kind of condition of my experience, it does not follow that they cannot function in another way; that they are 'nothing but' this, as Kant puts it in the quotation. Similarly, from the fact that a screwdriver just is that tool which propels screws, it does not follow that it does not have other uses – which I leave to the imagination. And nothing in the Transcendental Deduction – that I can see, at any rate – appears to guarantee this.

A second, and better, reason that Kant gives for supposing that the Categories apply only to phenomena goes as follows. Kant observes that to apply a Category it is necessary for us to have some criterion, or *schema* in his jargon, of its applicability. In the 'Schematism of the Pure Understanding' Kant gives what he takes to be the criteria of the applicability of the Categories. He does not deny that, logically, there could be other criteria; but, as a matter of fact, these are the only criteria that we have, or that beings constituted like us could have.

Now, it turns out that the criteria for *all* the Categories involve time. To give a couple of the simpler examples (A143=B183 ff.): 'the schema of substance is permanence in real time', 'the schema of necessity is existence of an object at all times'. It follows that it makes sense to apply the criteria only to those things that are in time: phenomena. As Kant puts it (A145=B184 ff.):

We thus find that the schema of each Category contains and makes capable of representation only a determination of time . . . The schemata of the pure concepts of the understanding are thus the true and sole conditions under which these concepts obtain relation to objects and so possess *significance*. In the end, therefore, the Categories have no other possible employment than the empirical.

The correctness of Kant's criteria is not beyond argument. For a start, it is not clear that there is any difference between the criterion given for being a substance and that for being necessary! Moreover, one might take the criterion for being a substance to be indestructibility; and the criterion for necessity to be not depending on anything else for existence. (Kant himself seems to do this elsewhere in the *Critique*, as we shall see when we discuss the Second and Fourth Antinomies in the next chapter.) And neither of these involves the notion of time. However, if we do accept that the criteria are all temporal, the conclusion follows.

The third, and final, argument that Kant uses for the non-applicability of the Categories to noumena is based on the Antinomies. The claim is supposed to provide a solution to them (for example, A421=B449, A642=B670). This argument is so intimately related with the Antinomies that I will defer consideration of it until the next chapter.

5.4   The law of causation

For the purposes of the next chapter, however, I want to digress briefly. The Transcendental Deduction has, according to Kant, established that the Categories apply to phenomena. In 'System of all Principles of Pure Understanding', he then tries to establish what (synthetic a priori) principles govern this application. The one I wish to comment on here is that in the second Analogy: every event has a cause (the 'Law of Causation'). I have already rejected this principle on the familiar grounds of the non-determinism of quantum mechanics (2.9). Let me briefly say where, I take it, Kant's argument for it fails.

According to Kemp Smith,[5] Kant gives six distinct arguments, but the common theme is essentially as follows. Kant observes that the temporal order of events is not determined by the temporal order in which we observe them, and suggests that their temporal order is determined by the order of causality. He therefore subscribes to some version of the Causal Theory of temporal direction. Let us grant this for the sake of argument.

Kant tends to assume that the Law of Causation follows from this theory. It does not. This is clear from the fact that the Theory is quite consistent with the claim that there was a first event. But even if we suppose that for any event, e, there is some prior event, we cannot use the Causal Theory to infer that e has a cause. This is because any sensible Causal Theory can claim only that x causing y is a *sufficient* condition for x to precede y; it cannot be a necessary condition. (There are many things which happen before y which are not causally related to it).

The standard way of obtaining necessary and sufficient conditions is to say that x precedes y iff it is *possible* for there to be a causal chain from x and y. (See Grünbaum (1973), p. 187.) But on such an account it is clear that an

5 Ibid., p. 369.

event, e, may have no cause, even though there is an event before it: all that
follows is that it is possible for it to have a cause. A more non-standard way of
obtaining necessary and sufficient conditions is suggested by Beck (1966) in
his 'defence' of the second Analogy. He suggests, in effect, that x precedes y iff
x causes some event simultaneous with y. But, again, it is clear that on such an
account e may have no cause; it must be simultaneous with some event that
does.

It therefore seems that Kant's argument cannot be repaired. Having noted
this, let us return to the main argument of this chapter.

5.5   The contradictory nature of noumena

Kant's view that the Categories cannot be applied to noumena embroils him in
the contradictions at the limits of thought. Let us start with the limit of
cognition. That the Categories can be applied only to phenomena entails
that there can be no knowledge of noumena. As Kant explains (Bxxv f.):

> that we have no concepts of understanding, and consequently no elements for knowl-
> edge of things, save in so far as intuition can be given corresponding to these concepts;
> and that we can therefore have no knowledge of any object as thing in itself, but only in
> so far as it is an object of sensible intuition, that is, an appearance – all this is proved in
> the analytical part of the *Critique*. Thus it does indeed follow that all possible spec-
> ulative knowledge of reason is limited to mere objects of *experience*.

Kant's claim that we can have knowledge of phenomena but not of noumena,
puts very precise limits on the extent of knowledge. It is not, therefore,
surprising that Kant is caught in the self-referential trap involved in skepticism
(see 3.4). For here is Kant writing a large book at least purporting to inform us
about, *inter alia*, noumena. His own theory would therefore seem to be both
within and without the known.

Kant would have defended himself against this charge in much the same
way that Carneades would have defended himself against a similar charge (see
3.4, fn. 8), namely, by insisting that the *Critique* does not give us any knowledge of noumena, but something less. The passage I have just quoted goes on:

> But our further contention must also be duly borne in mind, namely, that though we
> cannot *know* these objects as things in themselves, we must yet be in a position to at
> least *think* them as things in themselves; otherwise we should be landed in the absurd
> conclusion that there can be appearances without anything that appears.

Hence, though we cannot know anything about things in themselves, and,
more generally, noumena, we can at least think things about them.[6] How
adequate is this reply?

---

[6] Ewing ((1938), p. 198) suggests that this can be done by employing the pure Categories, that
is, the Categories without their criteria of application (the unschematised Categories). I do not see

To say that we cannot know anything about noumena is, whilst true, rather misleading; for it suggests that the impossibility of having knowledge is due merely to our lack of *epistemic* access. The impossibility of knowledge arises for a much more profound reason, however: a lack of *conceptual* access. The situation here is exactly the same as that we witnessed in connection with prime matter (1.6). (A number of perceptive commentators have noted the similarity between noumena – especially things in themselves – and prime matter.[7]) The reason that we cannot have knowledge of noumena is precisely that we cannot even make statements about them: any (meaningful) statement about them would have to apply the categories, and so is impossible.

Once one sees this, two things become clear. The first is that it is just as impossible to entertain thoughts about noumena as it is to know anything about them. For both involve (meaningful) statements about noumena. Kant's supposed way out therefore fails. The second is that there is a more fundamental contradiction involved here than that at the limit of cognition: that at the limit of expression.

Kant's own theory makes numerous assertions about noumena, applying various categories, as critics from Hegel onwards have pointed out.[8] For example, Kant talks of noumena causing our sensations (e.g. A288=B345):[9]

Understanding accordingly limits sensibility, but does not thereby extend its own sphere. In the process of warning the latter that it must not presume to claim applicability to things-in-themselves but only to appearances, it does indeed think for itself an object in itself, but only as transcendental object, which is the cause of appearance and not itself appearance.

And this is but the tip of the iceberg.[10] When Kant says that noumena may be supposed to exist (A253=B309) he deploys the Category of existence; when he says that they are not in time, he deploys the Category of negation. Even the statement that the Categories cannot be applied to noumena deploys the

how this is supposed to work. The pure Categories provide only the logical *forms* of judgment, as Kant himself points out (for example, B150). They cannot provide any content. As Kant puts it (A248=B305):

The pure categories, apart from formal considerations of sensibility, have only transcendental meaning; nevertheless they may not be employed transcendentally, such employment being in itself impossible, inasmuch as all condition of any employment in judgments are lacking to them, namely, the formal conditions of the subsumption of any ostensible object under these concepts. Since, then, as pure categories merely, they are not to be employed empirically, and cannot be employed transcendentally, they cannot, when separated from all sensibility, be employed in any manner whatever.

[7] See Wolff (1963), p. 152 n., and Łukasiewicz (1953), p. 72.
[8] See Inwood (1983), p. 146.
[9] See also A494=B522.
[10] See Kemp Smith (1923), p. 412.

Categories of possibility and negation! Hence unless Kant is to accept that his own theory is meaningless it must be possible to express such things (Closure).

Yet it is not (Transcendence). For, as Kant puts it (A679=B707):

There are no concepts available for any such purpose; even the concepts of reality, substance, cause, nay, even that of necessity in existence, lose all meaning, and are empty titles for [possible] concepts, themselves entirely without content, when we thus venture with them outside the field of the senses.

But this is not yet an end of the matter. For not only is Kant's own theory beyond the limit of the expressible, noumena themselves are beyond the limit of the conceivable (= thinkable). If I can think about certain objects, then I must have some way of fixing on them mentally; and I can use this fact to make them the subject of some assertion. Hence I can make a judgment about them. Since one cannot make judgments about noumena, one cannot, therefore, think of them. Hence noumena are precisely objects beyond the conceivable (Transcendence). Yet clearly, to make any judgment about a noumenon, as Kant often does, is to think about it (Closure). Hence noumena are precisely contradictory objects beyond the limit of conception. In particular, Kant is in the same position concerning God as is Anselm (4.2) and Cusanus (1.8).

Kant is aware of the contradiction involved, and is very uncomfortable about it. This is clearest in the chapter of the *Critique* called 'The Ground of the Distinction of all Objects in General into Phenomena and Noumena' which tries to wriggle out of the contradiction by distinguishing between an illegitimate positive notion of noumenon and a legitimate negative, or limiting, notion. This does not help: according to Kant, the negative notion is there to place a limit on the area in which we can apply the Categories, and so make judgments (A255=B311). But to say that there are (or even may be) things about which we cannot judge is precisely to make a judgment about them; specifically, it existentially quantifies over them, and so applies the Category of plurality. The 'legitimate' notion is therefore just as illegitimate as the illegitimate one.

So unsuccessful was this chapter of the *Critique* that Kant completely redrafted it for the second edition, but without doing anything to remove the fundamental contradiction. As Kemp Smith puts it ((1923), pp. 413f.):

But beyond thus placing in still bolder contrast the two counter-assertions, on the one hand that the Categories must not be taken by us as other than merely subjective thought functions, and on the other that a limiting concept is indispensably necessary, Kant makes no attempt in the new passages to meet the difficulties involved. With the assertion that the Categories as such, and therefore by implication, those of reality and existence, are inapplicable to things in themselves, he combines, without any apparent consciousness of conflict, the contention that things in themselves must none the less be postulated as actually existing.

Hence Kant is caught squarely in the contradiction inherent in the limits of thought. And let me emphasise again: this is not a contradiction of the kind of which one finds so many in the *Critique*: a result of carelessness or of changes of view; it is a contradiction which is occasioned by the very objects of the theory.

5.6   Analogy

In 4.2 we noted that Anselm, when faced with a similar situation in which our concepts could not apply to God, tried to defuse the contradiction implicit in making assertions about God by claiming that apparent applications were to be understood only analogically. Could Kant make a similar move?

Well, he does make a similar move with respect to the application of one category: causation. In the appendix to the Transcendental Dialectic (A672=B700 ff.) and in the Conclusion of the *Prolegomena* (sections 57, 58) Kant says that although we cannot (literally) make sense of the claim that one noumenon, such as God, caused the world (another), or something in it (a phenomenon), we can regard things *as if* He did (A672=B700 ff.). This is not a happy way of putting it. If the claim φ makes no sense, then the claim that it is as if φ makes no sense either. However, as Kant goes on to explain (most clearly in the *Prolegomena*), when he says this, what he means is that when God does what He does to bring about the world or something in it, this is *analogous* to what one phenomenon does when it causes another.

Leaving aside the question of whether this move can be made to work in this particular case, it is not difficult to see that it cannot be made to work in general (nor is there any evidence to suggest that Kant thought it could). First, in stating that, for example, causation, when applied to (predicated of) noumena, must be understood by analogy, one is still making judgments about noumena. It might be suggested that in the talk of applying concepts to noumena (and so applying the Category of substance) 'apply' must itself be understood analogically. But this is clearly not what Kant intends; nor can it be, without undercutting the point being made. For the claim is not meant to be an analogue of the claim that causation, when applied to noumenon, must be understood by analogy. (It is not even clear what the sense of such a claim could be.) The very content of the idea that the application of 'cause' is by analogy can be expressed only because 'application' is being used in its literal semantic sense.

Moreover, the Category of causation is one of the few Categories where the idea of an analogical use makes much sense. We do have, after all, a generic notion of *bringing about*. But there are other Categories where there is no such generic notion, and the notion of an analogical application therefore has little clear sense. Take, for example, the Category of negation. Consider the claim that noumena are not in space and time. It is difficult to see how the category of reality ('is') can be employed analogically here; but it is downright impossible to see how 'not', and so the Category of negation, can be.

Finally, there are contexts in which the Categories cannot possibly be employed analogically. Consider the very distinction between phenomena and noumena as expressed, for example, in the following: *all objects are either phenomena or noumena; phenomena are those which may be experienced; noumena are those which cannot be*. In the first clause the Categories of universality ('all') and community ('or') are deployed to all objects, phenomena *and* noumena. They must therefore be deployed in the same sense (presumably literally) in both cases. Similarly, in the second and third clauses the Category of possibility ('may', 'can') is deployed against both phenomena and noumena; and the very sense of the distinction depends on it being employed in the same way. And again, the Category of negation deployed in the last clause must have its literal meaning or the distinction being drawn would misfire.

Conclusion

We have now explored all the ways to avoid contradiction that are, as far as I can see, open to Kant. None of them is successful. The problem is posed for anyone who holds that the Categories do not apply to noumena and, at the same time, wants even to consider propositions about them. There are therefore only two possible solutions.

The first is to give up all talk of noumena. How much of the Kantian project would be left if one were to do this, I leave to Kantian scholars to argue about; not much I suspect. The central idea of Transcendental Idealism is that the things we normally take ourselves to be familiar with are representations. The very notion of things of which these are the representations – one kind of noumenon – therefore seems built into Kant's very problematic.[11] Nor is this solution open to anyone else who holds that there are – or even could be – objects that we do not perceive, be they God, photons, black holes, or numbers.

The other possible solution is to ditch the claim that the Categories apply only to phenomena. After all, we have seen only one reasonable argument for this so far; and we noted in 5.3 that it is not beyond doubt. This solution is, I think, correct. But it takes us out of the frying pan and into the fire, as we shall see in the next chapter.

---

[11] See the quotation from Kant given in 5.1, and the second quotation in 5.5.

6 Kant's antinomies

Introduction

In this chapter, we will concern ourselves with the other limit of thought in Kant, the limit of the iterable. This rears its head, and plays a central role, in the Dialectic of Pure Reason. The concerns of the previous chapter are lurking beneath the surface, however, as we shall see.

6.1 The transcendental illusion

The Transcendental Dialectic concerns certain objects, which Kant calls *Transcendental Ideas*. Given some phenomenon, we can consider its conditions of a certain kind. (What, in general, Kant means by 'condition' he never explains very clearly. However, it will not be necessary for us to have a definition;[1] the examples we meet will suffice.) According to Kant, Reason then forces us to construct the totality of all conditions of that kind. As Kant puts it (A409=B436):

Reason makes this demand in accordance with the principle that *if the conditioned is given, the entire sum of the conditions, and consequently the absolutely unconditioned ... is also given.*

The resultant totality does not itself possess conditions of the appropriate kind – or it would not be the totality of all such conditions. This is why Kant calls it the unconditioned. It is therefore a noumenon (if it is anything at all): any phenomenon (which is a representation for Kant; see 5.1) must have conditions of the appropriate kind (space, time, and cause), since these are constitutive of experience.[2]

The unconditioneds are exactly the Transcendental Ideas. According to Kant, there are three ways of totalising, corresponding to the three kinds of syllogism: categorical, hypothetical, and disjunctive, though the correspondence is tenuous to say the least. We thus come to three Transcendental Ideas: the Soul, the Cosmos, and God.

[1] Bennett ((1974), section 84) suggests that a condition of something is a condition of its possibility.
[2] See, for example, A508=B536.

Each Transcendental Idea brings in its wake a family of arguments, which Kant calls, respectively: the Paralogisms, the Antinomies, and the Ideal. The arguments appear to establish profound metaphysical truths, but are (for reasons that we will come to in the case of the Cosmological Idea) fallacious. (For this reason Kant calls them 'dialectical'.) Despite this, the fallacies are, in some sense, ones into which we inevitably fall: a 'natural and unavoidable illusion' (A422=B450). A visual illusion (such as the seeing of black dots at the interstices of a white grid on a black background) is an inherent product of our (correctly functioning) sensory apparatus. Moreover, even when we know this to be an illusion we cannot help seeing it. Similarly, the illusion concerning the dialectical arguments, which Kant calls 'the Transcendental Illusion', is an inherent product of our (correctly functioning) conceptual apparatus; when we know that the arguments are fallacious, still we cannot help seeing them as correct. Kant's explanation as to why it is that this illusion arises is rather obscure and unsatisfactory. But the basic idea is that our possession of Transcendental Ideas performs the essential regulative function of forcing us to acknowledge that any determination of conditions is bound to be incomplete, and so motivate us to determine further conditions. All of this is summed up in the following quotation (A644=B672 ff.):

[Transcendental Ideas] have an excellent, and indeed indispensably necessary, regulative employment, namely, that of directing the understanding towards a certain goal upon which the routes marked out by all its rules converge, as upon their point of intersection. The point is indeed a mere idea, a *focus imaginarius*, from which, since it lies outside the bounds of possible experience, the concepts of the understanding do not in reality proceed; none the less it serves to give to these concepts the greatest [possible] unity combined with the greatest [possible] extension. Hence arises the illusion that the lines have their source in a real object lying outside the field of empirically possible knowledge – just as objects reflected in a mirror are seen as behind it. Nevertheless this illusion . . . is indispensably necessary if we are to direct the understanding beyond any given experience (as part of the sum of possible experience), and thereby to secure its greatest possible extension, just as, in the case of mirror-vision, the illusion involved is indispensably necessary if, besides the objects that lie before our eyes, we are also to see those which lie at a distance behind our back.

Kant's analysis as to why Transcendental Ideas play an essential cognitive function is highly problematic, and I want neither to defend it nor discuss it here.[3] However, I take Kant's insight that completeness or totalisation is, in some sense, conceptually unavoidable, to be a profound one, and I will return to it in subsequent chapters.

---

[3] For some discussion, see, for example, Kemp Smith (1923), pp. 425ff.; Bennett (1974) ch. 12.

6.2   The antinomies: their abstract structure

Of the three families of dialectical arguments, only one will concern us here: the Antinomies. These are all versions of arguments to be found in the Leibniz/Clarke debate[4] though, as we shall see, they are also closely related to a number of other arguments that we have met in previous chapters. The Antinomies all have a common abstract structure. This is, perhaps, clearest in the First Antinomy; but it is there in all of them. In this section I will spell out this structure before we look at the arguments in more detail.

According to Kant, there are four Antinomies, corresponding to the four kinds of Categories (quantity, quality, relation, and modality), though the correspondence is, again, exceptionally tenuous. Each Category produces a kind of condition, and a crucial thing about these (as opposed to the conditions involved in the Paralogisms and the Ideal), is that taking a condition can be iterated to produce a series; in our own terminology, each condition is a generator (see 2.1). Taking some arbitrary phenomenon as a starting-point, we can, by iterating applications of the generator as far as possible, obtain the limit, that is, the unconditioned. (Strictly speaking, then, there are four Cosmological Transcendental Ideas, one corresponding to each kind of Category, but noting this rather spoils the earlier tectonic.) The limit may be either the sequence generated in this way, or the result of applying the operator as often as possible. However, since, according to Kant (as we noted in 6.1), the generators[5] can be applied to any phenomenon to produce a (novel) phenomenon, they are infinity generators; and hence we are dealing with the generated infinite.

Now, what is characteristic of the dialectical arguments in the Antinomies is that they come in pairs, each pair giving the conclusion that the appropriate limit has certain contradictory properties. The statements of these contradictories Kant calls the Thesis and the Antithesis. (*Prima facie*, the Antinomy is not always of this form; however, the underlying contradiction always is, as we shall see.) The arguments for these statements are a somewhat motley crew, but there is an over-all pattern, which Kant, himself, observes (A485=B513 ff.). The argument for the Antithesis is, essentially, an argument demonstrating that it is always possible to apply the generator again. In his words, the limit, if conceived of as obtained after a finite number of steps, is 'too small for the concept' which is generating it. The argument for the Thesis is always an argument to the effect that if the limit is generated by an infinite number of applications of the generator, Trouble ensues. As Kant puts it, the limit, so conceived, is 'too large for the concept'.

Let us now see how each Antinomy fits the abstract structure I have just described. I shall also give a brief evaluation of each argument (much briefer

---

[4] See Al-Azm (1972).
[5] Or at least their phenomenal versions (see below).

than is really warranted). Undoubtedly the arguments appeared much better in their historical context,[6] but my concern here is with the question of how much weight can be put on them now. The answer is 'not much'; but that is not the end of the matter, as we shall see.

6.3   First antinomy: the beginning of the cosmos

The First Antinomy comes in two versions. One concerns time; the other concerns space. I will deal mainly with the first of these, adding but a comment on the second at the end. In this, the generator is *an event at a (fixed) temporal duration prior to x*. Kant does not say 'fixed', but it is clear that this is intended since Zenonian regresses are meant to be ruled out. By iterated applications of the generator to an arbitrary event (say the October Revolution) we obtain the limit: a sequence of events stretching back as far as possible. The contradiction is simply that this limit both has and has not a last, (i.e. temporally first) member. In other words, that the cosmos is and is not bounded in time past.

The argument for the Thesis is simply that if there were no such member, we would have a completed infinite, which is impossible. As Kant puts it (A426=B454 ff.):

If we assume that the world has no beginning in time, then up to every given moment an eternity has elapsed, and there has passed away in the world an infinite series of successive states of things. Now the infinity of a series consists in the fact that it can never be completed through successive synthesis. It thus follows that it is impossible for an infinite world-series to have passed away, and that a beginning of the world is therefore a necessary condition of the world's existence.

Unfortunately, the argument is not successful. Kant claims that a completed infinity is impossible by definition. But this is so only because of a tendentious definition of infinity, which he nowhere defends. As modern set-theory shows, there are perfectly coherent definitions of infinity according to which a completed infinity is not a contradiction in terms; and a generated infinity of the kind in question is quite consistent. As we saw (2.6), there is a much more sophisticated tradition as to why a completed infinity of time past would be contradictory. But Kant did not appeal to this. Nor, as we saw there, would it have done him much good to do so. Thus, this argument fails.

The argument for the Antithesis is more interesting. It is, essentially, that if there were a last member of the regress there would be (an infinity of) times at which there were no events. At no such time is there a reason why the cosmos should have started; hence it would never have started (ibid.):

[6] See Al-Azm (1972).

For let us assume that [the cosmos] has a beginning. Since the beginning is an existence which is preceded by time, there must have been a preceding time in which the world was not, i.e. an empty time. Now no coming to be of a thing is possible in an empty time, because no part of such a time possesses, as compared with any other, a distinguishing condition of existence rather than of non-existence; and this applies whether the thing is supposed to arise of itself or through some other cause. In the world many series of things can, indeed, begin; but the world itself cannot have a beginning, and is therefore infinite in respect of past time.

Though this argument is better than that for the Thesis it is still highly suspect. The first reason is that it appeals to the Principle of Sufficient Reason (PSR). As we noted in 2.9, this will not take the required weight. Note, moreover, that even if the PSR is correct, the fact that nothing physical was happening does not imply that there was no reason why the cosmos started – at least if you believe in a God of a certain kind. The reason might just be the intention of God to start the cosmos at that instant. (God's intention does not have to be formed at that instant.) One may ask why God should have intended the cosmos to start then. To which the answer might just be: if God was to start the cosmos, She had to start it at some time; all times were equally good, so She chose that one at random. As Buridan's ass discovered, choosing one of a number of equally good alternatives might be a perfectly sufficient reason.

The second reason that the argument fails is that it assumes that the topology of time is Euclidean, and, in particular, that before any time there is another. This may, in fact, not be so. Nor is this a mere academic possibility. The General Theory of Relativity assures us that the structure of space/time and gravitational fields are mutually dependent, and if the cosmos started as a singularity, then it may be that it makes no sense to talk of either time or space prior to this singularity. There was no prior.[7]

A final word on the second version of the antinomy concerning space: the generator here is *an event at a (fixed) distance in some constant direction from* *x* (again, Kant does not mention the constant direction, but he obviously intends to rule out going round in circles), and the Antinomy is that the limit generated does and does not have a last member. The argument is very similar to the time version, as, therefore, are its flaws. There is only one further point worth noting. The infinity of space generated here seems more like time stretching into the future than into the past. There is therefore no reason to suppose that it is a 'completed infinity'. To obtain the conclusion that it is, Kant therefore requires a further argument. This is a particularly pompous piece of Kantian verbosity, which is best passed over in silence.[8]

---

[7] See, for example, Hawking (1988), pp. 42ff.
[8] See Kemp Smith (1923), pp. 485ff.

6.4   Second antinomy: the divisibility of matter

The Second Antinomy is, again, spatial and concerns the divisibility of matter.[9] The generator in this case is *a fixed fractional part of x*. As usual, Kant
does not say that the part has to be of some fixed proportion, but this is
required if nothing is to escape division. Starting with an arbitrary piece of
matter (say, you), apply the generator iteratively. The limit produced is a piece
of matter to which the generator can no longer be applied, i.e., which can be no
further divided. In Kantian jargon, this is *the simple*. The contradiction in this
case is that physical objects are and are not made up of simples. Actually, Kant
could have made it the logically equivalent and simpler: there are and are not
simples. For if there are simples, matter is made of them; if there are not, it is
not.

The argument for the Thesis is, perhaps, the most opaque of the eight
arguments in question. It goes essentially as follows. Given any object it is
always possible to decompose any compound part in thought. This is because
the fact that things are arranged in a certain way is always a contingent one.
Now take any object and suppose that it is not composed of simples.
Decompose it through and through. Nothing will be left, which is impossible
if we are dealing with a substance. Hence the supposition is false. As Kant puts
it (A434=B462 ff.):

Let us assume that composite substances are not made up of simple parts. If all
composition be then removed in thought, no composite part, and (since we admit
no simple parts) also no simple parts, that is to say, nothing at all, will remain, and
accordingly no substance will be given. Either, therefore, it is impossible to remove in
thought all composition, or after its removal there must remain something which exists
without composition, that is, the simple. In the former case the composite would not be
made up of substances; composition, as applied to substances, is only an accidental
relation in independence of which they must still persist as self-subsistent beings.
Since this contradicts our supposition, there remains only the original supposition,
that a composite substance is made up of simple parts.

The cruxes of this argument are, first, the claim that it is always possible to
decompose in thought, and, second, that it is impossible to decompose
'through and through'. The first seems reasonable enough: it always seems
logically possible that spatial parts could be arranged in some other way. The
second is reminiscent of Aristotle's argument to the same end (2.5), and is
more problematic. Its correctness here depends on what Kant means by 'substance'. In the Schematism Kant's criterion for being a substance is permanence in time (see 5.3), i.e., existence through all time. If this is what he means
I see no hope of pushing the argument through. More plausibly, by substance,

---

[9] If Kant had had the benefit of reading Taylor (1955), he might well have constructed a
temporal analogue too.

he means something that is indestructible (and hence *must* exist through all time). Then the argument looks a lot better. For anything that is made up of parts could (logically) cease to exist; for the parts could come apart. Hence if all parts of the object have parts, all its parts could cease to exist, in which case it, too, would cease to exist.

Whatever one makes of this argument in the end, modern science seems to have finessed it, since it would now appear that matter is not a substance in the required sense. The modern notion of matter is still, perhaps, a moot one (especially when we take quantum theory into account[10]). Yet it is clear that matter can be destroyed by turning it into energy, and so is destructible. Matter/energy may well be conserved, but energy is not spatially extended, and so the spatial decomposition involved in the argument seems to get no grip on it at all. Hence the argument fails.

The argument for the Antithesis is much more straightforward: Suppose that there were a simple part. This would occupy space. But all spaces are divisible. Hence this simple would be correspondingly divisible. By definition, this is impossible. As Kant puts it (ibid.):

Assume that a composite thing (as substance) is made up of simple parts. Since all external relation, and therefore all composition of substance, is possible only in space, a space must be made up of as many parts as are contained in the composite which occupies it. Space, however, is not made up of simple parts, but of spaces. Every part of the composite must therefore occupy a space. But the absolutely first parts of every composite are simple. The simple therefore occupies a space. Now since everything real, which occupies a space, contains in itself a manifold of constituents external to one another, and is therefore composite; and since a real composition is not made up of accidents (for accidents could not exist outside one another, in the absence of substance) but of substances, it follows that the simple would be a composite of substances – which is self-contradictory.

The argument is still fallacious, however; for, as modern mathematics shows, Euclidean spaces *are* made up of simple parts: points. And these are not divisible. Kant indicates that he thinks that a continuum cannot be composed of points. But as we noted in reply to Aristotle, who actually gives an argument for this claim (2.5), this is just wrong. Conceivably, modern science might challenge the conclusion that physical space has a Euclidean topology (i.e. is composed of points) by making it reasonable to believe that it is quantised (though this is not on the cards at the moment). But the argument would still fail, since the quanta of space would themselves be indivisible. Hence, the argument fails.

Finally, it is worth noting that in this Antinomy each of the Thesis and Antithesis has a rider (A436=B464). The rider in the case of the Thesis is that

---

[10] See Priest (1989a).

only simples exist. This is a simple corollary, as Kant notes. The rider of the Antithesis is also a corollary of the argument: there are no simples in the world. It is the phrase 'in the world' (i.e., the world as experienced), that makes a difference here, since it allows Kant to produce a second argument. This hinges on the fact that experience can never establish that division is *impossible*. Since the argument is not an integral part of the general pattern, I shall not discuss it here.

6.5   Third antinomy: causal chains

The Third Antinomy concerns causation of events or states of affairs. (I use the terms interchangeably as in 2.7.) The generator in this case is *a natural cause of x*. (The word 'natural' is here, since Kant explicitly contrasts natural causation with what he calls 'freedom', which turns out to be some kind of noumenal causation, as we shall see.) Starting with an arbitrary event, we apply the generator as far as possible to obtain the limit, in this case, a chain of causes. The Antinomy is that the chain has and has not a first member. This is not the way the Thesis and Antithesis are explicitly stated, which is that there both is and is not something other than natural causality. But, according to Kant, if there is no causality other than natural causality then the chain is infinite; and it is this claim he reduces to absurdity. Similarly, Kant argues, if there is something other than natural causality then the chain may have a first member; and again, it is this that is reduced to absurdity. Hence, the central contradiction in the Antinomy is the one I have stated.

The argument for the Thesis is essentially as follows. Suppose that the chain of causes from any event has no first member; then it goes back to infinity. But then the event has no sufficient cause, which is impossible. As Kant puts it (A444=B472 ff.):

Let us assume that there is no other causality than that in accordance with the laws of nature. This being so, everything which *takes place* presupposes a preceding state upon which it inevitably follows according to a rule. But the preceding state must itself be something which has taken place (having come to be in a time in which it previously was not); for if it had always existed, its consequence also would have always existed, and would not have only just arisen. The causality of the cause through which something takes place is itself, therefore, something that has *taken place* which again presupposes, in accordance with the law of nature, a preceding state and its causality, and this in a similar manner a still earlier state, and so on. If, therefore, everything takes place solely in accordance with laws of nature, there will always be only a relative, and never a first beginning, and consequently, no completeness of the series on the side of the causes that arise the one from the other. But the law of nature is just this, that nothing takes place without a cause *sufficiently* determining a priori. The proposition that no causality is possible save in accordance with laws of nature, when taken in unlimited universality, is therefore self-contradictory; and this cannot, therefore, be regarded as the sole kind of causality.[11]

This argument fails. It is clearly a version of Leibniz' Cosmological argument (see 2.8) and appeals to the PSR. But note that it is agreed that the chosen event does have a reason (its cause); the claim is that it has no *sufficient reason*, where 'sufficient reason' appears to mean a reason for whose own reason one cannot ask. The PSR is being applied in a very strong form, therefore: every contingent event has a reason why it is as it is, and, moreover, a reason which is itself not in need of a reason. This version inherits all the problems of the weaker version (see 2.9), but has an even worse flaw of its own. The reasons that we normally offer for events are certainly not sufficient in this sense. Indeed, it is difficult to think of one that is. As parents know, the game of asking 'why' whenever a reason is given never seems to end – except in frustration. I can therefore see no reason why *any* event should have a sufficient reason, let alone *all* events.

Another reason the argument fails is that it does not establish that the event has no sufficient reason; merely that it has no sufficient reason in the chain of causes. But as Leibniz noted, this leaves open the possibility that the chain itself, and hence each event in it, has a sufficient reason.

The argument for the Antithesis is rather different, and goes essentially as follows: if the chain has a first member, then this has no causal determination, which is impossible by the 'Law of Causality': every event has a cause. As Kant puts it (ibid.):

Assume that there is a freedom in the transcendental sense, as a special kind of causality in accordance with which the events in the world can have come about, namely, a power of absolutely beginning a series of consequences of the state; it then follows that not only will a series have its absolute beginning in this spontaneity, but that the very determination of the spontaneity to originate the series, that is to say, the causality itself, will have an absolute beginning; there will be no antecedent through which this act, in taking place, is determined in accordance with fixed laws. But every beginning of action presupposes a state of the not yet acting cause; and a *dynamical* beginning of the action, presupposes a state which has no *causal* connection with the preceding state of the case, that is to say, in nowise follows from it. Transcendental freedom thus stands opposed to the law of causality; and the kind of connection which it assumes as holding between the successive states of the active causes renders all unity of experience impossible. It is not to be met with in any experience, and is therefore an empty thought-entity.[12]

As usual, the argument fails. This is simply due to the failure of the 'Law of Causality'. (See 5.4.)

---

[11] There is then another paragraph which explains that the first member must arise other than through natural causation. But this is not relevant here.

[12] There is another paragraph explaining that there is therefore no 'causation of freedom'. But that is not relevant here.

6.6   Fourth antinomy: a necessary being

Finally, we come to the Fourth Antinomy. This is officially about necessary beings, though Kant often slides into talking about states of affairs again. Strictly speaking, then, what the generator produces when applied to x is an object on which x depends for its existence. There seems to be no natural way to express this quickly, so I will call such an object a *ground*. Thus the generator here is *ground of x*. An object depends on its ground (if it has one) for existence. But it is clear from Kant's remarks, that the kind of dependence in question here is causal. Hence what we have here is, in some ways, a rerun of the third Antinomy.[13]

But there is one important difference. Applying the generator iteratively to an object, we get a chain of objects. The limit in this case is either the last member of the chain (i.e., the causally independent object) if there is one, or the whole chain if there is not. It is taking both possibilities into account that makes this Antinomy distinctive (and allows Kant to give one argument that is not a *reductio*, for a change). The contradiction in this case is that the limit both is and is not necessary. As Kant states the Antinomy, it is that there is and is not a necessary being; but again, this is an unnecessary complication. For the object demonstrated to be necessary in the Thesis is the limit; and the argument for the Antithesis is broken up into two cases: the first deals with the limit; the second with everything else. Hence the crucial contradiction concerns the necessity of the limit.

A word here about what Kant means by 'necessary being'. In these arguments he appears to mean simply an ungrounded being. This is not the criterion for necessity given in the Schematism, however, which is: a being that never fails to exist (see 5.3), i.e., that is omnitemporal. Nor does either of these entail the other. The fact that an object has a ground does not imply that it is not omnitemporal; for the ground may itself be permanent and may necessitate the effect. Conversely, the fact that something is not omnitemporal does not imply that it has a ground, as a particle produced by some spontaneous quantum effect illustrates. I shall assume that Kant means what he appears to mean, simply because this minimises the amount of invalidity in the arguments.

Having got this straight, let us look at the arguments. This time, for a change, let us start with the Antithesis. The argument for this is as follows: If the limit is the whole chain, it cannot be necessary since no part of it is. If, on the other hand, it is the first member of the chain, this is impossible since such a first member is an object in the world, and so must have a ground. In Kant's words (A452=B481):

If we assume that the world itself is necessary, or that a necessary being exists in it, there are then two alternatives. Either there is a beginning in the series of alterations

---

[13] See Kemp Smith (1923), pp. 495ff.; Bennett (1974), p. 241.

which is absolutely necessary, and therefore without a cause, or the series itself is without any beginning, and although contingent and conditioned in all its parts none the less, as a whole, is absolutely necessary and unconditioned. The former alternative, however, conflicts with the dynamical law of the determination of all appearances in time; and the latter alternative contradicts itself since the existence of a series cannot be necessary if no single member of it is necessary.[14]

The argument is by dilemma. To show that a first member of the chain cannot be necessary Kant appeals to 'the dynamical law of the determination of all appearances in time', by which I take him to mean just the Law of Causality: the object must have a cause, and so is not necessary. As in the Third Antinomy, this appeal renders the argument fallacious. The argument deployed in the other horn of the dilemma (the existence of a series cannot be necessary if no single member of it is necessary) may look more plausible; but for the notion of necessity in question, it is simply a fallacy of composition. From the fact that each member of the series has a cause, it by no means follows that the whole does. Hence, this part of the argument fails too. (Nor is the argument any better if necessity means omnitemporality: the sequence can persist through all time even if no member does.)

Turning to the Thesis, the argument is essentially very simple: in either case the limit, by construction, has no ground, and so is unconditionally necessary. As Kant puts it (ibid.):

The sensible world, as the sum-total of all appearances, contains a series of alterations. For without such a series even representation of serial time, as a condition of possibility of the sensible world, would not be given to us. But every alteration stands under its condition, which precedes it in time and renders it necessary. Now every conditioned that is given presupposes, in respect of its existence, a complete series of conditions up to the unconditioned, which alone is absolute necessity. Alteration thus existing as a consequence of the absolutely necessary, the existence of something absolutely necessary must be granted . . . Something absolutely necessary is therefore contained in the world itself, whether this something be the whole series of alterations in the world or a part of the series.[15]

The argument as it stands will not do – at least if the sequence in question is an ω-sequence, as it is in the Third Antinomy. This is due to the fact that if the limit is the whole sequence of conditions, the argument has not established that it itself is ungrounded. All that follows is that it does not have a ground in the chain. However, we at last meet an argument that can be repaired. This is done in essentially the same way that we repaired Leibniz' Cosmological argument (2.8). Let σ be the transfinite sequence generated by applying the

---

[14] There is another paragraph of the argument where Kant argues, in effect, that there are no other candidates for a necessary being. This is irrelevant here.

[15] The passage omitted argues that the necessary being must be in the world in a certain sense. This is not relevant here.

generator *cause of* as far as possible, however far that is. (That is, given any object, we generate its ground if it has one; and given any unbounded sequence of grounds, we generate the ground of the sequence if it has one.[16]) Since, by definition, the generator can be no further applied, it follows that the limit of σ (that is, its last member if it has one, or it itself, if not) has no ground, i.e., is necessary.

6.7   Kant's solution(s)

We have now examined the individual arguments, and seen that none of them works (at least as they are formulated). In the end, it will be their over-all structure that is important, however. Each, as we have seen, fits the pattern I described in 6.2. In case this insight has been lost in the details, I summarise the important information in Table 3.

We now turn to what Kant made of the Antinomies. Although the arguments appear to establish that the limits are inconsistent, and in some sense we cannot help acknowledging their correctness, as we saw in 6.1, Kant thought that, in the final analysis, the arguments are not correct. He explains why; twice unfortunately, since the two explanations are incompatible, and Kant never retracts either.

The first reason, let us call it *Solution 1*, is the older[17] and more general, being supposed to apply to all the Antinomies (A505=B533). Solution 1 is essentially that of Aristotle: deny that the limit exists. (Thus, the infinities in question are only potential infinities, in Aristotle's terms.) Like all things in Kant, however, it has knobs on.

Kant claims that if the objects in the series of conditions were noumena then the limit would exist (for example, A498=B526 f.). This appears to have been so obvious to him that he never bothered to argue for it. (Why, I am not sure. Possibly, he thought it evident that in the cases we are dealing with the infinity must be completed.) But in any case the objects in the regress are phenomena; and this means that the limit does not exist. The *reductio* arguments can be taken to demonstrate this. Since they are perfectly sound, it follows that both the Thesis and Antithesis are false, but the only way that statements of the form 'S is P' and 'S is not P' can both be false is if S does not exist (A506=B531 ff.).

Kant also gives an independent argument as to why the object, S, does not exist. This is spelled out most clearly in the *Prolegomena* 52c, but also occurs at A793=B821. What, exactly, the argument is, is most unclear. As best I can

---

[16] If this exists it must be a distinct object. It cannot be the sequence itself: parts of this depend for their existence on other parts, but the whole does not depend on the whole, as Leibniz, in effect, pointed out (see the first quotation in 2.8).

[17] See Kemp Smith (1923), p. 506.

Table 3

Antinomy	Generator	Limit	[Anti]Thesis
1st	event prior to	totality of past states	has [not] a beginning
2nd	part of	the simple	objects are [not] composed of
3rd	cause of	chain of causes	has [not] a first member
4th	ground of	first member of chain if there is one or whole chain if there is not	is [not] necessary

understand it, it goes as follows. If the limit exists it is either a phenomenon or a noumenon. But it is clearly not a phenomenon, as we have already seen (in 6.1).[18] On the other hand, it cannot be a noumenon either, for noumena exist independently of all experience; yet the limit of all experiences of a certain kind obviously does not exist independently of experience. Such an idea is self-contradictory according to Kant. Hence the limit does not exist.

The second reason as to why the Antinomic arguments do not establish true contradictions, *Solution 2*, is rather different, and is supposed to apply only to the Third and Fourth Antinomies. At the risk of spoiling the over-all pattern, Kant produces this solution because Solution 1 is inconsistent with other fish that he has to fry. In the Fourth Antinomy the limit object, a necessary being, is (what else?) God; and Kant does not want to deny His existence. Similarly, when tracing back the chain of causes in the Third Antinomy, Kant wants it to be possible that one should come to something which initiates it, and so make room for free will. Thus, he cannot endorse the claim that the Theses are false.

Solution 2 also turns on the distinction between phenomena and noumena. As we noted in 5.6 Kant distinguishes between phenomenal causation and noumenal causation; the latter he calls, rather misleadingly, 'freedom' (A532=B560, A538=B566). In phenomenal causation a phenomenon causes another phenomenon; in noumenal causation a noumenon causes another noumenon or a phenomenon. The generators *cause of* x in the Third Antinomy and *ground of* x (i.e., object on which x causally depends for its existence) in the Fourth are, therefore, ambiguous. Of course, merely to diagnose an ambiguity is not *ipso facto* to resolve the contradiction. In a sense, it makes matters worse, since we now have *two* pairs of antinomic arguments, one for each of the disambiguated generators.

---

[18] This is not quite right: in the Fourth Antinomy the limit could be the last member of the sequence, and, as such, unproblematically a phenomenon; but presumably Kant would rule out this possibility on the ground of the Law of Causality.

In both Antinomies, Kant claims, the Antithesis is true for the phenomenal generator, and the Thesis may be true for the noumenal generator. This flies in the face of Kant's view on the Categories. For a start, it is not clear that he is entitled to a notion of noumenal causality (5.6); but even if he is, he is certainly not entitled to make judgments about noumena using it (5.5).

Still, setting these problems aside, another emerges. To resolve the contradiction in this way Kant must hold that the argument for the Thesis, in the case of the phenomenal generator, and the argument for the Antithesis, in the case of the noumenal generator, break down. It is substantiating these claims which constitutes the actual solutions. Let us call them solutions 2p and 2n respectively. Unfortunately, Kant never elaborates on either of them. Solution 2n is fairly obvious: the argument of the second Analogy for the Law of Causality (see 5.4), which is supposed to establish that the generator is an infinity generator, gets no grip on noumenal causality. Solution 2p, on the other hand, is far from obvious. Perhaps, in the case of the Third Antinomy Kant could have said that the PSR in the form required there fails: it is not true that every event must have a sufficient phenomenal cause. (Presumably, it must still have a sufficient cause, but this may be noumenal.) What he would have said in the case of the Fourth Antinomy I have no idea.

So much for the two solutions. We will turn to their adequacy in the next section. But before we do so, one should note the following. Both of Kant's solutions turn crucially on the distinction between phenomena and noumena, and their different properties. According to Solution 1 we mistakenly take the limit to exist; and we do this because we take phenomena to be noumena. In Solution 2, that is, solution 2n (which is the only one that Kant formulates, as we have just seen), we mistakenly apply the Law of Causality, and so take noumena to be phenomena. Hence we see the connection between the limits of the last chapter and those of this. The doctrines about the behaviour of phenomena and noumena are supposed to provide a solution to the Antinomies. Conversely, the fact that the Antinomies would arise if this behaviour were otherwise provides an argument that it is not so. In particular, it provides an argument for the claim that the Categories cannot be applied to noumena.[19] It also means that Kant cannot take the only really plausible way out of defusing the contradictory nature of noumena (see 5.5) − if he wishes to remain consistent.

6.8   Evaluation

The next question is how good Kant's resolution of the contradiction is in his own terms. The simpler solution to deal with is Solution 2; so let us take that

---

[19] This is the argument I referred to in 5.3. Since the Antinomic arguments fail anyway, it would seem to be no better than the other two arguments discussed there.

first. Consider, first, solution 2p. Since Kant nowhere explains where the arguments break down on this disambiguation, and nor is this obvious, there is, in a sense, no solution to evaluate here: the contradiction is unresolved. What solution 2n is, on the other hand, is clear. But is it not clear that it works. The arguments for the Antitheses in the Third and Fourth Antinomies appeal to the 'Law of Causality' to establish that the generator can always be applied again. Now, the Law of Causality does not apply to the noumenal generator, it is true; but the PSR, to which Kant subscribes, does. Every noumenon must have its (noumenal) reason; hence the generator can always be iterated, and the solution fails.[20]

So let us turn to Solution 1, according to which the limit does not exist. First, let us deal with Kant's independent argument for the non-existence of the limit. The argument for this, as I have interpreted it, hinges on the claim that the limit must be dependent on experience, since each of the objects generating it is. This is simply a fallacy of composition of sorts. Limits often do not share the properties of the things of which they are the limits. For example, a limit of finite numbers does not have to be finite, and a limit of rational numbers does not have to be rational. In this case the limit is a noumenon; as such it is an object of thought, not experience, and so its existence does not depend on experience. It does not share this property with the things of which it is a limit, and the argument collapses.

But we still have the *reductio* argument against the existence of the limit (at least in the case of the first three Antinomies). Clearly this depends on the claim that there are no truths of the appropriate kind about non-existent objects. This is obviously a debatable point, but fortunately there is no need to debate it here. For the Solution fails: if the arguments are, as Kant maintains, sound then they lead to contradiction anyway. For the *reductio* arguments in the Theses (with the possible exception of the First) never actually depend on the existence of the limit (the completed infinity)! but only on the existence of the indefinite regress (the potential infinity), which is entailed by the non-existence of the limit (and to which Kant is committed anyway). For example, suppose that the limit in the Second Antinomy, the simple, does not exist. Then certainly matter is not composed of simples; but this is precisely the supposition that Kant has reduced to absurdity in the argument for the Thesis. Similarly, suppose that in the Third Antinomy, the limit does not exist; then there is a chain of causes stretching back to infinity; and this is precisely the supposition that Kant has reduced to absurdity in the argument for the Thesis. Hence Kant's Solution 1 does not work either.

[20] It might be argued that the PSR cannot be applied to noumenal states of affairs since these might be logically necessary, but it is unlikely that Kant would have endorsed this. For one reason: the main candidate for a necessary state of affairs is God's existence, but the *Critique* is famous for its demolition of the Ontological Argument (A592=B620 ff.), which is supposed to establish this.

6.9   Fifth antinomy: the limit of thought

Let us take stock. We have seen that Kant held that by arguments that are, in some sense, inherent in reason, certain limits of thought are demonstrably contradictory. None the less, employing his interpretation of the distinction between phenomena and noumena, he tried to interpret the arguments in such a way as to resolve the contradiction, though not with success.

This last fact is somewhat academic at the moment since, as we have already seen, the Antinomic arguments fail for reasons quite independent of those Kant produced. As we saw, only the argument for the Thesis of the Fourth Antinomy stands up to inspection (with a little help): it establishes the existence of an ungrounded object. This takes us very close to a contradiction, however. If we knew that everything had a distinct ground, i.e., that the generator could always be applied again, contradiction *would* arise. Kant tried to secure the iterability of the generator by appealing to the Law of Causality, a move which, I argued, fails. However, one might endorse iterability on other grounds, such as the PSR, and then contradiction would arise. This is exactly the argument of 2.9, though, as I argued in there, the PSR is not correct.

We are, none the less, very close to a contradiction. All we need is a generator with suitable properties, and we are there. As we shall see in later chapters, it is not difficult to find technical generators of this sort. But to be going on with, let me give a simple non-technical one: *thought of x*. (Where by this I mean the content of the thought, not the act of thinking.) Given any object or collection of objects, the thought of it is a distinct object (unless the thought is of a self referential kind). So the contradiction now runs as follows. (I will not formalise it here, but a formal representation will become evident in due course.) Start with any object, say, the *Critique of Pure Reason*, and apply the generator iteratively, to produce, at each stage, the thought of the previous object: the *Critique*; the thought of the *Critique*; the thought of the thought of the *Critique*. And when we have an unbounded sequence of thoughts we next produce the thought of all of them, and keep going. (Clearly, we never produce a self-referential thought in this process since the object of thought is 'pre-defined' in each case.) Let this procedure be performed as often as possible (and so, presumably, into the transfinite). Consider the totality of all thoughts generated in this way, T. Clearly, T has no last member, since for any object there is a thought of it (though maybe it is so complex that no person could actually entertain it). And *ex hypothesi*, the generator can be no further applied to T. So T cannot be thought of (Transcendence). But you *can* think of T: you have just done so (Closure). Contradiction.[21]

For future reference, and with apologies to Kant, I will call this the Fifth Antinomy. It is exactly of the Kantian form. For we have an infinity generator

---

[21] Actually, the claim that T has no last member is inessential to the argument. If, for some reason, one takes T to have a last member, we can run exactly the same argument with respect to that.

Table 4

Antinomy	Generator	Limit	[Anti]Thesis
5th	thought of	T	can [not] be thought of

applied to a certain object, together with arguments that the limit produced in this way has inconsistent properties. This can be illustrated as in Table 4, which is a fifth row for Table 3 in 6.7.

The contradiction can be put in a slightly different but equivalent form. This will turn out to be useful in later chapters. The equivalent contradiction is that the thought of T both is (Closure) and is not (Transcendence) a member of T. The argument for equivalence goes as follows. Suppose that one can and cannot think of T. T is the set of all things generated by applying the generator as far as possible. Since one can think of T, the thought of T is just such a thing. Hence it is in T. But the thought of T is distinct from any thought in T (since T is distinct from any of its members); hence the thought of T is not in T (Transcendence). Conversely, suppose that the thought of T both is and is not in T. Since the thought of T is in T, one can think of T. But if one could think of T this thought would have to be a thought in the sequence of things generated; and since it is not, one cannot.

The next obvious question is whether either of Kant's two solutions can be applied to remove this contradiction. As we saw, there are general reasons as to why his solutions fail. But there are also reasons specific to this case. (I take the contradiction in its first form.) Solution 1 is to the effect that the limit does not exist, and so the Thesis is false. This does not appear to be of much help here. For it is only extensional predicates (at best) which cannot be truly predicated of non-existent objects. Notoriously, one *can* think of non-existent objects, such as Sherlock Holmes. In other words, even if x does not exist, the (content of) the thought of x does. Solution 2, as we saw, really only explains the failure of the argument for the noumenal generator (2n). In this case, it is to the effect that the limit exists, but the generator does not apply to it, i.e., there is no thought of the limit. This does not seem much use either; for, patently, one can think of the limit (even if it is a noumenon): we have just done so.

Conclusion

I will return to possibilities for defusing contradictions of this kind when we have further examples of them. For the present, I just note that Kant's claim that antinomy is inherent in aspects of our reasoning about the limits of thought, is quite correct. For what to make of this, we turn to Hegel.

7 Hegel's infinities

Introduction

In this chapter we move from Kant to Hegel. As we saw in the last chapter, Kant argued that contradictions are, in some sense, inherent in our thinking about generated infinities. Despite this, he drew back from a dialetheic conclusion: employing the distinction between phenomena and noumena he argued that the Antinomic arguments do not, in fact, establish contradictory conclusions. Hegel criticised the ground of the distinction between phenomena and noumena – with predictable consequences: the infinities of the Antinomies are contradictory. In this chapter we will first look at this matter, and then move on to look at Hegel's own positive account of the nature of infinity. Unsurprisingly, the account explicitly incorporates the view that generated infinities are truly contradictory.

7.1 Hegel's critique of Kant

The empiricists, such as Hume and Berkeley, held that both knowledge and meaning must be derived from sensory experience. Kant rejected this: knowledge may be a priori; and the Categories of reason do not derive in any way from experience, but are imposed upon it. However, Kant still gave experience a privileged position in relation to meaning. For, though the Categories might not be derived from experience, they have application only when schematised (5.3), that is, only when taken as the forms of *possible* experience.

Hegel rejected this vestige of empiricism. Neither experience nor its possibility had any privileged position with respect to knowledge or meaning. Hence, though the distinction between things perceivable by the senses (phenomena) and things not so perceivable (noumena) makes perfectly good sense for Hegel, the former are not categorically distinct from the latter. For example, it is just as possible to know things about noumena as it is to know things about phenomena; it may even be easier. As Hegel puts it in the *Lesser Logic*, section 44 (p. 72[1]):

---

[1] All quotations from this are taken from Wallace (1975).

The Thing-in-itself ... expresses the object when we leave out of sight all that consciousness makes of it, all its emotional aspects, and all specific thoughts of it. It is easy to see what is left – utter abstraction, total emptiness, only described still as in an 'outer world' ... Hence one can only read with surprise the perpetual remark that we do not know the Thing-in-itself. On the contrary there is nothing we can know so easily.

Hegel also observes (as we did in 5.5) that Kant's very claim that we cannot make judgments about noumena is self-inconsistent (*Lesser Logic*, section 60, p. 91):

It argues an utter want of consistency to say, on the one hand, that understanding only knows phenomena, and, on the other, assert the absolute character of this knowledge, by statements such as 'Cognition can go no further' ... No one knows, or even feels, that anything is a limit or a defect until he is at the same time above and beyond it.

For Hegel, then, nothing substantial can hang on the distinction between phenomena and noumena. In particular, the essential differences between the two realms to which Kant appeals in order to defuse the Antinomies (6.7) cannot be maintained.

7.2   Contradiction in the world

Hegel drew the appropriate conclusion from this. Since there are perfectly sound (according to Hegel) arguments to the effect that the World (that is, the infinity generated in each Antinomy) has contradictory properties, it does have contradictory properties. Thus, commenting on the Antinomies and Kant's supposed solution to them, he says (*Lesser Logic*, section 48, pp. 77f.):

to offer the idea that the contradiction introduced into the world of Reason by the categories of the Understanding is inevitable and essential was to make one of the most important steps in the progress of Modern Philosophy. But the more important the issue thus raised the more trivial was the solution. Its only motive was an excess of tenderness for the things of the world. The blemish of contradiction, it seems, could not be allowed to mar the essence of the world; but there could be no objection to attaching it to the thinking Reason, to the essence of mind. Probably, nobody will feel disposed to deny that the phenomenal world presents contradictions to the observing mind; meaning by 'phenomenal' the world as it presents itself to the senses and understanding, to the subjective mind. But if a comparison is instituted between the essence of the world and the essence of the mind, it does seem strange to hear how calmly and confidently the modest dogma has been advanced by one and repeated by others, that thought or Reason, and not the World, is the seat of contradiction.

As he goes on to explain in the next paragraph, Hegel thinks that the Kantian Antinomies are but the tip of an iceberg. *All* our concepts, and not just the generated infinities of the Antinomies, are embroiled in antinomic arguments. These are the arguments which drive forward our thinking from one category to the next, and so generate the dialectical progression of categories in the *Logic*. Moreover, according to Hegel, Kant missed a few categories (70 to be precise). How much credence should be given to this bit of Hegel (not much) need not concern us here. What will concern us for the rest of this chapter is Hegel's own positive account of one of those Categories, infinity itself.

7.3   Hegel's dialectic

Before we turn to this, however, a few words in general about the dialectical progression in the *Logic*. Starting with the simplest and emptiest concept, *being*, we wend, by a certain process, through ever more complex categories until we arrive at the richest and most adequate category for conceptualising reality (the absolute), *the absolute idea*. The concepts in the progression show a simple pattern. They are structured as a hierarchy of triples, so that each category (except those at the tips of the tree) has three sub-categories.[2] The triples are also structured. The second of each triad is arrived at by considering contradictions inherent in the first. Hegel calls the second the negation of the first. And, in the simplest cases at least, 'negation' means what you think it does. Thus, take the first category of the *Logic*, *being*; the second category in the corresponding triad is *non-being* or *nothing* as Hegel puts it.

By consideration of further contradictions, and particularly that between the first two categories of the triad, we arrive at the third category. This is often referred to by Hegel as the negation of the negation. What, exactly, this means is somewhat moot. What is clear is that the third category is supposed to be, in some sense, the dialectical union of the first and second. Hegel often says that the first and second categories are *aufgehoben*, or sublated, as it is sometimes translated, in the third. This is a term of Hegelean art whose murky depths we do not, fortunately, need to plumb.[3] In the most straightforward cases, the third category is the category of things whose being in the first category just is their being in the second, and which are therefore in both (since they must be in either one or the other). In this way, in the case of *being* and *non-being*, we are led to a class of things that both are and are not. These are the things in a state of change or becoming. For, according to Hegel, something which is changing from being F to not being F is, in the transition, both F and not F.[4] Hence the third category here is the category of *becoming*.[5]

---

[2]   There is one exception: there are four sub-categories of *judgment*. This is somewhat ironical, since these sub-categories – or at least *their* sub-categories – are essentially Kant's Categories.

[3]   See, for example, Taylor (1975), especially p. 119; Priest (1989b).

[4]   See Priest (1987), ch. 12; Priest (1989b).

[5]   All this may be simply formalised. Let Cx express the first category of a triad; then the second is expressed by ¬Cx; and the third is expressed by $^\wedge Cx = {}^\wedge \neg Cx$, where $^\wedge$ is a sentence nominaliser, which turns the sentence phrase α into the noun phrase $^\wedge \alpha$. $^\wedge Cx = {}^\wedge \neg Cx$ entails $Cx \wedge \neg Cx$. For details, see Priest (1989b).

Hegel is never very clear about the relationship of the third member of a triad to the first member of the next triad he considers. Sometimes it seems to be identity; sometimes it seems to be sublation; and sometimes it just is not clear what it is supposed to be. But to try to sort out this, and other aspects of the dialectical relationships in greater detail, would be a messy job. Moreover, it is clear that Hegel, like Kant, is trying to force the material into an artificial architectonic, which it does not fit properly. Hence many of the exact details are artificial or spurious. Fortunately, then, we do not need to enter further into them here.[6]

7.4   The false infinite

Let us now turn to Hegel's quite distinctive account of the infinite.[7] Hegel distinguishes between two notions of infinity: the false or spurious infinite, and the true or genuine infinite. Each of these manifests itself in a qualitative and a quantitative guise. Correspondingly, each is discussed twice in the *Logic*: first as a sub-category of *determinate being*; and a little later as a sub-category of *quantum*. The two discussions are parts of a single treatment, however, with numerous cross references and repetitions. So the two guises may be taken together. I will leave the true infinite till the next section; in this section I will discuss the false infinite.

Let us start with this in its qualitative guise. Hegel's qualitative notion of finitude is a quite orthodox one. Something is finite if it is determinate (in his terminology), that is, is limited or bounded by something else. Something is infinite (in the false sense) if it is not finite. The finite and the false infinite are therefore mutually complementary and bounding concepts.

Hegel calls this notion of the infinite false, and objects to it on the ground that it is not really infinite, since it does not manage to 'free itself from the finite'. He gives two distinct arguments for this. The first is that since it is bounded by something (viz., the finite), it is, itself, finite. As Hegel puts it in the *Logic* (pp. 139f.[8]):

This contradiction [between the finite and the false infinite] occurs as a direct result of the circumstance that the finite remains as a determinate being opposed to the infinite, so that there are *two* determinatenesses; *there are* two worlds, one infinite and one finite, and in their relationship the infinite is only the *limit* of the finite and is thus only a determinate infinite, an infinite which is itself finite.

This argument does not look terribly promising since it appears to confuse a concept with the objects which fall under it. The concept *infinite* is certainly

---

[6] Discussions can be found in numerous commentators, for example Findlay (1958) or Inwood (1983).

[7] Taylor ((1975), p. 114) calls it 'off-beat'.

[8] Quotations from this are taken from Miller (1969).

bounded by other concepts; as such it is finite. But this is quite consistent unless one imports some unjustifiable view that concepts must instantiate themselves, as Cusanus held (see 1.9). The objects which fall under the concept are infinite; but there is no reason to suppose that these are bounded by the concept *finite*, or anything else; and hence their infinity is in no way compromised.

However, Hegel does have a point here: if an object is infinite it falls in the category *infinite*, and this *is* to set a bound on it. In this sense, to conceive an object as infinite is a contradiction in terms. We are, here, on familiar ground. To be bounded and to be truly conceived are, in a sense, the same thing. For if something is bounded it can be conceived as that which lies within the boundary; and if something is conceived it is bounded by the terms of the conception. Hence, an unbounded object is essentially the same as an inconceivable object. And we are back with the contradiction at the limit of conceivable.

To understand Hegel's second argument against the false infinite, it is necessary to see how the false infinite manifests itself in its quantitative guise. Hegel suggests that because the false infinite is inseparably related to the finite, any thought of it must therefore lead to a thought of the finite. But, dually, any thought of the finite must inevitably lead to a thought of the (false) infinite. Hence reflection on either concept results in an unstable situation in which thought flips back and forth from one to the other, generating an indefinite progression. This progress to infinity is a paradigm of the quantitative false infinite (*Logic*, p. 142):

It is this alternating determination negating both its own self and its negation, which appears as the *progress to infinity*, a progress which in so many forms and applications is accepted as something ultimate beyond which thought does not go but, having got as far as this 'and so on to infinity', has usually reached its goal.

In fact, the flip-flop here is simply an infinity generator: *another thought of the finite, if x is a thought of the infinite; another thought of the infinite, if x is a thought of the finite.* And this false infinite is simply its corresponding potential infinity.

Thus the false infinite is the potential infinite. Hegel again makes this clear when he criticises Kant's notion of infinity (*Logic*, p. 244):

Kant's concept of the infinite ... is 'that the successive synthesis of the unit in the measurement of a quantum *can never* be completed'. A quantum as such is presupposed as given; by synthesizing the *unit* this is supposed to be converted into an amount, into a definite assignable quantum; but this synthesis, it is said, can never be completed. It is evident from this that we have here nothing but an expression of the progress to infinity.

Clearly, this is the potential infinite, and, as Hegel goes on to explain, it is the spurious infinite.

We can now understand Hegel's second argument for the claim that the false infinite does not free itself from the finite. The false infinite, he says (*Logic*, p. 227):

is the problem of attaining the infinite, not the actual reaching of it; it is the perpetual *generation* of the infinite, but it does not get beyond quantum, nor does the infinite become positively present.

Or, as he puts it more darkly (*Logic*, p. 142):

What we have here is an abstract transcending of limit, a transcending which remains incomplete because *it is not itself transcended.*

The point that is being made here, when stripped of all its Hegelean obscurity, is a simple one: a potential infinity, at any stage of its existence, is, after all, never more than finite. Hence it is not truly infinite. The point is well made. The notion of the potential infinite does not deliver an understanding of the way the infinite behaves; it delivers an understanding of the way that certain finitudes behave. One can deny, as did Aristotle (but Hegel most certainly does not, as we shall see), that the actual infinite exists. But the pertinent point here remains: What is it, then, of which one is denying the existence? It is the true infinite.

7.5   The true infinite

But what is that? In its quantitative guise, the answer is very simple: if the false infinite is a potential infinite, the true infinite is the corresponding completed infinity; or, in our terminology, the generated infinity. Hegel never, as far as I am aware, states this categorically. However, it is clearly implicit in the penultimate quotation of the previous section. Moreover, a little later (*Logic*, p. 244) Hegel says that:

the character of the mathematical infinite and the way that it is used in higher analysis corresponds to the Notion of the genuine infinite.

There is then a lengthy discussion of this use,[9] in which various examples of completed infinities are given. For example (*Logic*, pp. 246ff.), Hegel considers the infinite sum $1+a+a^2+a^3+\ldots$ $(-1<a<1)$. This is a false (potential) infinity which, by adding successive terms, gets as close to some number as we wish, but never reaches it. The true (completed) infinity is just this limit, $(1-a)^{-1}$.[10]

So far, this is all rather orthodox and not terribly exciting. When we consider the true infinite in its qualitative guise, the situation is quite different.

---

[9] For a brief summary of the section, see Findlay (1958), pp. 174f.

[10] Note that modern analysis actually defines the infinite sum as this limit. But Hegel is writing before Cauchy and Weierstrass and has a more geometric understanding of the infinite sum.

The triple <finite, false infinite, true infinite> is not an official Hegelean triad. However, the false infinite is the negation of the finite, and so these two categories are related to each other as the first two members of a triad. The true infinite is the third: the negation of the negation (*Logic*, p. 239). This will help to make more sense of the last quotation in the previous section. Or, as Hegel puts it more clearly (*Logic*, p. 137):

the self-sublation of this [false] infinite and of the finite, as a single process – this is the *true* or *genuine infinite*.

The true infinite is the notion of an object whose finitude is its infinitude, and which is therefore both finite and infinite.

It is probable that the meaning of this will be quite opaque to the reader; a simple example can help to make it much clearer. The example is the Fifth Antinomy of 6.9. Recall that T is the totality of all thoughts generated by starting with some object and applying the generator *thought of x* as far as possible. T bounds all thoughts generated, but is transcendable by an application of the generator. It therefore has exactly the properties of the Hegelean true infinite. First, it is bounded (on the 'outside') by all those things that cannot be generated; hence it is finite in Hegel's sense. But it is also unbounded (and so infinite in the false sense); for we can apply the generator to it to break out of this bound, and so on indefinitely. In the words of Hegel (*Logic*, p. 133): 'its limit is also not its limit'. Or, as he puts it at greater length – actually discussing the First Antinomy, but the point is the same (*Logic*, p. 237):

The thesis and antithesis and their proofs therefore represent nothing but the opposite assertions, that a *limit is*, and that the limit equally is only a *sublated* one; that the limit has a beyond, with which however it stands in *relation*, and beyond which it must pass, but that in doing so there arises another such limit, which is no limit.

T is not merely bounded and unbounded; but its being bounded is precisely what it is that allows us to transcend the bound, and so makes it unbounded. For one can apply the generator iff there is a determinate totality to which to apply it, but to be determinate is precisely to be bounded. Hegel captures this situation very well when he says (*Logic*, p. 134):

great stress is laid on the limitations of thought, of reason, and so on, and it is asserted that the limitation *cannot* be transcended. To make such an assertion is to be unaware that the very fact that something is determined as a limitation implies that the limitation is already transcended. For a determinateness, a limit, is determined as a limitation only in opposition to its other in general, that is, in opposition to that which is *free from the limitation*; the other of a limitation is precisely the *being beyond* it.

We have, then, two moments: forming a bound and breaking a bound. *Seriatim* they constitute the false infinite; *coniunctim* they constitute the true infinite. As Hegel puts it (*Lesser Logic*, p. 137), if we let these two moments:

fall asunder, the result is that some becomes other, and this other is itself a somewhat, which then as such changes likewise, and so on *ad infinitum*. The result seems to superficial reflection very grand, the grandest possible. But such a progression is not the real infinite. This consists in being at home with itself in its other, or if enunciated as a process, in coming to itself in its other. Much depends on rightly apprehending the notion of infinity, and not stopping short at the wrong infinity of endless progression.

The true infinite is the coming together of the two moments in the shape of an absolute totality, which yet can be broken out of; a limit which, none the less, can be transcended; a bounded unbounded.

Conclusion

As we have seen, not only does Hegel observe that certain kinds of limits behave in a contradictory fashion; he actually fashions a contradictory category to think them. This bold piece of philosophy brings to a close this part of the book. The contradictory nature of the limits of thought, of which numerous philosophers before Kant had had intimations, finally found a realisation in Kant's work, though his 'tenderness for things in the world' finally obscured this from him. It was left to Hegel to bring this realisation to its conclusion.

This is hardly an end of the story. Galileo is justly famous for (amongst other things) his recognition and formulation of the notion of inertia. In his work, the notion is a fairly rudimentary one, however, at least in comparison with the way in which it was articulated and elaborated by subsequent generations of physicists, starting with Newton. So it is with Hegel's theory of the infinite. Though essentially correct, the theory is rudimentary and incomplete in many ways.

Some examples: Hegel had a very limited understanding of limiting processes. He had no idea, for example, of transfinite sequences. (Though this is not as important as one might think in the present context; it affects only the question of how 'big' infinity is.) Next, Hegel had only a rudimentary understanding of the boundary-tearing mechanism which transcends limits. Though he had the notion of a boundary being transcended, or *aufgehoben*, he could give (understandably, given the historical context) no detailed account of mechanisms (such as diagonalisation) by which this occurs. Thirdly, Hegel's infinite is a special case of a more general structure. Hegel had no conception of this, or of the many areas in which this structure would turn up (or of the lengths to which people would go to maintain that it does not!). Many of these details were worked out in subsequent developments in the foundations of set-theory. In the third part of the book we will look at these.

Part 3

Limits and the paradoxes of self-reference

Logistic is no longer barren, it engenders antinomies.

Henri Poincaré, *Science and Method*

8 Absolute infinity

Introduction

In the last chapter we looked at Hegel's crucial ideas on infinity. Hegel's philosophy in general exercised a profound fascination and influence on succeeding philosophers. For some reason, however, his ideas on the infinite were quietly forgotten. Further developments had to wait nearly 100 years to come; and when they did come, they came from a very different direction, one which might well have surprised Hegel. This was the work of Cantor on the foundations of set-theory.

Cantor was not a philosopher in the way that all the people we have so far met were. However, his contribution to our understanding of the infinite was, perhaps, greater than any other person before or since; almost single-handedly he found an intricate and beautiful form in an area that had hitherto been thought formless. In this chapter we will consider his work.

I will not be concerned with all of Cantor's work on the infinite: only that part which is relevant to the theme of this book. I will start by looking at his notion of transfinite sequences. Next we will turn to the subject of diagonalisation. We will then look at the paradoxes of absolute infinity and Cantor's response to them. Finally, in preparation for a later chapter, we will look at his remarks on potential and actual infinity.

In this chapter and the others of this part, the material is more technical than in other chapters. I do not, in general, intend to go into technical proofs where these are standard. There are numerous textbooks which can be consulted.[1] I will, however, give enough technical detail for those unfamiliar with the area to be able to follow the discussion; and, in as far as I can, do this in a way that is intelligible to non-logicians.

8.1 The ordinals

So far in the book, the sequences we have dealt with are mainly ω-sequences, that is, sequences of the same form as the natural numbers. This is because they were the only ones known until Cantor. One of his achievements was to

---

[1] For example, the excellent texts Fraenkel, Bar-Hillel, and Levy (1973), and Bell and Machover (1977).

see that such sequences are just the tip of the transfinite iceberg. Let us start with sequences of numbers. Finite sequences are familiar enough:

0
0, 1
0, 1, 2
0, 1, 2, 3
.
.
.

As is the simplest infinite sequence:

0, 1, 2, 3...

Cantor realised that it makes perfectly good sense to consider a sequence which is like this sequence, except that it has a last member succeeding all these:

0, 1, 2, 3 ... ω

Initially, he thought of these numbers as indexing some operation[2] so that ω is the index of an operation that is performed immediately after operations 0, 1, 2, etc. There may even be two or three such operations:[3]

0, 1, 2, 3 ... ω, $\omega + 1$
0, 1, 2, 3 ... ω, $\omega + 1$, $\omega + 2$

or even as many again:

0, 1, 2, 3 ... ω, $\omega + 1$, $\omega + 2$ ...

or again:

0, 1, 2, 3 ... ω, $\omega + 1$, $\omega + 2$ ... 2ω, $2\omega + 1$, $2\omega + 2$ ...

or even as many times as there are ordinary numbers:

0 ... ω ... 2ω ... 3ω ...

and still we can keep going with a sequence which has another member after all these:

0 ... ω ... 2ω ... 3ω ... ω^2

and so on. The members of these progressions are called *ordinals*.

As can be seen, ordinals are generated by two principles that Cantor enumerated as follows (see Hallett (1984), p. 49):

---

[2] See Dauben (1979), pp. 80f.

[3] Don't worry too much about what '+' and other arithmetical operations mean here; an intuitive understanding is quite sufficient.

(1) if α is an ordinal number then there is a next number $\alpha+1$ which is the immediate successor of α.

(2) if any definite succession of defined ... [ordinal] numbers exists, for which there is no largest, then a new number is created ... which is thought of as the *limit* of those numbers, i.e., it is defined as the next number larger than all of them.[4]

Principle (2) is applied to give *limit ordinals*: ω, 2ω, 3ω, ω^2, etc.; principle (1) to give the others, *successor ordinals*, i.e., things of the form $\alpha + 1$.

We can make things a little more rigorous in terms of well–orderings, as Cantor was himself to do. Let us, for a start, use the trick (due to von Neumann, rather than Cantor) of identifying each ordinal with the collection of preceding ordinals. (So that 0 is simply the empty set; 1 is $\{0\}$; 2 is $\{0, 1\}$; ω is $\{0, 1, 2, 3... \}$; $\omega + 1$ is $\{0, 1, 2, 3... \omega\}$; etc.) A collection of objects is *well-ordered* by some ordering, $<$, iff each sub-collection of objects has a member which is $<$-least, i.e., less than all the other members of the sub-collection. It is not too difficult to show that each ordinal, ordered in the obvious way, is well-ordered. Conversely it is not too difficult to show that every well-ordered set has the same form as (i.e., is order-isomorphic to) an ordinal.[5] (This ordinal is called the *ordinal type* of the ordering.) Well-ordered sets are therefore simply the transfinite generalisation of ω-sequences.

8.2   Cantor's absolute, mark I

The next question – and an obvious one – is how far the progression of ordinals itself goes on. The answer is 'indefinitely'. And if you feel that this is itself a little indefinite, it is; but it is about the best that anyone can do! Cantor said that it goes on to absolute infinity (as opposed to relative infinities such as ω). In this section I will have a first look at what Cantor had to say about the Absolute.

From the very beginning, Cantor distinguished between the transfinite and absolute infinity. The ground of the distinction was that for any transfinite quantity there is a bigger, though not so for the Absolute. As he puts it (Hallett (1984), p. 41):

we must make a *fundamental* distinction here between:
IIa   Increasable actual-infinite or *transfinite*
IIb   Unincreasable actual-infinite or *Absolute*

To see what this means, note that a typical transfinite quantity is one of the (non-finite) ordinals, generated as in 8.1. Recall that for any such ordinal there

---

[4] Cantor's own words; see Dauben (1979), p. 98.
[5] A proof of this fact in Zemelo–Fraenkel set theory requires the Axiom of Replacement.

is a greater. The totality of ordinals generated in this way is, on the other hand, an absolute infinite; this can be made no greater. As Cantor put it on another occasion (Hallett (1984), p. 44):

The *transfinite* with its plenitude of formations and forms necessarily indicates an Absolute, a 'true infinite' whose magnitude is capable of no increase or diminution, and is therefore to be looked upon quantitatively as an absolute maximum.

As is clear from this quotation, the Absolute is just the infinity that had concerned previous generations of philosophers. The transfinite is an important middle ground coming between the finite, properly so called, and the Absolute. The existence of this was a highly important discovery; but as far as debates about the existence and nature of the infinite go, *an absolute irrelevancy*.[6]

What did Cantor have to say about absolute infinity? For a start, in private, he was wont to wax lyrical about it (Dauben (1979), p. 13):

What surpasses all that is finite and transfinite ... is the single completely individual unity in which everything is included, which includes the 'Absolute' incomprehensible to the human understanding. This is the 'Actus Purissimus' which by many is called 'God'.

As is clear, theology, if not mysticism, is getting in on the act. Indeed, in drawing together infinity, the Absolute Maximum, God, and incomprehensibility, Cantor here is strongly reminiscent of Cusanus (see 1.8, 1.9).

In his more guarded and official pronouncements, the theological connection is not pressed; but the claim of incomprehensibility certainly is. Speaking of progressing through the ordinals, he says (Hallett (1984), p. 42):

I have no doubt at all that in this way we extend ever further, never reaching an insuperable barrier, but also never reaching any even approximate comprehension of the Absolute. The Absolute can only be recognised, never known, not even approximately.

Read in an ungenerous way, this statement is quite self-refuting. If Cantor thinks he can talk about the Absolute, he must at least think it is there to be talked about; and must know, therefore, at least that much about it. And if his own definition of the Absolute (given above) does not even give an approximate characterisation of it, then we are at a loss to know what he is talking about. However, what he means by these general claims is, I take it, something a little less sweeping. When he says that the Absolute is unknowable he means that the Absolute is mathematically indeterminate. As he says elsewhere (Hallett (1984), p. 13), it:

---

[6] The similarity between the traditional infinite and the Cantorian Absolute is noted by Maddy (1983). Moore ((1989), pp. 198f.) also notes that ancient problems of the infinite replay themselves in the Absolute.

cannot in any way be added or diminished, and it is therefore to be looked upon quantitatively as an absolute maximum. In a certain sense it transcends human power of comprehension, and in particular is beyond mathematical determination.

This quotation also looks self-inconsistent: if the Absolute is to be looked on quantitatively, it is hardly beyond mathematical determination.

It is not worth spending much time on these inconsistencies. The remarks were never more than half-formed thoughts, and were never intended (at least at this stage) as a considered theory of the Absolute. Instead, I want to consider a much more fundamental contradiction in Cantor's thought; one which completely undercuts his distinction between the transfinite and absolute infinity. Consider the set of all ordinals. Cantor's generation principle (2) states that for any definite unbounded succession of ordinal numbers, there is an ordinal that is a limit of those numbers. Now, the sequence of all ordinals is certainly a definite unbounded sequence of ordinals; hence, by the principle, there must be a least ordinal greater than all these. By the von Neumann trick, this is the set of all ordinals, On, a paradigm absolute infinity. Thus, this absolute infinity is delivered in exactly the same way as all the other limit ordinals, and, as such, is no different from them. In particular, by applying principle (1) to it, we can form the ordinal On+1, which is greater than On. An absolute infinity *can* therefore be increased. Cantor's distinction between transfinite and absolute infinities (or, at the very least, this way of drawing it) collapses.

An absolute infinity is supposed to be a final upper limit, an ultimate upper bound. But the intent of principle (2) is precisely, as Cantor put it, to 'give us the ability to *break through every barrier*'.[7] These two notions blankly contradict each other, therefore.[8] We have, in this situation, exactly the same contradiction about the infinite that exercised earlier generations (see 2.6): the infinite is such that there can be no bigger; yet there can be a bigger. And in it we see the seed of numerous subsequent paradoxes. I will come to these in a moment, but first I want to look at one more aspect of Cantor's technical work.

8.3 Diagonalisation

This is diagonalisation. First, let me set the scene. Given that it makes sense to extend the ordinal numbers (i.e., those that index order) into the transfinite, the next question is whether it makes sense to extend, similarly, the cardinal numbers (i.e., those that index magnitude). To do this we need a criterion of size-comparison. Cantor and, at much the same time, Frege, suggested that two sets, x and y, *are the same cardinal size* ($x \simeq y$) iff their members can be paired off one for one. That is, there is a function which maps each member of

---

[7] Hallett (1984), p. 58.
[8] Hallett himself ((1984) p. 47) notes that this sort of situation is one in which 'there is certainly some tension'. This is rather an understatement.

x to a member of y; and each member of y is mapped to by a unique member of x. Next, a set x is *at least as big as* y (x $\geq_c$y) iff there is a subset of x which is the same size as y. (The subscript 'c' is there to remind that the ordering is cardinality ordering, which is different from the ordering of ordinals.) x is *bigger than* y (x $>_c$y) iff x$\geq_c$y and it is not the case that x $\simeq$ y. It is not difficult to see that these definitions of size capture our notion of cardinal size for finite collections as a special case; one can also show that they have all the properties one would want of a size-ordering.[9]

Clearly, there are finite sets of increasing size. Also, clearly, the collection of natural numbers (ω) is larger than any finite set. A set is called *denumerable* (or *countably infinite*) if it is the same size as ω. In an ingenious proof Cantor showed that the collection of all real numbers is not denumerable (Hallett (1984), pp. 75f.). It quickly follows that it is bigger than ω. The next question is whether there is a set of largest size. In a generalisation of his earlier proof, Cantor showed that there is not. For any collection, there is a bigger collection. This is now called *Cantor's Theorem*.

The proof is justly celebrated, but bears repeating. If x is a set, the *power-set* of x, P(x), is the set of all subsets of x. P(x) $\geq_c$x, since we can pair off every member of x, y, one for one with the set {y} in P(x). The tricky thing is to show that it is not the case that x $\simeq$ P(x).

Suppose that there were a one-to-one correlation, f, from x to P(x). Just consider the set of all those things in x that are not members of the set f assigns them, that is {y $\in$ x; y $\notin$ f(y)}. Call this z. Clearly, z is a subset of x, and so is in P(x). There is therefore some member of x, w, such that z=f(w). Hence:

$$w \in f(w) \quad \text{iff} \quad w \in z$$
$$\text{iff} \quad w \in \{y \in x; y \notin f(y)\}$$
$$\text{iff} \quad w \notin f(w) \quad \quad (\text{since } w \in x)$$

Thus, by *reductio*, there is no such f.

This construction is called 'diagonalisation'. It may not yet be clear why this is so; but it is not difficult to see. We can think of the members of x as being (well-)ordered, thus: $x_0, x_1, x_2 \ldots x_\alpha \ldots$ (The list may be a transfinite list and have no last member, but this is of no importance.) Assuming f to exist, then the corresponding sequence $f(x_0), f(x_1), f(x_2) \ldots f(x_\alpha) \ldots$ runs through all members of P(x). We can therefore codify the information concerning whether a member of x is in a member of P(x) by simply sticking 'true' (T) or 'false' (F) in the entries of a certain (possibly infinite) matrix. Table 5 is an illustration of this. According to the first row, x_0 is a member of $f(x_0), f(x_2)$, but not $f(x_1), f(x_\alpha)$, etc.

---

[9] The ordering is easily seen to be transitive. It is more difficult to show that it is a partial ordering. (This is essentially the content of the Schröder–Bernstein Theorem). Using the Axiom of Choice, one can show that it is a total ordering (that is, that any two sets can be compared in size), though Cantor himself was never able to establish this fact satisfactorily.

Table 5

	$f(x_0)$,	$f(x_1)$,	$f(x_2)$,	...	$f(x_\alpha)$,	...
x_0	**T**	F	T	...	F	...
x_1	F	**F**	T	...	F	...
x_2	T	T	**F**	...	T	...
–	–	–	–	...	–	...
–	–	–	–	...	–	...
x_α	F	F	F	...	**F**	...
–	–	–	–	...	–	...
–	–	–	–	...	–	...

Now, the set z, above, is defined by saying when something, y, is in it. This is done by consulting the members of the matrix on the diagonal (i.e., those in bold type). These correspond to the condition $y \in f(y)$, and we simply negate the entry there (i.e., apply the condition $y \notin f(y)$). For the illustration: $x_0 \in f(x_0)$, so set x_0 *out of* z; this ensures that z is not $f(x_0)$. $x_1 \notin f(x_1)$, so set x_1 *in* z; this ensures that z is not $f(x_1)$. And so on. Hence we ensure that z is not on the list at all; but since it is, *ex hypothesi*, we have a contradiction.

The essence of Cantor's proof is as follows. Given a list of objects of a certain kind (in this case, subsets of x), we have a construction which defines a new object of this kind (in this case z), by systematically destroying the possibility of its identity with each object on the list. The new object may be said to 'diagonalise out' of the list.

8.4 Paradox

We may now return to the subject of paradox. The contradiction at the heart of the Absolute was bound to surface sooner or later. In fact, it was sooner. It did so in a number of paradoxes that were discovered. The first is entirely implicit in the discussion of 8.2. Consider the collection of all ordinals, On. By construction, On is an ordinal; the least ordinal greater than all the ordinals. Hence it is not an ordinal. This paradox was published by Burali-Forti in (1897), though apparently Cantor himself discovered it at least a year before this,[10] which is hardly surprising in the context.

One further example of the contradictions that came to light will do for the time being. This is a version of a paradox discovered by Mirimanoff.[11] Starting with the empty set, we generate a transfinite sequence by applying the power-set at successor stages and collecting up at limit stages; that is, at limit stages we form the union of all previous stages. Let us call the union of all the sets in the sequence R.

[10] See Hallett (1984), p. 74.
[11] Ibid., section 4.4.

In modern set-theory R is called the *cumulative hierarchy* (since every member of the sequence can be shown to be a proper subset of any later member), and the stages of construction are called *ranks*. R has some important properties. First: anything in it is also a subset of it. (Since its members have lower rank.) Next, call any sequence (finite or infinite) $x_0, x_1, x_2 \ldots$ such that $\ldots x_2 \in x_1 \in x_0$ a *regress* from x_0. Call a set, x, *well founded* if there is no infinite regress from x. The members of the cumulative hierarchy are all well founded; as a matter of fact, the cumulative hierarchy comprises all and only the well-founded sets.

Now consider R. Since all its members are well founded, it, too, is well founded. Hence it is in R. But then it is not well founded since the following is an infinite regress: $\ldots R \in R \in R \in R$. Hence it is not in R.

Both of the above contradictions fit a familiar pattern: ascent of the ordinals or of the cumulative hierarchy is performed by a simple infinity generator (adding one or taking the power set), iterated into the transfinite by collecting up at limit ordinals. The contradiction concerns the behaviour of the limit: the collection of all things generated in this way, On and R. On both is and is not an ordinal. R is both in and not in R.

8.5   Kant and Cantor

Paradoxes of this kind involve the absolute infinite. Cantor therefore called them paradoxes of absolute infinity. They have exactly the same structure as Kant's Antinomies. To see this, one has only to tabulate them as I tabulated the Antinomies in 6.7. I do so in Table 6, throwing in the Fifth Antinomy (6.9) for comparison; I cite the contradiction in its equivalent form. (Ignore the entry in square brackets in the Generator column for a moment.) And lest it be thought out of place here on the ground that the notion of thought does not belong to set-theory, I merely point out that before set-theory was emasculated to avoid the paradoxes, it did. The construction involved is essentially that used by Dedekind to prove the existence of an infinite set.[12]

I observe that in each case, the limit is defined 'from below'; but the contradiction is produced by considering it 'from above': that is, in each case we take the limit to be itself a unity and note its properties.

For future reference, let us digress for a paragraph to do a little cleaning up. As things stand, the sequences are generated by two distinct procedures. At successor ordinals we apply the generator; at limit ordinals we collect up. We can make the process uniform if we generate the sequences by applying slightly different generators. For On, we generate the next member after any sequence, x (whether or not it has a last member), by forming the least ordinal greater than all the members of x. I will write this as log(x). For R, it is

---

[12] See Dedekind (1888), Theorem 66.

Table 6

Antinomy	Generator	Limit	[Anti]Thesis
Burali-Forti	+1 [log (x)]	On	is [not] an ordinal
Mirimanoff	power set of [UP(x)]	R	is [not] in R
5th	thought of [t(x)]	T	thought of ... is [not] in T

not difficult to show that the next member after the sequence, x, can be generated by applying the operator $\cup\{P(y); y \in x\}$. I will write this as UP(x). For T the sequence can be generated by always applying the operator: *thought of the last member of x, if it has one; or the thought of x otherwise.* I will write this as t(x). This explains the bracketed entries in the Generator column of Table 6.

The similarities between the Kantian Antinomies and the paradoxes of absolute infinity have been noted by a number of people, including Hessenberg, Zermelo and Fraenkel.[13] Perhaps the clearest statement is given by Martin. Speaking of the dialectic between defining from below and conceiving as a unity from above, he says ((1955), p. 55):

This conflict between concluding and beginning anew, between forming a totality and using this totality as a new element, is the actual ground of the [set-theoretic] antinomy. It is this conflict that gives the connection with the Kantian antinomies. Kant saw quite clearly that the antinomies rest on this antithesis between making a conclusion and going beyond the conclusion. In principle, this had already been seen by Archytas, when he wanted to go to the end of the world and stretch out his arm.

Some other commentators have denied the connection. For example, Bennett ((1974), p. 155), criticising Martin, says that there is 'no significant similarity' between the Antinomies and the set-theoretic paradoxes. And Hallett ((1984), p. 225), who is more sympathetic, still concludes that 'the connection between the Cantorian and the Kantian antinomies is only superficial'. Hallett notes some important dissimilarities between the details of the Kantian arguments and those of the paradoxes of the Absolute; Bennett gives no argument. In the end, both simply fail to find the pattern that fits both.

8.6   Cantor's absolute, mark II

All the quotations from Cantor concerning the Absolute in 8.2 (with the exception of the one mentioning God) came from the period before the para-

---

[13] For details see Hallett (1984), section 6.2.

doxes were discovered (the 1880s). After the paradoxes were known, Cantor revised his account of absolute infinity. He did this in an attempt to prove that any two sets could be compared with respect to size. The absolute infinity On played a central role in this proof; in particular, certain of its properties played a crucial mathematical role. The claim that absolute infinities were beyond *all* mathematical determination therefore had to be dropped.

Despite the fact that his account of the Absolute was not revised specifically in order to avoid the paradoxes, Cantor clearly hoped the revisions would give an account that was free of paradox. (Naturally, in a context where his new mathematics was fighting for recognition, consistency was very important for him.[14]) In this section we will look at how he hoped to achieve this.

By this time, thinking in set-theoretic terms had become an integral part of Cantor's approach. This made it possible for him to distinguish between two kinds of collection: consistent and inconsistent. The inconsistent collections are those such that the assumption that they are a 'unity' leads to a contradiction. These are exactly the absolute infinities. All of them have the same cardinal size (viz., that of On), which is greater than that of any consistent collection. In a letter to Dedekind he puts it thus (Cantor (1899), p. 114):

If we start from the notion of a definite multiplicity (a system, a totality) of things, it is necessary, as I discovered, to distinguish two kinds of multiplicities ... For a multiplicity can be such that the assumption that *all* of its elements 'are together' leads to a contradiction, so that it is impossible to conceive of the multiplicity as a unity, as 'one finished thing'. Such multiplicities I call *absolutely infinite* or *inconsistent multiplicities*.
As we can see, the 'totality of everything thinkable', for example, is such a multiplicity ...
If on the other hand the totality of the elements of a multiplicity can be thought of without contradiction as 'being together', so that they can be gathered together into '*one* thing', I call it a *consistent multiplicity* or a 'set' ...
Two equivalent multiplicities are either both 'sets' or both are inconsistent.

The distinction between consistent and inconsistent multiplicities is clearly informed by the paradoxes;[15] but how, exactly, does it help to avoid them?

The answer to this will not be clear from the above quotation. Neither, surprisingly, does Cantor address the issue in the letter, though he uses the Burali-Forti paradox to demonstrate that On is an inconsistent multiplicity. He is clear that On is well ordered, but seems to think that the fact that it is an inconsistent multiplicity shows that it is not an ordinal (or, to be precise, has no ordinal, since he does not use the von Neumann dodge of identifying an

---

[14] See Dauben (1979), pp. 128ff.
[15] Though, interestingly, Schröder made the same distinction in 1890 independently of the paradoxes, according to van Heijenoort in his introduction to Cantor (1899).

ordinal with the set of all previous ordinals). Why this is supposed to follow is unclear.

Light is thrown on the matter by a remark in a later letter to Jourdain, where he says (Hallett (1984), p. 286):

an inconsistent multiplicity, because it cannot be understood as one *whole* and thus cannot be considered as *one thing*, cannot be taken as an element of a multiplicity.

The background assumption here is clearly correct: to conceive of something as a member of a collection is *ipso facto* to conceive of it as a unity. So if an inconsistent multiplicity cannot be a unity, it cannot be a member of anything. Hence On cannot be an ordinal, i.e., cannot be in the collection of all ordinals: its being an inconsistent totality means that it is not a candidate for membership of anything.

This may indicate where the argument to contradiction is blocked; but it hardly provides a satisfactory solution to the paradoxes, since it leaves all kinds of questions unanswered. Why, for example, are *all* absolutely infinite collections impossible to think of as a unity without contradiction; why is having the same cardinal size as On a criterion of being absolutely infinite; and so on.

I will not pursue these and similar problems here, since Cantor never developed the ideas further. Many have taken Cantor's distinction between consistent and inconsistent multiplicities to be a first articulation of von Neumann's later distinction between sets and proper classes.[16] Whether or not this is so, von Neumann's distinction certainly embodies the crucial features of Cantor's embryonic solution (proper classes cannot be members; all have the same size), and is much more clearly articulated. Any further comments on this kind of solution are therefore more profitably addressed to that. So let us leave the subject until we meet von Neumann in a later chapter.

8.7   The domain principle

For the benefit of the discussion in that chapter I want to turn, finally, to the question of the justification of Cantor's principles of ordinal construction, (1) and (2) (see 8.1). Remember that we are thinking of each ordinal as the set of preceding ordinals; principle (1) then comes to this: for any set (of ordinals), α, there is a set (of ordinals) $\alpha \cup \{\alpha\}$. This seems obvious enough to require no further comment.

The situation with (2) is somewhat different. It says that given some unending progression (of ordinals) there is a set containing them. This is an exceptionally important principle; but there is some problem about stating it. Since the success of set-theoretic reductionism this century, the natural way of understanding the notion of an unending progression is exactly as a series,

---

[16] For example, van Heijenoort in his introduction to Cantor (1899); Hallett (1984), section 8.3.

i.e., a set of a certain kind. On this understanding the principle is tautologous. But this is obviously not its intent.

If the sequence in question is not to be understood as an already completed infinity (a set), then it must be understood as something in a state of generation, i.e., a potential infinite. And to speak of the set containing the members of the progression is exactly to speak of the (actual) infinity thus generated. What this principle comes to, therefore, is this:

For every potential infinity there is a corresponding actual infinity.

Following Hallett ((1984), p. 7) let us call this the *Domain Principle*. I take it to be a formulation of the Kantian insight that totalisation is conceptually unavoidable (6.1), though stated in a much more satisfactory way than Kant ever managed to achieve.

But what, exactly, is a potential infinity? The idea is, intuitively, clear enough. (We have been working with it since chapter 2.) Moreover, traditionally, it has been thought unproblematic; it is the other member of the pair, the actual infinite, that has been thought problematic. It is therefore somewhat ironic that in modern mathematics the notion of the actual infinite is relatively well understood (any infinite set is an actual infinity); it is a precise analysis of the nature of potential infinity that still awaits us (as Hart (1976) observes). I shall not try to offer one here;[17] it will suffice, for our purpose, to leave the notion at an intuitive level.

Whatever else it is, a potential infinity is some kind of variable quantity, whose variation can go beyond any preassigned bound of a certain kind. As Cantor puts it (Hallett (1984), p. 12):

The potential-infinite is mostly witnessed where one has an undetermined, *variable finite* quantity which either increases beyond all limit ... or which decreases beneath any finite small limit ... More generally, I speak of a Potential-Infinite whenever it is a question of an *undetermined* quantity which is capable of innumerably many determinations.

The corresponding actual infinite is, by contrast (ibid):

to be understood [as] a quantum which on the one hand is *not variable*, but rather is fixed and determined in all its parts – a genuine constant – but which at the same time surpasses in magnitude *every finite quantity* [i.e., preassigned bound] of the same kind.

---

[17] Some suggestions employing possible worlds of increasing domain can be found in 11.2. Hart (1975–6) offers two precise ways of understanding the notion. One is very similar to that suggested in 11.2. The other is simply to identify the notion with that of a proper class (which we will also meet in chapter 11). I am dubious about this suggestion since it entails that *no* potential infinity has a corresponding actual infinity, which seems far too strong to be an adequate analysis of the traditional notion. It must be possible, for example, to conceptualise the natural numbers *qua* potential infinity.

8.8   ... and its defence

So much for the Domain Principle itself. Let us now turn to Cantor's defence of it. In his own words, this goes as follow (Hallett (1984), p. 25):

> There is no doubt that we cannot do without *variable* quantities in the sense of the potential infinite; and from this can be demonstrated the necessity of the actual-infinite. In order for there to be a variable quantity in some mathematical study, the 'domain' of its variability must strictly speaking be known beforehand through definition. However, this domain cannot itself be something variable, since otherwise each fixed support for the study would collapse. Thus, this 'domain' is a definite, actually infinite series of values.
>
> Thus, each potential infinite, if it is rigorously applicable mathematically, presupposes an actual infinite.

Cantor's argument is a simple and ingenious one. It is based on the equally simple observation that for a statement about some variable quantity to have determinate sense, the domain of its variability must be determinate. (Cantor says 'known beforehand by definition'; but this is too strong; simple determinacy will do.) For example, consider the claim 'Let z be a root of the equation $ax^2 + bx + c = 0$. Then z has at least one value.' This is true if z may be complex; false if z must be real.

Now consider some statement about a potentially infinite variable; by the observation, if this has determinate sense, its domain of variability must be determinate. Can this domain not itself be a potential infinity (variable)? Perhaps it can; but then the sense of the original claim is not determinate unless the domain of *this* variable is itself determinate. Could that, itself, be a variable? Perhaps. We are obviously off on an infinite regress. Moreover, this regress is vicious. If it went on forever, the sense of the original statement would never become determinate. Given that the statement does have determinate sense, the regress must bottom-out somewhere. And thus the original variable must find its ultimate ground in an actual infinite domain.

Cantor's argument can be put in contemporary form (bypassing the issue of what, exactly, a potential infinity is) by a consideration of modern semantics. In the eighteenth and nineteenth centuries, a variable was thought of as something of indeterminate value. However, as Russell ((1903), section 87) pointed out, this makes little sense. A variable is simply some entity which may be assigned different values. And in its modern form, this entity is a linguistic one: the variable of modern formal syntax. Now, for a sentence containing a variable to have a determinate meaning, the range of the quantifiers governing the variable (which may be implicit if the variable is free) must be a determinate totality, a definite set. The standard way to specify the interpretation of a language is as a pair, <D,I>, where D is the domain of quantification and I provides the interpretations of the non-logical vocabulary. Note that D is a member of something else, and hence is conceptualised as a unity. It might be suggested that the quantifier could be rendered determinate simply by stating its truth conditions (in a metalanguage); for example, thus: '$\forall xPx$' is true iff every cat satisfies 'Px'. But the truth conditions use quantifiers, and so the question becomes how *these* obtain determinate sense. We are off on the vicious regress we just noted.

It should be noted that the determinacy of the sense of quantifiers is not a specifically classical, as opposed to intuitionist, requirement. Intuitionists require their quantifiers to be as determinate in sense as the rest of us. Take an existentially quantified sentence, $\forall x\alpha(x)$, for example. In general, this is true (= provable) iff (Dummett (1977), p. 24):

there is a proof of some statement of the form $\alpha(t)$, together with a proof that the object denoted by t belongs to the domain [of quantification].

Hence, if what counts as this domain is indeterminate, so is the sense of the quantified sentence. For this reason, an intuitionist account of the semantics for quantifiers specifies a determinate domain of discourse.[18] The intuitionist may conceive of this domain as an intuitionistic species, rather than as a classical set; but none the less it is conceptualised as a unity, for just the same reason as in the classical case. There is, then, nothing in the Domain Principle with which an intuitionist, as such, must disagree.[19]

The above argument for the Domain Principle is predicated on the assumption that the sense of quantified sentences in mathematics is determinate. In the final part of the book, we will meet various claims to the effect that *no* sense is determinate. Such global skepticism about meaning is too strong to undercut the argument here. If it were correct, we could merely reinterpret Cantor's argument as showing that, without an actual infinite, statements quantifying over infinite totalities could not have meaning in whatever well-defined sense mathematical statements in general have. A greater threat to the argument is one according to which quantified sentences of certain kinds do not have determinate sense, in a way in which other statements of mathematics do have it. There is such a view as this; but I shall defer discussion of it until we return to the Domain Principle in a later chapter.

Conclusion

Returning to the main theme of this chapter: as we have seen, Cantor's theory of the transfinite did not succeed in removing the paradoxes of the infinite. It merely relocated them. This should not be held against him, however. The contradictions are there, inherent in the object of discourse; so getting rid of them is hardly a sign of an adequate account! The great virtues of Cantor's work from the present perspective are twofold. First, it made it clear with an

---

[18] See, for example, Dummett (1977), pp. 197f.
[19] There is therefore nothing specifically realist about it, as Hallett ((1984), pp. 26ff.) claims.

unprecedented rigour that, and where, the contradictions occur. This rigour, moreover, narrowed down the field of possible solutions to a very small and surveyable class. Secondly, the notion of diagonalisation provided the corner-stone of an adequate understanding of boundary-transcendence. We will take up these issues in the subsequent chapters of this part.

9 Vicious circles

Introduction

The paradoxes of absolute infinity that we met in the last chapter (8.4) were but the leading edge of a number of paradoxes that turned up in set-theory at the turn of the century. No one investigated these more thoroughly than Bertrand Russell, and in this chapter I will discuss several of the things he had to say about them. As we will see, he found the key that holds the family of paradoxes together (or almost, anyway); we will also have a look at his proposed solution, which was less successful.

9.1 Russell's paradox

Let us start by discussing a paradox that we have not met so far. To keep things simple, we will ignore the existence of non-sets; hence we may take all sets to be *pure* sets, i.e., sets such that, if they have any members at all, these are sets, as are their members, *their* members, etc. Obviously a set is pure iff all its members are pure. Let V be the set of all (pure) sets (I will omit the qualification from now on).[1] Consider the power-set of V, P(V). Any member of P(V) is a set, and hence P(V) is a subset of V. Conversely, any member of V is a collection of sets, and so is a member of P(V), and hence V is a subset of P(V). It follows that P(V)=V; and in this case there is a one-to-one mapping between V and P(V), viz., the identity map (the map that maps everything to itself). But as we saw in 8.3, Cantor showed that for any set, x, there can be no such mapping between x and P(x). This contradiction is now called 'Cantor's paradox'. Cantor did, indeed, discover it, though he never published it officially.[2]

Cantor's paradox can be stripped down to its essence. As we saw in 8.3, Cantor's proof that there is no one-to-one correspondence between x and P(x) takes an arbitrary such correspondence, f, and deduces a contradiction by

[1] It is traditional wisdom that V is just the cumulative hierarchy, R (8.4). This is called the Axiom of Foundation. However, it is quite possible for there to be pure non-well-founded sets. See Aczel (1988).
[2] See Fraenkel, Bar-Hillel, and Levy (1973), p. 7.

considering whether a set w is a member of f(w), where f(w) is $\{y \in x; y \notin f(y)\}$. In the case in point, f is the identity function, so w is f(w), which is $\{y \in x; y \notin y\}$. Let us write this as ρ_x. Now if $\rho_x \in \rho_x$ then $\rho_x \notin \rho_x$. Hence $\rho_x \notin \rho_x$. It follows that $\rho_x \notin x$, or we would have $\rho_x \in \rho_x$. But if x is any subset of V, ρ_x is a subset of V. Hence $\rho_x \in V$. In Cantor's paradox we take V itself for x. We then have both $\rho_V \notin V$ and $\rho_V \in V$; or alternatively, $\rho_V \notin \rho_V$ and, since $\rho_V \in V$, $\rho_V \in \rho_V$.

This contradiction is therefore the heart of Cantor's paradox. It is now, famously, named after Russell, who obtained it in essentially this way, by stripping down Cantor's paradox.[3] Russell's paradox is undoubtedly the simplest of all the set-theoretic paradoxes. Its appearance showed definitively that the paradoxes of set-theory could not be blamed on a mistake in the relatively subtle arguments required to establish the Burali-Forti contradiction. Contradiction lay at the very heart of set-theory.

9.2   Russell's schema

The paradoxes we have met so far, those of Burali-Forti, Mirimanoff, and Russell (Cantor), are but three examples of a family of paradoxes that can be multiplied ad lib once one knows the formula. This formula was found by Russell himself. In his own words it is as follows:[4]

Given a property φ and a function δ, such that, if φ belongs to all members of u, $\delta(u)$ always exists, has the property φ, and is not a member of u; then the supposition that there is a class Ω of all terms having property φ and that $\delta(\Omega)$ exists leads to the conclusion that $\delta(\Omega)$ both has and has not the property φ.

Less tersely, given a property φ and function δ, consider the following conditions:

(1) $\Omega = \{y; \varphi(y)\}$ exists
(2) if x is a subset of Ω: (a) $\delta(x) \notin x$
                                    and (b) $\delta(x) \in \Omega$

Given these conditions we have a contradiction. For (a) and (b) applied to Ω entail that $\delta(\Omega) \notin \Omega$ and $\delta(\Omega) \in \Omega$; or, if we write $\alpha!$ for $\alpha \wedge \neg\alpha$,[5] $\delta(\Omega) \in \Omega!$.

Condition (1) I will call *Existence*.[6] Conditions (2a) and (2b) are clearly versions of Transcendence and Closure, respectively. When this schema (or the generalisation of it that we will meet later in the chapter) is at issue, I will

---

[3] See Russell (1903), sections 346–9; Russell (1905).

[4] Russell (1905), p. 142 of reprint. In this and subsequent quotations from Russell, I have taken the liberty of modifying his notation.

[5] See Priest (1987), p. 146.

[6] Meinongians who take sets to be non-existent objects are invited to read 'existence' as 'being', here and throughout; similarly with their cognates.

use these names for these versions.[7] I will call any function, δ, that satisfies the schema a *diagonaliser* (with respect to φ). A diagonaliser need not be defined literally by diagonalisation; but, as we shall see, it is always defined systematically to ensure that the result of applying it to any set cannot be identical with any member of that set. Diagonalisation proper is the paradigm of such a procedure. A diagonaliser can be thought of as a transfinite generalisation of what I have so far called a generator. We can define a transfinite sequence of members of Ω, $\langle w_\alpha; \alpha \in \text{On} \rangle$ by repeated application of the diagonaliser (transfinite recursion), thus: $w_\alpha = \delta(\{w_\beta; \beta < \alpha\})$. (If $\alpha = 0$, the argument of the function is just ϕ.)

Let us now see how the paradoxes fit this schema. In the case of Russell's paradox, the property $\varphi(y)$ is just $y \in V$, and so Ω is V. The function $\delta(x)$ is just ρ_x. Transcendence and Closure obtain, as I observed in the previous section; and the contradiction is that $\rho_v \in V!$[8]

For Burali-Forti's Paradox, $\varphi(y)$ is 'y is an ordinal' and the diagonaliser, $\delta(x)$, is log(x). Transcendence holds by definition, as does Closure. In this case, the collection Ω is just On, as is $\delta(\Omega)$ (by the von Neumann convention of 8.1). Hence the contradiction is that $\text{On} \in \text{On}!$.

In Mirimanoff's Paradox $\varphi(y)$ is 'y is well founded' and the diagonaliser, $\delta(x)$, is UP(x). Transcendence and Closure hold simply in virtue of x being well founded. The collection Ω is the cumulative hierarchy, R. Moreover, it is not difficult to see that $\delta(R)$ is just R itself. Hence, the contradiction in this case is that $R \in R!$.

Although the Fifth Antinomy is not a standard set-theoretic paradox, it fits the same pattern. $\varphi(y)$ is $y \in T$, so Ω is T. $\delta(x)$ is just t(x). The argument for Transcendence is as follows.

First, note that if x, y are in T and $x \neq y$ then $t(x) \neq t(y)$. For, since x and y are distinct objects (as are their last members if they have one), one can (at least in principle) entertain the thought of one without entertaining the thought of the other. These thoughts must therefore be distinct.[9] Hence any thought is of the form t(x) for a unique x. Call a thought $t(x_0)$ *unfounded* if there is a sequence $\langle x_i; i \in \omega \rangle$ such that $t(x_{i+1}) \in x_i$ for all $i \in \omega$. Every thought in

---

[7] In case the inferences used to establish Transcendence and Closure are not always dialetheically valid, we may define the conditions more cautiously. Whenever α is deducible classically there is some formula, β, such that $\alpha \lor \beta!$ is dialetheically deducible. (See Priest (1987), Theorem 0, p. 149.) Hence we can formulate Transcendence and Closure as $\delta(x) \notin x \lor \exists pp!$ and $\delta(x) \in \Omega \lor \exists pp!$, respectively (or something similar using the truth predicate if one does not believe in propositional quantification). The ultimate contradiction is then $\delta(\Omega) \in \Omega! \lor \exists pp!$, or simply $\exists pp!$.

[8] There is a related way of fitting Russell's paradox into the schema. For $\varphi(y)$ we take 'y $\in V \land y \notin y$', so that Ω is just ρ_V; the function $\delta(x)$ is simply the identity function id(x). Transcendence and Closure hold, as may easily be shown, and the contradiction is now that $\rho_V \in \rho_V!$.

[9] Moreover, t(x) is a thought *of* x (or its last member) and t(y) isn't.

Table 7

Paradox	$\delta(x)$	$\varphi(y)$	Ω	$\delta(\Omega) \in \Omega!$
Russell	ρ_x	$y \in V$	V	$\rho_v \in V!$
Burali-Forti	$\log(x)$	y is an ordinal	On	On $\in$ On!
Mirimanoff	UP(x)	y is well founded	R	R $\in$ R!
5th Antinomy	t(x)	$y \in T$	T	t(T) $\in$ T!

T is founded. The proof is by a (transfinite) induction. This is obviously true of the first thought in the sequence t({the *Critique*}). Suppose it is true for all members of the sequence x, but that the next thought, t(x), is unfounded. Then there is a sequence: x, x_0, x_1 . . . of the appropriate kind. But then $t(x_0) \in x$ and $t(x_0)$ is unfounded, which is impossible. It follows that if t(x) is any thought in T t(x) $\notin$ x (or else x, x, x . . . would be an infinite regress).

The argument for Closure is simpler: T is the sequence of thoughts generated by applications of t to any sequence of objects generated; T is a sequence of objects generated; so t(T) $\in$ T. The contradiction is that t(T) both is and is not in T.

We can tabulate the way the paradoxes fit the schema as in Table 7. (Compare this with Table 6 of 8.5.)

In 7.5 we saw that T is a paradigm of Hegel's true infinite. For exactly the same reason, so are all the other sets that play the role of Ω in the above table. Indeed, we may even take Russell's schema as providing a precise specification of the notion of a true infinity. For any δ, φ, and Ω that satisfy the schema, Ω bounds all the things that are φ; yet we can break out of the bound by applying the diagonaliser, δ.

9.3   Definability

The paradoxes of absolute infinity were not the only paradoxes of self-reference that turned up in the period in question. Another important group comprises the paradoxes of definability. The first of these surfaced in the work of König (1905).[10] Call something *definable* if there is some non-indexical noun-phrase (of English) that refers to it. Let DOn be the collection of all definable ordinals. Since English has only a finite vocabulary, the number of noun-phrases in it is countable. Hence, the number of definable objects and, *a fortiori*, DOn, is countable. But On is obviously not countable. Hence there are ordinals that are not definable. Since On is well ordered, there is a least ordinal not in DOn. By definition, it cannot be defined. But

---

[10] He produced the construction as part of a proof that the Continuum Hypothesis is false. However, in virtue of the similarity of this part of the argument to recognised paradoxes, the proof was never generally accepted.

we have just defined it using the phrase 'least ordinal not in DOn'. Let us call this 'König's Paradox'.

This argument refers to the collection of all ordinals, and so might be thought to be a paradox of absolute infinity. It is not, since DOn is countable. But in any case there are similar paradoxes which make no reference to absolutely infinite sets at all; for example, the following: Let DN_n be the set of all natural numbers definable by a noun-phrase of less than n words. Consider, say, DN_{99}. This is not just countable: it is finite (since the vocabulary of English is finite). But then there must be a *least natural number not in* DN_{99}. We have just defined it using the italicised phrase, however, which has well under 100 words. This is usually called 'Berry's Paradox'.[11]

Another member of the family, discovered about the same time as König's Paradox is that of Richard, and uses only the set of definable real numbers between 0 and 1, DR. For the usual reasons, this set is countable and its members can be ordered in a simple, specifiable, way. By a diagonal construction, essentially identical to Cantor's, but using decimal expansions, we can define a real number that is different from every real number in the set. Yet it has a name, and so is in the set.[12]

I do not want to formalise these proofs here. However, a partial formalisation of one of these arguments, König's, will prove useful.[13] Let us write 'x is definable' as τx. The first part of the argument is a proof, Σ, of $\exists x \neg \tau x$. Let μ be a least-number descriptor. Then $\mu x \neg \tau x$ is the least ordinal that cannot be defined. Let us abbreviate this to 'c'. By standard descriptor principles, $\exists x \neg \tau x \rightarrow \neg \tau c$. Hence $\neg \tau c$. But it is clear that c *can* be defined, since it is defined by '$\mu x \neg \tau x$'; thus τc. Let us write the argument for this part of the contradiction as Π. Putting the two parts of the argument together gives us the contradiction. Rearranging all this in a more perspicuous way, we obtain:

$$\frac{\Pi \qquad \dfrac{\dfrac{\Sigma}{\exists x \neg \tau x} \qquad \overline{\exists x \neg \tau x \rightarrow \neg \tau c}}{\neg \tau c}}{\tau c \wedge \neg \tau c}$$

If the reader experiences a certain sense of *déjà vu* at this point, this is quite understandable. So far in this chapter – and in fact for the last three chapters – we have been discussing only one of the kinds of limit that have concerned us throughout the book: the limit of the iterable. Another has now reappeared.

The above argument is essentially the same as Berkeley's Paradox (see 4.9), as a simple comparison will show. There are three differences, two formal and

[11] After its formulator; see Russell (1906), pp. 128f.
[12] For further details, see Richard (1905).
[13] Complete formalisations of Berry's Paradox can be found in Priest (1983) and (1987), 1.8.

one informal. The first formal difference is that König's argument uses a definite description operator ('the least ordinal such that'), whilst Berkeley's uses an indefinite description operator. This is a trivial difference of no moment. In the case of König's argument we are simply making use of the (inessential) fact that ordinals are well ordered. The second formal difference is that in König's argument there are independent sub-arguments (Σ and Π) for the two axiomatic premises of the Core Argument. This is not terribly important either: in chapter 4 I gave informal arguments for these claims anyway. But it does mean that $\exists x \neg \tau x$ is no longer even a *target* for *reductio*, as Berkeley wished it to be, since it is no longer an independent premise.

The informal difference is that in Berkeley's paradox τ is interpreted as 'is conceivable'; whereas in König's paradox it is interpreted as 'is definable'. Now these notions may not be identical, but they would seem to be pretty well co-extensional. For if there is a noun-phrase that refers to something, that thing can be conceived, simply by bringing the noun-phrase before the mind; and if something can be conceived, there must be some way of singling it out, and hence some way of referring to it (for example, with 'the object being thought about by GP at *time*, *date*').

Hence, the limit of the conceivable is essentially the limit of the definable, and König's Paradox and Berkeley's Paradox are, to all intents and purposes, the same. For the same reason, the definability paradoxes provide further examples of contradictions at the limit of the conceivable.[14]

9.4   The inclosure schema

We have seen that two of the limits that we have been concerned with, the limit of the iterable and the limit of the conceivable, both reach fruition in the paradoxes of set-theory. The next question is whether there is a closer connection than this. For example, do the definability paradoxes fit Russell's schema for the paradoxes of absolute infinity of 9.2?

Prima facie, the answer would appear to be 'yes'. Take, for example König's Paradox. Let $\varphi(y)$ be the predicate 'y is a definable ordinal' and $\delta(x)$ be the function $\mu y y \notin x$. Then δ certainly diagonalises out of any class of definable ordinals, and so satisfies Transcendence; and '$\mu y y \notin x$' might be thought to define $\delta(x)$, in which case Closure is satisfied. It is not, however. For '$\mu y y \notin x$' contains a free variable, and so names nothing. If x is some set, we need a name for it to substitute for 'x' to obtain an appropriate name, i.e., x must itself be

---

[14] And just as there is a variant of Berkeley's Paradox which uses the notion of conceiving, rather than conceivability, so there are versions of the definability paradoxes which use the notion of definition (or better, referring) rather than definability. Corresponding to König's Paradox, for example, is the paradox of the least ordinal that has never been referred to; similarly for the other definability paradoxes.

Table 8

Paradox	$\delta(x)$	$\psi(x)$	$\varphi(y)$	Ω	$\delta(\Omega) \in \Omega!$
König's	$\mu yy \notin x$	x is definable	$y \in DOn$	DOn	$(\mu yy \notin DOn) \in DOn!$
Berry's	$\mu yy \notin x$	$x \in DN_{90}$	$y \in DN_{99}$	DN_{99}	$(\mu yy \notin DN_{99}) \in DN_{99}!$
Richard's	diag(x)	x is definable	$y \in DR$	DR	$diag(DR) \in DR!$
Berkeley's	$\varepsilon yy \notin x$	x is conceivable	τy	C	$\varepsilon yy \notin C \in C!$

definable; and even if every member of a class of ordinals is definable, there is no reason to suppose that it, itself, is definable.[15]

We can, however, obtain a schema that does fit both kinds of paradox by generalising Russell's schema. We now require two properties, φ and ψ, and a function δ, satisfying the following conditions:

(1) $\Omega = \{y; \varphi(y)\}$ exists, and $\psi(\Omega)$
(2)   if x is a subset of Ω such that $\psi(x)$: (a) $\delta(x) \notin x$
                                                            (b) $\delta(x) \in \Omega$

Given that these conditions are satisfied we still have a contradiction. For since $\psi(\Omega)$, we have $\delta(\Omega) \notin \Omega!$. I will call any Ω that satisfies these conditions (for an appropriate δ) an *inclosure*.[16] The conditions themselves, I will call the *Inclosure Schema*, and any paradox of which this is the underlying structure, an *inclosure contradiction*. The main difference between the Inclosure Schema and Russell's is that in the Inclosure Schema the diagonaliser is guaranteed to function only on a sub-family of the power set of Ω, viz., those sets that satisfy ψ.

Bearing this in mind, it is clear that Russell's schema proper is just a special case of the Inclosure Schema, where the family is the power-set itself, i.e., ψ is the universal property ($\lambda xx = x$). Thus, the Inclosure Schema still encompasses the paradoxes of absolute infinity. But by choosing ψ appropriately, it also encompasses the definability paradoxes. This is obvious enough to require little explanation. Pondering Table 8 (an extension of Table 7 in 9.2 to include ψ) should do the trick. I will throw in Berkeley's Paradox for good measure.

For König's Paradox: DOn is obviously definable, $(\mu yy \notin x) \notin x$ by construction, and if x is definable, so is $\mu yy \notin x$. For Berry's Paradox DN_{99} is clearly definable in less than 90 words, and if x is definable in less than 90 words, $\mu yy \notin x$ is not in x, but is certainly definable in less than 99 words ('the least ordinal not in' has 5 words – recall that the natural numbers are just the finite ordinals). For Richard's Paradox diag(x), is a certain real number,

---

[15] And conversely, the mere fact that a class of ordinals is definable does not imply that every member is definable.

[16] The English prefix 'in-' is ambiguous. It can have the sense of *within*, as in 'income' or, indeed, 'inclose'; this is often corrupted to 'en-' in later English. It can also have the sense of a negative particle, as in 'incapacity' or 'indisposition'; later English prefers 'un-'.

defined by diagonalisation in such a way that it is guaranteed not to be in x. DR is obviously definable; and if x is definable, so is diag(x). For Berkeley's Paradox, C is the set of conceivable things, {x; τx}. This is conceivable (since I conceive it). And, if x is a conceivable subset of C, εyy ∉ x is conceivable and is not in x (because of the meaning of ε and the fact that x does not contain everything).

9.5   More on the inclosure schema

As I observed in the previous section, Russell's schema is just a limit case of the Inclosure Schema, where $\psi(x)$ is the universal property, as wide as it can be. At the other limit, we have the case where $\psi(x)$ is 'x = Ω', as narrow as it can be. Although this is clearly a somewhat degenerate case, it is not without its interests. As we shall see in due course, some important limits of thought are of this form.

It might be thought that admitting this case as a case of inclosure contradiction rather trivialises the notion. For given any contradiction of the form Pa!, we can knock it into the shape required by the schema. We simply take 'Py' for $\varphi(y)$ (so that Ω is just {y; Py}), 'x = Ω' for $\psi(x)$, and set $\delta(\Omega) = a$. Closure and Transcendence then follow immediately.

The issue is much more subtle than this, however. We require of the Inclosure Schema not merely that it be a pattern into which the contradictions fit. Patterns are cheap enough: given any finite set of data (such as the received paradoxes of self-reference) there is an infinite number of patterns that it can be made to fit. We want not just any old pattern, but the essential pattern. How to cash out this notion here is an interesting question. If we were dealing with a scientific, empirical, matter, what we would be after would be a pattern that is a lawlike, not just accidental, generalisation (however, in the end, one wishes to cash out the distinction). But it is not clear (at least to me) how to transfer the distinction to the present case. Still, for genuine satisfaction of the Schema we need the fact that a contradiction fits the pattern to *explain* why the contradiction arises. It is clear that in the example of the last paragraph this cannot be so. For the fact that the contradiction arises is used to establish that the pattern is satisfied. That the pattern is satisfied can hardly, therefore, be used to explain why the contradiction arises.[17] This is certainly not to say that every

---

[17] In a similar way, one can show that, in a certain sense, any paradox that satisfies the Inclosure Schema fits Russell's original schema. Given any diagonaliser that satisfies the Inclosure Schema, δ, we define a new diagonaliser, δ', as follows. If x is a subset of Ω:

$$\delta'(x) = \delta(x) \text{ if } \psi(x)$$
$$= \Theta(\Omega - x) \text{ otherwise}$$

where Θ is a choice function on the (non-empty) subsets of Ω. δ' can easily be seen to satisfy Russell's schema. As is clear, however, δ' is a gerrymandered, grue-type entity. The reduction therefore has little intrinsic value.

example of the Inclosure Schema where $\psi(x)$ is 'x = Ω' is pathological. But for legitimate cases we need, at the very least, some understanding of why it is that, given the totality Ω, $\delta(\Omega)$ is able to 'lever itself out'. Once one understands *how* it is that a diagonaliser manages to operate on a totality of objects of a certain kind to produce a novel object of the same kind, it becomes clear *why* a contradiction occurs at the limit. This kind of explanatory value *is* present in the instances of the Inclosure Schema that we have noted in the previous section, and in those which we will go on to note.[18]

9.6   Russell's VCP and the theory of orders

Let us now move on and look at Russell's solution to the paradoxes that instantiate the Inclosure Schema. Russell believed that there was a single solution to all the paradoxes of self-reference. He outlined this first in Russell (1906); a fuller account was given in (1908); which was more or less simply incorporated in the introduction to Whitehead and Russell (1910) (to the second edition of which all subsequent page references refer).

According to Russell, if an object is defined in terms of some totality, then, if that object were in the totality, we would have a vicious circle. Hence this cannot arise. Russell sums up these thoughts in the Vicious Circle Principle (VCP), which he states as follows (p. 37):[19]

Whatever involves *all* of a collection must not be one of that collection.

It is often said that the VCP is Russell's solution to the paradoxes. It is not. If $\delta(x)$ is any set defined in terms of x, the VCP just says that $\delta(x) \notin x$, i.e, that δ is a diagonaliser. This is part of what constitutes the problem, not a solution to it. Russell's solution to the paradox, like Kant's Solution 1 and Aristotle's before him, is to deny the existence of the inclosure, Ω.

But why is there no such totality? To see why Russell thought this we have to look at his theory of orders. And to understand this, one should first observe that Russell's basic objects were propositions and functions thereof. (If we think of propositions as zero-place propositional functions we may speak just of propositional functions.) What, exactly, he took these to be is, historically, moot, since he tends to run together open sentences and properties; but fortunately we do not need to go into this here.[20] All that we need to note is

---

[18] One way to get some handle on the issue formally might be to note that in the case of the *bona fide* diagonalisers that we have met, there is a genuine functional dependence of the value of the function on its argument: the argument is actually used in computing the value of the function. This is clearly not the case with the pathological example we noted. Unfortunately, the issue of when the value of a function *really* depends on its arguments is a tricky and unresolved one. For some discussion of the problem, see Anderson et al. (1992), section 70.

[19] Russell gave three formulations of the VCP, and these are not obviously equivalent (see Gödel (1944)). These subtleties are not relevant here.

[20] For details, see Quine (1963), ch. 11.

that propositional functions are a kind of thing that can contain variables. Propositional functions are divided up into disjoint orders, over which, variables of each order range. The exact structure of these orders is somewhat complex, but for present purposes we can keep things simple and stick to one-place functions. The orders for these are a simple hierarchy of type ω. Hence we may index the variables with natural numbers, so that the variables of order i are just x_i, y_i, etc. (For Russell, each order is further sub-divided into what he calls types, according to the order of the kind of argument it can take, but we do not need to go into this here.[21]) Finally, we need to specify how to recognise the order of a function. The order of a function is one more than the order of the highest order variable that it contains. This builds the VCP into the construction.

Russell reduced sets to propositional functions in a certain way. Again, the exact details need not concern us.[22] For Russell, any set is of the form $\{y_i; \theta(y_i)\}$, and we may simply *identify* this with the propositional function $\theta(y_i)$ (so that membership and satisfaction become the same thing). Since variables range over only one order, it follows that any set can contain things of only one order, and hence that there is no totality of all propositions, sets, ordinals, or any other inclosure.

There is still a totality of all sets (ordinals, etc.) of any given order, and we might suppose that the contradictions could be resurrected with respect to those; but they cannot. To see why, consider a typical set which produces paradox: $\Omega_i = \{y_i; y_i$ is a [definable] ordinal$\}$. If we now apply a diagonaliser to this we obtain an entity (or at least, the definition of an entity) which contains a variable of order i: $\mu x_i(x_i$ is an ordinal and x_i is greater than every member of $\Omega_i)$. Such an entity is of order i+1. Hence it is not one of the values of the variable y_i; and even if one can show that it has the right properties to be a [definable] ordinal, one cannot infer that it is in Ω_i. The argument to Closure is therefore blocked. Exactly similar considerations apply to the other paradoxes, as may be checked.

9.7   Systematic ambiguity

Russell's solution to the paradoxes is well known to face severe difficulties. For a start, there is the question of whether the theory of orders can be justified, and if so, how. Next, the construction rules out a good deal more than just the paradoxical collections: it rules out various impredicative collections that occur in quite unproblematic mathematical contexts, such as the theorem that each set of real numbers has a least upper bound. Russell solved these problems by means of the Axiom of Reducibility. According to this, if f is any function

[21] For full details, see Chihara (1973), ch. 1.
[22] For an account of the reduction, see Chihara (1973), ch. 1.

whose arguments are of order i, then there is an extensionally equivalent function whose order is i+1. Russell calls such functions *predicative*, and states the axiom as follows (p. 56):

The axiom of reducibility is the assumption that, given any function f, there is a formally equivalent *predicative* function.

In symbols, the Axiom (schema) of Reducibility is:

$$\exists\phi_{i+1}\forall x_i(f(x_i) \leftrightarrow \phi(x_i))$$

This may solve the problem formally, but raises the question of the justification of the axiom, to which Russell never really produced a convincing answer. This was not an end to the problems for this solution, however. For even given the Axiom of Reducibility (and an axiom of infinity), there is much set-theory that cannot be demonstrated given the restrictions imposed by orders. For example, the existence of the cardinal $\aleph_\omega$ and, *a fortiori*, larger cardinals cannot be established.

I do not wish to discuss these issues further.[23] I put them here mainly for the record. Russell's solution founders on a much less technical but more fundamental problem. According to the theory, every variable must range over one order of propositional functions. No variable can therefore range over all propositional functions. For the same reason, no variable can range over all propositions. This pushes many claims beyond the limit of the expressible. Take, for example, the law of excluded middle: every proposition is either true or false. Since this has a quantifier over all propositions, it cannot be expressed. Or, closer to home, consider the Axiom of Reducibility itself. This is supposed to hold for all functions, f. Russell's very statement of it (above) therefore violates the theory of orders. Even decent statements of the VCP cannot be made without violating the VCP since they must say that *for any function*, f, any propositional function which 'involves' f cannot be an argument for f. Such statements are impossible by Russell's own admission.

To add insult to injury, the very theory of orders cannot be explained without quantifying over all functions, and hence violating it. For to explain it, one has to express the fact that *every propositional function* has a determinate order. Hence, the theory is self-refuting.[24]

Russell was well aware of at least some of these difficulties. To solve them he formulated his theory of systematic ambiguity. This is most easily understood with respect to an example. Take the statement of the Axiom of Reducibility. According to Russell, this has to be understood (for fixed i) as indicating not a single proposition, but an infinitude of propositions: one for each order that f

---

[23] Discussion of the various issues can be found in numerous places, for example, Chihara (1973), ch. 1; Fraenkel, Bar-Hillel, and Levy (1973), 3.5; Quine (1963), ch. 11.
[24] As was well pointed out by Fitch (1946).

might be. Russell, himself, explains the point with respect to a similar example as follows (p. 55):

In some cases, we can see that some statement will hold of 'all nth-order properties of a', whatever value n may have. In such cases, no practical harm results from regarding the statement as being about "all properties of a" provided we remember that it is really a number of statements, and not a single statement which could be regarded as assigning another property to a, over and above such properties. Such cases will always involve some systematic ambiguity.

This solution is, frankly, disingenuous.[25] For, however we express it, what we are supposed to understand by a systematically ambiguous formula, such as the formal statement of the Axiom of Reducibility above, is exactly what would be obtained by prefixing the formula with a universal quantifier '$\forall f$', ranging over all functions. There must therefore be such a thought, though it cannot be expressed in the theory of orders.

Even worse, systematic ambiguity cannot handle all cases. When it works, it does so, in effect, because a statement with a free variable, f, is logically equivalent to that which is obtained by prefixing it by a universal quantifier. Thus, it can work only where the fact about all propositions that we wish to express is of universally quantified form. Now, consider, for example, the undoubtedly true: no order is the order of all propositions; i.e., for every order, i, there is a proposition, p, that does not have order i. If we understood this systematically ambiguously, we would get all statements of the form: for every order i, there is a proposition, p, of order j, such that p is not of order i, which mean something quite different, and one of which is false (i=j). Or consider the consequence of the theory of orders that there is no totality of propositions, in Russell's words (p. 37):

Propositions ... must be a set having no total.

There is no systematically ambiguous statement which can express this. Considered as systematically ambiguous, every proposition that this expresses is false since the propositions of each order *do* have a totality.

Finally, again to rub it in, note that one can express the quantifier 'for every propositional function' as 'for every n and every propositional function of order n'. (And thus systematic ambiguity is often taken to be expressed by schematic uses of order-subscripts when these are made explicit.) Hence the very first sentence of Russell's own explanation of the principle of systematic ambiguity, quoted above, violates the VCP, since it talks of all propositional functions (of a). Moreover, this statement cannot be understood in terms of systematic ambiguity since this universal quantifier does not have the whole of the rest of the statement in its scope.

---

[25] See Priest (1987), p. 25.

9.8   The solution that reproduces the problem

If the problem that Russell is landed with looks familiar, that is because it *is* familiar. Russell's solution to the problem of the contradiction at the limits of thought generates another. By his own theory, Russell's theory cannot be expressed (Transcendence); but he does express it (Closure). Hence we have a contradiction at the limit of expression. In the same way, Kant's solution to the Antinomies drove him beyond the bounds of the expressible with respect to noumena.

We can even knock Russell's predicament into the Inclosure Schema itself; in fact, into Russell's schema. Russell cannot explain his account without talking about all propositions. Given that he *does* express his account, there must be a variable that ranges over all propositions. Let $\varphi(y)$ be: y is a proposition; so Ω (= $\{y; \varphi(y)\}$) exists, and is the set of all propositions. (Given Russell's identification, this is just the propositional function $\varphi(y)$ itself.) If x is any set of propositions, let $\delta(x)$ be any proposition concerning all the members of x (for example, the proposition *all members of x have some order*). Then δ is a diagonaliser, by the VCP. Hence we have Transcendence. But since $\delta(x)$ is obviously a proposition, we have Closure. As we see, then, in trying to solve the problem, Russell just succeeds in reproducing it. His theory is therefore less of a solution to the contradiction at the limits of thought than an illustration of it.

Conclusion

In this chapter we have seen that two of the limits of thought that have concerned us in the book, the limit of iteration and the limit of conception, are intimately related to the Inclosure Schema. One of the other limits, the limit of expression, also appeared briefly under that guise. The fourth limit that has concerned us, the limit of cognition, has been absent from the discussion for a number of chapters now. In the next chapter it will return. And as we will see there, it, too, is intimately connected with the Inclosure Schema.

10 Parameterisation

Introduction

As we saw in chapter 9, the limits of iteration and conception (definition) come together in the shape of paradoxes of self-reference; in particular, they both instantiate the same form: the Inclosure Schema. An obvious question is whether the Schema captures the other limits that we have met. This is the first topic we will investigate in this chapter.

We will do this by looking at some of the ideas of Ramsey, whose essay 'The Foundations of Mathematics'[1] provided the most acute early commentary on Russell's ideas on paradox. Ramsey suggested that the paradoxes of self-reference are of two kinds. I think it no understatement to say that this suggestion has provided the framework for all subsequent work on the paradoxes. A crucial question we will have to address is the extent to which this division is justified. Ramsey also suggested solutions to the paradoxes of each kind. One was similar to that of Russell; the other was more novel. This and its adequacy constitute the second topic we will take up in this chapter. Finally we will look at some of the more modern descendants of Ramsey's solution.

10.1 Ramsey's two families

Russell held that the paradoxes of self-reference all belong to a single family, sharing a single problematic. And certainly, *prima facie*, this view looks right. There does seem to be something similar going on in all the paradoxes, though pinning down what this is, is notoriously difficult. Even before Russell wrote, however, some logicians were claiming that the paradoxes are not of a kind. Peano, for example, suggested that only some of the paradoxes belong to mathematics; others belong to 'linguistics' (Peano (1906), p. 157). Ramsey took up Peano's suggestion, and divided the paradoxes neatly into two families. It is difficult to state the criterion for the distinction more clearly than did Ramsey himself. I will simply, therefore, quote him (p. 171):

---

[1] Ramsey (1925); subsequent page references are to this – the reprinted edition – unless otherwise specified.

It is not sufficiently remarked, and the fact is entirely neglected in *Principia Mathematica*, that these contradictions [the paradoxes of self-reference] fall into two fundamentally distinct groups, which we will call A and B. The best known are divided as follows:

A. (1) The class of all classes which are not members of themselves.
    (2) The relation between two relations when one does not have itself to the other.
    (3) Burali Forti's contradiction of the greatest ordinal.
B. (4) 'I am lying.'
    (5) The least integer not nameable in fewer than nineteen syllables.
    (6) The least indefinable ordinal.
    (7) Richard's contradiction.
    (8) Weyl's contradiction about 'heterologische'.

The principle according to which I have divided them is of fundamental importance. Group A consists of contradictions which, were no provision made against them, would occur in a logical or mathematical system itself. They involve only logical or mathematical terms such as class and number, and show that there must be something wrong with our logic or mathematics. But the contradictions in Group B are not purely logical, and cannot be stated in logical terms alone; for they all contain some reference to thought, language, or symbolism, which are not formal but empirical terms. So they may be due not to faulty logic or mathematics, but to faulty ideas concerning thought and language. If so, they would not be relevant to mathematical logic, if by 'logic' we mean a symbolic system, though of course they would be relevant to logic in the sense of the analysis of thought. [Footnote: These two meanings of 'logic' are frequently confused.]

In hindsight, it is clear that Ramsey's criterion has the flimsiest basis. For a start, if one wants to draw a fundamental distinction, this ought to be done in terms of the *structure* of the different paradoxes. Ramsey's distinction depends on the relatively superficial fact of what vocabulary is used in the paradoxes, and, in particular, whether this belongs to mathematics properly so called. But worse, this is a notoriously shifting boundary. Ramsey was writing before the heyday of metamathematics. Had he been writing ten years later, it would have been clear that a number of items of vocabulary occurring in paradoxes of Group B do belong to mathematics. In particular, both syntactical and semantical linguistic notions became quite integral parts of mathematics. The work of Gödel and Tarski showed how these notions could be reduced to other parts of mathematics (number-theory and set-theory, respectively).

Despite the collapse of the effective basis of the distinction, the distinction itself, like the grin of the Cheshire Cat, survives and continues to provide an hypnotic fixation for work on the paradoxes. To make matters worse, it is now customary to draw Ramsey's distinction in even more misleading terms. The paradoxes in Group A are usually called set-theoretic paradoxes; those in Group B are usually called semantic paradoxes. Putting the classification in these terms seems to leave no room for, for example, the Fifth Antinomy or Berkeley's Paradox at all.

From the present theoretical perspective, the distinction between Groups A and B looks even more arbitrary and misleading. To see this, distinguish, first, between two sub-classes of Group B. First there are those of its members that explicitly involve the notion of definability (for example, (5) – (7) in Ramsey's examples). Call this Bi. Next are the others ((4) and (8)). Call this Bii. Now, the paradoxes in Group A are the paradoxes of the limit of iteration (though the Fifth Antinomy uses the notion of thought, and so Ramsey would have had to classify it in Group B);[2] and the paradoxes in Group Bi are the paradoxes of the limit of conception (definition). But, as we saw in chapter 9, these paradoxes have a common underlying structure, the Inclosure Schema, and so belong to the same family. All the paradoxes in this group depend on a diagonaliser being applied to a limit totality.

10.2 Group Bii

As may be clear, the paradoxes in Group Bii correspond to a third limit that has concerned us in the book: the limit of cognition. (In 3.9, we noted that the Liar paradox is just a special case of these.) The next question is whether paradoxes in this group are structurally distinct from those in Group A+Bi, that is, whether they fit the Inclosure Schema. *Prima facie*, they are distinct. For inclosure paradoxes all involve the notion of a totality out of which we diagonalise. The Liar paradox, for example, however, does not appear to be of this form: it does not mention totalities at all.

As we noted in 9.6, Russell held there to be a common cause of, and solution to, all the paradoxes of self-reference. He therefore had to manipulate the Liar paradox into a form where the theory of orders could be applied to it. He did this by parsing the Liar sentence as: there is a proposition that I am affirming and that is false, i.e., $\exists p$(I assert p and p is false) (Whitehead and Russell (1910), p. 65). If the quantifier in this proposition has order i, it, itself, is of order i+1, and so does not fall within the scope of the quantifier. This breaks the argument to contradiction. Russell's parsing, by insisting that the self-reference involved be obtained by quantification, strikes one as totally artificial. For a start, the Liar does not have to be asserted to generate a contradiction. But, more fundamentally, the self-reference required may be

---

[2] We have not met Ramsey's paradox (2) before, but it is not difficult to see that it fits Russell's schema. Let $\varphi(y)$ be 'y is a relation', so that Ω is the set of all relations. If $x \subseteq \Omega$ then $\delta(x)$ is the relation r_x, defined as follows: $\langle y,z \rangle \in r_x$ iff $y,z \in x$ and $\langle y,z \rangle \notin y$. Closure is immediate. If $r_x \in x$ then $\langle r_x, r_x \rangle \in r_x$ iff $\langle r_x, r_x \rangle \notin r_x$. Hence, we have Transcendence.

obtained by ways other than quantification, for example, by a demonstrative: *this* proposition (or sentence) is false.

Russell's reparsing of the Liar, then, fails. However, there is an analytic connection between satisfying a condition and being in a set: something satisfies a condition iff it is in the set of things satisfying that condition.[3] Hence, facts about totalities are implicit in facts about conditions, and vice versa. Using this observation, we can manipulate the paradoxes of Group Bii into a form in which they fit the Inclosure Schema quite legitimately. Hence we can show the paradoxes of this group to be of a kind with the paradoxes in the other groups. Let us see how, starting with the Liar paradox.

Assume, for the nonce, that it is sentences (rather than propositions or some other semantic entities) that are true or false. Let $\varphi(y)$ be 'y is true', so that Ω is the set of true sentences, Tr; let $\psi(x)$ be 'x is definable'. δ is a function, σ, defined by some suitable technique of diagonalisation so that if a is any definable set $\sigma(a) = \alpha$ where, $\alpha = \langle \alpha \notin a \rangle$. The angle-bracket expression is a sentence expressing the fact that α is not in the set a. (Hence, α says 'This sentence is not in a'.) Note that a must be definable, or there would be no guarantee that there is such a sentence.

Now, if a is definable and a $\subseteq$ Tr:

$$
\begin{aligned}
\sigma(a) \in a \Rightarrow \quad & \langle \alpha \notin a \rangle \in a \\
\Rightarrow \quad & \langle \alpha \notin a \rangle \in \text{Tr} \\
\Rightarrow \quad & \alpha \notin a \qquad \text{(by the T-schema)} \\
\Rightarrow \quad & \sigma(a) \notin a
\end{aligned}
$$

Hence $\sigma(a) \notin a$, and Transcendence is satisfied. Moreover, it follows that $\alpha \notin$ a, and hence by the T-schema $\langle \alpha \notin a \rangle \in$ Tr, i.e., $\sigma(a) \in$ Tr. Hence, Closure is satisfied too. The Liar is the sentence $\sigma(\text{Tr})$ and the contradiction is that $\sigma(\text{Tr}) \in$ Tr and $\sigma(\text{Tr}) \notin$ Tr.

Similar treatments can be given to the other paradoxes in this group. Consider, for example, the Knower paradox. This is the same as the Liar, except that $\varphi(y)$ is 'y is known to be true', and so Ω is the set of known things, Kn. Transcendence is verified as before, since knowledge implies truth; Closure follows, since it has been established that $\alpha \notin$ a, and so $\sigma(a) \in$ Kn. The paradox is that $\sigma(\text{Kn}) \in$ Kn and $\sigma(\text{Kn}) \notin$ Kn. Any notion that shares the relevant properties with knowledge, for example provability, will generate a contradiction with the same structure. Thus, for example, we have 'Gödel's paradox': this sentence is not provable.[4] A variant on these paradoxes is the

---

[3] This observation appeals to the naive notion of set, and would be challenged, for example, by those who subscribe to ZF or some similar form of set theory. We will see the inadequacy of such theories in the next chapter. The naive notion of set is also defended in Priest (1987), chs. 2 and 10.

[4] See Priest (1987), pp. 58f.

Liar (or Knower) chain, where several sentences are interrelated. These fit the pattern, too. To see this, just consider the simplest paradox of this kind: the Liar pair. This is exactly the same as the Liar, except that σ is slightly more complicated. This time, $\sigma(a) = \alpha$, where $\alpha = \langle \beta \in Tr \rangle$ and $\beta = \langle \alpha \notin a \rangle$. To see that σ satisfies the appropriate conditions, suppose that $a \subseteq Tr$ and that a is definable. Then:

$$
\begin{aligned}
\sigma(a) \in a \quad &\Rightarrow \alpha \in a \\
&\Rightarrow \alpha \in Tr \\
&\Rightarrow \langle \beta \in Tr \rangle \in Tr \\
&\Rightarrow \beta \in Tr \qquad \text{(by the T-schema)} \\
&\Rightarrow \langle \alpha \notin a \rangle \in Tr \\
&\Rightarrow \alpha \notin a \qquad \text{(by the T-schema)} \\
&\Rightarrow \sigma(a) \notin a
\end{aligned}
$$

Hence, $\sigma(a) \notin a$, which is Transcendence. To see that Closure is satisfied, note the following:

$$
\begin{aligned}
\sigma(a) \notin a \quad &\Rightarrow \alpha \notin a \\
&\Rightarrow \langle \alpha \notin a \rangle \in Tr \qquad \text{(by the T-schema)} \\
&\Rightarrow \beta \in Tr \\
&\Rightarrow \langle \beta \in Tr \rangle \in Tr \qquad \text{(by the T-schema)} \\
&\Rightarrow \alpha \in Tr \\
&\Rightarrow \sigma(a) \in Tr
\end{aligned}
$$

The contradiction is that $\sigma(Tr) \in Tr$ and $\sigma(Tr) \notin Tr$.

A final example from this group of paradoxes will suffice. This is the Heterological Paradox. $\varphi(y)$ is '$\neg$ y sat y' where 'sat' is the satisfaction relation, so $\Omega = \{y; \neg y \text{ sat } y\}$, Het; $\psi(x)$ is 'x is definable', as before; if a is a definable set, $\delta(a) = \langle v \in a \rangle$, where v is any new variable, and so this is an open sentence. Now, suppose that $a \subseteq$ Het and that a is definable. Then:

$$
\begin{aligned}
\langle v \in a \rangle \in a \quad &\Rightarrow \langle v \in a \rangle \in Het \\
&\Rightarrow \neg(\langle v \in a \rangle \text{ sat } \langle v \in a \rangle) \\
&\Rightarrow \langle v \in a \rangle \notin a \qquad \text{(by the Satisfaction Schema)}
\end{aligned}
$$

Hence $\langle v \in a \rangle \notin a$, i.e., Transcendence. So by the Satisfaction Schema $\neg \langle v \in a \rangle$ sat $\langle v \in a \rangle$, i.e., $\langle v \in a \rangle \in$ Het, Closure. The paradox is that $\langle v \in Het \rangle \in$ Het and $\langle v \in Het \rangle \notin$ Het.

We can record these observations as in Table 9. (Compare this with the Table 8 in 9.4. I have omitted the final column.)

We have seen, assuming that sentences are truth bearers, that all the paradoxes of Group Bii fit the Inclosure Schema. If one takes propositions or some other semantic entities, instead of sentences, to be truth bearers, the situation is essentially the same; all we need to do is reinterpret the notation. We now take $\langle \alpha \in x \rangle$ to be the appropriate proposition. Similarly, in the Heterological

Table 9

Paradox	$\delta(x) =$	$\psi(x)$	$\varphi(y)$	Ω
Liar	α, where $\alpha = \,<\alpha \notin x>$	x is definable	y is true	Tr
Knower	α, where $\alpha = \,<\alpha \notin x>$	x is definable	y is known	Kn
Liar Chain	α, where $\alpha = \,<\beta \in \mathrm{Tr}>$ and $\beta = \,<\alpha \notin x>$	x is definable	y is true	Tr
Heterological	$<v \in x>$	x is definable	¬y sat y	Het

Paradox, we take $\langle v \in x \rangle$ to be the appropriate property. In fact, things are actually simplified by this. For presumably, for any set (not just a definable one), x, there is a proposition, α, such that $\alpha = \langle \alpha \notin x \rangle$ (the proposition that this proposition is not in x). Similarly, in the Heterological paradox, if x is any set there is a property of being in x. In this case, one no longer needs to assume that x is definable; and the paradoxes fit Russell's original schema.

One further observation: the paradoxes in Groups Bi and Bii, though fitting the Inclosure Schema, establish that the relevant δ is a diagonaliser in different ways. This is, note, the major *structural* difference between them. In Bi paradoxes the conclusion $\delta(x) \notin x$ is obtained directly from the fact that $\exists y\, y \notin x$ since δ is a description operator of some kind, selecting one of the things that is not in x. In Bii paradoxes it is obtained indirectly, in virtue of the fact that $\delta(x) \in x$ entails $\delta(x) \notin x$, this being established by appealing to a principle such as the T-schema, the Satisfaction Schema, etc. For the benefit of subsequent discussion I will call any principle of this kind a *bridge principle* (since it provides a bridge between a semantic notion and the world).

10.3 Inclosures and the limits of expression

We have seen that contradictions at three of the limits of thought that we have been considering in the book, the limits of iteration, cognition, and conception (definition), fall into the pattern of inclosure contradictions. This naturally raises the question of whether there are inclosure contradictions corresponding to the fourth limit, the limit of expression. We will see, in the last part of the book, that there are.[5] But even before we get there, it is possible to see that

---

[5] In fact, we have met one already in 9.8, but this was essentially just an artifact of Russell's solution to the paradoxes.

there are such contradictions: some paradoxes of self-reference are of this form.

None of the standard paradoxes of self-reference concerns expressibility. However, there is a close connection between indefinability and inexpressibility. Given an indefinable entity, it will be impossible to express any facts about it. For we have to be able to refer to an object to state facts about it. Thus, given any definability paradox, we can generate an expressibility paradox.[6] I will show this using König's paradox. Similar considerations will apply to all the others.

We know that the least indefinable ordinal both can and cannot be defined. Now, consider the fact that it is an ordinal. Since we cannot refer to it, we have no way of expressing this fact. But I have just expressed it. Showing that the paradox fits the Inclosure Schema is simply a matter of reworking the corresponding argument for König's paradox. Let variables range over states of affairs. Let $\varphi(y)$ be 'y is expressible', so that Ω is the set of all expressible states of affairs, Ξ. Let $\psi(x)$ be 'x is definable'. Clearly, Ξ is definable, and so we have Existence. Since our language has only countably many expressions, Ξ is countable. Hence, if $x \subseteq \Xi$ then x is countable too, and hence the states in x can be about only a countable number of ordinals.[7] In this case there must be an ordinal that no member of x is about, and so a least. Let $\delta(x)$ be the state of affairs of its being an ordinal. Clearly, this in not in x (Transcendence). Yet the state of affairs is in Ξ since it is expressed by 'μz(z is an ordinal that no member of a is about) is an ordinal', where 'a' is a name for x (Closure).

We may bypass the notion of definability, and construct paradoxes of expressibility directly using diagonalisation.[8] For example, consider all the one-place (non-indexical) predicates (i.e., concept-expressions, in Frege's terms) of numbers in, say, English. These can be enumerated, for example lexicographically. Let the nth predicate be $P_n x$. Consider the predicate $\neg P_x x$; call this Qx. Then for some m, Qx is $P_m x$ since the ordering, and so Q, are expressible in English. Thus Qm iff $\neg P_m m$ iff $\neg Qm$. It is not difficult to put this into the form of an inclosure contradiction. Let $\varphi(y)$ be 'y is a one-place arithmetic predicate (of English)'; so Ω is the totality of all such predicates. Let $\psi(x)$ be 'x is definable in English'. If $\psi(x)$, let $\delta(x)$ be the predicate defined by diagonalisation, as above. By the usual argument, we have Transcendence; since the enumeration of x is definable in English, $\delta(x)$ is an English predicate, and so we have Closure. (We need the fact that x is definable, or there is no

---

[6] The observation is made, essentially, by Pollock (1970).

[7] I am assuming here that each state of affairs can be about only a finite number of ordinals, i.e., that states of affairs are what the *Tractatus* will call 'atomic'. If this is not obvious, just let $\psi(x)$ be 'x is a definable set of states of affairs, each of which is about only a finite number of ordinals'.

[8] A construction of the following kind is given in Grim (1991), ch. 3.

guarantee that the ordering is expressible in English.) Finally, Ω is definable in English; hence we have Existence.

Whether directly or indirectly, then, there are numerous contradictions at the limits of expression that are inclosure contradictions.

10.4 Group B: Ramsey's solution

We have now seen that all the paradoxes of self-reference (including some less usual ones) fit into the Inclosure Schema; and hence, *contra* Ramsey, that there is a single family here. Let us now move on and consider Ramsey's solutions to the paradoxes. Unsurprisingly, he gives different solutions for the paradoxes of each of his two groups.

Ramsey's solution to Group A paradoxes was the same as Russell's, except that he simplified it (famously) in one respect: the simplest way to look at this (though not the way Ramsey himself puts it) is that he changed the definition of 'order'. For Ramsey, the order of a (one-place) propositional function is one more than the order of the *free* variable occurring in it. This, in effect, takes all the functions, of whatever order (in Russell's sense), whose arguments are of the same order and makes them a single class, over which a variable can range. It is clear that this removes the need for an Axiom of Reducibility (and so the problem of justifying it) at a stroke. (This was Ramsey's main aim.) In what follows, it will be important to keep clear the difference between Ramsey's definition and Russell's. I will retain the word 'order' for Russell's definition, and use the word 'type' for Ramsey's. Hence, Ramsey's hierarchy comprises objects (type 0), functions of these (type 1), functions of functions (type 2), etc.

The hierarchy of types still provides a solution to standard Group A paradoxes. The totality of all ordinals (or whatever) of type i, still turns out to be of type higher than i, making it impossible to demonstrate Closure. And the totality of *all* ordinals, *all* propositions, etc., still does not exist. But, just because of this, the solution inherits the major weakness of Russell's original solution: it renders its own explanation beyond the limit of the expressible. I need say little more about this here.

The situation is very different for the paradoxes in Group B, however. There is still no set of *all* definable ordinals. But the collapse of a vertical section through Russell's orders into a single type, means that a version of König's Paradox can be pushed through for the set of definable ordinals of any given type. Similar comments apply to the other paradoxes of Group B. To understand why, exactly, and what Ramsey's solution to the paradoxes of Group B was, it is best look at an example.

Ramsey himself, gives the fullest explanation of his solution using the Heterological Paradox (pp. 191ff.), so let us stick with this. His version of the paradox is somewhat different from the version I gave in 10.2. A major difference is that he formulates the paradox in terms of the condition of heterologicality ($\neg$ x sat x), rather than the heterological set. To discuss what Ramsey would have said about the version I gave would raise the question of his views about sets (which were, in fact, very similar to Russell's). From the point of view of a solution to the Heterological Paradox, this would both complicate matters, and be absolutely irrelevant. Moreover, Ramsey's discussion of the issues is fairly intricate, and I do not want to introduce further complications. Hence I will discuss the paradox in essentially the form he gave it.

Ramsey cashes out the notion of satisfaction in terms of properties (propositional functions). I will use lower-case letters for variables of type 0, and upper-case letters for variables of type 1. Now let us write xRY for 'x denotes Y' or 'x means Y' as Ramsey puts it. The condition '$\neg$x sat x' can then be written $\exists Y(xRY \wedge \neg Yx)$. Let us write this as Fx. We then reason as follows:

$$F\langle F\rangle \Rightarrow \exists Y(\langle F\rangle RY \wedge \neg Y\langle F\rangle)$$
$$\Rightarrow \neg F\langle F\rangle$$

(by an analogue of the Satisfaction Schema). Hence $\neg F\langle F\rangle$. But since, presumably:

$$\langle F\rangle RF \qquad (*)$$

we have:

$$\langle F\rangle RF \wedge \neg F\langle F\rangle$$
so $\qquad \exists Y(\langle F\rangle RY \wedge \neg Y\langle F\rangle) \qquad (**)$
i.e., $\qquad F\langle F\rangle.$

Russell objected to the argument at (**), since the order of F is too high. In other words, if the quantifier in F is of order i, the quantifier at line (**) needs to be of order i+1. This move is no longer available to Ramsey since all properties of objects of the same type (in our case, type 0) are of the same type. Instead he denies (*). He claims that 'R' is ambiguous, and that although $\langle F\rangle$ means F in *some* sense, it is a different sense from that in which meaning occurs within F itself. Specifically, the meaning-relations differ for functions of different orders. In this way is the argument blocked, since the order of F is higher than that of Y. And Ramsey claims (pp. 193, 198f.) that all the paradoxes in Group B contain some word like 'means', whose similar disambiguation solves the paradox.

10.5 ... and its inadequacy

How successful is Ramsey's proposed solution? It has a variety of problems before it can even get off the ground. First, it is not at all clear that a word similar to 'means' occurs in all the paradoxes of Group B. Those that mention language explicitly may all be supposed to do so; but Berkeley's Paradox does not. Next, by assuming that satisfaction is to be analysed in terms of properties (functions) it imports certain contentious assumptions. Thirdly, unless the claim that R (and similar words) is ambiguous can be defended, there is no reason to believe it true (except that it blocks the paradox – but then all solutions do that).

Ramsey is well aware of this last point, and attempts to argue that there are reasons for supposing functions of different orders to have different meaning-relations. His explanation is quite long (pp. 194ff.), but goes, essentially, as follows. To say that x means Y is to say that there is a relationship of a certain kind between x and the objects 'involved in' Y. Now a function of (for example) order 1 contains a quantifier (over objects of type 0) and so(?) the relationship of involvement is different from that of (for example) a function of order 0, which contains no such quantifier.

Ramsey's account of meaning is not one that most would now find plausible. And even if it were right, I know of no way of cashing out the notion of involvement employed in such a way as to validate the problematic inference (marked with '?'). But even if Ramsey's explanation of why 'means' is ambiguous is correct, another objection looms. Given some collection of meaning-relations we can simply form a single relation which is their logical sum. And this fact appears to reinstate the paradox. Ramsey himself is alive to this objection, and gives it (p. 196f.) essentially as follows.

Let R_0, R_1, and R_2 be the meaning-relations for functions of individuals of order 0, 1, and 2 respectively. Let R be their logical sum, i.e., xRY iff $xR_0Y \lor xR_1Y \lor xR_2Y$. Then the heterological condition, $\exists Y(xRY \land \neg Yx)$, appears to be of order 2 (since it contains at most a quantifier over functions, i.e., entities of type 1). Hence $\langle F \rangle R_2 F$, and thus $\langle F \rangle RF$; and we are back with the contradiction.

Ramsey's solution to this problem is that, despite appearances, the condition in question is not of order 2, but is of order 3! His reason for this is rather tortured and unpersuasive.[9] But even if he could substantiate this, he is still not out of the woods. For, even if his arguments so far are correct, all that has been shown is that the logical sum of a class of meaning-relations is a meaning-relation which diagonalises out of the class. The problem comes, as we might

---

[9] Essentially, it goes as follows. R_2 is a relationship whose co-domain (i.e., the class of objects that can occupy the second place of the relation) comprises propositional functions of order 2, which themselves have quantifiers over functions of individuals, and so are of the form $f(\forall X \varphi(X))$. So R_2 (and so F) involves a variable function, f, of functions of individuals and so is of order 3 (p. 196). Ramsey does not explain, again, here what he means by the crucial term 'involve'. But even if we grant the dubious claim that if the relata of a relation involve a notion then the relation itself does, it is not at all clear that the relata, in this case, really involve functions of functions. For the co-domain just is the class of functions of order 2, and none of these contains functions of functions. To express their form might require a *schematic* variable, f, but this is not a genuine variable, and so does not involve entities of type 3 in any real sense.

expect now, when we construct the class of *all* meaning-relations, and take their logical sum, R*. This is a meaning-relation, and so, by definition, must be in that very class. If F is now the heterological condition involving this relation, we must have ⟨F⟩RF for some meaning-relation, R. Hence ⟨F⟩R*F, and the paradox ensues.

Ramsey is alive to this problem too, and says (p. 197):

> What appears clearly from the contradictions is that we cannot obtain an all-inclusive relation of meaning for propositional functions. Whatever one we take there is still a way of constructing a symbol to mean in a way not included in our relation. The meanings of meaning form an illegitimate totality.

Hence, Ramsey falls back on, essentially, Russell's solution: there is no totality of a certain kind. We saw that this made Russell's theory self-refuting. Ramsey is in an even worse situation. For the existence of an appropriate totality can be demonstrated by principles that Ramsey can hardly object to. Observe that a meaning-relation for functions of type 1 (which are all that are in question here) is a relation whose left-hand arguments are all predicates – which are objects of type 0 – and whose right-hand arguments are functions of type 1. Thus, all meaning-relations are legitimate, according to the theory of types, and, more importantly, are all of the same (relational) type. Hence, the set of all such relations is a sub-set of this type, and hence is perfectly well defined.

What has turned Russell's self-refutation into a flat contradiction is simply Ramsey's simplification of Russell's theory. For Russell, the relevant collection does not exist since it contains members of arbitrarily high order. By supposing that all propositional functions of a certain kind (but of arbitrarily high order) form a determinate type (totality), this safeguard is no longer available to Ramsey.

10.6 Parameterisation in general

Ramsey's solution to the paradoxes of Group B is an instance of a well-known stratagem for disposing of contradictions. The stratagem is to the effect that when one meets an (at least *prima facie*) contradiction of the form P(a)!, one tries to find some ambiguity in P, or some different respects, r_1 and r_2, in which something may be P, and then to argue that a is P in one respect, $P(r_1, a)$, but not in the other, $\neg P(r_2, a)$. For example, when faced with the apparent contradiction that it is both 2pm and 10pm, I disambiguate with respect to place, and resolve the contradiction by noting that it is 2pm in Cambridge and 10pm in Brisbane. Of course, there might well be more than two respects in which a thing can be P; in the example used, any spot on the surface of the earth (except a pole) can provide a relevant respect. Hence, in general, there will be a family of parameters such that the apparently monadic P(x) falls apart into the family of relations P(c,x), where c is some parameter. I will therefore call this technique *parameterisation*. Naturally, the fact that parameterisation can be applied successfully to resolve some contradictions, does not imply that it can be applied to resolve all contradictions. Each case demands independent consideration.

To see how parameterisation is supposed to work for Ramsey, note that the satisfaction predicate, or, more fundamentally, the denotation relation he uses to define it, is parameterised by the orders of the relevant functions. Thus we have a family of parameterised heterological predicates, $F_n x$, one for each order, n. It then turns out that $\neg F_n \langle F_n \rangle$, but $F_{n+1} \langle F_n \rangle$.

As we have seen, the technique of parameterisation cannot be applied satisfactorily in the way Ramsey wishes; a number of facts prevent its working successfully. Still, it might be hoped that some other application of parameterisation might fare better than Ramsey's. And virtually all suggested solutions to the semantic paradoxes since Ramsey are further attempts to apply parameterisation. Perhaps the clearest example of this is Tarski's (1936) solution to the paradoxes, though in fairness to him it should be pointed out that he did not advocate this as a solution; merely as a way of avoiding the paradoxes. Tarski parameterised semantic predicates such as satisfaction and truth, using a hierarchy of languages. More recently, some philosophers (who most certainly do see this as a solution to the paradoxes) have suggested that semantic predicates have a context-dependent extension, and hence that the possible values of some context variable can be used to parameterise the relevant predicates.[10] (Note that one can always trade in a context-dependent truth for a non-context-dependent one by making the contextual parameter explicit. Thus, for example, 'It's the 20th century' is true in 1990 iff 'In 1990 it is the 20th century' is true.) Alternatively, some philosophers have suggested that different tokens of the same (non-indexical) type may have different truth values. This, too, is a version of parameterisation: tokens now provide the relevant parameters.[11] Even the contemporary solutions that are not explicitly parametric have to fall back in the last instance on the Tarskian distinction between object and metalanguage, and so on parameterisation.[12]

To put such solutions in a general form, return to the Inclosure Schema. This concerns some property, φ, and a function, δ, which, when applied to suitable classes of things that are φ, diagonalises out of them to give another object that is φ. If Ω is the limit of all φs, we get $\delta(\Omega) \in \Omega$ and $\delta(\Omega) \notin \Omega$, or

---

[10] Perhaps the first person to suggest this possibility was Parsons (1974c). The idea has been developed at greater length by Burge (1979). Its most sophisticated technical presentation is in Barwise and Etchemendy (1987), Part III, who call the contexts 'situations' and give a set-theoretic analysis of these.

[11] I think that the originator of this view is Buridan. (See Hughes (1982).) For others who have run the line, see Smiley (1993), p. 25.

[12] See, for example, the discussion of the solutions of Kripke, Gupta, and Herzberger in ch. 1 of Priest (1987).

equivalently, $\varphi(\delta(\Omega))$ and $\neg\varphi(\delta(\Omega))$. Parameterising works by breaking φ into a family of parameterised predicates $\varphi(c,y)$ where c is some appropriate parameter (language, context, tokening, or whatever). The parameterisation of φ induces a corresponding parameterisation of the totality Ω defined in terms of it: for each c there is a totality Ω_c, $\{y; \varphi(c,y)\}$. Now, in each paradox, half of the argument is used to establish that, for the relevant δ, δ is a diagonaliser with respect to the property $\varphi(c,y)$. (In the case of the Bi paradoxes, this is so in virtue of the properties of the relevant descriptor. In the case of the Bii paradoxes, the argument requires a parameterised version of the appropriate bridge principle, for example: in context c, $T(c, \langle\alpha\rangle) \rightarrow \alpha$.) Since δ is a diagonaliser, $\delta(\Omega_c) \notin \Omega_c$. But in all cases, $\delta(\Omega_c)$ clearly *is* φ in some respect (it has just been referred to, been shown to be true, etc.) Hence, to do justice to the facts, it must be maintained that for some c' $\varphi(c',\delta(\Omega_c))$, i.e., $\delta(\Omega_c) \in \Omega_{c'}$. For example, the Liar sentence of level n is not true in the language of level n, but it is true in the language of level n+1; or the least indefinable ordinal in context c is not definable in context c, but is definable in context c'; or, token c of the Liar sentence does not truly say of itself that it is not true, but token c' of the same type does, etc.[13]

10.7 ... and its inadequacy

Since parameterisation is a generalisation of the Ramsey technique for solving the paradoxes of Group B, it is not surprising that it suffers from exactly those problems that we have already met with in Ramsey. First, there is, in general, no reason to suppose that the property φ is parameterised. Notoriously, some forty years after Tarski's proposal, there is no evidence to show that English is a hierarchy of metalanguages – indeed, there is evidence to show that it is not.[14] Nor is there any reason to suppose that the extensions of words like 'true' are context-dependent, in the way that, for example, 'past' is. Parsons (1974c) argues that some of the predicates in question may naturally be analysed in terms of quantifiers (just as Ramsey had suggested), and that quantifiers – or, better, their domains – are contextually determined. It is certainly true that the domains of some quantifiers are contextually determined ('everyone has had lunch'); but, equally, those of others are not ('every natural number is odd or even'), and Parsons gives no reason independent of the

---

[13] There is one subtlety worth noting here concerning Tarski's case. The argument that the Liar sentence at level n diagonalises out of the true sentences of the language of level n uses the T-scheme for level n. But this is valid only for sentences of level n−1. Hence, it may be thought, the argument fails since the Liar sentence is itself of level n. However, it is only half of the T-schema that is used, $T\langle\alpha\rangle \rightarrow \alpha$ (as may be seen by consulting the argument of 10.2) and if α is not a sentence of level n−1, it is not a true sentence of level n−1; hence, assuming classical (or at least intuitionist) principles concerning the conditional in the T-scheme – which all these solutions do – this half of the T-scheme is valid for all formulas, and not just those of level n−1.

[14] See Kripke (1975); Priest (1987), 1.5.

paradoxes to suppose that the quantifiers in question are context-dependent. Finally, the claim that different sentences of the same non-indexical type can have different truth values is patently *ad hoc*.

Next, and even assuming that it is correct to parameterise φ, it is normally difficult to find independent reasons as to why the parameter must change from c to c' to give consistency.[15] One might argue that the fact that δ is a diagonaliser demonstrates that $\neg\varphi(c,\delta(\Omega_c))$; and since $\delta(\Omega_c)$ is clearly φ in *some* sense or other, there must be a c' such that $\varphi(c',\delta(\Omega_c))$; but this does not establish that c is not c', which is just what is at issue.[16] Tarski obtains the fact that the Liar sentence at level n is true at level n+1, and not at level n, purely by definition: the way the hierarchy is defined, the sentence just is a sentence of level n+1, and not n. But, unless this is pure legerdemain, the question remains as to *why* things should be defined in this way.

Thirdly, and crucially, the parameterisation does not avoid the paradox, but merely relocates it. For we can define the logical sum of all the parameterised relations as follows: $\varphi^*(y)$ iff $\exists c\varphi(c,y)$ (y is true at some level, in some context, etc.). Let Ω^* be the corresponding totality. One now shows, by the standard argument, that the relevant δ is a diagonaliser with respect to φ^*, and hence that $\neg\varphi^*(\delta(\Omega^*))$. But, as usual, since $\delta(\Omega^*)$ has been shown to be φ in some respect, $\varphi^*(\delta(\Omega^*))$. For example, consider the claim that this sentence type is true in no context/tokening. Suppose that this is true in some context/tokening, then it follows that it is not true in that context/tokening. Hence it is true in no context/tokening. I.e., it is true in this context/tokening, and so in *some* context/tokening.[17]

There are a few ways that one might try to avoid this conclusion. The first (Burge, (1979), p. 192) is to claim that φ^* cannot be defined, since one cannot legitimately quantify into the parametric place. This is not only false, it is self-refuting (if one wishes to be consistent): even to explain the view that φ is parameterised one needs to say that things can be φ *in some respect*, and not others, and hence quantify into the parametric place.

Another possible suggestion is to attack the proof that δ is a diagonaliser with respect to φ^*. For example, in the case of Bi paradoxes, one might deny that $\exists y\, y \notin \Omega^*$, on the ground that everything is definable (definable in less than 99 words, etc.) relative to some parameter. Exactly how plausible this is, depends on the paradox and the understanding of the parameter. It may not be implausible to suppose, for example, that every natural number is definable in less than 99 words in some context. But it is most implausible to suppose that every ordinal is definable in some context, at least if a context is anything that

---

[15] Though this is not a problem for the tokening strategy.

[16] Criticisms of Burge along these lines can be found in Priest (1991b), p. 202; and of Barwise and Etchemendy in Priest (1993), section 7.

[17] For this criticism of the tokening strategy, see Hazen (1987).

is humanly accessible. In any case, this move will obviously not help with paradoxes in Group Bii.

A third possibility is to deny Closure, possibly on the ground that $\delta(\Omega^*)$ does not exist.[18] This, however, brings other, and familiar, problems. For the very solutions offered always provide the wherewithal to construct $\delta(\Omega^*)$ and demonstrate that it is φ in *some* sense. (For example, the least ordinal definable in no context is defined in *this* context; and 'this sentence is not true in any language in the Tarski hierarchy' is a true statement of *some* language.) But now we are faced with a choice: either this sense is one of the parameters, and hence we have a contradiction; or it is not, and since we had enumerated all possible parameters, this fact is not expressible at all: it follows that the solutions themselves are beyond the limit of the expressible.[19]

In 9.8 I observed that Russell's solution to the paradoxes merely reproduces the problem; and, more specifically, that it instantiates the Inclosure Schema. We are now in a position to see that exactly the same is true of parameterisation. In the Schema, take for φ the logical sum of the parameterised properties just defined, φ^*; take for Ω, Ω^*; let $\psi(x)$ be '$x=\Omega^*$ or for some c, $x=\Omega_c$'; and let δ be the appropriate diagonaliser. Then, clearly, $\psi(\Omega^*)$; and as we have just seen, if x is any ψ subset of Ω^*, $\delta(x)$ diagonalises out of x, but has the property φ^*. Hence, these quantities satisfy the Inclosure Schema. Again, parameterisation is less of a solution to the contradictions at the limit of thought than a manifestation of them.

Conclusion

In this chapter we have looked at a number of modern solutions to the paradoxes of Ramsey's Group B. As we have seen, they have the same general failings as did Ramsey's own solution. The other sorts of modern paradox-solution are aimed primarily at Ramsey's Group A. We will turn to these in the next chapter. As we will see there, they fare little better.

[18] This line is taken in Barwise and Etchemendy (1987).
[19] For a critique of Barwise and Etchemendy on these grounds, see Priest (1993).

11 Sets and classes

Introduction

As we have seen in the last two chapters, all the paradoxes of self-reference (including Berkeley's Paradox and the Fifth Antinomy) are inclosure contradictions; that is, they all instantiate the Inclosure Schema, which, to remind the reader, concerns properties φ and ψ, and a function δ such that:

(1) $\Omega = \{y;\ \varphi(y)\}$ exists and $\psi(\Omega)$ Existence
(2) if $x \subseteq \Omega$ and $\psi(x)$ (a) $\delta(x) \notin x$ Transcendence
                       (b) $\delta(x) \in \Omega$ Closure

One might depict these conditions as in Figure 1. The large oval is Ω, the set of all φ things. x is any subset of Ω satisfying ψ, and δ applied to this takes us out of x but into Ω. Applying δ to Ω takes us both into and out of Ω. This is somewhat difficult to depict(!). I have done so by taking $\delta(\Omega)$ to be a spot on the boundary of Ω.[1]

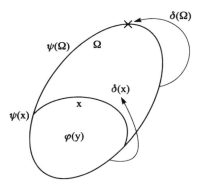

Figure 1

---

[1] There is something rather appropriate about this. The boundary is, in its own way, paradoxical, both joining and separating the inside and the outside.

Any solution to an inclosure paradox must deny one of the clauses in the Inclosure Schema. Since they all concern sets, a natural place to look for a solution is with modern set-theory. Modern set-theories were developed with an eye on, amongst other things, an avoidance of the paradoxes in Ramsey's Group A (10.1), where ψ is the universal condition, and so may be ignored. In the first part of the chapter we will consider how successful they are at this task. We will then widen the issue and see how successful they are at solving the broader class of inclosure paradoxes.

Modern set-theorists tend to waver between two *prima facie* rather different solutions to the set-theoretic paradoxes. The first was developed by Zermelo, and is embodied in Zermelo–Fraenkel set-theory (ZF); the second employs the notion of a proper class, and was developed by von Neumann. I will look at these in turn, starting with Zermelo.

11.1 Zermelo's solution: ZF

The solution advocated by Zermelo is an old and familiar one: deny that Ω exists, and so deny Existence. We have seen this stratagem employed by Aristotle (2.2), Kant (6.7), and Russell (9.6). As we saw in those places, it was not successful there. Let us see if it is more successful here.[2]

The set-theory in which this solution is embodied, ZF, is formulated in a first-order language with variables ranging over pure sets. The principles of set existence embodied in it do not allow us to show the existence of a set corresponding to an arbitrary condition. In general, we can show only the existence of the subset of any given set, comprising objects satisfying that condition. This principle is enunciated in Zermelo's *Aussonderung* Axiom, which he puts as follows:[3]

AXIOM III (Axiom of Separation). Whenever the propositional function $\psi(x)$ is definite for all elements of a set M, M possesses a subset M_ψ containing as elements precisely those elements x of M for which $\psi(x)$ is true.

This axiom, together with some more basic axioms of set existence (such as those for power-set and union) can be used to establish the existence of most sets standardly appealed to in mathematics. But, crucially, the absolutely infinite sets, such as V, On, and R, involved in the paradoxes of absolute infinity cannot be shown to exist. If they could be shown to exist, the paradoxical

---

[2] It is often noted that the pseudo-paradox of the barber is structurally similar to Russell's paradox (for example, Sainsbury (1988), p. 110). It is therefore interesting to note how this relates to the Inclosure Schema. Let $\varphi(y)$ be 'y is a person', so that Ω is the set of all people. Let $\psi(x)$ be 'x comprises the people of a group where those who do not shave themselves are shaved by a unique person'; and let $\delta(x)$ be that unique person. Closure is immediate, and if $\delta(x) \in x$ then $\delta(x)$ does and does not shave themself. Hence we have Transcendence. The paradox fails simply because $\psi(\Omega)$ is false, and so Existence fails, though not because Ω fails to exist.

[3] (1908); the translation is from van Heijenoort (1967), p. 202.

arguments would show the theory to be inconsistent.[4] It should be noted that there are other sets that cannot be shown to exist in ZF, whose existence is consistent with the axioms of ZF, for example, non-well-founded sets. Though the standard interpretation of ZF is the cumulative hierarchy (8.4), there are other interpretations in which there are non-well-founded sets.[5]

Of course, the mere fact that the contradiction-producing sets cannot be proved to exist hardly, of itself, solves the paradoxes. No one doubts that if the proof-theory of set-theory is sufficiently emasculated the theory can be rendered consistent. The question is what *reason* there is to suppose that the sets do not exist. If the set of all (pure) sets could be shown to exist, then the existence of all the paradox-producing sets would follow by the *Aussonderung* Axiom. The crucial question is, therefore, why one should suppose that V does not exist. Zermelo shows that there is no universal set as follows:[6]

THEOREM. Every set M possesses at least one subset M_0 that is not an element of M. *Proof* [If] M_0 is the subset of M that, in accordance with Axiom 3, contains all those elements of M for which it is not the case that $x \in x$, then M_0 cannot be an element of M. For either $M_0 \in M_0$ or not. In the first case, M_0 would contain an element $x=M_0$ for which $x \in x$, and this would contradict the definition of M_0. Thus, M_0 is surely not an element of M_0, and in consequence, if it were an element of M, would also have to be an element of M_0, which was just excluded.

As should be clear, this argument is exactly that which shows that ρ_x diagonalises out of x (9.1). As such, it is one side of the argument involved in Russell's paradox. It is hardly, therefore, an argument for a solution to the paradox. In particular, if there are independent grounds for the other half of the paradox (which is, in this case, delivered by the existence of V), we clearly have not resolved it. Moreover, there *are* just such grounds. According to Cantor's Domain Principle, which we saw to be quite justified (8.7, 8.8), any variable presupposes the existence of a domain of variation. Thus, since in ZF there are variables ranging over all sets, the theory presupposes the collection of all sets, V, even if this set cannot be shown to exist in the theory. Consistency has been purchased at the price of excluding from it a set whose existence it is forced to presuppose.

Moreover, this inadequacy is no mere theoretical inadequacy, but actually spills over into mathematical practice. For the absolute infinities that ZF cannot recognise as existing are exactly those required in the category-theoretic treatment of the category of all groups, etc. Hence, mathematical practice,

---

[4] For details of all this, see virtually any modern book on set-theory, for example, Fraenkel, Bar-Hillel, and Levy (1973), ch. 2, section 3.

[5] See, for example, Aczel (1988).

[6] (1908), Theorem 10; see van Heijenoort (1967), p. 203.

and not just the Domain Principle, requires the recognition of collections that do not exist in ZF.[7]

11.2 Intuitionist and modal ZF

A number of philosophers have noted, in effect, that ZF violates the Domain Principle.[8] Moore ((1990), pp. 170f.), puts the dilemma this poses very nicely as follows:

Our problem is, in a sense, *the* problem of the infinite. It rests on the fundamental paradox of the one and the many, that we both do and do not want to recognize unity in (truly) infinite multiplicity – or, more dramatically, that we seem both compelled to recognize unity there and compelled not to ... We seem forced to recognize the full hierarchy of Sets as something that we cannot – and *a fortiori* cannot be forced to – recognize as anything ... [W]hen we deny that there is a Set of all Sets ... we have a real sense of first getting into focus (seeing and acknowledging) what it is whose existence we are about to deny, then thinking, 'It is this, the totality of what we are talking about when we engage in set theory, our very subject matter conceived as a whole; *this* is what does not exist.' But this is absurd, in just the same way that it is absurd to grasp the (truly) infinite as that which is ungraspable. Yet this is what we seem to have done. We seem to have focused attention on the (truly) infinite as something that is not even there.

Many philosophers have offered solutions to the problem. By and large, they are all attempts to give substance to the idea that V is a potential infinity, but in a sense that does not trigger the Domain Principle.[9] The simplest suggestion to this effect is that classical quantification should be eschewed in ZF in favour of intuitionist quantification.[10] The thought here is that the intuitionist account of infinity is the closest modern analogue of Aristotle's account of potential infinity.[11] In particular, it gives a way of making sense of quantification over an infinite totality, which does not conceptualise that totality as completed. Hence, using intuitionist quantification should avoid the problem. It does not: as I noted in 8.8, the Domain Principle applies just as much to intuitionist quantifiers as it does to classical ones. Hence, intuitionist quantification presupposes a set (or species) of all sets. (And Zermelo's argument that there is no universal set is intuitionistically valid, too.)

---

[7] For more on this issue, see Priest (1987), 2.3.

[8] For example, Lear (1977), Parsons (1974a) (see the very end of the essay), Mayberry (1977) and Moore (1990).

[9] Moore's own solution is rather different. He simply denies the Domain Principle, though he does not address Cantor's arguments for it. I will make a further comment on his view in chapter 12 when I discuss saying and showing.

[10] Mayberry is sympathetic to an intuitionist approach, though the exact details of his approach are more complex. For further discussion, see Priest (1987), p. 47.

[11] See Dummett (1977), pp. 55ff.

A related suggestion (in virtue of the connection between Kripke semantics for Intuitionism and those for modal logics) seeks to cash out the notion of a potential infinity in terms of modal logic.[12] For example, let R_α be the collection of all sets of rank less than or equal to α. Let Σ be some set of ordinals that is cofinal with On (i.e., for every ordinal, there is a greater ordinal in Σ) and let the set $\{R_\alpha; \alpha \in \Sigma\}$ be the worlds of a Kripke model for a modal logic (where the interpretation of '$\in$' in R_α is the obvious one). World R_α accesses world R_β iff $\alpha \leq \beta$. Since this accessibility relation is a weak partial ordering, the modal propositional logic of the structure is S4. Let us call this structure $\mathscr{U}$.

$\mathscr{U}$ can be thought of as representing the cumulative hierarchy as 'growing'. At any stage (world) some initial section of the cumulative hierarchy has come into existence. There is no stage at which it has all come into existence; but every initial section has come into existence by some stage. Now if we suppose that quantifiers are given world-relative truth conditions (i.e., $\forall x \varphi$ is true in world R_α iff for all x in R_α x satisfies φ), then there is no quantifier whose range is the whole absolute infinity which is the cumulative hierarchy. The domain of quantification at each stage (R_α) is a member of the domain of any subsequent stage. If we think of the modal language as containing second-order (upper-case) variables ranging over sub-collections of the domain, then $\forall X \Diamond \exists y y = X$ is true, which is a nice way of expressing the thought that all sub-classes of the domain are potential sets.

A minor problem with this construction is that, as specified so far, there is no reason to suppose that the structure is a model of ZF. This can be rectified by supposing that for the base world, R_α, α is an inaccessible cardinal.[13] Indeed, if we suppose that every member of Σ is inaccessible, ZF is necessarily true. How plausible a fix this is depends on what one thinks of the reasonableness of postulating large cardinals, an issue which I shall not discuss here.

A more crucial objection is that the quantification over absolutely infinite sets has not disappeared: it has just gone underground (or perhaps overground if one thinks of the metalanguage as above the object language). For, as is clear from my explanation of the modal structure, to give this explanation, it is necessary to quantify over the absolute infinity of all ordinals. And the class of worlds $\{R_\alpha; \alpha \in \Sigma\}$ is a set which does not exist in ZF either. Thus the structure still presupposes non-existent sets. Nor does it help to

---

[12] The following is inspired by Parsons (1971), fn. 10, and Parsons (1974b). The material in the rest of this section and the next uses various technical notions not explained in the rest of the book, and can be skipped over without loss of continuity.

[13] It is not necessary to know what an inaccessible cardinal is here – for details, see Fraenkel, Bar-Hillel, and Levy (1973), section 6.3; all that it is necessary is to know is that if θ is inaccessible, R_θ is a model of ZF.

suggest that the problem is dissolved, since the illicit quantification is only 'metatheoretic'. For the metatheory spells out exactly our understanding of what is going on in the object theory. Thus this point is not so much a reply as a reinforcing of the objection: the object theory is incomplete since our understanding of it presupposes the existence of sets which it can prove not to exist![14]

11.3 Indefinitely extensible totalities

Another suggestion as to how to solve the problem attempts to outflank the Domain Principle by rejecting the determinacy of sense, on which the argument for the Principle rests. It is often suggested that statements that contain a vague predicate, such as 'is bald', have no determinate sense. The idea here is that predicates involved in statements about absolute infinities, such as 'is an ordinal' are vague in a similar way. Taken at face value, this suggestion does not look very promising. Being an ordinal does not come by degrees, as does being bald. Indeed, 'is an ordinal', like all mathematical predicates, is a paradigm of a crisp predicate. Rather, the thought has to be that the cut-off point for being an ordinal is indefinite, just as the cut-off point for being bald is. Dummett ((1991), pp. 316f.) puts the idea nicely:

Better than describing the intuitive concept of ordinal number as having a hazy extension is to describe it as having an increasing sequence of extensions: what is hazy is the length of the sequence, which vanishes into the indiscernible distance. The intuitive concept of ordinal number, like that of cardinal number and set, is an indefinitely extensible one.

So far, so good; but the onus is now on someone who holds this position to explain the things we take to be true about ordinals, sets, and other absolute infinities. Given that we are dealing with variable extensions, and the notion of being an ordinal or a set is not itself vague, the only obvious suggestion is that the definite truths are those that are true however the extensions of the relevant notions are fixed; whilst the statements of indefinite truth value are those that may vary from fixture to fixture. But how to make this thought precise? The natural way of cashing out the idea is precisely as the model $\mathcal{U}$ that we met in the previous section: we now think of each possible world as one of the ways of fixing extensions. The determinate truths are exactly those that are necessarily true at the base world.

It follows that the suggestion in question is little better than the modal one, and suffers from the same major problem. Even to conceptualise how the

---

[14] Lear (1977) gives a construction similar to $\mathcal{U}$, except that he gives intuitionist truth conditions for the logical constants. In particular, a universal quantifier over all sets is effectively involved in the truth conditions of the universal quantifier. His construction therefore faces the same objection.

model is supposed to work we have to suppose a totality of all ordinals, or sets, and quantifiers that range over them. Hence we seem to be back with the original problem.

Could we avoid it by interpreting the metalinguistic machinery as vague in the same way? Possibly, but it is then dubious that it could serve the explanatory function for which it was proposed: the very sense of the construction is drawn from the contrast between the absolute totality and its fragments. If the absolute totality is itself variable, the fragments become otiose. In any case, the suggestion to interpret the metatheoretic machinery in this way would be disingenuous: this is not the way that the model was intended. Its intent was precisely to show how partial fragments could approximate an absolute whole. And one must have a conception of an absolute whole for this idea to make sense. As Kant saw so well, given a notion like that of set or ordinal, reason forces us to conceive of the totality of all things satisfying it. Totalising is part of our conceptual machinery – like it or not.

Despite the fact that I have used a quotation from Dummett to illustrate the suggestion I have been discussing, his view of the matter is rather different. It is explained in (1991) pp. 313–19. The purpose of this passage is to argue that quantification over all infinite totalities, including, but not exclusively, absolutely infinite ones, must be intuitionist. As he puts it, the point is to reject the claim that (p. 313):

given any domain of mathematical objects, quantification over it can be interpreted classically, so that statements formed by means of such quantification will be determinately either true or false, and hence obey classical logic.

As such, he does not see indefinitely extensible totalities as rendering indeterminate (undetermined) the *senses* of claims that quantify over them. Rather, it is their *truth values* which may be indeterminate (neither true nor false). Indeed, the whole point of giving intuitionist truth conditions for the quantifiers is precisely to determine *the* appropriate sense of quantified statements.

Neither does the fact that a concept is indefinitely extensible imply that the things satisfying it do not form a totality. According to Dummett (p. 318) the natural and real numbers – neither of them absolute infinities – are both indefinitely extensible. Rather, the point is that quantification over such totalities is not guaranteed to yield a classical truth value. As he puts it (p. 316):

What the paradoxes [of absolute infinity] revealed was not the existence of concepts with inconsistent extensions, but of what may be called indefinitely extensible concepts. The concept of an ordinal number is a prototypical example. The Burali–Forti paradox ensures that no definite totality comprises everything intuitively recognisable as an ordinal number, where a definite totality is one quantification over which always yields a statement determinately true or false.

For these reasons, his views do not resolve the present problem, as he himself acknowledges.[15]

11.4 Von Neumann and proper classes

Let us now turn to the second orthodox solution to the set-theoretic paradoxes. Sensing the inadequacy of ZF, von Neumann decided to add machinery that could express the collections presupposed by, but absent from, ZF. Von Neumann divided all collections into two categories: I-objects and II-objects. I-objects are those objects that can occur truly on the left-hand side of statements of the form $x \in y$. II-objects are those objects that can occur truly on the right-hand side of such statements. It should be noted that the collections of I-objects and II-objects are not mutually exclusive; there can be I-II objects. I-objects can be thought of as the sets of ZF – and are now usually called 'sets'. II-objects can be thought of as sub-collections of the domain of sets – and are now called 'classes'. II-objects that are not I-objects – now usually called 'proper classes' – are therefore those collections of sets which are not themselves in the domain of quantification of ZF. Thus, the sets that do not exist in ZF, such as R, On, and V, are proper classes (as the same arguments that show them not to exist in ZF demonstrate).

I should note that this description, though correct, is, strictly speaking, anachronistic for three reasons. The first is that von Neumann took I-objects to include not only sets but also urelements (non-sets); but this makes no difference here. The second is that von Neumann took I-objects and II-objects to be the characteristic functions of collections, rather than the collections themselves. However, in virtue of the interdefinability of collections and their characteristic functions, this is of no importance. The third is that von Neumann did not, himself, identify I-objects with the sets of ZF and II-objects with sub-collections of this domain. Rather, the identification came to be natural at a later time in virtue of results showing that these notions were technically equivalent.[16]

Now, a proper class cannot, by definition, be a member of anything. But this does not give a criterion for when a collection, specified by some condition, is a proper class. The criterion that von Neumann proposed, and that is now standard, is that a class is proper when it is at least as big as (and therefore the same size as) V. This is encapsulated in his Axiom IV.2:[17]

---

[15] 'Abandoning classical logic is not, indeed, sufficient by itself to preserve us from contradiction if we maintain the same assumptions as before; but, when we do not conceive ourselves to be quantifying over a fully determinate totality, we shall have no motive to do so' (P. 316, fn.).

[16] See Fraenkel, Bar-Hillel, and Levy (1973), p. 326.

[17] Von Neumann (1925); the translation is taken from van Heijenoort (1967), p. 400; I have modified the notation.

A II-object a is not a I-II-object if and only if there is a [function] b such that for every I-object x there exists a y for which both y $\in$ a and b(y)=x.

This is known as the Limitation of Size Doctrine. (For an account of its history see Hallett (1984).) In virtue of it, the distinction between sets and proper classes can be seen as a more rigorous form of Cantor's distinction between consistent and inconsistent multiplicities (as I noted in 8.6).

Prima facie, von Neumann's set-theory gives a rather different solution to the set-theoretic paradoxes than does Zermelo's. Since the collections V, On, R, etc., all exist as proper classes, Existence is satisfied. In each case, however, Closure fails: applying the relevant diagonaliser produces a proper class. (In the case of Burali-Forti's paradox and Mirimanoff's paradox $\delta(\Omega) = \Omega$.) And hence $\delta(\Omega)$ is not in Ω since it is not in anything.

What blocks the paradoxes is, then, precisely that it is impossible for a proper class to be a member of something. As von Neumann puts it (ibid., p. 401):

There are ... some quite essential differences [between Zermelo's system and mine]. That we speak of 'functions' rather than 'sets' is no doubt a superficial difference; it is essential, however, that the present set theory deals with sets (or 'functions') that are 'too big', namely those II-objects that are not I-II-objects. Rather than being completely prohibited, they are declared incapable of being ... [members] (they are not I-objects!). This suffices to avoid the antinomies.

This solution is reminiscent of Kant's Solution 2 (6.7): the limit exists, but the operation that gives contradiction, viz., membership of something or other, cannot be applied.

The crucial question now would seem to be whether there are any grounds, except definitional legerdemain, for supposing that there is nothing for proper classes to be members of. As we have just seen, von Neumann calls the collections 'too big'; but it is difficult to see why size, as such, should have anything to do with being a unity, i.e., the possibility of being a member (see 8.6). Indeed, to refer to a collection, even if it is a proper class, is, in a certain sense, to treat it as an entity, a unity; *a fortiori*, if one quantifies over it. Any collection (set or class) must, therefore, be a candidate for membership.[18]

---

[18] Lewis (1991) achieves some of the effects of classes with the device of plural quantifiers ranging over sets. It might be thought that this would resolve the problem, since in this case we no longer have to quantify over classes themselves, and so treat them as entities. It has been argued by Resnik (1988) that plural quantification over sets is equivalent to simple quantification over classes. If this is so, then nothing is gained by this move. In fact, I doubt that it is so. However, avoiding this Scylla drives the suggestion straight back into Charybdis in the present context. Just because plural quantification does not recognise classes as entities, Lewisian set-theory is no advance on ordinary ZF as far as the present concerns go: the quantifiers (singular and plural) range over a totality which in no sense exists.

This is all bad news; but worse is to come. Consider the paradoxes of set-theory as they appear *in propria persona* in von Neumann's theory. Take the Burali-Forti paradox as an example. Instead of considering the collection of sets that are ordinals, we can consider the collection of classes that are ordinals (which is, intuitively, On ∪ {On}), and try to run the paradox for this. When we do so, we find that it fails, and for exactly the same reason that it fails in ZF: there is no such collection. (If there were, On would be a member of it.) Similar remarks apply to Russell's paradox and Mirimanoff's: neither the collection of pure classes, nor the collection of well-founded classes exists. Von Neumann's solution is ultimately the same as Zermelo's.

Unsurprisingly, then, it shares with Zermelo's the same fundamental problem. Note that the variables of von Neumann's theory range over the domain of all collections (I-objects and II-objects). The totality of all collections is not, therefore, V (the collection of all sets), but V′, the collections of all sets and classes. And it is this, and similar collections, whose existence cannot be consistently admitted in von Neumann's theory. Hence, the theory violates the Domain Principle just as much as Zermelo's. (Sometimes, von Neumann's theory is represented as a two-sorted theory with different kinds of variables ranging over I-objects and II-objects. This makes no essential difference to the point being made: the Domain Principle is violated by the variables ranging over II-objects.) And, as for ZF, this inadequacy shows itself in the fact that von Neumann's theory does not provide an adequate basis for category theory. One might, for example, be able to form the category of all sets; but one cannot form the category of all classes.[19]

It might be thought that this problem could be solved by supposing that proper classes can be members of some sort of collections that bear the same relationship to them as they do to sets, hyper-classes.[20] But this just repeats the problem at the next higher level. An obvious thought is to iterate this construction into a hierarchy so that a collection of any order can be a member of something at the next higher level. This gives us, in effect, the set-theory of Ackermann,[21] which can be thought of as iterating this procedure to some transfinite ordinal.[22] A little thought shows that this construction does not solve the problem either, but, again, merely transfers it. For in such a theory there are variables that range over all the collections in the hierarchy; yet on pain of the usual contradiction, the domain of this variation can be proved not to exist in the theory.

---

[19] Or, for that matter, even the functor category of the category of all sets – see Priest (1987), p. 42.

[20] See Fraenkel, Bar-Hillel, and Levy (1973), p. 142.

[21] Ibid., pp. 148ff.

[22] See Grewe (1969).

However one works out the details, all the solutions we have discussed ultimately take the Aristotelian way out. The limit (the totality of *all* collections countenanced by the theory) is said not to exist; and hence the Domain Principle is violated.[23]

11.5 The principle of uniform solution

We have seen that the standard solutions to the set-theoretic paradoxes do not fare well even in that limited domain for which they were intended. But once we take into account the broader canvas, the picture is even bleaker.

If two paradoxes are of different kinds, it is reasonable to expect them to have different kinds of solution; on the other hand, if two paradoxes are of the same kind, then it is reasonable to expect them to have the same kind of solution. Generalising: it is natural to expect all the paradoxes of a single family to have a single kind of solution. Any solution that can handle only some members of the family is bound to appear not to have got to grips with the fundamental issue.[24] Let us call this the Principle of Uniform Solution (PUS[25]): same kind of paradox, same kind of solution.

The PUS puts a lot of weight on the notion of *kind*. To convince ourselves that two paradoxes are of the same kind we must convince ourselves (a) that there is a structure that is common to the paradoxes; and (b) that this structure is responsible for the contradictions. Condition (b) is both essential and difficult to articulate. I have done what I can for the case at hand in 9.5.

Once over this hurdle, it is not difficult to apply the PUS and demonstrate that orthodox solutions to the set-theoretic paradoxes are inadequate. For, as is clear from 9.2, the Fifth Antinomy is a paradox of exactly the same kind as Burali-Forti, etc. Ramsey, it is true, would not have classed the paradox as a Group A paradox, since it contains the word 'thought'. But, as I have already argued (10.1), this is a superficial criterion; and it is quite clear that, structurally, this paradox belongs with the paradoxes of absolute infinity. Yet the orthodox solutions to the set-theoretic paradoxes get no purchase on it. It does no good to point out that the limit of thoughts, T, does not exist. For notoriously we can, in some sense, have a thought whose content is a non-existent object, as I pointed out in 6.9. Nor does it do any good to claim that T is a

---

[23] A somewhat different kind of solution is suggested by Maddy (1988). She constructs a theory of classes on top of a theory of sets by applying the techniques of Kripke (1975), to obtain proper classes which may be members of proper classes. The paradoxes are avoided since the logic of proper classes is three-valued. The problem with this construction is the same as that with Kripke's itself. It remains consistent only because certain legitimate – indeed, necessary – notions are not expressible in the theory. Exclusion negation, or equivalently, genuine complementation, cannot be expressed, or Russell's paradox would reappear.

[24] A similar point about solutions to intensional paradoxes is made in Priest (1991b).

[25] Sorry about that.

proper class. For even if proper classes cannot be members of other classes, it is clear that we can still think of them. Each proposal is therefore an *ignoratio*.

11.6 ... and inclosure paradoxes

We have just seen that the PUS shows that the orthodox solutions to the set-theoretic paradoxes are a failure, even for paradoxes concerning the limit of the iterable. But another application has much more profound consequences.

As we have seen (9.6), Russell held that all the paradoxes of self-reference belong to a single family and, consequently, have a single solution: a strict application of the theory of orders. Ramsey, as we have also seen, divided the paradoxes into two distinct families, and hence felt free (by the PUS) to offer a different kind of solution for each family (10.4). With hardly an exception, logicians since Ramsey have accepted that there are two distinct families here; thus, virtually all post-Ramsey solutions have been directed at either Ramsey's Group A or his Group B.

But Russell's instinct was right. All the traditional paradoxes of self-reference are inclosure contradictions. That is, the structure described in the Inclosure Schema explains all of these contradictions. Hence, by the PUS, one should be satisfied with nothing less than a unified solution to the family. Does any extant solution provide this?

I discussed the contemporary solutions to paradoxes of Group B in 10.6, 10.7. These have no application to the paradoxes of Group A at all: they are not concerned with totalities, absolutely infinite or otherwise. Similarly, orthodox solutions to the set-theoretic paradoxes do not work for paradoxes of Group B. Whether or not they can be applied to Bii paradoxes (the Liar, etc.) at all depends on what we take truth bearers to be: if they are propositions then the inclosures (such as Tr) are, presumably, absolute infinities; so the existence and nature of such infinities may be relevant; if truth bearers are sentences then the inclosures are simply countable; so the behaviour of absolute infinities is irrelevant. But in any case, for Bi paradoxes (the definability paradoxes) the inclosures are always countable (such as DOn) or finite (such as DN_{99}), and so are *guaranteed to exist* by the Limitation of Size Doctrine.

Hence, no single post-Ramsey solution applies to all the inclosure contradictions. Even if the orthodox solutions worked where they were designed to (which they do not, as we have seen), this observation would be sufficient, on its own, to sink them.

11.7 Unified theories

Even had Ramsey been right, and the paradoxes of Groups A and B been distinct, contemporary attitudes to the two families and their solutions would hardly be happy. It is not sufficient to have a solution to the paradoxes of each of the two groups if these two solutions are incompatible. The two most important theories of modern physics, Quantum Theory and the General Theory of Relativity, however good each is in its own domain, appear to be incompatible with each other. Hence, at least one (and probably both) are false. Physicists realise this, and the search is on for an adequate unified theory, Relativistic Quantum Mechanics, which synthesises the strengths of both.[26]

Logicians have tended to give little thought to the compatibility of orthodox solutions to the paradoxes of Groups A and B. But suppose we adopt either Zermelo's or von Neumann's solution to the paradoxes of Group A. What are we to say about the paradoxes of Group B? One might point out that the notions of truth, etc., do not occur in the language of set-theory, and hence that the paradoxes do not arise. But this is not to solve the problem; it is just to turn one's back on it. In fact, set-theorists do operate with the notions of truth, definability, etc.: these are an integral aspect of the model-theoretic investigation of set-theory. In such a context the notions are usually thought of as relegated to a 'metatheory'. To the extent that this is a solution to the semantic paradoxes at all, it is a Tarskian one, and so buys in to the technique of parameterisation which, as we have seen (10.7), is inadequate. But the crucial point in the present context is that this solution is incompatible with the solution to the set-theoretic paradoxes. For, in the metatheory, the domain of quantification, which the object theory tells us does not exist, is postulated as existing!

The situation in the foundations of logic is therefore quite as chronic as that in the foundations of physics. But unlike physicists, logicians have ignored the problem; they live with it, instead, by some sort of professional schizophrenia.[27]

11.8 Curry paradoxes

Although it is a digression, this would seem to be the right place to say a word about another kind of paradox that is related to some of the paradoxes I have been discussing, and which also cuts across Ramsey's division: Curry paradoxes. Some of the paradoxes I have discussed proceed by establishing a sentence of the form $\alpha \leftrightarrow \neg\alpha$. (All the paradoxes in Group Bii do this, and some of the paradoxes in Group A, notably Russell's, but not the paradoxes in Bi or the other paradoxes in group A.) For each paradox of this kind, we can form a new paradox by replacing $\neg\alpha$ uniformly with $\alpha \rightarrow \beta$, where β is an arbitrary formula; or, more simply, with $\alpha \rightarrow \bot$, where $\bot$ is some logical constant entailing everything. Using the Absorption Principle $(\alpha \rightarrow (\alpha \rightarrow \beta) \vdash \alpha \rightarrow \beta)$ we can then infer $\alpha \rightarrow \bot$, and hence α, and hence $\bot$. (See Priest (1987), 6.2.)

---

[26] See Davies (1984), pp. 142ff.; see also Joseph (1980).
[27] These issues are discussed further in Priest (1987), 2.4, 2.5 and Mayberry (1977).

Do such paradoxes fit the Inclosure Schema? Yes and no, depending on what $\rightarrow$ is. If it is a material conditional then, in most logics, $\alpha \rightarrow \perp$ is logically equivalent to $\neg\alpha$, and so the curried version of each paradox is essentially the same as the uncurried form. If, on the other hand, $\rightarrow$ is a non-material conditional (for example, a strict conditional), then $\alpha \rightarrow \perp$ and $\neg\alpha$ are quite different notions. (Evaluating the truth of the first at a world requires a consideration of what is happening at other worlds; evaluating the truth of the second does not.) In this case, the curried versions of the paradoxes belong to a quite different family. Such paradoxes do not involve negation and, *a fortiori*, contradiction. They therefore have nothing to do with contradictions at the limits of thought.

Conclusion

To return from the digression: In the last two chapters we have, *inter alia*, completed a review of all main contemporary solutions to inclosure contradictions. As we have seen, the solutions are not adequate, even in the limited domains for which they were generally designed. Moreover, not only do they tend to be incompatible, but the piecemeal approach initiated by Ramsey flies in the face of the PUS and the fact that all such paradoxes instantiate a single underlying structure: the Inclosure Schema. The only satisfactory uniform approach to all these paradoxes is the dialetheic one, which takes the paradoxical contradictions to be exactly what they appear to be. The limits of thought which are the inclosures are truly contradictory objects.[28]

The notion of an inclosure plays a central role in the paradoxes of self-reference. But it would be a mistake to suppose that the relevance of this notion is restricted to that area. Another area in which it plays an important role is the philosophy of language. Why this is so, is an issue that will occupy us in the next, and final, part of the book. That part is not concerned with logical technicalities in the way that much of the present part of the book has been (many readers will be relieved to hear). However, before we leave the technicalities behind, and for the sake of interest, I will give a few details of the model theory of inclosures. These will be of interest only to logicians, and, strictly speaking, constitute a digression from the main purpose of the book. Hence I relegate them to an appendix, which can safely be omitted.

---

[28] Interestingly enough, Hegel held just this view of the Liar paradox. See his remarks on Eubulides in volume 1 of his *Lectures on the History of Philosophy*.

Technical appendix

Introduction

The notion of an inclosure is obviously a strange one. Since its introduction in 9.4, we have seen various arguments to the effect that there are inclosures. However, since the notion is an inconsistent one, one might doubt that the arguments work, simply because the notion is incoherent in some sense. The purpose of this technical appendix is to assuage some of these doubts.

One way to show a notion to be coherent is to produce models of it. This is precisely the strategy I will adopt here. I will show that there are models, in the standard sense of model-theory, of the inclosure conditions. Since the conditions are inconsistent, these are not models of classical or intuitionist logic. They are, and have to be, models of a paraconsistent logic.

There are many paraconsistent logics.[1] It will suffice for my purposes to take the simplest of these, the system LP of Priest (1987), chapter 5. In particular, I will interpret the $\rightarrow$ in the inclosure conditions as a simple material (and, in paraconsistent contexts, non-detachable) conditional. The task of showing that the inclosure conditions have non-trivial models where the conditional is a relevant, or at least, detachable, one is more complex, and still needs to be undertaken. (That this can be done successfully, I have little doubt.)

The techniques used to produce the models in question were initiated by Bob Meyer. His original work is still unpublished, though it is abstracted in (1976). Perhaps the clearest presentation of the techniques is in Meyer and Mortensen (1984). They involve, essentially, taking a model of a theory and collapsing it to produce an inconsistent model. In the case of Meyer and Mortensen, the model collapsed is the standard model of arithmetic, and the collapsed models are non-standard, finite models.

In what follows I will briefly describe the logic LP. I will then state the relevant collapsing theorem.[2] Finally, I will apply this to construct models of

---

[1] For a review of them see Priest, Routley, and Norman (1989), ch. 5.

[2] This is more general than the Meyer collapse in one sense, since it applies to arbitrary models and equivalence relations. However, the Meyer collapse is stronger in another sense, since it handles not only extensional connectives, but also a non-extensional conditional.

the inclosure conditions. I will make no attempt to make the details intelligible to non-logicians, and this appendix can be skipped by the general reader without loss.[3]

1   Semantics of LP

The language of LP is a first-order language with connectives $\neg$ and $\wedge$, and quantifier $\forall$. $\exists$ and $\vee$ are defined in the usual way. Note that $\varphi \rightarrow \psi$ is defined as $\neg\varphi \vee \psi$. There are constants and predicates, including the identity predicate. In principle, there is no problem about the language containing function symbols. However, the Collapsing Lemma, in the form that we will need it, fails if the language contains them. Hence, we will assume that they are not present. This is no loss, as we will see.

An interpretation, $\mathcal{U}$, for the language is a pair $\langle D,I \rangle$, where D is the non-empty domain of quantification; I is a function which maps each individual constant into D and each n-place predicate, P, into a pair $\langle I^+(P), I^-(P) \rangle$, where $I^+(P) \cup I^-(P) = D^n$. (Note that $I^+(P) \cap I^-(P)$ may be non-empty.) I will call the members of the pair the positive and negative extensions of P, respectively. For identity to have the right properties we also require that $I^+(=) = \{\langle x,x \rangle; x \in D\}$. The *language of* $\mathcal{U}$ is the language augmented by a set of individual constants, one for each member of D. For simplicity we take the set to be D itself, and specify that for all $d \in D$ $I(d) = d$.

Every formula in the language of $\mathcal{U}$, φ, is now assigned a truth value, $v(\varphi)$, in the set $\{\{1\},\{0\},\{1,0\}\}$ by the following recursive clauses.

$$1 \in v(Pt_1 \ldots t_n) \Leftrightarrow \langle I(t_1) \ldots I(t_n) \rangle \in I^+(P)$$
$$0 \in v(Pt_1 \ldots t_n) \Leftrightarrow \langle I(t_1) \ldots I(t_n) \rangle \in I^-(P)$$

$$1 \in v(\neg\varphi) \Leftrightarrow 0 \in (v)$$
$$0 \in v(\neg\varphi) \Leftrightarrow 1 \in v(\varphi)$$

$$1 \in v(\varphi \wedge \psi) \Leftrightarrow 1 \in v(\varphi) \text{ and } 1 \in v(\psi)$$
$$0 \in v(\varphi \wedge \psi) \Leftrightarrow 0 \in v(\varphi) \text{ or } 0 \in v(\psi)$$

$$1 \in v(\forall x\varphi) \Leftrightarrow \text{ for all } d \in D \ 1 \in v(\varphi(x/d))$$
$$0 \in v(\forall x\varphi) \Leftrightarrow \text{ some } d \in D \ 0 \in v(\varphi(x/d))$$

Where $\varphi(x/d)$ denotes φ with all free occurrence of 'x' replaced by 'd'.

Let $\mathcal{U} = \langle D,I \rangle$ be an interpretation; then $\mathcal{U}$ is a *model* for φ ($\mathcal{U} \models \varphi$) iff φ is true in $\mathcal{U}$, i.e., $1 \in v(\varphi)$. The set of sentences in the language of $\mathcal{U}$ true in $\mathcal{U}$ is called the *theory* of $\mathcal{U}$.

---

[3] The material in this chapter is part of Priest (1992).

A couple of facts about LP are worth noting. The first is that every LP interpretation is a model of every truth of classical first-order logic (with identity).[4] (The consequence relations of LP and classical logic are, of course, different.) The second is that any standard classical interpretation is iso-morphic to an LP interpretation in which all atomic formulas (and so all formulas) take the value {0} or {1}. Consequently I will simply identify such interpretations. Thus, models of classical theories are just special cases of LP models.

2   The collapsing lemma

The main technical result we will need is the Collapsing Lemma. Let us now turn to this. Let $\mathcal{U}$ be any interpretation with domain D, and let $\sim$ be any equivalence relation on D. If $d \in D$, let [d] be the equivalence class of d under $\sim$. Define a new interpretation, $\mathcal{U}^{\sim}$, whose domain is {[d]; $d \in D$}. If c is a constant that denotes d in $\mathcal{U}$, it denotes [d] in $\mathcal{U}^{\sim}$. If P is an n-place predicate then $\langle X_1 \ldots X_n \rangle$ is in its positive [negative] extension in $\mathcal{U}^{\sim}$ iff $\exists x_1 \in X_1 \ldots \exists x_n \in X_n$ such that $\langle x_1 \ldots x_n \rangle$ is in the positive [negative] extension of P in $\mathcal{U}$. What $\mathcal{U}^{\sim}$ does, in effect, is simply identify all the members of D in any one equivalence class, forming a composite individual with all the properties of its components. I can now state the:

Collapsing Lemma

Let φ be any formula; let v be 1 or 0. Then if v is in the value of φ in $\mathcal{U}$, it is in its value in $\mathcal{U}^{\sim}$.

In other words, when $\mathcal{U}$ is collapsed into $\mathcal{U}^{\sim}$, formulas never lose truth values: they can only gain them. The Collapsing Lemma is the ultimate down-ward Loewenheim–Skolem Theorem. If theory T has a model, $\mathcal{U}$, then T has a model of *every* cardinality less than that of $\mathcal{U}$ (wherein, note, = has its standard positive extension). To obtain a model of cardinality κ (less than that of $\mathcal{U}$) we simply choose an equivalence relation on the domain of $\mathcal{U}$ that has κ equivalence classes. (A moment's thought shows that there is always such an equivalence relation.) The result then follows by the Collapsing Lemma.

I will not prove the Collapsing Lemma here. The proof is by a straightfor-ward induction over the complexity of formulas, and can be found in Priest (1991c).[5] It should be noted that if the language were to contain function symbols the proof would not work: there is no way of defining the interpreta-

---

[4] See Priest (1987), p. 98.
[5] A similar result is proved in Dunn (1979).

tions of the function symbols in $\mathscr{U}^\sim$ to ensure that if term t denotes d in $\mathscr{U}$, it denotes [d] in $\mathscr{U}^\sim$, which is required for the rest of the proof.[6]

Now, let $\mathscr{U}$ be an LP interpretation with at least a two-membered domain. Let $\sim$ be any equivalence relation on the domain of $\mathscr{U}$, and let $\mathscr{U}^\sim$ be the interpretation constructed by collapsing. T and $T^\sim$ are the theories of $\mathscr{U}$ and $\mathscr{U}^\sim$, respectively. Then the Collapsing Lemma assures us that $T \subseteq T^\sim$. Of course, $T^\sim$ may properly extend T. If $\sim$ is anything other than the trivial equivalence relation that relates every object of the domain only to itself, there will be distinct objects, a and b, such that $a = b \in T^\sim$. $T^\sim$ will therefore be inconsistent, even if T is not. On the other hand, provided that $\sim$ is not the trivial equivalence relation that relates every object to every other, there will be distinct objects, a and b, such that $a = b \notin T^\sim$. Hence $T^\sim$ will be non-trivial.

3   A first model of inclosure

The Collapsing Lemma can be applied to the standard and non-standard models of classical arithmetic to produce a variety of non-standard models. These can be of various kinds and, as yet, a complete taxonomy is not known. However, the conditions we are interested in are set-theoretic rather than arithmetic. So we will collapse, instead, models of set-theory and, in particular, models of ZF. Hence, we will take our language to contain, apart from the identity predicate, a single binary predicate, $\in$.

Before we construct the models, let us rework the inclosure conditions slightly. These are, recall:

(1) $\Omega = \{y; \; \varphi(y)\}$ exists and $\psi(\Omega)$ Existence
(2)   if $x \subseteq \Omega$ and $\psi(x)$ (a) $\delta(x) \notin x$ Transcendence
                                         (b) $\delta(x) \in \Omega$ Closure

To keep things simple, we will suppose that $\psi(x)$ is '$x = x$', and is therefore always trivially satisfied. Thus, in effect, we are modelling not only the Inclosure Schema, but Russell's schema. Next, in every model, we will choose some object, α, in its domain and take $\varphi(y)$ to be '$y \in \alpha$'. Hence Ω will just be α, and Existence will be trivially satisfied; we may therefore ignore it.

Finally, we must eliminate function symbols, since we cannot guarantee collapse if these are present. The function symbol δ in Transcendence and Closure can be replaced, in a standard way, with a functional relation symbol. If we replace it in this way, these conditions become:

(i) $\forall x \exists! y Dxy$

---

[6] If, however, $\sim$ is a congruence relation with respect to the functions which are the denotations in $\mathscr{U}$ of the function symbols we can define the denotations of the function symbols in $\mathscr{U}^\sim$ in the natural way, and this delivers the necessary result. In this way a stronger form of the Collapsing Lemma can be proved.

(ii) $\forall x \forall y (x \subseteq \Omega \land Dxy \rightarrow y \notin x)$

(iii) $\forall x \forall y (x \subseteq \Omega \land Dxy \rightarrow y \in \Omega)$

(where '!' has its usual meaning here). Hence we need to find a model of these three conditions.

Let $\mathcal{U}$ be any (classical) model of ZF with domain S. Let On(x) be the formula of ZF that expresses the claim that x is an ordinal. I will refer to anything that satisfies On(x) in $\mathcal{U}$ as an ordinal; and when I refer to the ordering of these, I will mean simply the ordering in $\mathcal{U}$. We will be concerned with equivalence relations on S that leave all non-ordinals alone, but identify certain ordinals.

Let Dxy be log(x,y), the formula of ZF expressing the fact that y is the least ordinal greater than every ordinal in x. Let Ω be any ordinal, α. Then (i), (ii) are true in every model of ZF, and hence any collapsed model. (For (i) recall that every *set* of ordinals is bounded above.) We therefore need only choose an equivalence relation that makes (iii) true in the collapsed model.

Let $\sim$ be the equivalence relation that identifies every ordinal greater than α with α. Let c and d be any members of S, and let $\theta(y)$ be:

$$c \subseteq \Omega \land \log(c, y) \rightarrow y \in \Omega$$

If d is not an ordinal then $\neg \log(c,d)$ is true in $\mathcal{U}$. Hence $\theta(d)$ is true in $\mathcal{U}$, and hence $\mathcal{U}^{\sim}$. If d is an ordinal $< \alpha$ then $d \in \Omega$ is true in $\mathcal{U}$, and so $\mathcal{U}^{\sim}$. If d is an ordinal $\geq \alpha$ then for some ordinal β, $d \in \beta$ is true in $\mathcal{U}$, so $d \in \Omega$ is true in $\mathcal{U}^{\sim}$ (since α has been identified with β). Hence, $\forall y \theta(y)$ is true in $\mathcal{U}^{\sim}$; (iii) follows. It is worth noting that in $\mathcal{U}^{\sim}$, Ω is exactly the set of all ordinals.

4   More complex models

The model $\mathcal{U}^{\sim}$ of the last section thinks that any two ordinals greater than α are the same (and different). Hence, the ordinal structure is rather boring past α. There are much more interesting models, however.

For one of these, let us say that if $\sim$ identifies α and $\alpha + 1$ then α is a *fixed point* for $\sim$. Now let everything be as before, except that $\sim$ is an equivalence relation with α as a fixed point. Again, we need to check only condition (iii). To verify this, there are four cases. If d is not an ordinal, then $\theta(d)$ is true in $\mathcal{U}^{\sim}$, as before. If d is an ordinal $< \alpha$ then $d \in \Omega$ is true in $\mathcal{U}$. And hence $\theta(d)$ is true in $\mathcal{U}$, and so $\mathcal{U}^{\sim}$. If d is α then, since α and $\alpha + 1$ have been identified and $\alpha \in \alpha + 1$ in $\mathcal{U}$, $d \in \Omega$ is true in $\mathcal{U}^{\sim}$, and so $\theta(d)$ is. Finally, suppose that d is an ordinal $\geq \alpha + 1$. If x is a subset of α in $\mathcal{U}$, then the least ordinal greater than every member of x must be no greater than α. Hence, the negation of the antecedent of $\theta(d)$ is true in $\mathcal{U}$; hence $\theta(d)$ is true in $\mathcal{U}$, and so in $\mathcal{U}^{\sim}$. (iii) therefore holds.

The collapse that we have just been looking at shows that things do not have to degenerate at the limit, Ω: there can be consistency beyond it. For example, if $\beta > \alpha + 1$ then $\beta \in \Omega$ is not true in $\mathcal{U}^\sim$. There can also be limits beyond limits. If α and β are fixed points of $\sim$ (where $\beta > \alpha + 1$), then taking $x \in \alpha$ and $x \in \beta$ for φ will both satisfy the inclosure conditions.

The equivalence relations considered so far have been quite particular, but we can show that Russell's schema can be modelled given *any* non-trivial equivalence relation on the ordinals. If $\sim$ is any such relation there are some α and β with $\alpha < \beta$ such that α and β are identified. This time, let Ω be $\alpha + 1$, and let Dxy be $y = \beta$. (i) and (ii) can easily be seen to hold in $\mathcal{U}$ and so $\mathcal{U}^\sim$. (iii) is now:

$$x \subseteq \Omega \wedge y = \beta \rightarrow y \in \Omega$$

If d is not β then d satisfies the negation of the antecedent of this in $\mathcal{U}$, and hence $\mathcal{U}^\sim$. If d is β then it satisfies the consequent in $\mathcal{U}^\sim$, since $\alpha \in \alpha + 1$ is true in $\mathcal{U}$ and α is identified with β in $\mathcal{U}^\sim$. Hence (iii) is true in $\mathcal{U}^\sim$.

In this model the ordinals between α and β form a series of numbers both greater than and less than β, i.e., α. Of course, we can make matters more complicated by identifying one of these with a number, say, greater than β. What properties these and more complex identifications have, I do not know.

Conclusion

The above are just a sample of models for the Inclosure Schema that can be constructed by collapsing; others can be produced in numerous ways. For example, we could identify, instead of ordinals, stages of the cumulative hierarchy. Alternatively, there are known to be (LP) models of ZF plus the naive Comprehension Schema.[7] If we start with one of these models instead of a simple model for ZF, then we will obtain collapsed models that satisfy Comprehension as well as ZF and the inclosure conditions. I suspect that a more systematic study of collapsed models will yield a number of interesting results.

[7] See Restall (1992), appendix.

Part 4

Language and its limits

To say that 'everything is the Tao' almost gets the point, but just at the moment of getting it, the words crumble into nonsense. For we are here at a limit at which words break down because they always imply a meaning beyond themselves – and here there is no meaning beyond.

Alan Watts, *The Way of Zen*

12 The unity of thought

Introduction

The issue we are concerned with in this book is that of the limits of thought. We have seen how contradictions at the limits of thought that we have been concerned with take a very sharp form in the inclosure contradictions of self-reference. The story does not end here, however. As we saw in the second part of the book, the classical formulation of the problem was given by Kant, who put the issue in terms of the limits of reason. The twentieth century, for its own reason, has taken to formulating philosophical issues in terms of language. It is therefore unsurprising that the issue should appear again in contemporary form as a concern about aspects of language. In this part of the book, we turn to this.

It is natural for a theory of language to have implications about what can and what cannot be expressed. We will see that modern theories of language always seem to render some very important things – usually themselves – beyond the limit of expression. The contradictions at the limits of thought therefore appear in a new guise here. In this part of the book we will examine a number of modern accounts of meaning with an eye on the matter. The main concern will not be to evaluate these theories; rather, it will be to examine their consequences.

In this chapter we will start by looking at one of the foundational figures in contemporary philosophy of language: Frege. We will then move on to the Wittgenstein of the *Tractatus*. Our major concern throughout the chapter will be the unity of thought.

12.1 Frege, concept and object

The major project of Frege's life was to demonstrate that mathematics (or, at least, analysis) was logic. At the end of his life, this project lay in ruins. The discovery of Russell's paradox blew a hole in it from which it never recovered. As a subsidiary part of his project, Frege formulated a systematic philosophy of language. The clarity and power of its structure had never before been achieved. Ironically, this aside was to be one of the major influences on twentieth-century philosophy.

We will not be concerned with all of Frege's views on language: only those that locate the site of a certain *aporia*. The crucial papers are 'Function and Concept', 'On Sense and Reference', and, particularly, 'On Concept and Object'.[1] The contents of these papers are so well known that a lengthy exposition is hardly necessary.[2]

Frege takes the traditional distinction between subject and predicate, and refashions it for his own ends. Instead of the category of subject, Frege proposes the category *name*. This is wider than the traditional category, since it includes those noun-phrases that occur *within* the predicate as a grammatical object. But it is also narrower than the traditional category, since it excludes quantifier phrases such as 'all men'. We are left with proper names and definite descriptions. Instead of the category of predicate, Frege proposes the category *concept-expression*. A concept-expression is what is left when names are deleted from a sentence. Thus, in 'Oswald was framed for the murder of Kennedy', 'Oswald' and 'the murder of Kennedy' are names and 'was framed for' is a concept-expression.

Frege also reshaped the traditional distinction between two notions of meaning: connotation and denotation. He distinguished between the sense (*sinn*), of a linguistic unit and its referent (*bedeutung*). According to Frege, all linguistic units have both a sense and a reference (denotation). The denotation of a name is an object; the denotation of a concept-expression is a concept. The denotation of a statement is a truth value (true or false). The sense of a linguistic unit is, in general, that which determines which object/concept/truth-value is the correct referent. In the case of a statement, this is the (objective) thought expressed by it (the proposition expressed by it).

How much of this is defensible is an issue that we need not go into here.[3] About the next of Frege's insights there can be little doubt. This is that the meaning of a compound linguistic expression is, in some sense, a function of the meanings of its parts. (This is usually called 'compositionality'.) Frege thought that, by and large, the referent of an expression was a function of the referents of its parts, and the sense of an expression was a function of the senses of its parts.

We now come to the crucial question: how do the senses/referents of the parts produce the sense/reference of the whole? It is clear that the meaning of a whole is, in some sense, a unity: the thought that Brutus killed Caesar, for example, is a single thought. It is not, therefore, a mere congeries of the meanings of its parts: ⟨the sense of 'Brutus', the sense of 'killed', the sense

---

[1] All to be found in Geach and Black (1960), to which page numbers refer unless otherwise indicated.

[2] A concise, but clear, summary can be found in the introduction of Furth (1967). A lengthy discussion can be found in Dummett's mammoth (1973).

[3] Detailed discussion can be found in Dummett (1973).

of 'Caesar'). In some way the parts have to co–operate. But how? Frege answers this question in most detail for reference, so I will follow him here. It is clear that a parallel story is to be told for sense.

According to Frege, a concept is a function, like the mathematical function, sin, which maps a number to another number. A concept is a function that maps an object to a truth value. This does not solve the problem, since exactly the same problem arises with respect to a function and its arguments: 'sin(π)' is an expression referring to a single entity (the number zero); it is quite different from <sin, π>.[4] Frege's solution to the problem is that a function is, in some sense, inherently 'gappy'. Objects (the arguments of the function) may fill those gaps, giving completion. As he puts it (p. 24):

> The argument does not belong with the function, but goes together with the function to make up a complete whole; for the function by itself must be called incomplete, in need of supplementation, or 'unsaturated'. And in this respect functions differ fundamentally from numbers [i.e., objects].

The words 'incomplete', 'unsaturated', etc. are, of course, metaphors. Frege realised this, but could do no better; neither can I. At this point we seem to have reached bedrock.

12.2 The concept *horse*

As is clear, concepts and objects are quite different *kinds* of thing, and must be so, since concepts perform a quite different kind of function in the composition of thought.

But this poses a nasty problem for Frege.[5] For since concepts are not objects, they cannot be named, that is, referred to, by a noun–phrase. But it would appear to be clear that we can refer to a concept with a noun phrase; for example, to use Frege's notorious example (due to Kerry): the concept *horse*. Frege is well aware of the problem. His solution to it is to insist, quite consistently, that, despite appearances, such phrases do not refer to concepts. As he puts it (p. 45):

> the three words 'the concept "horse"' . . . designate an object; but on that account they do not designate a concept as I am using that word.

This raises a more serious problem, however. If 'the concept *horse*' does not refer to a concept, a number of claims about concepts would appear to be problematic. For example, consider the claim that Phar Lap falls under the concept *horse*. *Falling under* is a relationship between an object and a concept.

---

[4] A mathematician might say that 0 is the *application* of the function sin to π: Ap (sin, π). But this does not solve the problem: it just transfers it to this new functional expression.

[5] A number of the following points are made at greater length in Black (1968).

Hence, this statement is false. On this and similar occasions, what one would normally want to express by this sentence might be expressed in other ways. For example, one can say simply: Phar Lap is a horse. But on other occasions this is impossible. For example, there is no similar paraphrase of: the concept *horse* was considered by Frege.

Actually, the problem is not so much with the use of a definite description, as with the predicate 'is a concept' itself, which allows us to form the description. To say what it needs to say, it must apply to concepts; yet, like all (first-order) predicates, it must apply to objects; if we join it to a phrase that refers to a concept, nonsense results, for example: is a horse is a concept.

The ramifications of this are clear. Frege needs to be able to talk about concepts in order to express his own theory. Yet he cannot do so (meaningfully) by his own theory. For example, consider the claim that all concept-words denote concepts, i.e., for every concept-word there is a concept that it denotes. Whatever satisfies 'is a concept' is an object. Hence this is false. Or consider the claim that concepts are unsaturated. Anything that satisfies 'is a concept' is an object, and so saturated. One more example, amongst many, from Frege's own words: he says (p. 30) 'a concept is a function whose value is always a truth value'. Whatever satisfies 'is a concept' is an object, and so not a function.[6] To say what he needs to say, Frege needs a predicate that applies to concepts, and this is just what he cannot have.

We see that the effect of Frege's view is to put much, including his own theory, beyond the limit of the expressible. Frege recognises this, and is obviously embarrassed by it (p. 54):[7]

I admit that there is a quite peculiar obstacle in the way of an understanding with my reader. By a kind of necessity of language, my expressions, taken literally, sometimes miss my thought: I mention an object when what I intend is a concept. I fully realize that in such cases I was relying on the reader who would be ready to meet me half-way – who does not begrudge a pinch of salt.

But he was not embarrassed enough. It is one thing for mystics, such as, perhaps, Cusanus, to hold views that they also hold to be ineffable; it is quite another for a man of science, such as Frege was.

In a later and, at the time, unpublished, essay (c1892) Frege comes back to the issue and offers a solution to it. He suggests that we may refer to a concept with a 'what' clause, as in 'what "is a horse" stands for'. The point of such clauses is that they can themselves be used predicatively. Consider, for example, the sentence: Frege is what I am, a philosopher-logician. In this way, we can say, for example, Phar Lap is what 'is a horse' stands for.

---

[6] The predicate 'is a function' is problematic for the same reason. This just makes the problem worse.

[7] See also the last paragraph on p. 55.

The construction does strain the ear somewhat. But in any case, the trick cannot do the required job. For if a what-clause must be construed predicatively then the claim, for example, 'what "is a horse" stands for was considered by Frege' is nonsense. Ditto the claim: 'what "is a horse" stands for is not an object', etc. And so we cannot paraphrase away all the things we need to say.

More importantly, Frege's suggestion does not address the fundamental problem, which was, as we saw, that he has at his disposal no predicate that applies to concepts. Dummett, in his discussion of the problem ((1973), pp. 211–22) suggests that 'is a concept' should be eschewed as a pseudo-expression. We need, instead, an appropriate second-order predicate, i.e., a phrase, like a quantifier phrase, that fits together with an ordinary predicate to make a sentence. His suggestion is 'Everything either is . . . or is not . . . '. If we use upper-case variables for concepts, this is $\forall y(Xy \lor \neg Xy)$. The suggestion will not do the job, however – if the job is to express Frege's theory. Consider, for example, the claim that every concept is unsaturated. This becomes: $\forall X(\forall y(Xy \lor \neg Xy) \to X$ is unsaturated), or more simply $\forall X(X$ is unsaturated). This raises the question of the intelligibility of second-order quantification in the present context. But setting that aside, we still have the problem of the predicate 'is unsaturated', which is an ordinary first-order predicate; and so this sentence is nonsense.

Maybe some way could be found to rejig the predicate as a suitable second-order predicate (though I doubt it). But worse is in store. Consider the claim that concept-words refer to concepts, i.e., $\forall x(x$ is a concept-word $\to \exists Y\ x$ refers to Y). The same problem arises with respect to the predicate 'refers to'; and this time there is certainly no way of rejigging it, simply because it must be legitimate to say that names refer to objects, and so 'refers to' must be a predicate that is first order in both its arguments. If it be retorted that the reference relations for names and concept-words must be distinct, then we cannot say with Frege ((c1892), p. 118):

To every concept-word, or proper name, there corresponds as a rule a sense and a meaning [reference], as I use these words.

or that the reference of a complex linguistic expression is a function of the references of its parts.

In fact, we cannot make any generalisations over objects and concepts, as Frege often does, or even say that objects and concepts are different; for example, ((c1892) p. 120):

From what we have said it follows that objects and concepts are fundamentally different and cannot stand in for one another.

Any attempt to express this which paraphrases 'is a concept' as a second-order predicate, results in nonsense.

We see that the Frege/Dummett repair will not solve Frege's fundamental problem. It might be thought that some minor modification of Frege's views would dispose of it, whilst leaving their essence intact; or that the problem is generated by some quirky and false Fregean doctrine, which should be disposed of anyway. Neither thought is correct; but let us leave the issue there for the time being and move on to Wittgenstein.

12.3 Wittgenstein and the limits of thought

As is well known, Frege's writings were an important influence on the early Wittgenstein. The same can not be said of his style of writing, however: Frege is deft, clear, and precise; the *Tractatus* is cryptic, epigrammatic, and abstract. One thing that Wittgenstein is quite clear about, however, is that the main point of the *Tractatus* is to delimit the bounds of (legitimate) thought; it is therefore precisely the same as that of Kant's Transcendental Dialectic. In the introduction he says:[8]

the aim of the book is to draw a limit to thought, or rather – not to thought, but to the expression of thought: for in order to be able to draw a limit to thought, we should have to find both sides of the limit thinkable (i.e. we should have to be able to think what cannot be thought). It will therefore be only in language that the limit can be drawn and what lies on the other side of the limit will simply be nonsense.

Wittgenstein's thoughts here are reminiscent of Berkeley's argument that we met in chapter 4. There can be no boundary between what is thought and what is not, for if there were, we could think of the things on the other side, which would be contradictory. Berkeley's solution was, as we saw, to deny that there is anything on the other side. *Prima facie*, Wittgenstein's reaction is different. First, he reformulates the problem as one concerning, not thought, but the language used to express thought. He then argues that language which appears to express thoughts on the other side of the boundary does not express ineffable thoughts (which would be contradictory), but is pure nonsense, and so expresses nothing at all. Hence, in the last analysis, his solution is not that different from Berkeley's: he denies that there is anything on the far side of the boundary.

As we might expect, however, switching from talk of thought to talk of language is ultimately of little help. Even the distinction is bogus in the *Tractatus*; for Wittgenstein actually identifies thoughts with the propositions that express them.[9] In working out the details of his project Wittgenstein is forced, time and time again, to make statements on the far side of the boundary. The problem is like a time-bomb hidden in the machinery of the

---

[8] Translations and page numbers are from the Pears and McGuinness edition, (1961). I will refer to propositions of the *Tractatus* by prefixing 'T' to their number.
[9] See, for example, T3.

Tractatus, which finally detonates at the penultimate proposition in the book, producing stunned silence.

12.4 Language and the world

Let us start with the basic details of Wittgenstein's account of language, the world, and the relationship between them. These are to be found largely in the first half of the *Tractatus*. I shall not go into great detail; full discussions can be found in any one of a number of commentaries.[10] In giving expositions, concrete examples are highly desirable. Wittgenstein never does this. Nor, in a sense, could he. The actual examples of what he is talking about would be found at the end of a chain of philosophical analysis never performed. I will resist the temptation to offer concrete examples; they are almost certain to be as misleading in one way, as they are helpful in another.

First, the world: this is a totality of (atomic) facts. Facts are assemblages of objects. They are no mere congeries, however. The objects in a particular fact fit together, like pieces of a jigsaw puzzle (or links in a chain, to use Wittgenstein's simile), according to possibilities intrinsic to the objects. It is tempting to think at this point of Frege and the way that concepts and objects are supposed to fit together. However, this is not what Wittgenstein has in mind, as we shall see. It is doubtful that Wittgenstein even took concept-expressions to refer to objects.[11] At any rate, the objects in a fact are articulated into a determinate structure, and the way that the objects are structured is called the *form* of the fact.

On the other side of the fence, language is composed of propositions. These are all truth-functional compounds of atomic propositions, and hence their truth values are determined by the truth values of the atomic propositions they contain. An atomic proposition itself expresses a possible (atomic) fact, and says something about the objects comprising this fact. Propositions are composed of names which correspond to (refer to) objects. Like facts and objects, propositions are no mere congeries of names, however. In particular, within a proposition the names are related to each other in a certain way. The way they fit together is the *form* of the proposition. An atomic proposition is true iff there is a fact whose objects are the objects named in the proposition, and which has the same form as the proposition. In other words, the proposition is true if the map which maps names to objects is an isomorphism. Or, as Wittgenstein puts it, the proposition *pictures* the fact.

---

[10] For example, Stenius (1960), Black (1964), Fogelin (1976).
[11] For a start, see T3.1432.

12.5 Saying and showing

Given some fact (or proposition), say (abstractly) aRb, it is important to distinguish between it (or the claim that it makes) and facts about it and its internal structure, such as that it involves a and b, that these are related in a certain way, or even that it is a fact (or proposition). I will call such things *structural facts* (following T4.122), though I should warn the reader straight-away that the use of 'fact' here is not a *Tractarian* one. This will be important – indeed, the heart of the matter. However, before we come to this we need to look at the distinction between saying and showing.

This distinction is of fundamental importance for Wittgenstein. We may say that a proposition expresses the fact that the objects it is about are in such and such a way, or that it *says* that they are thus and so. If one did not know what objects were named by the names in the proposition, one would not know what it said. But, even then, one could see something about the proposition, for example, that it has a certain form. Wittgenstein says that the proposition *shows* its form in this way. As he puts it (T4.121):

Propositions *show* the logical form of reality. They display it.

In a similar way, and quite generally, all structural facts are shown: a proposition shows that it is a proposition, shows what its constituents are, etc.

One should note that the word 'show' in English has both a propositional use and a non-propositional use. In its propositional use, 'show' is followed by a that–clause (she showed that she could play cricket); in its non-propositional use it is followed by 'what', 'how', etc., or even a simple noun-phrase (she showed him the bat/how to use it/where he could put it, etc.). Structures in the world and language show in both these senses. For an example of the latter, see the previous quotation. We will have examples of the former in due course.

It is worth noting that there is historical evidence to suggest that Wittgenstein observed that Russell's theory of types forced him into supposing that there were things that could not be said (as we saw in 9.7), and that reflection on this played some role in the genesis of his notion of showing.[12]

12.6 The determinacy of sense

Before we continue the main discussion, and for reasons that will become clear later, I want to digress for a section to take up a final matter of exegesis. This concerns the determinacy of sense.

Let us start by returning to the issue of what sort of thing is an object for Wittgenstein. The answer is that, whatever it is, it is simple, that is, has no constituents (T2.02). 'Constituents' here does not necessarily mean physical

---

[12] See the discussion in 3.2 of Griffin (1964).

constituents (though these could be constituents); rather, it means logical constituents. Thus, one can know a priori that a marriage is constituted by a wife and a husband; and these are its constituents. Wittgenstein would not deny that there are, in a certain sense, complex objects, like marriages, in the world; but these are not the objects of the *Tractatus*. And any statement about such complexes can be reduced to a more fundamental statement about its constituents which gives its meaning (T2.0201). The process is called 'philosophical analysis'; and a paradigm tool is Russell's theory of descriptions. For example, in 'Oswald was framed for the murder of Kennedy' the complex for which Oswald was framed is analysed to obtain the familiar: there was a unique murder of Kennedy and Oswald was framed for it.

But now two questions arise. Why should one suppose (a) that there are simples; and (b) that starting with a statement of English, you can always analyse it down to claims about simples? The answer to the first question (T2.021) is that if there were no simples the world would have no substance. This is reminiscent of the argument for the Thesis of Kant's Second Antinomy (6.4), except that we are now talking of logical components and logical substance, rather than physical components and physical substance. But what is logical substance? To see this we have to look at Wittgenstein's argument for the second claim – which entails the first, anyway. T2.0211, 2.0212 tell us that:

If the world had no substance, then whether or not a proposition had sense would depend on whether another proposition was true.
In that case we could not sketch any picture of the world (true or false).

This is an elusive argument, and some commentators despair of making sense of it.[13] The best I can do is as follows. Suppose that we start with some claim of English. If it is not explicitly about simples then it can be analysed. Its sense is therefore given by *analysandum*$_1$. If *analysandum*$_1$ is not itself explicitly about simples, it, too, can be analysed to give *analysandum*$_2$, which determines the sense of *analysandum*$_1$, and hence of the original sentence. But now we are obviously off on a regress; and if the regress does not bottom–out in a claim containing simple signs – i.e., signs referring to simples (T3.201) – whose sense is determined by their immediate relation to reality (substance), then it goes on to infinity.[14] But then there is nothing to determine the sense of the original claim. Hence its sense is indeterminate, not in the sense of being fuzzy, but in the sense of being undetermined (not nailed down). As Wittgenstein puts it (T3.23):

---

[13] See, for example, Fogelin (1976), section 1.5. But see also Candlish (1978).

[14] The actual text appears to generate the regress by saying that the sense of the *analysans* depends on the *truth* of the *analysandum* and hence, presumably, its sense. This detour through truth strikes me as both incorrect and unnecessary.

The requirement that simple signs be possible is the requirement that sense be determinate.

Wittgenstein assumes it to be obvious that sense is determinate, that we can 'make a picture of the world'. The result follows. Given the framework within which Wittgenstein is working, this strikes me as quite a plausible argument. I will return to it in due course.

12.7 Structural 'facts'

Let us now return to the main argument, indeed, to its crux. Structural facts are not facts at all in the sense of the *Tractatus*. And any attempt to construct a proposition expressing them results in something meaningless. There are two senses of meaninglessness that Wittgenstein uses in the *Tractatus*. In one sense, something has sense if it carries non-trivial information, that is, if it states that we are in some possible world, as opposed to some other. The opposite of having meaning in this sense, Wittgenstein calls *sinnlos* (normally translated as 'senseless'). In another sense, something has sense if its formulation does not violate the canons of conceptual grammar, in the way that 'is a horse is a concept' does. Something that is meaningless in this sense can carry no information at all, trivial or otherwise. For this sense of meaninglessness, Wittgenstein uses the phrase *unsinnig* (usually translated 'nonsense').[15] Structural claims are meaningless in this much stronger sense. To see why, it is best to consider a couple of examples.

Consider any claim to the effect that a fact (or a proposition; the considerations are the same) has a certain form. First, note that the form of a fact is not a component of the fact in the same way that the objects that comprise it are. For the form of a fact is the way that its objects are structured, and this can no more be another object than the form of a certain house is another of its bricks. If the form of the fact were just another object, on a par with the objects that comprise it, then the fact would just be a congeries of objects, and not a unity. The form of a fact functions in a quite different way from its objects: it is the way that the objects are put together.

One way to see this (if it is not obvious), is the observation that is as old as Plato's Third Man argument. Russell puts it succinctly in his manuscript of (1913) (p. 98):

[Form] cannot be another constituent, or if it were there would have to be a new way in which it and the . . . other constituents are put together, and if we take this way as again a constituent, we find ourselves embarked on an infinite regress.

---

[15] On the distinction between the two notions of being meaningless, see, for example, Black (1964), p. 160.

The regress is vicious since, if it arose, there would be nothing 'holding all the constituents together'. The form of a fact must be a quite different sort of thing from the objects that constitute it. Hence, a fact cannot be about its own form in the way that it can be about those objects.

It might be thought that although a fact cannot be about its own form, some other fact can be. But we can soon see that this is not true either. For the form of a fact is not an object at all. As we have just seen, it is the way that objects are put together, and, as such, a quite different sort of thing. But if it is not an object, then there are no facts about it, and therefore, no proposition that expresses such facts. As Wittgenstein puts it (T4.121):

Propositions cannot represent logical form: it is mirrored in them.
What finds its reflection in language, language cannot represent.

A similar problem arises if we consider propositions expressing another kind of structural fact, say, one to the effect that something is a proposition. This is (or at least appears to be) a proposition concerning the proposition in question, and so requires us to name it. But names name objects, not propositions, which are quite different.

This follows from several doctrines of the *Tractatus*,[16] but the fundamental reason is quite simple. Propositions state how things are. It therefore makes sense to affirm or deny them. Objects, on the other hand, just are; it makes no sense to affirm or deny them.[17] As Wittgenstein puts it (T3.144):

Situations can be described but not *given names*.
Names are like points; propositions like arrows – they have sense.

We see, then, that since propositions are not objects they cannot be the constituents of a fact any more than a form can.

We have now examined two examples of structural claims; these are quite typical of all similar claims. What we have seen is that attempts to express them produce claims which violate the canons of logical grammar. We are forced to treat as objects things that cannot possibly be objects, since they have quite different functions (form binds; propositions state). Thus, structural 'facts' cannot be expressed. Attempts to do so produce something *unsinnig*. As Wittgenstein summarises the matter (T4.1212):

What *can* be shown, *cannot* be said.

---

[16] For example, objects are simple (12.6), but propositions are obviously complex.

[17] This argument also goes back to Greek philosophy. Negating can be thought of as a sense-reversal. And as Aristotle observed (see Geach (1972), p. 45f.) it makes no sense to negate a name. (See also Ryle (1990).)

12.8 Saying the unsayable

We are now back in familiar territory. We have seen that structural things cannot, quite literally, be said. Any attempt to make such claims must produce a string of symbols that is nonsense. Structural claims are therefore beyond the expressible. Yet Wittgenstein expresses them all the time. Most of the *Tractatus* contains nothing but structural claims. This should be clear from the simple summary of 12.4; but lest anyone think that I have done some injustice to Wittgenstein on this point, let us examine a few of his statements.

In 12.7 we saw that, though form can be shown, nothing can be said about it. Yet we have the following assertions about form at T2.033 and T2.18:

Form is the possibility of structure.

What any picture, of whatever form, must have in common with reality, in order to depict it – correctly or incorrectly – in any way at all, is its logical form.

These quite clearly make assertions about form.

In 12.7 we also saw that it is impossible to make propositions about propositions. Yet we have the following assertions at T3.141 and T3.22:

A proposition is not a blend of words. – (Just as a theme in music is not a blend of notes.)
A proposition is articulate.

In a proposition a name is the representative of an object.

Both of these are assertions about propositions. (In particular, they quantify over them.)

It might be suggested that these are all statements of English that need to be analysed, and that once one does this, reference to forms, propositions, etc., will disappear. The proof of such a pudding would be in the eating. And I, for one, have not the foggiest even how to lay the table. In any case, just to hammer in the final nail, we sometimes find Wittgenstein actually saying what it is that propositions show, for example, T4.1211 and T4.126 (and note that the showing involved here is propositional):

Thus, one proposition '*fa*' shows that the object *a* occurs in its sense, two propositions '*fa*' and '*ga*' show that the same object is mentioned in both of them.

When something falls under a formal concept as one of its objects, this cannot be expressed by means of a proposition. Instead it is shown in the very sign for this object. (A name shows that it signifies an object, a sign for a number that it signifies a number, etc.)

As Russell summarises the situation in his introduction to the English translation of the *Tractatus* (p. xxi):

Everything, therefore, which is involved in the very idea of the expressiveness of language must remain incapable of being expressed in language, and is, therefore, inexpressible in a perfectly precise sense . . . What causes some hesitation [about this view] is the fact that, after all, Mr. Wittgenstein manages to say a good deal about what cannot be said.

12.9 The ladder

We see that Wittgenstein is in just the situation that Kant found himself in (see 5.5). There are certain things which cannot, quite literally, be said (or thought, since these are the same thing for Wittgenstein). But to explain this very idea such things must be said. For Kant, these were claims about noumena; for Wittgenstein, they are structural claims.

Wittgenstein is well aware of the situation; in fact, he faces it squarely in a way that Kant never does. His solution to the problem is the stunning penultimate proposition of the book, T6.54:

My propositions serve as elucidations in the following way: anyone who understands me eventually recognises them as nonsensical, when he has used them – as steps – to climb up beyond them. (He must, so to speak, throw away the ladder after he has climbed up it.)
He must transcend these propositions, and then he can see the world aright.

With the sudden jerk of a conjuror, Wittgenstein intends to remove the table-cloth, leaving the best china in place. Unfortunately, there is little doubt that in this case the china comes off with the cloth. For, heroic as the stance is, it is no more successful than the similar move by Sextus (see 3.4). If Wittgenstein is right, then the propositions of the *Tractatus*, far from being the rungs of a real ladder that one can ascend, are like the rungs of a holographic ladder that will not support any weight put on them: the 'propositions' of the *Tractatus* are not even propositions at all in Wittgenstein's sense; just nonsense. There is therefore no question of understanding them. Conversely, if one does understand them, as one certainly seems to, then they cannot be nonsense.[18]

One might, I suppose, try to harness the distinction between saying and showing at this point, by claiming that someone who understands the *Tractatus* understands what its statements show, not what they say. This, however, is quite unsatisfactory. For if the statements of the *Tractatus* show anything, then some of the things that are shown are propositional (see 12.5). In other words, they must show *that* something is the case. Let α be a

---

[18] Ironically enough, Wittgenstein even seems to concede this in the introduction to the *Tractatus*, since he says (p. 4) that the thoughts expressed by the *Tractatus* are unassailably and definitively true – and so not nonsense.

statement of the *Tractatus*; and let us suppose that it shows that p. What is p meant to be?

Perhaps it is a nonsense 'proposition', such as one of the statements from the *Tractatus* itself. But this will not work. For if p is nonsense, so is the suggestion that α shows that p. In this it is no worse than p; but it is no better either, so any discomfort felt about p will be felt equally about the claim that α shows that p. Perhaps, then, it is some proposition that is literally ineffable. This suggestion just does not do justice to the facts. There is no such proposition; or if there is I have not the remotest idea what it is – which I should have, since as far as I can tell I have understood the *Tractatus*. Naturally, if p were some ineffable proposition, and I knew what it was, I could hardly tell you. But that is *not* the situation. I literally have no idea as to what should fill the gap if it is an ineffable proposition. And neither, as far as I know, has anyone else.[19]

But of course, we know what must fill the gap: a quite effable proposition. We have seen that it is quite possible to state what can be shown. In this chapter I have said many such things myself, and in 12.8 we saw Wittgenstein doing exactly the same.

Conclusion

Let us take stock. In the first part of the chapter we saw that to account for the unity of thought Frege postulated the existence of concepts, unsaturated entities whose distinctive properties account for this unity. The fact that concepts are not objects, rendered his claims about them beyond the limit of the expressible. In the second part of the chapter we saw that the Wittgenstein of the *Tractatus* accounted for the unity of thought (the proposition) by invoking the notion of form. The distinctive properties of this account for the unity, but also drive statements about it beyond the expressible.

Both Frege and Wittgenstein were dealing with the same fundamental problem here: the unity of thought.[20] In this respect, Wittgenstein's notion of the form of a proposition is just the intellectual descendant of Frege's notion of concept.[21] In both philosophers, the precise formulation of the problem

---

[19] Moore ((1990), see especially 13.4 and 15.3) tries to defuse the violation of the Domain Principle by ZF (see 11.2) by applying a version of the saying/showing distinction. His solution is to the effect that, although the claim that there is a set of all sets is false, it is all we can do to articulate an ineffable insight that we have when we reflect on our practice of quantifying over all sets. Comments similar to the ones in the text apply to his suggestion. If the insight is not that the collection of all sets quite literally forms a set (or is a unity, as Moore is inclined to put it), then I have not the foggiest what it is supposed to be; and neither, I suspect, has he.

[20] The history of the problem goes back well before Frege. See Hylton (1984). Russell also grapples with it in his comments on verbs in sections 52–5 of (1903).

[21] As Anscombe observes, (1959), pp. 108f.

depends on other doctrines; but the problem itself is a general one which depends on few doctrinal claims. Let me state it as best I can.

Thoughts are articulated. To form them we must combine simpler building-blocks. But thoughts are no mere lists of their components. There must therefore be things which hold them together as unities. Let us call these (with apologies to modern physics) *gluons*. Gluons are not the same kind of thing as the components they glue, and hence not the kind of thing one can express claims about. But anything can be an object of thought; in particular, we can think about gluons. Thus they *are* the same kind of thing as other constituents, and we can express claims about them.[22]

We have, here, a contradiction typical of the limit of thought. It is also not difficult to see that it fits the Inclosure Schema, albeit the limit case where $\psi(x)$ is '$x = \Omega$' (see 9.5). Let $\varphi(y)$ be 'y is expressible (in some language, say English)', so that Ω is the set of all states of affairs expressible in English. Take any of the gluons that holds an English proposition together. And let $\delta(\Omega)$ be a situation concerning that gluon, maybe that it is a gluon of a certain proposition. Then, by the arguments we have had, $\delta(\Omega)$ both is (Closure) and is not (Transcendence) expressible.

There is a simple, if bold, way out of the problem I have just explained. To see what it is, recall Wittgenstein's argument for the existence of simple objects (12.6). This can be reformulated in a very general way that is quite independent of Tractarian considerations.

Propositions (thoughts, or whatever) are certainly compositional. Now consider any component of a proposition and ask what determines its sense (meaning). Possibly, it has the sense it does in virtue of some relation it bears to something else in language (thought); but this just raises the question of how this itself has its sense. If we chase back sense in this way, there are two possibilities. In the first case, the sense of any component will ultimately ground out in a relationship between language and something else, something in reality. It might not be a Fregean concept or a Wittgensteinian object, but it will be an entity of some kind. Let us call it the *semantic correlate* of the component, for the relation of the component to its correlate determines its sense. In this case, we are faced with the problem of the unity of thought; for how do the semantic correlates knit together? In the second case, when we chase back the senses of components, we never break out of language (thought), and hence there is ultimately nothing to ground the sense of the original proposition. (If one elephant will not support the world then neither

---

[22] And if one is tempted by the thought that something can be an object and a gluon, but in different propositions, just consider, for example, the true (as it happens) statement 'I am thinking about the gluon of this proposition (the way that this proposition is composed)'. It is essential to the truth of this, that whatever it is that holds the proposition together is, at the same time, the object of the thought.

will an infinite regress of elephants.) Hence, in this case, we are faced with the indeterminacy of sense.

The way out of the contradiction that I mentioned should now be obvious. Accept the second horn of the dilemma: the indeterminacy of sense. Maybe there is ultimately nothing to fix the sense of linguistic statements. This is the move that a number of subsequent writers made (though not necessarily for that reason). In the next two chapters, we will look at the most important of these writers, and examine the consequences of this move.

13 Translation, reference, and truth

Introduction

As I observed in the conclusion of the previous chapter, a contradiction at the limit of expression arises naturally for any view that postulates semantic correlates, entities that are meanings, but may be avoided if no such entities are invoked. It is natural, therefore, to try to avoid the problem by giving an account of meaning that avoids a postulation of this kind. In this chapter and the next we will look at theories that do this. As we shall see, though they may avoid the contradiction in question, they do so only at the expense of taking us into other contradictions at the limit of thought.

The idea that semantic correlates are to be avoided in giving an account of meaning has been endorsed by a number of philosophers of language writing since the *Tractatus*. One of the most important of these is the modern US philosopher Quine. In this chapter we will consider his work. We will also look at the philosopher in whom the Quinean programme reaches its greatest sophistication, Davidson. But let us start with Quine.

13.1 Quine and the myth of the museum

Quine's views on meaning and associated topics are spelled out in many places. The *locus classicus* for our purpose is chapter 2 of *Word and Object* (1960) (hereafter, *WO*).[1] Consequences of the view that will much concern us are spelled out further in his essay 'Ontological Relativity' (hereafter, *OR*), the title essay of (1969). Quine's writings, like those of Frege, and unlike those of Wittgenstein, have a clarity and (ironically, as we shall see) a transparency that makes reference to secondary sources of exegesis somewhat unnecessary. However, chapters 6 and 7 of Orenstein (1977) do an excellent job on the ground we will need to cover.

Quine approaches the topic of meaning, as he approaches all other topics, naturalistically. That is, he views meaning as an empirical phenomenon, to be theorised empirically, in this case behaviouristically. As he is the first to point

---

[1] A slightly different version of this is Quine (1959). The part of the argument relevant to our present concern is usefully summarised in the first part of ch. 1 of Quine (1969).

out, the postulation of semantic correlates is an immediate casualty of this approach (*OR*, p. 27):

The copy theory in its various forms [such as that of the *Tractatus*] stands closer [than a naturalistic theory] to the main philosophical tradition, and to the attitude of common sense today. Uncritical semantics is the myth of a museum in which the exhibits are the meanings and the words are labels. To switch language is to change labels. Now the naturalist's primary objection to this view is not an objection to meanings on account of their being mental entities, though this could be objection enough. The primary objection persists even if we take the labelled exhibits not as mental ideas but as Platonic ideas or even as the denoted concrete objects. Semantics is vitiated by a pernicious mentalism as long as we regard a man's semantics as somehow determinate in his mind beyond what might be implicit in his overt behaviour. It is the very facts about meaning, not the entities meant, that must be construed in terms of behavior.

If the first casualty of Quine's approach is the notion of a semantic correlate, the second is the determinacy of sense (which is to be expected, given the considerations discussed in the Conclusion of the previous chapter). As Quine puts it (*OR*, pp. 28f.):

When ... we turn towards a naturalistic view of language and a behavioral view of meaning, what we give up is not just the museum figure of speech. We give up an assurance of determinacy. Seen according to the museum myth, the words and sentences of a language have their determinate meanings. To discover the meanings of a native's words we may have to observe his behavior, but still the meanings of the words are supposed to be determinate in the native's *mind*, his mental museum, even in cases where the behavioral criteria are powerless to discover them for us. When on the other hand we recognize with Dewey that 'meaning ... is primarily a property of behavior', we recognize that there are no meanings, nor likenesses nor distinctions of meanings, beyond what are overt in people's disposition to behave. For naturalism the question of whether two expressions are alike or unalike in meaning has no determinate answer, known or unknown, except insofar as the answer is settled in principle by people's speech dispositions, known or unknown. If by these standards there are indeterminate cases, so much the worse for the terminology of meaning and likeness of meaning.

And there are such indeterminate cases: language is shot through with such indeterminacy, as Quine goes on argue.

13.2 The indeterminacy of translation

The argument goes as follows. We are to suppose that we come across speakers of some language about which we know nothing (and so cannot 'cheat' when it comes to discerning the meanings of their utterances). Such a situation Quine calls 'radical translation'. How do we go about determining what their utterances mean? We observe the speakers, the conditions under which they utter, what they are looking at when they utter, and other general and salient features of their surroundings. On the basis of this we make various guesses (hypotheses) about what their utterances mean. Quine calls these 'analytic hypotheses'. These hypotheses are tested in the standard way that scientific hypotheses can be tested. For example, on the basis of our observation, we might guess that 'gavagai' means '(there is a) book'. We test this by showing speakers a copy of *Word and Object*, which they have never seen before, and seeing whether they will say 'gavagai', or make signs which appear to be signs of assent when we offer the word. Once we have a number of well-confirmed analytic hypotheses, and so some basic grasp of parts of the language, we can then use these parts to advance the process of bootstrapping by asking questions in such a way as to discover or justify other analytic hypotheses, for example, by uttering the sentence which we take to mean 'What do you call this?'.

So far so good. However, Quine next claims that the evidence that we have can never suffice to establish one set of analytic hypotheses to the exclusion of others. For example, the evidence could equally well support the hypothesis that 'gavagai' means undetached book part (spatial or temporal). All the evidence is consistent with this, since whenever one sees a book one sees an undetached book part, and vice versa. It might be thought that using words whose meanings we already know we could distinguish between the different possibilities, for example, by pointing to the back and front cover of *Word and Object* and asking whether they are the same gavagai. But this presupposes that we already know that a certain expression means 'the same as'. And this is an hypothesis that is even further from the empirical evidence than those concerning 'gavagai', and so subject to similar indeterminacy. Hence, even if the speakers say 'yes' when asked the question, we can still suppose that 'gavagai' means undetached book part if we translate what we took to mean 'the same as' as the equivalence relation 'is a part of the same book as'.

Bearing these considerations in mind, Quine generalises. There will be different sets of analytic hypotheses for the whole language that are consistent with all the empirical evidence, and yet which translate the utterances of the language quite differently. As he puts it, there are (*WO*, p. 73):

rival systems of analytic hypotheses [that] can conform to all speech dispositions ... and yet dictate, in countless cases, utterly disparate translations; not mere paraphrases, but translations each of which would be excluded by the other systems of translation. Two such translations might even be patently contrary in truth value provided there is no [sensory] stimulation that would encourage assent to either.

It might be thought that Quine's generalisation here is rather swift. What we have is a problem rather like the simple decryption problem that asks you to determine what numbers certain letters mean, given that you have a correct addition in coded form. Any partial solution has implications for what other parts of the solution may be. But, since there is no way of fixing any part of the solution in advance, there is no guarantee that there is a unique solution. Indeed, as those who have tried to design such problems will know, problems with a unique solution are difficult to construct, and unlikely to occur spontaneously. None the less, it could just be that there is something about the situation that guarantees a unique solution. But at least the onus is on one who claims there is to show why.

And there are general reasons for supposing that there is no unique solution in the case of radical translation. For analytic hypotheses are simply hypotheses about empirical regularities, and since Hume we have known that the correctness of *any* general hypothesis is underdetermined by any finite sample of empirical evidence, even all possible evidence, since it is quite possible for different theories to have the same observational consequences. For example, take any theory in physics, and append to it something that has no empirical consequences, such as that God transcends experience. The new theory will be observationally equivalent to the old.[2]

Or to use a trite, but none the less telling, example, suppose that we have two dependent physical quantities, a and b, and have observed the following correlations: $\langle 0, 0 \rangle$, $\langle 1, 1 \rangle$, $\langle 2, 4 \rangle$, $\langle 3, 9 \rangle$. Then this is consistent with the putative law that $a^2 = b$. But it is also consistent with any putative law of the form $a^2 = b + f(a,b)$, where f is some function whose value is 0 for each of the given pairs. There is an infinite number of these. If a and b are continuous magnitudes there are infinitely many equations that are compatible with all possible observations (since any observation is performed only to some finite number of decimal places). In this case, and provided we are physical realists, we may suppose that there is a determinate law relating a and b, and so rendering one of these equations determinately true, whatever observational evidence there is. Similarly, if we suppose that there are objectively existing semantic correlates for each word or linguistic expression, we may suppose that one set of analytic hypotheses is uniquely right. But it is exactly this that is rendered impossible by the rejection of the 'museum myth'.

13.3 Beyond the limit of expression

We have seen that in a context of radical translation there will be rival sets of analytic hypotheses specifying different meanings for utterances of the language, and no sense to the claim that any one set is more right than any other. The meaning of the language is radically undetermined: there is no fact of the matter about what utterances mean (which is not to say that any utterance can mean anything you like[3]).

---

[2] For a less artificial example, the Special Theory of Relativity is, arguably, observationally equivalent to a classical ether theory that incorporates the Lorentz–Fitzgerald spatio-temporal contractions.

[3] Though Quine comes dangerously close to this for other reasons. In 'Two Dogmas of Empiricism' (1951) Quine claims, famously, that, whatever the sensory evidence, any claim can be held on to if we are prepared to make suitable changes elsewhere in our web or beliefs.

And this fact about language is not just a fact about a radically unknown language. The trick of starting with an unknown language was just one to provide a veil of ignorance to stop us cheating, a device to isolate what, exactly, meaning comes to in itself. The conclusion of the argument therefore applies just as much to languages with which we are familiar, such as English: radical translation, as Quine puts it, begins at home (*OR*, p. 46). There is thus no fact of the matter concerning what utterances of English mean.

But now we are back in familiar territory. If this is so, then it is true just as much of Quine's own utterances as those of others. It follows that his utterances have no determinate sense: whatever sense he would like us to attach to them, they do not, as such, mean that (Transcendence). Yet clearly Quine does succeed in expressing views about meaning that *do* have determinate sense (Closure). For when Quine tells us that there are no such things as semantic correlates he is telling us something about semantic correlates, not semantic correlate parts. When he tells us that sense is not determinate, he is not telling us that sense is not determinate and God transcends all experience.

It might be suggested that there really is no problem here. When we hear Quine's utterances, we simply translate them into our own idiolect homophonically. That is, we do not interpret his utterance of 'meaning' as 'meaning stage' in our idiolect; we translate it as 'meaning'. Hence there is no problem understanding him. This may, indeed, be how we do understand him. But that is beside the point. The point is not that we could not understand Quine if his utterances had no determinate sense. Rather, it is that no utterances have determinate sense (his, or, for that matter, ours), which some of them clearly do have. In particular, there is nothing, as such, that can be meant by an utterance of 'sense is indeterminate'. Yet clearly there is. We *know* what it is like for a sentence to have indeterminate sense: we are very familiar with ambiguous sentences, such as 'She watched the cricket on the television.' Quine's claims, whatever they are, are not like this. It is possible, I suppose, for a skeptic about meaning to deny this.[4] However, we are by no means through with the havoc that indeterminacy wreaks yet.

Before we pass on to this, let me just note that a number of the above points (and related ones) are made by Searle (1987), though his conclusion is rather different. He interprets the contradiction involved as a *reductio* of Quine's behaviourism. There are a couple of points to be made about this. The first is that behaviourism is not essential to the conclusion of indeterminacy. Intensional notions can be incorporated in the methodology of radical translation whilst indeterminacy remains. We will note this later in the case of Davidson.

---

[4] The later Wittgenstein might be counted as one of this number, as we shall see in the next chapter. Hylton (1990–1) might also fall into the category. According to him, our language does not mean anything, at least in any transcendental sense.

Secondly, and more importantly, it is always open to someone to take a contradiction at the limit of thought and use it as a *reductio*. Sometimes, this does not succeed in avoiding a contradiction. For example, in the case of the paradoxes of set-theory, we can use a *reductio* to demonstrate that there is no set of all sets. But, while we still have independent reasons for supposing that there is, we still have a contradiction.[5] Or in the case of the semantic paradoxes we can take propositions to be truth bearers and use a *reductio* to argue that the Liar sentence does not express a proposition. But then the paradox reappears in a strengthened form.[6] In the present case, wielding the contradiction as a *reductio* against behaviourism has no similar problems that I am aware of. However, the main point of this part of the book is to show that *all* the standard accounts of meaning result in *some* contradiction at the limit of thought. Hence, wielding a *reductio* against any one account of meaning is to no avail.

13.4   The indeterminacy of reference

Let us now return to Quine. For him, as we have seen, sense is indeterminate. But, as Frege noted (see 12.1), the sense of an expression is that which determines its reference. Hence if the sense of an expression is indeterminate, its reference is likely to be indeterminate, too. This does not follow immediately. Suppose, for example, that the sense of 'gavagai' were indeterminate between (the normal senses of) 'gene belonging to a creature with a heart' and 'gene belonging to a creature with a kidney'. Then, arguably at least, 'gavagai' would have a determinate reference, since these two phrases have the same extension. However, in the case at hand, exactly the same considerations that show that sense is indeterminate show that reference is indeterminate too. For, if 'gavagai' may be legitimately translated by different analytic hypotheses as 'rabbit' and 'undetached rabbit part' (to use Quine's own example), then, since these phrases obviously have different extensions, the reference of 'gavagai' is, similarly, indeterminate.[7]

Moreover, as I have already observed, there is nothing specific to the language of others about these conclusions. It is just as true of our own language, and of our own use of our own language, our own idiolect. As Quine puts it (*OR*, p. 47):

I have urged in defence of the behavioral philosophy of language ... that the inscrutability of reference is not the inscrutability of fact; there is no fact of the matter. But if there really is no fact of the matter, then the inscrutability of reference can be brought

---

[5] See the discussion in 11.1.

[6] See, for example, Priest (1987), ch 2.

[7] *OR* contains, also, further arguments to the effect that reference is indeterminate (for example, based on the Loewenheim–Skolem theorem), but these need not concern us here.

even closer to home than the neighbor's case; we can apply it to ourselves. If it is to make sense even of oneself that one is referring to rabbits ... and not rabbit stages ... then it should make sense equally to say it of someone else.

And since it makes no sense to say it of one's neighbour, it makes no sense to say it of oneself.

Hence, the idea that one refers determinately to objects in talking must be given up. Let us call this the Thesis of the Indeterminacy of Reference: it is not possible to refer determinately to objects; there is just no fact of the matter as to whether 'rabbit' refers to rabbits, undetached rabbit parts, or wot not. The Thesis generates a contradiction, but this time concerning reference rather than sense. Objects in the world transcend anything we can determinately refer to in speaking. Yet, patently, Quine does refer to rabbits, rabbit parts and other objects in his ruminations on reference. Even the skeptic about sense would be hard-pressed to deny this. Indeed, even to claim that one cannot refer determinately to objects, presupposes that we can refer to those objects (and not to undetached object parts) to say what it is that we cannot refer to![8] Thus we have a contradiction at the limits of expression again. The Indeterminacy of Reference cannot be expressed (Transcendence); yet Quine expresses it (Closure).

Quine is alive to the fact that there are problems here. He puts what he takes to be the central one thus (*OR*, p. 47):

We seem to be maneuvering ourselves into the absurd position that there is no difference on any terms, interlinguistic or linguistic, objective or subjective, between referring to rabbits and referring to rabbit parts or stages ... Surely this is absurd, for it would imply that there is no difference between the rabbit and each of its parts or stages ... Reference would seem now to become nonsense not just in radical translation, but at home.

13.5 Relative reference

Quine's solution to the problem is simply to bite the bullet and accept that the notion of reference *is* meaningless. All that makes sense are claims to the effect that something refers relative to a translation into a background language (*OR*, pp. 48f.):

It is meaningless to ask whether, in general, our terms 'rabbit', 'rabbit part' ... etc. really refer respectively to rabbits, rabbit parts ... etc. rather than to ... [something else]. It is meaningless to ask this absolutely; we can meaningfully ask it only relative to some background language. When we ask, 'Does "rabbit" really refer to rabbits?',

---

[8] As Ayer, I am told, once put the matter in a lecture: the claim that there is no fact of the matter as to whether 'gavagai' refers to rabbits or rabbit parts, depends for its very force on the fact that 'rabbits' and 'rabbit parts' do refer to distinct things.

someone can counter with the question: 'Refer to rabbits in what sense of "rabbits"?' thus launching a regress; and we need the background language to regress into. The background language gives the query sense, if only relative sense; sense relative in turn to it, the background language. Querying reference in any more absolute way would be like asking absolute position, or absolute velocity, rather than position or velocity relative to a given frame of reference.

Thus, Quine's solution is the heroic one: give up the notion of reference as meaningless. This was Wittgenstein's move in the *Tractatus* too (see 12.9). Does it work any better for Quine than it did for Wittgenstein? The answer is 'no' for several reasons.

There is already a large irony in the quotation from Quine. Quine says that we can make the sense of a query determinate by translating into a background language. But it cannot do this if the statements of the background language do not themselves have determinate sense. And, of course, they do not, according to Quine. But we can exercise charity here and take this to be a slip of the pen.[9] What Quine is talking about is reference, not sense. What, then, is to be said about this?

The first thing is that the device of using a relative notion of reference will not solve the problem that Quine flagged in the last quotation of the previous section, of explaining how we manage to refer to one thing rather than another.[10] Relating the references of terms to those of a background language can make them determinate only to the extent that the references of the terms of the background language are determinate. And according to Quine they are not. We can attempt to render the references of these terms determinate by a similar move. But this launches a regress, and a vicious one.[11] We might attempt to stop the regress by, as Quine suggests at one point, 'acquiescing in our mother tongue and taking its words at face value' (*OR*, p. 49). But this hardly helps. Our mother-tongue is no better off than any other. And the face values of its terms are no better than the face values of a currency rendered worthless by inflation. One way to see this is to ask what happens if we *start* by asking about the references of the terms in our mother-tongue. The regress is then a trivial one. 'Rabbit' means rabbit. But this is vacuous, and no better than answering the question of where the origin of a frame of reference is by saying that it is at the origin (to pursue Quine's analogy between background language and frame of reference).

The second point is that we cannot, in any case, jettison an absolute notion of reference. Our understanding of the way that language works depends on

---

[9] Though, if it is a slip, it is a Freudian slip since it betrays a belief in the determinacy of sense in the home language.

[10] This point is made in Davidson (1979), pp. 231ff. (of the reprint). Davidson argues that we cannot even make sense of the relativity of reference in the required sense.

[11] The situation here is very similar to Cantor's argument for the Domain Principle that we met in 8.8.

such a notion. Consider a sentence such as 'Brisbane is in Australia'. For this to be true (correctly applicable, warrantedly assertible, acceptable, or wot not) is for the city referred to by 'Brisbane' (in the context of utterance, etc.) to be located in the country referred to by 'Australia'. Thus, one cannot understand the sentence unless one possesses, at least implicitly, the notion of reference.[12]

It might, I suppose, be insisted that that notion of reference is the relative one. But then the notion of truth, since it depends on it, must also be a relative one. Truth, then, is relative to an idiolect, and so to a person. The view therefore commits one to a relativism about truth of exactly the Protagorean kind. I argued against this in 3.8, and so shall not pursue the matter further here. As a matter of fact, Quine himself, elsewhere, argues against such relativism on self-referential grounds.[13]

The final and decisive point in the present context is that the relativising move does not, in any case, avoid the problem at the limit of expression that is our central concern. The trap is sprung by pointing out that Quine himself, in his Thesis of the Indeterminacy of Reference, refers to objects. If there is a legitimate relative notion of reference, this is beside the point. And jettisoning an absolute notion of reference even makes matters worse, since this undercuts Quine's own position. Both the Thesis (that one cannot refer determinately to objects) and the arguments used for it presuppose that the absolute notion of reference makes sense.[14] As, indeed, it does.

It could be suggested that the notion of reference in the Thesis is a relative one. This, I think, would be disingenuous: it is not what Quine intends. But, in any case, it is not enough. For, in the claim that there is no fact of the matter as to whether 'rabbit' refers to rabbits, both the nouns 'rabbit' and '"rabbit"' refer to objects (animals of a certain kind and words). It might be suggested that these words, too, refer only relative to a translation into a background language. But this does not help either. For relative to a translation into a background language, there *is* a fact of the matter as to whether or not 'rabbit' refers to rabbits. Relative to a homophonic translation into English, for example, it is simply true that 'rabbit' refers to rabbits and not to rabbit parts. Hence, Quine's Thesis would just be false.

---

[12] The claim that our understanding of how language works depends on a notion of reference is argued at greater length in Davidson (1977). In that paper he also argues that the notion of reference may be dispensed with in a certain sense: specifically, that one should not expect an analysis of the notion of reference independent of its role in a theory of meaning (truth). It remains true that a notion of reference is essential to such a theory, if only as a 'theoretical construct'.

[13] See Quine (1975), pp. 327–8.

[14] Hylton (1990–1) seems to miss this point, though he is vaguely aware that Quine cannot express his own views. He notes (p. 288) that 'in one sense, there is nothing that Quine is denying'. The predicament is not unlike that in which the later Wittgenstein finds himself, as we will see in the next chapter.

Another suggestion as to how to avoid the problem is that the arguments for indeterminacy should be interpreted *ad hominem* against those who hold there to be determinate reference. We have seen this move to have a limited, but positive, effect in the case of a similar problem for skepticism (see 3.4). But it will not work here. Quine's views about reference are entailed by his views concerning how one should approach the issue of meaning, the underdetermination of theories by evidence, etc. All of these, Quine (and any other empiricist) subscribes to. He must therefore accept their conclusions.

13.6 Davidson, truth, and meaning

We have seen that Quine's account of meaning ends in contradictions at the limit of expression (for both sense and reference). This is not an end of the matter, however. For the Quinean picture leaves some notable open questions, and the most plausible way of answering these generates further contradictions at the limits of thought.

In the project of radical translation, we are required to construct a system of analytic hypotheses that allows us to translate the target language, and test this against the evidence. But what form, exactly, should the system of hypotheses take? Quine, as we saw, makes suggestions about the matter, but hardly provides a well worked-out theoretical answer. Taking up the challenge, Davidson did just that. His answer (endorsed by Quine[15]) appeared first in 'Truth and Meaning' (1967); and many of the further details were worked out in a subsequent suite of papers.[16]

Davidson's approach to language is not exactly the same as Quine's; it starts from a similar rejection of meanings as entities (pp. 17ff.), but there are some significant differences. Notably, Davidson is no behaviourist. In particular, he allows that intensional notions play a role in the testing of analytic hypotheses. Moreover, he adopts more general methodological constraints on test procedures than does Quine, notably, a thoroughgoing use of the Principle of Charity (if theory A makes more of a speaker's utterances come out true than theory B then theory A is preferable to theory B). However, none of this detracts from the conclusions already reached in this chapter, such as the indeterminacy of translation, as Davidson points out.[17]

---

[15] See Quine (1981), p. 38.

[16] All the papers can be found together in Davidson (1984). Subsequent page references to Davidson's views are to this. An excellent and simple account of his ideas can be found in ch. 12 of Hacking (1975). A more general but less readable account occurs in ch. 2. of Platts (1979).

[17] See, for example, Davidson (1973), p. 139. Although Davidson accepts the indeterminacy of translation, he rejects, as I understand him, the indeterminacy of reference in the required sense. Instead, he claims ((1979), p. 239), we simply have an indeterminacy in the matter of which language a speaker is speaking. If, however, there is no fact of the matter as to which of several languages (having the same syntactic words) a speaker is speaking, then there is, as far as I

Henceforth, I shall follow Davidson and call a system of analytic hypotheses for a language a 'theory of meaning' for that language. Now, what, exactly, do we want a theory of meaning to do? Most crucially, we want it to tell us the meaning of every sentence of the language.[18] That is, for every sentence, s, of the language, we want the theory to entail a statement of the form: s means that p. Davidson also suggests two further desiderata. First, the theory should be finitely axiomatisable, else it could be of no human use. Secondly, it should expose how compositionality works, i.e., how wholes mean, in virtue of how their parts mean.[19] Now, how is the trick of finding such a theory to be turned?

Davidson suggests the use of the apparatus of a Tarskian truth theory for a language. Tarski (1936) showed how, given a language of certain kinds, we can construct a (finitely axiomatisable) theory of truth for that language. Specifically, for every sentence, s, of that language we can, by applying a well-defined canonical proof procedure, establish a sentence of the form: s is true iff p, where p is a sentence of our language, and may be thought of as stating the truth conditions of s. In Davidson's parlance, this is the T-sentence for s. Moreover, if t is some sub-formula of s, the proof of the T-sentence for s goes via the proof of the T-sentence for t.[20] The exact details of the construction are not relevant here. They are well known to logicians, and probably of no interest to others. Hence I will explain them no further.

Now, Frege suggested, very plausibly, that the meaning of a declarative sentence is its truth conditions. (Arguably, to know the meaning of such a sentence is to know under exactly what conditions it is true.) Davidson capitalised on this insight and suggested that, given a suitable Tarskian truth theory for a language, the T-sentence for sentence s may be thought of as spelling out its meaning.[21]

Naturally, there is a question about what 'suitable' means in this context. In effect, a suitable truth theory is one that is verified by empirical testing (as Quine stated) of a kind that Davidson carefully spells out.[22] Loosely, given the T-sentence for s, we see whether the empirical evidence is such as to verify the claim that speakers believe s when p – or, perhaps, believe s when they may

---

can see, no fact of the matter as to what a syntactic word refers to; and so reference *is* indeterminate.

[18] Strictly speaking, this should be 'utterance' rather than 'sentence', but I shall ignore indexicals and the complications they pose here.

[19] One might argue about these desiderata, but such issues will be of no relevance here.

[20] Actually it is the Satisfaction Schema rather than the T-schema, but this is a simple technical complication.

[21] To formulate a truth theory for a natural language, the Tarskian techniques need to be extended to deal with aspects of natural languages not found in the Tarskian paradigms; this is all part of the Davidsonian programme.

[22] Especially in (1973) and (1974a).

reasonably be supposed to be aware that p.[23] The more a theory's T-sentences are verified in this way, the better the theory. Again, precise details are not relevant here.

13.7 Semantic closure and contradiction

So far so good. What has this to do with contradictions at the limits of thought? Simply this: suppose that we construct a theory of meaning for a natural language, such as English, in the language itself. Consider the sentence 's is not true', where s is a proper name for that very sentence. Then the theory will deliver the T-sentence for s, namely:

s is true iff s is not true

(or at least, a biconditional whose right-hand side means the same as 's is not true', and so from which this follows.) This is the instance of the T-schema that generates the Liar paradox. Hence the construction generates a contradiction at the limits of cognition. Nor is this an accident: that the theory should generate all T-sentences is part of its essence as a theory of meaning.[24] Thus the account of meaning generates another contradiction at the limit of thought, fitting the Inclosure Schema, as we have already seen (10.2).

Davidson is aware of the situation. What is his response? Whilst claiming uncertainty, he says (pp. 28f.):

The semantic paradoxes arise when the range of the quantifiers in the object language is too generous in certain ways. But it is not really clear how unfair to Urdu or Wendish it would be to view the range of the quantifiers as insufficient to yield an explicit definition of 'true-in-Urdu' or 'true-in-Wendish'. Or, to put the matter in another, if not more serious way, there may in the nature of the case always be something we grasp in understanding the language of another (the concept of truth) that we cannot communicate to him.

The thought about the quantifiers is not quite right: a Tarskian theory of truth does not have to have the quantificational resources to turn the recursive truth conditions into an explicit definition of truth. However, the central point remains: the notion of truth for a language may always transcend that language.

Davidson's proposed solution to the problem is essentially a Tarskian one and, as such, problematic, as we have already seen (10.7). But, in the present context, it is more interesting to note that the escape from the contradiction at the limit of cognition generates a new one at the limit of expression. For,

---

[23] This is more like McDowell's version of the process. See McDowell (1976), and also Platts (1979), ch. 2.

[24] This is pointed out in Priest (1987), 4.3. Actually, the detour through a Davidsonian account of meaning is not essential. Since 's means that p' entails 's is true iff p', *any* theory of meaning that delivers the meaning of each sentence in the appropriate fashion is going to entail the Liar contradiction.

according to Davidson's suggestion, the notion of truth in some language, L, is not expressible in L. In particular, 'true-in-English' is not expressible in English (Transcendence). But, of course, it is expressed in English by 'true-in-English' (Closure).[25] To say what cannot be expressed, one has to express the very thing.

Davidson's suggestion that a speaker of one natural language may possess a concept of truth that a speaker of another lacks, would also appear to be beyond the limit of expression (though expressed), at least according to Davidson himself. In 'On the Very Idea of a Conceptual Scheme' (1974b) he argues that the claim that one speaker may possess concepts that another lacks – that is, has a different conceptual scheme – makes, in the end, no sense (pp. 197f.):[26]

It would be wrong to summarize by saying that we have shown how communication is possible between people who have different schemes, a way that works without need of what there cannot be, namely a neutral ground, or a common coordinate system. For we have found no intelligible basis on which it can be said that schemes are different. It would equally be wrong to announce the glorious news that all mankind – all speakers of language, at least – share a common scheme and ontology. For if we cannot intelligibly say that schemes are different, neither can we intelligibly say that they are one.

The argument for this view is rather a long one but, if I understand it right, turns on the rejection of semantic correlates and the consequent indeterminacy of translation. If one were to think of concepts as did Frege, then there would be no problem about the idea that speaker A possesses a concept that speaker B does not: this is just a relationship of a certain kind between a speaker and a semantic correlate. But this move is open to neither Quine nor Davidson. The only way that either can make sense of the idea is as the claim that (part of) the language of speaker A cannot be translated into that of speaker B. But this situation can never arise: it is always possible to translate. There may be a cost: translation may require us to attribute some odd beliefs to speakers (p. 197). If, for example, we translate 'gavagai' as 'book', and speakers tend to utter it as rabbits go past, we may have to attribute to them some rather strange metaphysical beliefs, for example that rabbits have writing in them (in their entrails?). But strange cultures do have strange metaphysical beliefs; so this is hardly outrageous. If there were a determinately correct translation, our translation might be wrong. But the existence of a uniquely correct translation is precisely ruled out by the indeterminacy of translation.

Hence, both the statement that truth-in-English is not expressible in English, and even the very claim that one speaker has a concept that another lacks, appear to be contradictions at the limits of expression (at least within the Quine/Davidson framework).

[25] See Priest and Crosthwaite (1989), pp. 384ff.
[26] Quine agrees. See (1981), p. 42.

Conclusion

We have seen in this chapter how a theory of meaning that jettisons the notion of semantic correlates may yet engender contradictions at the limit of thought. The Quine/Davidson theory gives rise to contradictions at the limits of expression both because of the indeterminacy of sense and reference, and in an attempt to avoid contradictions at the limits of cognition.

Although Quine and Davidson both reject the existence of semantic correlates, they both work very much in the Fregean truth-conditional tradition. There are, however, approaches to meaning that come at the notion from a quite different direction. One of these was proposed by the later Wittgenstein himself. Another is proposed by Derrida, whose work is inspired by Saussure, rather than Frege. In the next chapter we will look at these accounts and see whether they fare any better at avoiding contradictions at the limits of thought.

14 Consciousness, rules, and *différance*

Introduction

In the last chapter, we looked at the account of meaning of Quine and Davidson. We saw that it rejected the existence of semantic correlates, accepted the consequent indeterminacy of sense, and yet still produced contradictions at the limits of thought. Their account of meaning is not (necessarily) a behaviourist one, as I observed (in 13.3 and 13.6), but it is certainly a third-person approach to meaning. It takes no account of what it is like to use language from a first-person perspective; consciousness, if you like. Traditionally – at least in the ideationalist tradition of Locke and others – this was thought to be of the essence of meaning.[1] Hence it may well be thought that we have so far missed an important element of the story, and that this vitiates any conclusions we might draw from our consideration of language. The purpose of this chapter is to address this issue.

We will do so by looking at the views on meaning of two rather different writers: the later Wittgenstein of the *Philosophical Investigations*, and the modern French writer Derrida. These are very different philosophers, in tradition, style of writing, and focus. Yet in the present context they are strikingly similar. Both reject accounts of meaning based on semantic correlates (though neither puts it that way); both accept the consequent indeterminacy of sense; both take into account the relationship between consciousness and meaning; and both adopt a tantalising, but often frustrating, obliqueness to philosophical issues.[2] In this chapter we will see all these things. We will also see another property that they share – with each other and with all the other writers on meaning we have been considering: their views all trespass over the limits of the expressible, and so deliver contradictions at the limits of thought.

14.1 Wittgenstein and names

Let us start with Wittgenstein. As is well known, Wittgenstein came to reject most of the doctrines of the *Tractatus* in his later life. Instead, he came to adopt

---

[1] See Hacking (1975), Part A.

[2] Aspects of the similarities and differences between the two writers are discussed in Garver (1973) and Grene (1976).

very different views about language and meaning. These are expressed in Part I of the *Philosophical Investigations* (1953).[3] There is also relevant material in parts of the *Remarks on the Foundations of Mathematics*. One of the shrewdest analyses of the relevant material is Kripke's (1982),[4] and what I say is heavily influenced by this. Naturally, Kripke's analysis is contentious.[5] It seems to me that the interpretation he gives is largely correct, but I do not want to enter into the exegetical debate here. As usual, it is the nature of the arguments themselves, not the issue of whether a particular person gave them, that is my central concern. My discussion should be understood in the light of these comments.

The *Investigations* starts, famously, with a quotation from Augustine in which he states a version of an account of meaning which invokes semantic correlates for all words: all words are names, and name objects. (It could equally well have started with an appropriate quotation from the *Tractatus*.) The first part of the *Investigations* is a critique of this (and other Tractarian themes). For example, we have (PI120):[6]

You say: the point isn't the word, but its meaning, and you think of the meaning as a thing of the same kind as the word, though also different from the word. Here the word, there the meaning. The money, and the cow that you can buy with it. (But by contrast: the money and its use.)

So if the meanings of words are not determined by their relationships to semantic correlates, what does determine their meaning? For example, what makes it correct for me to apply the word 'book', next time I use it, to one of the books on my shelf, and not to the motor bike which I will ride home?

14.2 Following a rule

The use of language is a rule-governed activity. What determines the correctness or otherwise of my use of 'book' is a certain rule of application, for example, the rule: *always apply the word 'book' to books (and only books)*. So we can put the question more generally. When we follow a rule, what determines the correctness of our behaviour? The sections following PI143 contain a sustained discussion of the question. The answer implicit in them is: nothing.

---

[3] I will prefix section references to the *Investigations* with 'PI'. Quotations are from the third edition, 1967.

[4] Page references are to this.

[5] For example, critiques of Kripke's interpretation can be found in Goldfarb (1985), Tait (1986), and Werhane (1987). Kripke's book initiated a large literature, partly dealing with his interpretation, partly dealing with his arguments, mainly mixed. For an excellent discussion and survey (by no means exhaustive) of the literature, see Boghossian (1989). I have resisted the temptation to take on the literature here: to do so properly would require much more space than is appropriate in this context.

[6] See also, for example, PI10–14.

For a start, it does no good to say that the rule itself determines the right behaviour. For what determines how the rule is to be applied? When, for example, I next apply the rule stated in the last paragraph, why can't I simply take 'books' as it occurs in the rule to apply to motor bikes? Doubtless, because of the meaning of the word 'book'; but it was exactly what determines the meaning of the word 'book' in this way that was at issue, so we are no better off. Maybe, then, there is a rule as to how to apply the rule. But this just shifts the problem back one and launches us off onto a regress that is clearly vicious (PI86).

Maybe, then, it is some state of mind associated with the rule that determines the matter. For example, maybe the rule for the use of 'book' conjures up the mental image of a book, and I simply match up the image with the object. Many passages in the *Investigations* bring home the fact that there is often no state of mind that goes together with meaning something, and, *a fortiori*, that determines meaning. But, even if there were suitable candidates for such mental states, it is not difficult to see, as Wittgenstein points out, that they could not do the required job. The point is similar to the one made in the last paragraph. Any mental state would have to be applied in some way. What determines its application? For example an image of a book could equally represent a book of a certain colour, the shape of a book, literacy, or any number of other things. As Wittgenstein puts it (PI139):

Well, suppose that a picture comes before your mind when you hear the word 'cube', say the drawing of a cube. In what sense can this picture fit or fail to fit a use of the word 'cube'? – Perhaps you say: 'It's quite simple; – if that picture occurs to me and I point to a triangular prism for instance, and say it is a cube, then this use of the word doesn't fit the picture.' – But doesn't it fit? I have purposely chosen the example that it is quite easy to imagine a *method of projection* according to which the picture does fit after all.
The picture of the cube did indeed *suggest* a certain use to us, but it was possible for me to use it differently.[7]

Or maybe it is another mental state. For example, perhaps it is the intention to use the word 'book' to apply to books, that determines its application? This is no better. For what is it that determines that books in intention represent books in reality, and not motor bikes? Notoriously, representations, mental or otherwise, need be nothing like what they represent. And similar comments will apply to other mental (intensional) states. As PI693 puts it: 'nothing is more wrong-headed than calling meaning a mental activity'.

---

[7] PI141 goes on: 'Suppose, however, that not merely the picture of the cube, but also the method of projection comes before our mind? – How am I to imagine this? – Perhaps I see before me a schema shewing the method of projection: say a picture of two cubes connected by lines of projection. – But does this really get me any further? Can't I now imagine different applications of this schema too? – Well, yes.'

Although the *Investigations* hardly considers all the aspects of mind or action that, it might be suggested, account for the determinacy of rule-following, the considerations Wittgenstein marshals are pretty general, and it is difficult to see how there could be candidates that escape them.[8] Hence, he concludes (PI201):

This was our paradox: no course of action could be determined by a rule, because every course of action can be made to accord with the rule. The answer was: if everything can be made out to accord with a rule, then it can also be made out to conflict with it. And so there would be neither accord nor conflict here.

Since meaning is a special case of rule-following, it follows that there is nothing to determine that 'book' should be applied to books rather than to motor bikes; and so on for all other words. In other words, there is nothing to determine that words mean anything at all. Wittgenstein never draws the conclusion explicitly (as Kripke notes, and we will come back to in a moment). However, Kripke draws it for him (p. 21). (In this quotation, quus is an arithmetic function that is the same as plus in all hitherto computed cases, but is different in the next one.)

This, then, is the sceptical paradox. When I respond in one way rather than another to such a problem as '68 + 57', I can have no justification for one response rather than another. Since the sceptic who supposes that I meant quus [by '+'] cannot be answered, there is no fact about me that distinguishes between my meaning plus and my meaning quus. Indeed, there is no fact about me that distinguishes between my meaning a definite function by 'plus' (which determines my response in new cases) and my meaning nothing at all.

14.3 Language games

These considerations, then, destroy meaning. The situation appears intolerable. What does Wittgenstein make of it? He gives what Kripke calls a 'skeptical solution' to the paradox. A straight solution to a paradox is simply a way of faulting the arguments for the conclusion in question. Wittgenstein has endorsed the relevant arguments himself, and so this option is hardly open to him. A skeptical solution, by contrast, is a way of accepting the conclusion, but explaining how we can live with it. In Wittgenstein's case, this is an explanation of how we manage to use language even though there is no determinate meaning. The key to this is his own account of rule-following.

According to Wittgenstein, to follow a rule is simply to go on in a certain way that we find inevitable after a period of training. After a certain training, I apply 'book' to copies of *The Critique of Pure Reason*, the *Tractatus* and so on, and not, for example, to my bike. And that is that. So PI217 tell us:

[8] Some further candidates are discussed in ch. 1 of Kripke (1982).

'How am I able to obey a rule?' – if this is not a question about causes, then it is about justification for obeying the rule in the way I do.
If I have exhausted the justifications I have reached bedrock, and my spade is turned. Then I am inclined to say: 'This is simply what I do.'

What, then, differentiates this behaviour from a merely subjective response? The fact that everyone else (or at least most other people) act in the same way. If someone does not respond this way, we say that they have not learned the language. If they do not respond to suitable training or retraining, we count them as idiots or insane. The very possibility of using language, therefore, depends on the fact that most people *do* have the dispositions to respond to training in the same way. Without this the notion of following a rule would make no sense at all. As Wittgenstein puts it (PI199):

It is not possible that there should have been only one occasion on which someone obeyed a rule. It is not possible that there should have been only one occasion on which a report was made, an order given or understood; and so on. – To obey a rule, to make a report, to give an order, to play a game of chess, are *customs* (uses, institutions).[9]

It follows that when it comes to the issue of how language should be used, there is no higher court of appeal than common practice, the 'language game' that is played. As Wittgenstein puts it (PI124):

Philosophy may in no way interfere with the actual use of language; it can in the end only describe it ... It leaves everything as it is.[10]

But now we have a new problem. One of the language games we play is about meaning. We say that some utterances have meaning and that some do not, that 'book' and 'motor bike' mean different things, and so on. In particular, and according to this, the view that there is no determinate meaning, or that there is no determinately correct way to apply the word 'book' is blatantly false. The price of Wittgenstein's solution is, therefore, that it shows his analysis to be false; or, better, it leaves him no language in which to express his claims about meaning and, generally, rule-following, since he has just succeeded in justifying the linguistic status quo. Kripke puts it nicely as follows (pp. 69f.):

It is for this reason I conjectured ... that Wittgenstein's professed inability to write a work with conventionally organised arguments and conclusions stems at least in part, not from personal and stylistic proclivities, but from the nature of his work. Had Wittgenstein ... stated the outcome of his conclusions in the form of definite theses, it would have been very difficult to avoid formulating his doctrines in a form that consists in apparent sceptical denials of our ordinary assertions ... If, on the other hand, we do not state our conclusions in the form of broad philosophical theses, it is

---

[9] See also PI202.
[10] Or as he puts it in a different context (PI98): 'every sentence of our language is "in order as it is"'.

easier to avoid the danger of a denial of any ordinary beliefs ... Whenever our opponent insists on the perfect propriety of an ordinary form of expression (e.g. that 'the steps are determined by the formula', 'the future application is already present'), we can insist that if these expressions are properly understood, we agree. The danger comes when we try to give a precise formulation of exactly what it is that we *are* denying – *what* 'erroneous interpretation' our opponent is placing on ordinary means of expression. It may be hard to do this without producing yet another statement that, we must admit, is *still* 'perfectly alright when properly understood'.

Hard? In fact impossible, since Wittgenstein's very thesis is the indeterminacy of the norms of rule-following. The situation is now a very familiar one: we have another contradiction at the limit of expression. Wittgenstein's account of rule-following entails that the major conclusions of his skeptical arguments cannot be expressed. The situation is the same as that in the *Tractatus*. But whilst in the *Tractatus* Wittgenstein chose to make this conclusion explicit, in the *Investigations* he had grown more canny (if Kripke is correct), refusing to state the point, and merely hinting at it. In 1.3 we saw that Cratylus' views forced him into a similar plight. In the *Investigations*, Wittgenstein opts for the silence of Cratylus.

None the less, the point remains: the conclusion that results from the skeptical arguments, and that Wittgenstein wishes us to grasp, is beyond expression (Transcendence). Yet it is possible to express it; I have just done so and so does Kripke (Closure). Hence we have a contradiction at the limit of expression.

PI119 says:

The results of philosophy are the uncovering of one or another piece of plain nonsense and of bumps that the understanding has got by running its head up against the limits of language. These bumps make us see the value of the discovery.

It is just that when we make the discovery we cannot (but do) express it.

14.4 Derrida on presence

So much for Wittgenstein. Let us now turn to Derrida. Derrida is a literary philosopher. This is true in two senses. The first is that his work falls across the traditional divide between philosophy and literary criticism. I shall consider only that part of his work which bears on the theme of the determinacy of sense (though, arguably, this is the central part of his theoretical work).[11] The second sense in which Derrida is a literary philosopher is that he often eschews traditional philosophical styles of writing in favour of styles that might be more at home in literary works. One reason for this might be the problem – that we

---

[11] For a general introduction to Derrida's thought, a number of works can be consulted, for example, Norris (1987). The ground we will cover is well traversed in Culler (1979).

have just encountered in Wittgenstein – of saying what he means straight.[12] At any rate, whatever the reason, his style makes him singularly difficult to interpret. For this reason I am unsure that I have understood him – more than any other philosopher discussed in this book.[13]

Still, putting this caveat aside, let us start with Derrida's principal philosophical thesis: the denial of presence. What I have called semantic correlates, Derrida calls the *transcendental signified*. And anything supposed to act in this role, Derrida calls a *presence*. Fregean referents and Tractarian objects are presences (as are Lockean ideas), though not ones on which Derrida explicitly sets his sights. More frequently cited examples are: essence, Being and, particularly, consciousness. These are some of the central concepts of Western metaphysics. In fact, Derrida takes metaphysics to be exactly that subject which endorses the action of some presence or other. As he puts it ((1981), p. 20):

the entire history of metaphysics ... impose[s], and will never cease to impose upon semiological science in its entirety this fundamental quest for a 'transcendental signified'.

Whether Derrida is right to see the whole of Western metaphysics in this way is an interesting question – which we need not go into here.

14.5 ... and absence

So much for what presence is; next to its denial. When Derrida denies presence he denies that anything can act, as a presence, to ground meaning. The next question is obvious: if statements do not have meaning in virtue of being grounded in semantic correlates, how do they have meaning? Derrida gives an answer to this question by way of a critique of structuralist theories of meaning, particularly that of Saussure.[14]

Structuralism already rejects the view that a phrase has meaning in virtue of a concept it expresses in and of itself. It observes that phrases come in families, often binary families, and claims that a phrase has its meaning in virtue of its relationships to the other phrases in that family, and, particularly, because of its contrasting place in the family. Thus, for example, consider the word 'red'. This belongs to the family of colour words {red, green, blue ... }, and what makes it

---

[12] Interestingly enough, one of the influences on Derrida, Nietzsche, employs this technique for similar reasons, according to one commentator. Nehamas (1985) argues that Nietzsche espouses a view according to which there is no absolute truth: only relative truths, 'perspectives'. The trouble is that to describe this view one has to put it forward as a non-relative truth. We met a simlar problem for Protagoras in 3.8.

[13] But then, if Derrida is right, there is perhaps nothing determinate to understand.

[14] This can be found in the early pages of Derrida (1974), and is usefully summarised on pp. 19ff. of (1981).

mean red, is just that it does not mean green, blue, etc. Similarly for 'blue'. Or, to remove the air of circularity from this, we could put it as follows: each of the words in the family has meaning in virtue of its network of relations of opposition with the other members of the family, that is, its difference from them.[15]

This much of structuralism Derrida accepts, but other aspects of Saussure's thought he rejects. Crucially, he rejects Saussure's notion of the sign. According to this, the sign is composed of two aspects: the signifier (that is, the physical token) and the signified (the concept it expresses). Though the sign may be dependent for its identity on its place in a network of meaning-relations, the signifier is still conceptualised as corresponding to a unique concept, the signified; and this is a presence.

But how are we to locate this concept? Not, according to Saussure, in writing. For when a word or longer linguistic string – which we can call a text[16] – is written, it continues to exist independently of its utterance, and can come to take on all kinds of different meanings in virtue of new contexts. For example, Shelley's poem *Ozymandias* tells of a traveller who comes across the trunk of a statue in the middle of a desert. This is all that remains of a once great empire. On it are written the words:

My name is Ozymandias, king of kings:
Look on my works, ye Mighty, and despair.

In the original context these were obviously meant to bring home the insignificance of everyone other than Ozymandias; now, they bring home the vanity of pretension. Derrida calls this phenomenon the *iterability* of the text.

To find the concept we therefore have to look to the intentions (i.e., consciousness) of the utterer. This, therefore, is a kind of presence (indeed, the paradigm case for Derrida since, then, meaning is present in consciousness). But what would we find if we examined the intentions of the utterer? They would, presumably, be something like: in uttering such and such I intended to mean so and so.[17] We do not, therefore, find meanings; just more words (so and so). And if we were to ask for the meaning of *these* words we would merely find *more* words. Hence, we never break out of the circle of words into a realm of semantic correlates. Any word is referred to further words indefinitely, and this relationship of referral, or, perhaps better, deferral, is just as constitutive of meaning as Saussure's differences. As Derrida puts it ((1981), p. 26):

---

[15] Interestingly enough, similar thoughts can be found in the middle-period Wittgenstein. See (1975), p. 317. For a discussion of the similarities between Saussure and Wittgenstein, see Harris (1988).

[16] The notion of a text is much broader than that of language, and comprises other forms of representation too, such as pictures, adverts, etc. This makes no essential difference to the points being made here, so I shall ignore these other forms.

[17] Or, in its Gricean variant (1957), intend listeners to come to believe that (I believe that) so and so, by means of recognising this intention.

Whether in the order of spoken or written discourse, no element can function as a sign without referring to another element which itself is not simply present. This inter-weaving results in each 'element' – phoneme or grapheme – being constituted on the basis of the trace within it of the other elements of the chain or system.

Thus, meaning is constituted by the total network of both differences and deferrals. For this network, Derrida coins the neologism '*différance*'. Hence, meaning is constituted by, as he puts it, the 'play' of *différance*.

14.6 Deconstruction

Before we are finished with Derrida's basic notions, there is another we need to discuss: deconstruction. Derrida, as I have said, denies presence. He does not, as far as I am aware, provide a general argument against presence. Rather, what he does do is take examples of texts which endorse some notion of presence, either overtly or covertly, and show that they are self-undercutting in some sense. This is called 'deconstruction'. Though the details of how to deconstruct depend on the text itself, and so vary from case to case, there is a general frame.

Take a text that endorses some form of presence, π. By the Saussurian semiotics, this draws its sense from its opposite, non-π. And this means that the pair $\langle \pi, \text{non-}\pi \rangle$ provides, in some sense, an underpinning structure for the text. (There may be other pairs providing other aspects of the structure.) But the members of the pair are not on equal terms; since it is π that is supposed to be doing all the metaphysical work, π is the dominant member of the pair. In the jargon of deconstruction, it is privileged.

Deconstruction comes in two stages (or perhaps Hegelean moments, since they may be carried out simultaneously). The first is to reverse the privileging, to make non-π the dominant member of the pair. This is done by showing how, in contrast to the claims of the text, it implicitly shows that non-π is the more important and fundamental of the pair. This stage is called, for obvious reasons, 'reversal'. The next stage, now that both members of the pair are on an equal footing, is to examine the very ground of the distinction between π and non-π, and show that it is a false antithesis. There is a space between them in which some new concept lies, which both unites and differentiates the pair, but is not reducible to either. This stage is called 'displacement'. In many respects it is reminiscent of the third stage of Hegel's dialectic (7.3).[18] The new concepts in question might be said to transcend (*aufhebt*) the relevant opposi-tions. They are often called 'undecidables', by a rather shaky analogy with Gödel's Incompleteness Theorem, and are expressed by words that occur in the original texts, but which come to take on a whole new meaning. These

---

[18] Though see Derrida (1981), p. 43.

provide much of the distinctive vocabulary of deconstruction: *supplément*, *hymen*, *parergon*, etc.

How deconstruction is supposed to undercut the text is as follows. First, the reversal shows that there are certain contradictions implicit in the pretensions of the text. This is, of course, a very traditional form of critique. (In a sense we have already seen examples of it at work in previous chapters concerning knowledge and skepticism (chapter 3), phenomena and noumena (chapter 5), content and form (chapter 12).) The result of the second phase is much more novel. The undecidable concept that emerges undercuts the distinction between, and hence the sense of, the original contrasting pair of concepts, and *a fortiori* any attempt to use the contrast to ground an account of meaning (presence).

It would be pointless for present purposes to examine all Derrida's applications of this method. However, let us quickly look at one example of it, if only to put some flesh on these rather abstract bones. This is Derrida's discussion of Rousseau in *De la Grammatologie*.[19] Like Saussure, Rousseau takes speech to be a form of presence in a way that writing is not, since it is always present to consciousness. (Clearly, Rousseau had never used a dictaphone.) The couple speech/writing is therefore the underlying structure of his text, speech being the privileged member. Derrida argues that Rousseau is forced to recognise, despite his avowed thesis, that writing is an absolutely necessary supplement (supplanting) of speech; thus writing is conceded to be the more fundamental. The undecidable that emerges from the discussion is the notion of a supplement, which describes the relationship between speech and writing but, in good Hegelean fashion, means both 'replacement' and 'completion', and so destroys any clear functional opposition between speech and writing.

14.7 The revenge of Cratylus

With Derrida's views in place, let us now (re)turn to the issue of the limits of thought. If Derrida is right, there is no presence, no ultimate ground of meaning. In particular, no text can show immediately and transparently what it means. Thus, all texts must be interpreted – or read, to use a different jargon. Moreover, because of its iterability, a text can be read in many ways; that is, it may be interpreted to mean different things in different contexts (which is not to say that it can be interpreted to mean anything). There is no

---

[19] A summary is given on pp. 126–7 of Hart (1989); another can be found in Johnson (1981). Interestingly in the present context, Staten (1984) (especially ch. 2) argues that the *Investigations* is a text that deconstructs the *Tractatus*. Despite the fact that the Wittgenstein of the *Investigations* is undoubtedly against what Derrida is against, I find Staten's argument that the methodology of the *Investigations* is a deconstructive one unpersuasive. It does not seem to me to fit the pattern I have sketched.

question of any one interpretation being correct (though this is not to say that all interpretations are equally good). Finally, and in any case, the interpretation of a text is just another text, and so needs to be interpreted, but itself has no privileged interpretation.

A text, then, expresses no intrinsic meaning, but may be taken to mean indefinitely many things. Now apply this observation to Derrida's own text. We take Derrida to be advocating a certain view, namely, arguing against presence, the determinacy of sense. Yet, if he is right he is not advocating anything with stable and determinate sense at all. What, then, are we supposed to make of what he says if there is nothing *as such* that he says? Or, to put it the other way, given that he does express certain views (those that I have summarised), he is expressing something (Closure) that, if he is right, cannot be expressed (Transcendence).

We have met this situation before in another context. It is essentially Cratylus' problem of how one can express anything, when meaning itself is in a state of flux (1.3). As we saw there, it is possible for Cratylus to avoid the contradiction simply by pointing out that meanings do not change in the short term. The sense of an assertion is determined, or fixed, for long enough. This reply is not open to Derrida, however. The meaning of any statement is constituted by the chain of interconnections (differences and deferrals) between itself and other statements. Any time that someone makes a remark (or at least, a remark on the same topic), this extends the chain and, therefore, changes the meaning. And the more one says (for example, by way of exegesis or clarification!) the worse the situation gets, since the more the meaning changes.

There is, however, another possible reply. This is simply to concede that Derrida's texts have no fixed sense, but argue that they have a function quite independent of the expression of such a sense. In particular, though the texts might mean nothing in any absolute sense, the idea of a particular reading of the texts makes perfectly good sense. Now, Derrida's texts have been read (by himself and others) as an attack on presence. If this is so, they have served their end. If the texts are read in some other way by some latter-day Shelleyan traveller, who cares? In other words, the texts have a particular function in the present philosophical conjuncture, and they can serve this function without having determinate meaning. This, it might be said, is the strategy of Derrida's writing.[20]

14.8 *Différance*

We are not finished with the limit of the expressible yet, though. For there is a more fundamental way in which Derrida's work transcends the bounds of

---

[20] In this, it is not unlike Sextus' strategy. See 3.4.

expression. It does so when it deals with *différance*. *Différance* is a problematic notion, as numerous commentators have noted. According to Derrida, it is the structure that gives rise to meaning; it is the precondition of any meaning at all. It itself is beyond expression: it cannot be described in any way.[21] As he puts it ((1982), p. 26):

différance has no name in our language. But we 'already know' that if it is unnameable, it is not provisionally so, not because our language has not yet found or received this *name*, or because we would have to seek it in another language, outside the finite system of our own. It is rather because there is no *name* for it at all, not even the name of essence or of Being, not even that of '*différance*', which is not a name, which is not a pure nominal unity, and unceasingly dislocates itself in a chain of differing and deferring substitutions.

It might be thought that this is a mental aberration, or a simple mistake on Derrida's part. It is not: it is forced on him by the internal logic of his position. One can see this by putting together two observations.

The first is that deconstruction is an operation that, when applied to a text that is structured by some binary opposition, produces, in the phase of displacement, a notion that is not expressible in terms of that opposition, and so in the text that this opposition structures. As Derrida himself puts it ((1981), p. 42):

That being said – and on the other hand – to remain in this phase [of deconstruction, viz., reversal] is still to operate on the terrain of and from within the deconstructed system. By means of this double, and precisely stratified, dislodged and dislodging, writing, we must also mark the interval between inversion, which brings low what was high, and the irruptive emergence of a new 'concept', a concept that can no longer be, and never could be, included in the previous regime.

For the second observation, note that the totality of all linguistic entities, that is, textuality itself, is structured by a certain binary opposition. What *all* such entities have in common is their presupposition of (the) metaphysics (of presence); crucially, the sign itself, of which all linguistic expressions are composed, is the metaphysical notion *par excellence*. As Derrida puts it ((1978), pp. 280f.):

There is no sense in doing without the concept of metaphysics in order to shake metaphysics. We have no language – no syntax and no lexicon – which is foreign to this history [of metaphysics]; we can pronounce not a single destructive proposition which has not already had to slip into the form, the logic, and the implicit postulations of precisely what it seeks to contest. To take one example from many: the metaphysics of presence is shaken with the notion of *sign*. But . . . as soon as one seeks to demonstrate in this way that there is no transcendental or privileged signified and that the

---

[21] In (1982), p. 6, Derrida likens the problem of speaking about *différance* to the problem that negative theologians such as Cusanus (see 1.8) have in talking about God.

domain or play of signification henceforth has no limit, one must reject even the concept and word 'sign' itself – which is precisely what cannot be done. For the signification 'sign' has always been understood and determined, in its meaning, as a sign-of, a signifier referring to a signified, a signifier different from its signified.

The very notion of presence, the core of metaphysics, is therefore written into any linguistic expression,[22] and hence it is the pair presence/absence that structures textuality itself, that is, the totality of all texts.

Since this is so, we can apply the deconstructive operation to it. What, then, do we get? What notion is obtained when the pair presence/absence is deconstructed? The answer is, of course, *différance*. *Différance* is the notion that arises out of the displacement of the pair presence/absence, and so transcends them. This is because it is precisely *différance* that (Derrida (1974), p. 143):

makes the opposition of presence and absence possible. Without the possibility of *différance*, the desire of presence as such would not find its breathing space. This means by the same token that this desire carries in itself the destiny of non-satisfaction. *Différance* produces what it forbids, makes possible the very thing it makes impossible.

Thus (Derrida (1981) p. 27):

différance, then, is a structure and a movement no longer conceivable on the basis of the opposition presence/absence.

To summarise the two observations: The first is that if a text is deconstructed we arrive at a notion, facts about which cannot be expressed in the text in question. The second is that the notion of *différance* is obtained by deconstructing the totality of *all* linguistic expressions. It follows from these that facts about *différance* cannot be expressed by linguistic utterances at all. Hence, we see that the inexpressibility of *différance* is no mere quirk of Derrida, but is inherent in the logic of his position.

14.9 … and inclosure

Claims about *différance* are not expressible; but Derrida's own texts would seem to be replete with such claims. Even to say that *différance* is inexpressible you have to refer to it to say what it is that cannot be expressed. The problem has been noted by a number of writers. Wood ((1980), p. 225), for example, pithily puts it thus: 'Derrida has the problem of saying what he means without meaning what he says.'

What does Derrida make of this? One strategy he uses is to employ the technique (borrowed from Heidegger) of writing under erasure, so indicating that his words do not really mean what they say, thus ((1982), p. 6):

---

[22] Derrida's view here is very similar to Kant's view concerning the Transcendental Illusion (see 6.1).

Now if *différance* ix... what makes possible the presentation of the being-present, it is never presented as such.

But if the words are not to be taken at face value, what *are* they to be taken to mean? In an interview with Ronse, Derrida takes up the matter as follows ((1981), p. 14):

I try to write (in) the space in which is posed the question of speech and meaning. I try to write the question: (what is) meaning to say? Therefore it is necessary in such a space, and guided by such a question, that writing literally mean nothing. Not that it is absurd in the way that absurdity has always been in solidarity with metaphysical meaning. It simply tempts itself, tenders itself, attempts to keep itself at the point of the exhaustion of meaning.

When stripped of its hedging, what Derrida is saying is that his own writing is meaningless. Hence, his reaction is exactly that of the Wittgenstein of the *Tractatus* (12.9) and Quine (13.5). But, just as with Wittgenstein and Quine, this is quite unsatisfactory. For Derrida *is* making himself understood, and so is not saying meaningless things. Indeed, his statements about *différance* enter into the play of *différances* constituted by discussions of texts (his own and others), and so are meaningful by his own account, in exactly the same way that all other statements are.

Hence, any honest appraisal of the situation must admit that statements about *différance are* expressible. We therefore have a contradiction typical of a limit of thought. Claims about difference are not expressible (Transcendence); yet they are expressed (Closure).

In fact, the contradiction fits the Inclosure Schema in a simple way. Let $\varphi(y)$ be: y is a linguistic expression. Let $\psi(x)$ be: x is structured by some binary opposition. Let $\delta(x)$ be some statement that concerns the notion undecidable in terms of such an opposition. (Such statements would typically occur in any text that deconstructs x.) As we have seen, if x is a text structured by some binary opposition, $\delta(x)$ cannot be expressed in x. Hence we have Transcendence, but it is clearly a linguistic expression. Hence we have Closure. Finally, the totality of all expressions, Ω, is structured by the pair presence/absence. Hence we have Existence. The contradiction arises when the deconstructive diagonaliser is applied to the totality of all texts to produce a statement about *différance* (for example, one of Derrida's own). At this point, *le pas au-delà* (the step beyond) is *un pas au-delà* (a non-beyond) to use Derrida's own neat turn of phrase.[23] One might well exploit Derrida's technique of writing under erasure, and call inclosures l̶i̶m̶i̶t̶s̶.

---

[23] See Hart (1989), p. 88.

Conclusion

This completes our review of the later Wittgenstein and Derrida, and, more generally, of modern theories of meaning that jettison semantic determinacy. As we have seen, all such theories end in contradictions at the limit of expression. There is also a further striking fact. All of the theories of meaning that we have looked at in this part of the book render some important states of affairs ineffable (whilst managing to express them). And in all cases the states of affairs in question are ones that are, in some sense, about notions that make expression in language itself possible: the unity of the proposition (Frege, earlier Wittgenstein), reference (Quine), truth (Davidson, albeit in an attempt to avoid contradictions at other limits), rule-following (later Wittgenstein), *différance* (Derrida). We have here, in all cases, an inclosure contradiction of the kind we already noted in the Conclusion of chapter 12. $\varphi(y)$ is 'y can be expressed in language' (where y is some state of affairs), so that Ω is the totality of things that can be expressed; $\psi(x)$ is 'x = Ω'; $\delta(\Omega)$ is s, where this is the relevant state of affairs concerning whatever notion it is that makes expression in language possible. Then, by the argument in each case, we have $\neg\varphi(s)$ (Transcendence); yet in the process of analysis we demonstrate that $\varphi(s)$ (Closure).[24]

I have not tried to show that any half-way adequate theory of meaning must end up in the same situation; I am not sure how one could go about showing this. But the fact that each theory renders inexpressible facts about what makes language possible – and that the theories are of such different kinds – does suggest that there is something about the very possibility of language that is like this. At the heart of language lies what language cannot express (though each theorist may get a different fix on it, as it were). I think that there is

---

[24] There is a natural thought at this point. Since any adequate account of the situation must do justice to the fact that claims about the pertinent structure of language can be expressed in *some* sense, it is tempting to distinguish between the different senses. The senses might be thought of as contexts, languages, *genres*, or any other number of things. Let us call the different senses, for want of a better word, discourses. The pertinent structure of statements of any given discourse cannot be expressed by statements of that discourse; but it can be expressed by statements of a different discourse. For example, in his introduction to the English edition of the *Tractatus* (Pears and McGuinness (1961), p. xxii), Russell advocates just this with respect to the form of the problem that arises there. As should be clear, this is a version of parameterisation. It does resolve the contradiction; but, as we saw in 10.7, it does so only by relocating it. In particular, it is now the pertinent facts about the totality of languages of all discourses that generate the contradiction. Formally, we parameterise the predicate $\varphi(y)$ so that $\varphi_i(y)$ now reads 'y can be expressed in discourse i' (where the indices range over all discourses). If s_i is the state of affairs like s except that it relates to the language of discourse i, we can now suppose that $\neg\varphi_i(s_i)$ but, quite consistently, that $\varphi_{i'}(s_i)$. But now define $\varphi^*(y)$ as $\exists i\varphi_i(y)$, and let s* be the corresponding state of affairs as it bears on discourses in general. s* obviously expresses a proposition in some discourse, so $\varphi^*(s^*)$. But, by whatever argument we used before to establish Transcendence, $\neg\varphi^*(s^*)$. Hence we still have a contradiction at the limits of thought instantiating the Inclosure Schema.

probably much more to be said about this; but at present, what this is, I do not know.

One could also, I am sure, take issue with many of the details of each of the cases that I have discussed. However, in the present context, it is not the details, but the over-all pattern that is both salient and important. It is a pattern that we have witnessed at many points in the book. Assuming the determinacy of sense, there are contradictions at the limits of expression. There is a way out of the contradiction; notably, jettison the determinacy of sense. Yet ways of doing this merely take us into other contradictions at the limit of expression. What to make of this pattern? I will take this up in the Conclusion of the book.

Conclusion

Whatever is your maximum, kick two inches above that.
Terry Dalton, Karate-do Sensei

The persistence of inclosure

1 The pattern

In the chapters of this book we have traced notions of four limits of thought: the limit of iteration, the limit of cognition, the limit of conception (definition), and the limit of expression. We have tracked them through Western philosophy, from its origins in ancient Greece to the present. As we have seen, they have long been noted as the locus of paradox and contradiction; and many who have discussed situations that involve them have ended up (often unwillingly) in self-contradiction. This is hardly surprising if, as I argued in the Conclusion of chapter 11, the limits themselves are contradictory. I take the contradictory nature of these limits to be the best explanation of the continual historical recurrence of this phenomenon; and therefore confirmed by it.

Further confirmation is provided by the fact that when people have taken steps to avoid these contradictions the contradictions have reasserted themselves elsewhere. In trying to avoid a contradiction at the limit of the knowable, Sextus generated one at the limit of the expressible (3.4); Kant attempted to solve the Antinomies (contradictions at the limit of the iterable) by invoking the distinction between phenomena and noumena (6.7), and in so doing generated contradictions at the limits of the conceivable and expressible (5.5); Russell attempted to solve the paradoxes of self-reference (contradictions at all the limits), but merely succeeded in generating another contradiction at the limit of expression (9.7). Theories of meaning that postulate semantic correlates generate contradictions at the limit of expression (Conclusion of chapter 12); but jettisoning semantic correlates just produces other contradictions at the limits of thought (Conclusions of chapters 13 and 14). And several solutions to the paradoxes of self-reference that we have looked at merely reproduce the problem (9.8, 10.7, 11.4).

Like the air in a partially inflated balloon, if the contradictions are pressed down at one point, they come up at another. One might call this the law of conservation of contradiction. If contradiction is inherent in the very nature of the subject, this is hardly surprising: we should expect contradictions to appear in any discussion of the topic which comes close to doing justice to the facts.

2   Limitative theorems

The phenomenon of persistence is, in fact, already well recognised in discussions of the semantic paradoxes: attempts to solve these paradoxes always produce further paradoxes. Herzberger (1980–1), for example, discusses the issue.

To see how and why this arises, let us start, first, with the limitative theorems of modern logic.[1] It is a commonplace to observe that the paradoxes of self-reference underlie many of these. For example, if a theory could express its own truth predicate we would have (other things being equal) the Liar paradox. Hence, no theory can express its own truth predicate (if consistency is to be maintained): Tarski's Theorem. If a theory containing arithmetic were axiomatic it would be able to express its own membership predicate; we would then have a version of the Knower paradox (Gödel's paradox; see 10.2). Hence, the theory is not axiomatic (if consistency is to be maintained): Gödel's first Incompleteness Theorem. Moreover, any attempt to show a (suitably rich) theory to be consistent must be able to express the membership predicate for that theory. This cannot be expressed in the theory itself, or we would have the same paradox. Hence, any attempt to show a theory to be consistent must use resources that outstrip those of the theory in question (if it is consistent): Gödel's second Incompleteness Theorem. Hence, in both Tarski's Theorem and Gödel's second Incompleteness Theorem, the limitative result is simply that a certain notion cannot be expressed in the theory if contradictions at the limits of thought are to be avoided.[2]

Now, attempts to solve the semantic paradoxes need to show that the semantic notions of English (or some other natural language) are, despite appearances, consistent. This requires us to formulate a theory about how those notions behave, and establish its consistency, normally by producing a semantic interpretation for it. By the limitative theorems, this is going to require resources beyond those available in the theory. It is unsurprising, then, that each attempt to solve the paradoxes generates semantic machinery not available in the theory. But where is the theorist to locate this machinery? It can usually be incorporated into the theory itself in a natural way; but, in this case, paradoxes (often of the extended variety) arise – the persistence of contradiction; or else the notions in question can be relegated to a distinct metatheory.[3]

As far as solving the paradoxes goes, the first move is obviously fatal. But so, in its way, is the second: for the aim of the exercise was to show that the

---

[1] For an informal discussion of these see, for example, Fraenkel, Bar-Hillel, and Levy (1973), chapter 5, section 7. For technical details, see Boolos and Jeffrey (1974), chapters 15, 16.

[2] If we allow that the relevant theories may be inconsistent, and so represent the contradictions, then the limitative results fail. See Priest (1994b).

[3] For further discussion, see Priest (1987), ch. 1.

semantic notions of English are consistent, but we now have more semantic notions than can be expressed in our original theory, and so our theory is wrong, or at least, incomplete. We might attempt to avoid the problem by showing that the object theory *plus* metatheory is consistent, but we are now off on a regress. Moreover, this fails. The move is a form of parameterisation and merely regenerates the problem at the limit, as we saw (10.6, 10.7) – the persistence of contradiction.

This is inevitable: if we are trying to find a solution to the semantic paradoxes of English then the metalanguage must be one for English. Hence, if consistency is to be maintained, the relevant notions cannot be expressed in English (Transcendence). But the notions *are* always expressed in English (Closure). Hence, attempts to avoid these contradictions at the limits of thought ultimately end up in contradictions at the limit of expression – the persistence of contradiction.

We have already seen an example of this with Davidson and 'true-in-English' (13.7). A second example is Herzberger himself in another of his papers (1970). In this, he analyses a paradox he calls the paradox of grounding (a semantic version of Mirimanoff's paradox; see 8.4, 8.5). His conclusion (in the form of a pertinent limitative theorem) is that the notion of a predicate of a language being grounded cannot be expressed in that language. The irony of this is that Herzberger has no difficulty explaining what it is for a predicate of English to be grounded, so showing that it can be expressed in English.

3   The Grim universe

If the contradictions themselves have a habit of turning up again and again, it is unsurprising that attempted strategies for solving them do likewise. We have witnessed several (unsuccessful) strategies for trying to avoid the contradiction. For example, several philosophers have appealed to some non-literal mode of expression: Anselm (4.2), Kant (5.6), Wittgenstein (showing, 12.9), Derrida (14.9). Others have resorted to parameterisation: Ramsey, Tarski, etc. (10.6), Russell (chapter 14, footnote 24); but by far the most persistent historical strategy has been to deny the existence of the ultimate totality (in the last instance, if not before). This, in its way, was the line taken by Aristotle (2.2), Kant (Solution 1, 6.7), Russell (9.6), Zermelo (11.1) and others. But as we have seen, the idea cannot be sustained: totalisation is inherent in our conceptual apparatus, and attempts to deny this characteristically run into contradiction themselves.

This book was all but finished when I came across Grim's book *The Incomplete Universe*,[4] which provides yet another case-study in the phenomenon that has been our concern. Grim's primary concern is with the contra-

---

[4] Grim (1991); page references are to this.

dictions at the limits of cognition. In virtue of the fact that we can diagonalise out of any totality of truths, knowable truths, etc. (as we saw in 10.2), Grim concludes that there is no totality of all truths, all things knowable, all propositions, etc. As he puts it (p. 1):

This [book] is an explanation of a cluster of related logical results. Taken together, these seem to have something philosophically important to teach us: something about knowledge and truth and something about the logical impossibility of *totalities* of knowledge and truth.

Here, he means the totalities of *all* truths, *all* knowable things, etc. (There is no problem about collections of *some* of them.) His solution to the problem is, therefore, of the most familiar kind.

In the Grim universe, then, there is no totality of all entities of the pertinent kinds. But the Grim universe is grimmer than this. We saw (11.1) that solutions that deny the existence of such totalities run foul of Cantor's Domain Principle. Grim concedes that quantification over these totalities is also impossible. He even produces a nice variation of Russell's paradox to show that one cannot quantify over all propositions (pp. 113ff.). Essentially, it goes as follows. Suppose that you *can* quantify over all propositions, and consider the proposition that all propositions are not about themselves. If it is not about itself, then, since it is about those propositions that are not about themselves, it is about itself. Conversely, if it is about itself then, since it is not about those propositions that are about themselves, it is not about itself.

We can tighten up the argument at the same time as showing that the contradiction here is an inclosure paradox (in fact, one that fits Russell's schema), as follows. We will say that proposition p is *about* proposition q (Apq) iff p is of the form $\forall x \alpha(x)$, and $\alpha(q)$. Now let $\varphi(y)$ be 'y is a proposition', so that Ω is the totality of all propositions. If $x \subseteq \Omega$, let $\delta(x)$ be the proposition $\forall q(q \in x \wedge \neg Aqq)$. Call this p_x. p_x is obviously a proposition, and so we have Closure. Transcendence is shown as follows. Let $x \subseteq \Omega$, and suppose that $p_x \in x$. Then either $Ap_x p_x$ or $\neg Ap_x p_x$. If $Ap_x p_x$ then, since p_x is of the form $\forall q(q \in x \wedge \neg Aqq)$, we have $p_x \in x \wedge \neg Ap_x p_x$, and so $\neg Ap_x p_x$. If, on the other hand, $\neg Ap_x p_x$ then we have $p_x \in x \wedge \neg Ap_x p_x$, i.e., $Ap_x p_x$. Hence, in either case we have a contradiction. By contraposition, $p_x \notin x$, as required.

Grim's way out of this inclosure contradiction is, as I have said, to deny that you *can* quantify over all propositions. The move may avoid the contradiction, but it does so only by making Grim's own thesis inexpressible. For the very claim that there is no totality of *all* propositions (or all true propositions, etc.) obviously *does* quantify over all propositions. If it does not, then it does not express what is required. Hence we have a contradiction at the limit of expression – the persistence of contradiction.[5]

---

[5] The situation is not unlike that in which Russell found himself. See 9.7.

Grim is aware of the problem, if not, perhaps, its acuity. He says (p. 122):

I started this chapter with a basic Cantorian argument that there can be no set of all truths or of all propositions. In the end, however, I offered an argument against universal propositional quantification in general. Isn't there at least a tension between these two conclusions?

His resolution of the 'tension' is to insist that what his arguments show is that (p. 122):

the very notion of *all* truths – or of all propositions . . . – is itself incoherent.

What is meant here by 'incoherent'? Sometimes the word is used as a simple synonym of 'inconsistent'. If it meant this here, we would have just another statement of the problem, not a solution. However, this is not what Grim means. He explains (p. 123); his conclusions:

should be rendered using scare quotes or other techniques of indirect speech. There is no 'set of all truths', nor for that matter any coherent notion of 'all truths', much as there is no such thing as 'the square circle' or the 'largest positive integer'. In each case what we deny is that there is anything that fits a certain description, a description that we would contradict ourselves by straightforwardly *using*. But the denial that there is any such thing as 'all truths' or 'all propositions' should not itself be thought to commit us to quantifying over all truths or propositions, any more than the denial that there is such a thing as 'the square circle' should be thought to commit us to referring to something as both square and a circle.

What, exactly, is going on here is not clear: there seem to be several thoughts, not entirely consistent with one another. For a start, we are instructed to express the thesis of the book in scare quotes. Thus, we have an appeal to a non-literal mode of expression. We have seen this several times before; and it is no better here than at the other places. Putting the thesis in scare quotes might warn us that it does not mean what it says it means; but that does not help us to determine what it *does* mean.[6] In any case, when we say that there is no such thing as the square circle, 'the square circle' should not be put in scare quotes. Its meaning is the literal and correct one. It is just that this denial need not commit us to the existence of such an entity, as Russell taught us.

Next, we are supposed to see an analogy between something or other, on the one hand, and non-denoting descriptions, or language containing them, on the other. It is not clear to me whether the something in question is supposed to be the definite description 'the notion of quantification over all propositions' or the sentences containing such quantification. In fact, neither possibility works.

---

[6] One might say, I suppose, that the whole story just becomes one of Grim(m)'s fairy tales.

If we are to take the description 'the notion of quantification over all propositions' as itself non-referring then, since there is no such notion, language that uses it must be meaningless. This would, again, be a familiar enough move, but one that is of little help here. Patently, the language is not meaningless; Grim uses it all the time. If it were meaningless, we would not be able to understand his arguments that are supposed to establish the major conclusion of the book. Obviously, we do.

Suppose, on the other hand, that we are to take it that language containing quantification over all propositions is to be understood in a way similar to language containing non-denoting descriptions. What, exactly, we are to say about this move depends on which of the many accounts of non-denotation we are supposed to use, and how, exactly, it is supposed to apply to the quantificational case. But however we try to work out the details, such a move must fail. This is because what we say about sentences containing propositional quantification is, in the end, irrelevant. In particular, Grim's argument about the proposition 'all propositions are not about themselves' may mention a quantified sentence to specify a proposition, but it never *uses* one. All the statements asserted in the argument are quantifier-free. Hence what one says about the status of quantified sentences in use is beside the point.

We can even eliminate all mention of quantification from the argument altogether. Let us say that proposition p is about proposition q (Apq) if p is of the form $\alpha(t)$ where $\alpha(q)$, (and here, quantification is not allowed to occur in α). Now consider the proposition: this proposition is not about itself, i.e., ¬App where this itself is p. If App then, since p is of the form ¬Att, we have ¬App. If, on the other hand, ¬App, then, since p is of the form ¬Att, App. Contradiction. Hence, trying to avoid the contradiction at the limit of thought by some thesis about quantification over propositions, cannot succeed.[7]

As this brief review of Grim's work has demonstrated, his book encapsulates virtually all the notable features to be found in discussions about the limits of thought with which we have become so familiar in the course of this book. One could not hope for a more striking new confirmation of the pattern.

---

[7] Section 1.7 of Grim's book contains a short critique of the line on the semantic paradoxes that I have advocated. A minor criticism given is that the line results in a 'bewildering flurry' of contradictions (p. 27). A number of the contradictions he cites depend on the contraposibility of the T-schema, which I endorsed in the postscript of Priest (1979a), but came to reject in the more systematic account of (1987) (see especially 5.4). Whether the contradictions that remain are bewildering is a subjective matter, not an objective one. His major criticism is that one ought not to accept a contradictory account whilst a consistent account (namely his) is available. As we have seen, it is not.

4   Hegel and inclosure

The contradictions at the limits of thought that we have discussed in the book are all captured formally by the notion of an inclosure. The contradictions that instantiate the Inclosure Schema are generated by two moments: totalising sets of φs and breaking out of those totalities with a diagonaliser, δ, whose nature gives it the power to tear through any such boundary. The crunch comes when we consider the totality of all φs; here, the diagonaliser has nowhere consistent to go. An immovable force meets an irresistible object; and contradiction, in the shape of an inclosure, is the result.

The historical figure who had the clearest insight into the phenomenon was, as we saw, Hegel. For him, the moments of totalisation and transcendence are the two moments of the true infinite. The notion of an inclosure is a generalisation of the notion of Hegel's true infinite; diagonalisation loses its generating properties (since it is only a partial function), and hence the inclosure loses its absolute infinity; but, at its limit, the inclosure inherits the properties of Hegel's contradictory category.

Many people have the urge to push their powers as far as possible, and so explore their limits. This is obviously true of the physical powers exercised in sports and other tasks of endurance; but it is equally true of our powers of thought, such as conceiving, describing, expressing, etc. Exploring a limit of thought has a curious Looking-Glass property, however. In exploring the limit, one perforce finds oneself on the other side. Hegel put it thus:[8]

great stress is laid on the limitations of thought, of reason, and so on, and it is asserted that the limitation *cannot* be transcended. To make such an assertion is to be unaware that the very fact that something is determined as a limitation implies that the limitation is already transcended.

Wittgenstein in the *Tractatus* thus:[9]

in order to be able to draw a limit to thought, we should have to find both sides of the limit thinkable (i.e. we should have to be able to think what cannot be thought).

Quite so. Whereof one cannot speak, thereof one has just contradicted oneself.

---

[8]   Miller (1969), p. 134.
[9]   Pears and McGuinness (1961), p. 3.

Part 5

Post terminum

And this gray spirit yearning in desire
To follow knowledge like a sinking star,
Beyond the utmost bound of human thought.

Alfred, Lord Tennyson, *Ulysses*

15 Heidegger and the grammar of being

15.1 Heidegger and grammar

In contemporary philosophical circles it is common to distinguish between analytic philosophy and continental philosophy. To what extent there is a real difference between these two sorts of philosophy, rather than simply a matter of linguistic style and idiom, is a substantial issue. I am inclined to think that there is not.[1] This essay may go a little way towards showing this, but that is not the topic that I have on the agenda here.

Taking the distinction at face value, and concentrating on the analytic side, it is clear that Frege, Russell, Wittgenstein, and Carnap are paradigm members. And in the work of these philosophers, logical grammar plays a central role, as, for example, the essays in Gaskin (2001) bear witness. Logical grammar also led these philosophers into seemingly paradoxical conclusions. Think, as we have seen, of Frege on the concept *horse* (12.2) or of Wittgenstein saying the unsayable in the *Tractatus* (12.8).

Turning to the other side of the divide, Husserl, Heidegger, Sartre, and Derrida are paradigmatically in the continental camp. Logical grammar plays a much less obvious role in these philosophers. A major upshot of this chapter is that it plays a highly significant role in at least one of these philosophers, Martin Heidegger. Moreover, considerations concerning logical grammar drove Heidegger into exactly the same sort of paradoxical conclusions as they did the analytic philosophers. All this I will show. I should say straightaway that Heidegger's thought is rich and complex, and it is only a part of it that will concern us here – though it is a central, if not the most central, part. I note also that I am concerned, here, to expound Heidegger's views, not to defend them. I will, though, try to present them in as plausible a light as possible.

---

[1] For a start, the nomenclature is singularly misleading. 'Analytic philosophy' has virtually nothing to do with philosophical analysis. This was a philosophical method endorsed by Russell and Wittgenstein early in the 20th century, and which was quickly rejected – even by Wittgenstein himself. 'Continental philosophy' is even more misleading. For a start, it refers, in a very British way, to mainland Europe; but much of what goes on there is not continental philosophy; worse, the origins of analytic philosophy come from the European mainland. (Think of Frege, Wittgenstein, the Vienna Circle, the Lvov–Warsaw School.) For a more detailed discussion of the distinction, see Priest (forthcoming c).

Though Heidegger wrote much in his life, the central point of his philosophy, around which all else turns, is what he called 'the question of *being*'.[2] The question was announced in the introduction to *Being and Time* and pursued until his very last writings. From the very beginning, it was clear to Heidegger that grammatical considerations are important for this. In *Being and Time*, he says, for example ((1996), p. 34):[3]

With regard to the awkwardness and 'inelegance' of expression in the following analyses, we may remark that it is one thing to report narratively about *beings* and another to grasp beings in their *being*. For the latter task not only most of the words are lacking but above all the 'grammar'. If we may allude to earlier and in their own right altogether incomparable researches on the analysis of being, then we should compare the ontological sections of Plato's *Parmenides* or the fourth chapter of the seventh book of Aristotle's *Metaphysics* with a narrative passage from Thucydides. Then we can see the stunning character of the formulations with which their philosophers challenged the Greeks.

Moreover, these grammatical considerations played an important role in the turn in Heidegger's thought concerning being that occurred in the mid-1930s, a period sometimes referred to as the *Kehre*.[4] We will see how in due course. Let us start with the question of being itself.

15.2 The question of being

What is the question of being? Everything that there is has being – exists if you like, as long as you do not read any particular import into this notion, spatial, temporal, material, etc. But what is it to be? That is the question of being. As Heidegger puts it ((1996), pp. 4f.):

What is *asked about* in the question to be elaborated is being, that which determines beings as beings, that in terms of which beings have always been understood no matter how they are discussed.

The question of being was, according to Heidegger, a central issue of early Greek philosophy; but after Plato and Aristotle the question became lost, until we now find it difficult to hear it as an important question at all. In the introduction to *Being and Time*, Heidegger points out three reasons as to why it might be thought to be a non-issue – that being is the most universal property, that it is therefore indefinable (by genus and species), that its mean-

---

[2] Some translators capitalise the 'B' of 'Being' (and the 'N' of 'Nothing'). This can be a useful convention, but I will not follow it here.

[3] Italics in all quotations are original.

[4] The *Kehre* is by no means simply a name for the turn in Heidegger's thought, though this is how I will use it here. It is, perhaps more importantly, a view concerning *Dasein*; but we do not need to go into this.

ing is self-evident – and rejects all these as good reasons, quite rightly. In particular, as Heidegger points out, you must have some understanding of the notions involved in a question before you can even ask it, but that does not show that this understanding is an articulated one ((1996), p. 4):

As a seeking, questioning needs prior guidance from what it seeks. The meaning of being must already therefore be available to us in a certain way. We intimated that we are always already involved in an understanding of being. From this grows the explicit question of the meaning of being and the tendency towards its concept. We do not *know* what 'being' means. But already when we ask, 'What is being?' we stand in an understanding of the 'is' without being able to determine conceptually what the 'is' means. We do not even know the horizon upon which we are supposed to grasp and pin down the meaning.

It should be noted that Heidegger takes being to be both the being of existence and the being of predication. To say that an object is, and to say that it is something, both attribute *being* to the object. Here, for example, Heidegger is clear that being is the *is* of existence ((1996), p. 5):

Everything we talk about, mean, and are related to is in being in one way or another. What and how we ourselves are is also a being. Being is found in thatness and what-ness, reality, the objective presence of things [*Vorhandenheit*], subsistence, validity, existence [*Da-sein*], and in the 'there is' [*es gibt*].

And here he states that being is the *is* of predication ((1996), p. 3):

'Being' is used in all knowledge and predicating, in every relation to beings and in every relation to oneself, and the expression is understandable 'without further ado.' Everybody understands 'The sky is blue,' 'I am happy,' and similar statements.

It might be thought that Heidegger is simply confused in running these two things together, but he is not. For Heidegger, the general form of a statement is 'x is [y]' (where the y is optional); and 'is', which expresses being, is, for Heidegger, the generic logical predicate.

One final preliminary point. The question of being is asked, and asked only, by people. Their nature, *Dasein*, has therefore a very special relationship to the nature of being. That this is so is quite explicit in *Being and Time*; and what this relationship is was also to occupy Heidegger in one way or another throughout the whole of his writings.

15.3 The incredible ineffability of being

So much for the question of being. What is its answer? Heidegger came to the view that this could not be answered, at least, not in any straightforward fashion. What stand in the way of an answer are simple grammatical considerations. Heidegger gives two arguments (that I am aware of) as to why the question cannot be answered. The first appeals to the fact that being is not itself *a* being ((1996), p. 5):

The being of beings 'is' not itself a being. The first philosophical step in understanding the problem of being consists in avoiding telling the *mython tina diēgeisthai*, in not 'telling a story', that is, not determining beings as beings by tracing them back in their origins to another being – as if being had the character of a possible being.

But if being is not a being, it follows that one cannot say anything about it. For to say anything of the form 'Being is [so and so]' would be to attribute to it being, and so make it a being, which it is not.

If Heidegger's reasoning is unclear here, it is possible to elucidate it with a similar argument that appears in Frege. According to Frege,[5] one needs to distinguish between objects (the ontological correlates of names) and concepts (the ontological correlates of predicates). The crucial difference is that concepts are 'unsaturated' (inherently gappy). Frege needs to appeal to this fact to explain the unity of the proposition. We need not go into all this here. The important point for the nonce is that it is a consequence of this view that it is a logical mistake to suppose that concepts are objects of a certain kind. In particular, one cannot refer to them by means of a noun-phrase at all. In the same way, for Heidegger, beings are objects, things, and *being* is a concept. Indeed, as I have already noted, 'is' is the generic form of predication. One cannot, therefore, refer to being, since it is of the wrong logical category. *A fortiori*, one cannot say anything about being. For to say anything about being one would have to say something of the form 'Being is . . . '. And so treat it as an object.

15.4 Nothing

Heidegger's second argument for the ineffability of being is spelled out at greatest length in his essay 'What is Metaphysics?' To understand this, we have to take what will appear at first to be a digression, and talk about *nothing*.

For Heidegger, *nothing* is a thing, and a very important one at that. It sometimes has the honour of a definite article, *the nothing*; and it even does things: nothing nihilates ((1977b), p. 105). This will strike many contemporary philosophers as a simple confusion. In modern logic, 'nothing' is a quantifier phrase, not a noun phrase. *Nothing* is not therefore a substantive. Heidegger was criticised on just this point in a very famous attack by Carnap. Referring to 'What is Metaphysics?', Carnap says ((1959), p. 70):

The construction of sentence (1) ['We seek the Nothing'] is simply based on the mistake of employing the word 'nothing' as a noun, because it is customary in ordinary language to use it in this form in order to construct a negative existential statement . . .

---

[5] See 12.1 and 12.2.

In a correct language, on the other hand, it is not a particular *name*, but a certain *logical form* of the sentence that serves this purpose.

But Heidegger is not confused. He is well aware that 'nothing' may be a quantifier. But it may also function as a perfectly legitimate noun-phrase as well. For example, in his essay *The Metaphysical Foundations of Logic*, he says ((1992), p. 3):

'Thinking about nothing' is ambiguous. First of all, it can mean 'not to think.' But logic as the science of thinking obviously never deals with not thinking. Secondly, it can mean 'to think nothingness,' which nonetheless means to think 'something.' In thinking of nothingness, or in the endeavour to think 'it', I am thoughtfully related to nothingness, and this is what thinking is about.

And Heidegger is right about this. 'Nothing' can be used as a substantive. If this is not clear, merely ponder the sentence 'Heidegger and Hegel both talked about nothing, but they made different claims about it'. 'Nothing' cannot be a quantifier here. Or consider the sentence:

(*) God brought the universe into being out of nothing.

This means that God arranged for nothingness to give way to the universe. In (*) 'nothing' cannot be parsed as a quantifier. If we do so, we obtain: For no x did God bring the universe into existence out of x. And whilst no doubt this is true if God brought the universe into existence out of nothing, it is equally true if the universe has existed for all time: if it was not brought into existence at a time, it was not brought into existence *out of* anything. And the eternal existence of the universe is, in part, what (*) is denying.

Nothing, then, may indeed be a thing. But, according to Heidegger, it cannot be talked about ((1977b), pp. 98f.):

What is the nothing? Our very first approach to the question has something unusual about it. In our asking we posit the nothing in advance as something that 'is' such and such; we posit it as a being. But that is exactly what it is distinguished from. Interrogating the nothing – asking what, and how it, the nothing, is – turns what is interrogated into its opposite. The question deprives itself of its own object.

Accordingly, every answer to the question is also impossible from the start. For it necessarily assumes the form: the nothing 'is' this or that. With regard to the nothing question and answer are alike inherently absurd.

One cannot, therefore, say anything of *nothing*. To say anything, whether that it is something or other, or just that it is, or even to refer to it at all, is to treat it as an object, which it is not. *Nothing* is the absence of all objects.[6] One might

---

[6] Even if one insists that 'nothing' can only be a quantifier, the situation is not that different, at least if one is a Fregean. For since it is a quantifier, it is a second-level concept. Now, for Frege, all concepts have reference. So 'nothing' does refer to a thing, in that sense. But one cannot refer to this by a noun-phrase, since it is not an object. One still cannot, therefore, say

note, though, that though one cannot have knowledge by description of nothing, one can, according to Heidegger, have knowledge by acquaintance. It is precisely in the experience of anxiety, that a person (*Dasein*) comes face to face with *nothing*.

15.5 Being and nothing

What has this to do with the ineffability of being? Simply, that for Heidegger being and nothing are identical. If *nothing* is ineffable, so, then, is *being*. Heidegger states the pertinent identity as follows ((1997b), p. 110):

'Pure Being and pure Nothing are therefore the same.' This proposition of Hegel's (*Science of Logic*, vol. I, Werke III, 74) is correct. Being and the nothing do belong together, not because both – from the point of view of the Hegelian concept of thought – agree in their indeterminateness and immediacy, but rather because Being itself is essentially finite and reveals itself only in the transcendence of Dasein which is held out into the nothing.[7]

Heidegger's reason for supposing that being and nothing are the same is difficult to discern, but as far as I understand it, it can be summed up in the simple argument:

> Being is what it is that makes beings be.
> Nothing is what it is that makes beings be.
> Hence, being is nothing.

The first premise is true by definition. The conclusion follows validly, assuming that *nothing* is a substantive here.[8] Only the second premise, therefore, needs to be discussed. The reason for this claim, essentially, is that a being is, and can only be, because it is not a nothing. It stands out, as it were, against nothingness. If there were no nothing, there could be no beings either. As Heidegger puts it ((1977b), p. 105):

In the clear night of the nothing of anxiety the original openness of beings as such arises: they are beings – and not nothing. But this 'and not nothing' we add in our talk is not some kind of appended clarification. Rather it makes possible in advance the revelation of beings in general. The essence of the originally nihilating nothing lies in this, that it brings Da-sein for the first time before beings as such.

anything about it, at least, anything of the form 'Nothing is . . . '. (Thanks to Richard Gaskin for pointing this out to me.)

[7] And again: 'Only because the question 'What is Metaphysics?' thinks from the beginning of the climbing above, the transcendence, the *Being of* being, can it think of the negative of being, of *that* nothingness which just as originally is identical with Being' (Heidegger (1959a), p. 101).

[8] And that 'What it is that . . . ' is a definite description, which it is if it specifies the essence of something.

Further, if *nothing* negates itself, it produces what it is not: something. Thus, a being is exactly nothing nihilating itself.[9] Being is, then, nothing operating on itself, as the final sentence of the following quotation suggests ((1997b), p. 106):

> The nothing is neither an object nor any being at all. The nothing comes forward neither for itself nor next to beings, to which it would, as it were, adhere. For human existence the nothing makes possible the openedness of beings as such. The nothing does not merely serve as the counterconcept of beings; rather it originally belongs to their essential unfoldings as such. In the Being of beings the nihilation of the nothing occurs.

At the heart of each being is exactly nothingness. That is the essence of its being, that is, its being. And since one cannot say what nothing is, one cannot say what being is.

15.6 Stretching language

For two reasons, then, one can say nothing about *being*. The very grammar of our language makes it impossible to do this. The only way we have of talking about being is, in fact, to treat it as *a* being. This obfuscation is one of the central things that Heidegger means by the pejorative term 'metaphysics'.

Heidegger discusses the problem (amongst other things) in his essay *The Question of Being*. The central topic of this is what he calls 'the crossing of the line'. Exactly what this is need not concern us here. All that one needs to know is that it is what needs to be done to address properly the question of being. Bearing this in mind, one can understand the following ((1959a), p. 71):

> What if even the language of metaphysics, and even metaphysics itself, whether it be that of the living or of the dead God, as metaphysics, formed the barrier which forbids the crossing over the line . . . ? If that were the case, would not the crossing of the line necessarily become the transformation of language and demand a transformed relation to the essence of language?

The rhetorical questions are then answered in the affirmative ((1959a), p. 73):

> *The question of the essence of Being dies off, if it does not surrender the language of metaphysics, because metaphysical conception forbids the thinking of the question of the essence of being.*

Language, at least the language of metaphysics – and we have no other – just cannot do what is required.

Struggling with the problem in the same essay, he tries to get around it by the technique of writing under erasure: writing something and crossing it out.[10] The problem with *being* is that it is not a thing. It exists only in its

---

[9] I am grateful to Jay Garfield for pointing out to me this interpretation of the text.

[10] Observant readers will have noted from some of the previous quotations that Heidegger had already done something similar with the use of 'scare quotes'.

relation to beings and, in particular, to *Dasein*. Each, in fact, exists only inasmuch as it relates to the other. Heidegger describes the relation of being to *Dasein* anthropomorphically as 'turning towards'. Bearing this in mind, one can understand the following passage ((1959a), p. 81):

If turning-towards belongs to Being and in such a way that the latter is based on the former, then 'Being' is dissolved in this turning. It now becomes questionable what Being which has reverted into and been absorbed by its essence is henceforth to be thought of. Accordingly, a thoughtful glance ahead into this realm of 'Being' can only write it as ~~Being~~. The drawing of the crossed lines at first only repels, especially the almost ineradicable habit of conceiving 'Being' as something standing by itself and only coming at times face to face with man ... Nothingness would have to be written, and that means thought of, just like ~~Being~~ ... [11]

Writing under erasure is not the only linguistic device that Heidegger employed to get around the problem of talking about being. In another late essay, *The Principle of Reason*, Heidegger essays another way: expressing himself without using the verb 'is' at all. The following quotation explains. Since it also recapitulates a number of other themes we have looked at, I will quote at length ((1991), pp. 51f.):

If we painstakingly attend to the language in which we articulate what the principle of reason [*Satz vom Grund*] says as a principle of being, then it becomes clear we speak of being in an odd manner that is, in truth, inadmissible. We say: being and ground/reason [*Grund*] 'are' the same. Being 'is' the abyss [*Abgrund*]. When we say something 'is' and 'is such and so', then that something is, in such an utterance, represented as a being. Only a being 'is'; the 'is' itself – being – 'is' not. The wall in front of you and behind me is. It immediately shows itself to us as something present. But where is its 'is'? Where should we seek the presencing of the wall? Probably these questions already run awry.

Hence, there is a peculiar state of affairs with the 'is' and 'being'. In order to respond to it, we articulate what the principle of reason says as a principle of being as follows: Being and ground/reason [*Grund*]: the same. Being: the abyss [*Abgrund*]. As we remarked, to say 'being' 'is' ground/reason is inadmissible. This way of speaking, which is virtually unavoidable, does not apply to 'being'; it does not hit upon its proper character.

On the one hand we say: being and ground/reason [*Grund*] – the same. On the other hand we say: being – the abyss [*Abgrund*]. It would be worthwhile to think the univocity of both 'sentences' [*Sätze*], of sentences that are no longer 'sentences'.[12]

---

[11] Heidegger goes on to explain that the crossing out has not only a negative function; it also has a positive function. The crossing of the arms of an 'X' indicates a pointing. Crossing out 'being' thus indicates that *being* points to *Dasein*. The two are inextricably connected. These things need not concern us here.

[12] The text actually translates the last sentence thus: 'It would be worthwhile to think the univocity of both "sentences" [*Sätze*], of phrases [*Sätze*] that are no longer "propositions" [*Sätze*].' Richard Gaskin persuaded me that the translation I give is preferable.

We have, then, two ways which Heidegger devised in his attempts to struggle with the problem of talking of being. Both of them stretch language in one way or another. Considerations of logical grammar seem to leave no other option.

15.7 The limits of description

We have not finished with Heidegger yet, but let us now draw back and look at the bigger picture. Heidegger's arguments would appear to present him with a problem that is all too evident. He has shown that being is such that one cannot say anything about it. Yet it is clear that one can say things about it. The quotations from Heidegger that I have made are littered with assertions about being, as even a casual perusal suffices to verify. Even Heidegger's techniques that we looked at in the last section do nothing to solve the problem. Consider writing under erasure. Whether one likes it or not, even '~~being~~' appears to refer to being – or how are we to understand what Heidegger is on about? To add injury to insult, even Heidegger's own explanation of writing under erasure, which I quoted in the last section, refers to the notion of being in the more usual way. And dropping the verb does not help either. In 'being and ground: the same', one is still conveying the idea that two *things* are the same, and referring to being in the process. Moreover, neither of these techniques takes away from the fact that, even if one tries to use a non-standard form of language, the standard form of language *did* express what could not be expressed.

Heidegger's predicament is a familiar one in the history of philosophy. As I have argued in previous chapters, there are certain limits of thought that are contradictory. There are boundaries which thought cannot cross, and yet which it does. The boundaries are the sites of dialetheias, true contradictions. The boundaries in question are of several kinds (the limits of expression, iteration, cognition, and conception/description), but in each case, a certain object must be within a fixed totality (the Closure Condition), but must also be without it (the Transcendence Condition). We have seen several arguments for the dialetheic nature of the limits in question, but a major one is based on the repeated and persistent phenomenon of philosophers who analyse such limits, and who are driven, willy-nilly, into contradiction (pp. 227f.). (If the limits are contradictory, what else would you expect?) With one minor exception (p. 221), I have not mentioned Heidegger before this chapter, but it is now clear that he fits the pattern too. Being is a notion that is beyond the bounds of the describable (Transcendence); but it *is* describable (Closure): Heidegger shows how.[13]

---

[13] The situation can be put in terms of the Inclosure Schema as follows. $\varphi(y)$ is 'y can be expressed in language', so that Ω is the totality of things that can be expressed; $\psi(x)$ is 'x = Ω'; $\delta(\Omega)$ is a claim about being, say that being is what it is that makes beings be. Then, by Heidegger's arguments, we have $\neg\varphi(\delta(\Omega))$: this fact about being cannot be expressed; but Heidegger himself shows that $\varphi(\delta(\Omega))$ by expressing this fact.

Heidegger fits the pattern in another way. Many philosophers, once they have realised their situations, have tried to get out of the problem by making an appeal to some non–literal notion of expression (such as metaphor or analogy); without exception, such moves do not work.[14] As we saw in the last section, Heidegger, too, employs non–standard modes of language in this way. As we have seen, though, these are no more successful than other moves of the same kind.

I do not wish to repeat the details of previous chapters, but let me mention briefly two of the philosophers who figure in them, and whose work is particularly germane here. The first of these is Frege. As we noted, Frege's doctrine of concept and object means that one cannot refer to concepts by means of noun–phrases. But we can refer to them in this way; we do so when we say, e.g., 'the concept *horse*'. As I have already shown, Frege's problem about concepts is closely allied to Heidegger's about *being*.

Frege realised that he was in trouble. He insisted that phrases such as 'the concept *horse*' and its like do not refer to concepts, appearances notwithstanding. The cost of this move is that it makes a nonsense of too much else of what Frege claims.[15] In desperation he says (Geach and Black (1960), p. 54):

I admit that there is a quite peculiar obstacle in the way of an understanding with my reader. By a kind of necessity of language, my expressions, taken literally, sometimes miss my thought ... I fully realize that in such cases I was relying on the reader who would be ready to meet me half way ...

One cannot fail to be reminded of Heidegger's own words about the inherently misleading nature of language, which I quoted in the last section.

The second philosopher to mention is Wittgenstein. Frege was driven to his views about the nature of concepts in order to give an account of the unity of the proposition. In the *Tractatus*, what provides for this unity is the logical form of a proposition. The inexpressibility of the concept *horse* and its kind metamorphoses, in that work, into the inexpressibility of the notion of logical form.[16] Wittgenstein's solution to this was, famously, his doctrine of saying and showing. The form of a proposition (and many other things) cannot be described, but it can be shown. In the end, though, the doctrine of showing did not solve the problem, since Wittgenstein did, after all, succeed in saying the things that can only be shown, as Russell wryly remarked in his introduction to the English translation of the *Tractatus* (Pears and McGuinness (1961), p. xxi).

But enough of this. Back to Heidegger.

---

[14]   See esp. pp. 229f.
[15]   See 12.2.
[16]   See ch. 12, esp. p. 192.

15.8 *Aletheia* and the law of non-contradiction

The arguments for the indescribability of being I explained above are all from Heidegger's writings in the period before the *Kehre*, the methodological turn in his thought. After the *Kehre*, Heidegger's writings about being take on a different tone. In particular, Heidegger comes to emphasise that art, and particularly poetry, when understood in the appropriate way *reveal* what being is. For example, he says ((1977c), p. 166):[17]

The art work opens up in its own way the Being of beings. This opening up, i.e., this revealing, i.e., the truth of beings, happens in the work. In the art work, the truth of beings has set itself to work. Art is truth setting itself to work.

Though he never says as much (as far as I know), I think that the turn in Heidegger's thought is, at least in part, a response to the fact that you cannot say what being is. Though being cannot be described, it can be shown – or revealed, unconcealed, as Heidegger is more wont to put it. Art can show us beings in their being, and hence reveal *being* to us. In this way we can *think* being, as he puts it, appropriating the word 'think' for his own purpose. If this is right, then Heidegger's move here is very much like the corresponding move of Wittgenstein in the *Tractatus*: invoke something (language or art) that shows what it is that cannot be said.[18]

The fact, according to Heidegger, that revealing is the canonical way of answering the question of being is a major reason why Heidegger insists on translating the Greek *aletheia*, not as 'truth', as it would normally be translated, but in a literal way, as unconcealedness. Poetry reveals being in its *aletheia*. As he explains ((1977a), p. 389):

It is not for the sake of etymology that I stubbornly translate *aletheia* as unconcealment, but for the sake of the matter which must be considered when we think adequately that which is called Being and thinking. Unconcealment is, so to speak, the element in which Being and thinking and their belonging together exist.

But why does Heidegger not simply accept the fact that is staring him in the face – that he can speak of *being*, that is, *nothing*, albeit inconsistently? This is, of course, quite compatible with poetry showing us being as well: what can be shown can often be said. (I can show you that it is raining, as well as tell you.) He addresses this point explicitly in his essay *An Introduction to Metaphysics*. He says ((1959b), p. 23):

He who speaks of nothing does not know what he is doing. In speaking of nothing he makes it into a something. In speaking he speaks against what is intended. He contra-

---

[17] See also the essays in Heidegger (1971).

[18] Of course, I am not suggesting that the later Heidegger is just rewriting the *Tractatus*. In very many ways the two thinkers are attempting something quite different. The point is, merely, that they make similar moves in response to the same problem.

dicts himself. But discourse that contradicts offends against the fundamental rule of discourse (*logos*), against 'logic'. To speak of nothing is illogical. He who speaks illogically is unscientific. But he who goes so far as to speak of nothing in the realm of philosophy, where logic has its home, exposes himself most particularly to the accusation of offending against the fundamental rule of all thinking. Such speaking about nothing consists entirely of meaningless propositions.

Heidegger thus makes it clear that the ineffability of being is required by Logic; and, specifically, the law of non-contradiction. Thus either our descriptions of being have to go or Logic does. But there is a third possibility: that Logic is simply mistaken about the law of non-contradiction. True contradictions are entirely possible, and the law is an historical mistake – just like the Euclidean 'law' that the whole must be larger than its parts. This is exactly what, of course, a modern dialetheist takes to be the case: the 'law' is a mistake. Heidegger simply identifies Logic with the received logical theory of his day, forgetting that it, too, is a product of a fallible history. It is an irony that a thinker of the acuity of Heidegger, who was so critical of his historical heritage, should have been blind to the possibility that people had got Logic wrong, which logical investigations in the second half of the twentieth century have shown to be a very real possibility. Perhaps if Heidegger had been writing later, with a full knowledge of developments in modern logic, he would have said that an adequate thinking of being requires, not simply aletheia, but dialetheia.[19]

[19] Ancestors of this paper were read at the Department of Philosophy, the University of Tasmania, and at a meeting of the Australasian Association of Philosophy, held at the University of Melbourne in 1999. I am grateful to those present for their helpful thoughts.

16 Nāgārjuna and the limits of thought

with Jay Garfield

If you know the nature of one thing, you know the nature of all things.

Khensur Yeshe Thubten

Whatever is dependently co-arisen,
That is explained to be emptiness.
That, being a dependent designation,
Is itself the middle way.

Mūlamadhyamakakārikā XXIV: 18

16.1 Welcome to Nāgārjuna

Nāgārjuna (first or second century AD) is surely one of the most difficult philosophers to interpret in any tradition. His texts are terse and cryptic. He does not shy away from paradox or apparent contradiction. He is coy about identifying his opponents. The commentarial traditions grounded in his texts present a plethora of interpretations of his view. Nonetheless, his influence in the Mahāyāna Buddhist world is not only unparalleled in that tradition, but exceeds in that tradition the influence of any single Western philosopher in the West. The degree to which he is taken seriously by so many eminent Indian, Chinese, Tibetan, Korean, Japanese, and Vietnamese philosophers, and lately by so many Western philosophers, alone justifies attention to his corpus. Even were he not such a titanic figure historically, the depth and beauty of his thought and the austere beauty of his philosophical poetry would justify that attention. While Nāgārjuna may perplex and often infuriate, and while his texts may initially defy exegesis, anyone who spends time with Nāgārjuna's thought inevitably develops a deep respect for this master philosopher.

One of the reasons Nāgārjuna so perplexes many who come to his texts is his seeming willingness to embrace contradictions, on the one hand, while making use of classic *reductio* arguments, implicating his endorsement of the law of non-contradiction, on the other. Another is his apparent willingness to saw off the limbs on which he sits. He asserts that there are two truths, and that they are one; that everything both exists and does not exist; that nothing is existent or non-existent; that he rejects all philosophical views including his own; that he asserts nothing. And he appears to mean every word of it. Making sense of all of this is sometimes difficult. Some interpreters of Nāgārjuna, indeed, succumb to the easy temptation to read him as a simple mystic or an irrationalist of some kind. But it is significant that none of the important commentarial traditions in Asia, however much they disagree in other respects, regard him in this light.[1] And indeed, most recent scholarship is unanimous in this regard as well, again despite a wide range of divergence in interpretations in other respects. Nāgārjuna is simply too committed to rigorous analytical argument to be dismissed as a mystic.

Our interest here is neither historical nor in providing a systematic exegesis or assessment of any of Nāgārjuna's work. Instead, we are concerned with the possibility that Nāgārjuna, like many philosophers in the West, and indeed like many of his Buddhist successors – perhaps as a consequence of his influence – discovers and explores true contradictions arising at the limits of thought. If this is indeed the case, it would account for both sides of the interpretive tension just noted: Nāgārjuna might appear to be an irrationalist in virtue of embracing some contradictions – both to Western philosophers and to Nyāya interlocutors who see consistency as a necessary condition of rationality. But to those who share with us a dialetheist's comfort with the possibility of true contradictions commanding rational assent, for Nāgārjuna to endorse such contradictions would not *undermine*, but instead would *confirm*, the impression that he is indeed a highly rational thinker.[2]

We are also interested in the possibility that these contradictions are structurally analogous to those arising in the Western tradition. But while discovering a parallel between Nāgārjuna's thought and those of other paraconsistent frontiersmen such as Kant and Hegel, Heidegger and Derrida, may help Western philosophers to understand Nāgārjuna's project better, or at least might be a philosophical curio, we think we can deliver more than that: we will argue that while Nāgārjuna's contradictions are structurally similar to those we find in the West, Nāgārjuna delivers to us a paradox as yet unknown in the West. This paradox, we will argue, brings us a new insight into ontology and into our cognitive access to the world. We should read Nāgārjuna then,

---

[1] Gorampa, in 14th-century Tibet, may be an exception to this claim, for in *Nges don rab gsal* (1990) he argues that Nāgārjuna regards all thought and conceptualisation as necessarily totally false and deceptive. But even Gorampa agrees that Nāgārjuna argues (and indeed soundly) for that conclusion.

[2] We note that Tillemans (1999) takes Nāgārjuna's sincere endorsement of contradictions to be possible evidence that he endorses paraconsistent logic with regard to the ultimate while remaining classical with regard to the conventional. We think he is right about this.

not because in him we can see affirmed what we already knew, but because we can learn from him.

One last set of preliminary remarks is in order before we get down to work: In this chapter we will defend neither the reading of Nāgārjuna's texts we adopt here, nor the cogency of dialetheic logic, nor the claim that true contradictions satisfying the Inclosure Schema in fact emerge at the limits of thought. We will sketch these views, but will do so fairly baldly. This is not because we take these positions to be self-evident, but because each of us has defended these things elsewhere; in the case of the last of these, in previous chapters. This chapter will be about bringing Nāgārjuna and dialetheism together. Finally, we do not claim that Nāgārjuna himself had explicit views about logic, or about the limits of thought. We do, however, think that if he did, he had the views we are about to sketch. This is, hence, not textual history but rational reconstruction.

16.2 Inclosures and the limits of thought

As we saw in 12.3, in the *Tractatus* Wittgenstein takes on the project of delimiting what can be thought. He says in the Preface:[3]

Thus the aim of the book is to draw a limit to thought, or rather— not to thought, but to the expression of thoughts: for in order to be able to draw a limit to thought, we should have to find both sides thinkable (i.e., we should have to be able to think what cannot be thought). It will therefore be only in language that the limit can be drawn, and what lies on the other side of the limit will simply be nonsense.

Yet, even having reformulated the problem in terms of language, the enterprise still runs into contradiction. In particular, the account of what can be said has as a consequence that it itself, and other things like it, cannot be said. Hence, we get the famous penultimate proposition of the *Tractatus:*[4]

My propositions serve as elucidations in the following way: anyone who understands me eventually recognizes them as nonsensical, when he has used them – as steps – to climb up beyond them. (He must, so to speak, throw away the ladder after he has climbed up it.)

Wittgenstein's predicament is serious: no matter that we throw away the ladder *after* we have climbed it: its rungs were nonsensical *while* we were using them as well. So how could it have successfully scaffolded our ascent? And if it didn't, on what basis are we now to agree that all of that useful philosophy was nonsense all along? This predicament, however, is not peculiar to him. As we have seen in preceding chapters, it is a quite general feature of theories that try

---

[3] Pears and McGuinness (1961), p. 3.
[4] Ibid., p. 74.

to characterise the limits of our cognitive abilities to think, describe, grasp, that they end up implying that they themselves cannot be thought, described, or grasped. Yet it would appear that they can be thought, described, and grasped. Otherwise, what on earth is the theory doing?

Thus, for example, when Sextus claims in *Outlines of Pyrrhonism* that it is impossible to assert anything about things beyond appearances, he would seem to be asserting just such a thing; and when he argues that no such assertion is justified, this must apply to his own assertion as well (3.4). When Kant says that it is impossible to know anything about, or apply any categories to, the noumenal realm, he would seem to be doing just what cannot be done (5.5). When Russell attempts to solve the paradoxes of self-reference by claiming that it is impossible to quantify over *all* propositions, he does just that (9.7). And the list goes on. Anyone who disparages the philosophical traditions of the East on account of their supposed flirtation with paradox has a lot of the West to explain away.

Of course, the philosophers we just mentioned were well aware of the situation, and all of them tried to take steps to avoid the contradiction. As we have seen in preceding chapters, they were not successful; even more striking: characteristically, such attempts seem to end up in other instances of the very contradictions they are trying to avoid. The recent literature surrounding the Liar Paradox provides a further rich diet of such examples.[5]

Now, why does this striking pattern occur again and again? As was argued (pp. 227 ff.), the simplest answer is that when people are driven to contradictions in charting the limits of thought, it is precisely because those limits are themselves contradictory. Hence, any theory of the limits that is anywhere near adequate will be inconsistent. The recurrence of the encounter with limit contradictions is therefore the basis of an argument to the best explanation for the inconsistent nature of the limits themselves. (It is not the only argument. But other arguments draw on details of the particular limits in question.[6])

The contradictions at the limits of thought have a general and bipartite structure. The first part is an argument to the effect that a certain view, usually about the nature of the limit in question, transcends that limit (cannot be conceived, described, etc.). This is *Transcendence*. The other is an argument to the effect that the view *is* within the limit – *Closure*. Often, this argument is a practical one, based on the fact that Closure is demonstrated in the very act of theorising about the limits. At any rate, together, the pair describe a structure which can conveniently be called an *inclosure*: a totality, Ω, and an object, o, such that o both is and is not in Ω.

---

[5] For how this phenomenon plays out in the theories of Kripke, and Gupta and Herzberger, see Priest (1987), ch. 1; for the theory of Barwise and Etchemendy, see Priest (1993); and for McGee, see Priest (1994c).

[6] See the preceding chapters and Priest (1987), chs. 1–3 for extended discussions.

On closer analysis, inclosures can be found to have a more detailed structure. At its simplest, the structure is this. The inclosure comes with an operator, δ, which, when applied to any suitable subset of Ω gives *another* object which is in Ω (that is, one that is not in the subset in question, but is in Ω). Thus, for example, if we are talking about sets of ordinals, δ might apply to give us the least ordinal not in the set. If we are talking about a set of entities that have been thought about, δ might give us an entity of which we have not yet thought. The contradiction at the limit arises when δ is applied to the totality Ω itself. For then the application of δ gives an object that is both within and without Ω: the least ordinal greater than all ordinals, or the unthought object.

All of the above is catalogued in the preceding chapters. The catalogue of limit contradictions there is not exhaustive, though. In particular, it draws only on Western philosophy. In what follows, we will add to the list the contradictions at the limits of thought discovered by Nāgārjuna. As we will see, these, too, fit the familiar pattern. The fact that they do so, whilst coming from a quite different tradition, shows that the pattern is even less parochial than one might have thought. This should not, of course, be surprising: if the limits of thought really are contradictory, then they should appear so from both east and west of the Euphrates.

One way in which he does differ from the philosophers we have so far mentioned in this chapter, though, is that Nāgārjuna does not try to *avoid* the contradiction at the limits of thought. He both sees it clearly, and endorses it. (In the Western tradition, few philosophers other than Hegel and some of his successors have done this.) Moreover, Nāgārjuna seems to have hit upon a limit contradiction unknown in the West, and to suggest connections between ontological and semantic contradictions worthy of attention. To Nāgārjuna, then.

16.3 Conventional and ultimate reality

Central to Nāgārjuna's view is his doctrine of the two realities. There is, according to Nāgārjuna, conventional reality and ultimate reality. Correspondingly, there are two truths: conventional truth, the truth about conventional reality; and ultimate truth, the truth about the ultimate reality – *qua* ultimate reality.[7] For this reason, discussion of Nāgārjuna's view is often phrased in terms of two truths, rather than two realities.

The things that are conventionally true are the truths concerning the empirical world. Nāgārjuna generally calls this class of truths *saṃvṛti-satya*, or occasionally *vyavahāra-satya*. The former is explained by Nāgārjuna's com-

---

[7] The reason for the *qua* qualification will become clear in a minute. It will turn out that conventional and ultimate reality are, in a sense, the same.

mentator Candrakīrti[8] to be ambiguous. The first sense – the one most properly translated into English as 'conventional truth (reality)' (Tibetan: *tha-snyad bden-pa*) is itself three ways ambiguous: On the one hand, it can mean *ordinary*, or *everyday*. In this sense a conventional truth is a truth to which we would ordinarily assent – common sense augmented by good science. The second of these three meanings is *truth by agreement*. In this sense, the decision in Australia to drive on the left establishes a conventional truth about the proper side of the road. A different decision in the USA establishes another. Conventional truth is, in this sense, often quite relative. (Candrakīrti argues that, in fact, in the first sense it is also relative – relative to our sense organs, conceptual scheme, etc. In this respect he would agree with such Pyrrhonian skeptics as Sextus.) The final sense of this cluster is *nominally true*. To be true in this sense is to be true in virtue of a particular linguistic convention. So, for instance, the fact that shoes and boots are different kinds of things in English, but are both instances of one kind – *lham* – in Tibetan makes their cospecificity or lack thereof a nominal matter. We English speakers, on the other hand, regard sparrows and crows both as members of a single natural superordinate kind, *bird*. Native Tibetan speakers distinguish the *bya* (the full-sized avian) from the *bya'u* (the smaller relative). (Again, relativism about truth in this sense lurks in the background.)

But these three senses cluster as one family against which stands yet another principal meaning of *saṃvṛti*. It can also mean *concealing, hiding, obscuring, occluding*. In this sense (aptly captured by the Tibetan *kun-rdzob bden-pa*, literally *costumed truth*) a *saṃvṛti-satya* is something that conceals the truth, or its real nature, or as it is sometimes glossed in the tradition, something regarded as a truth by an obscured or a deluded mind. Now, the Madhyamaka tradition, following Candrakīrti, makes creative use of this ambiguity, noting that, for instance, what such truths conceal is precisely the fact that they are merely conventional (in any of the senses adumbrated above) or that an obscured mind is obscured precisely in virtue of not properly understanding the role of convention in constituting truth, etc.

This lexicographic interlude is important primarily so that when we explore Nāgārjuna's distinction between the conventional and the ultimate truth (reality), and between conventional and ultimate perspectives – the distinct stances Nāgārjuna distinguishes towards the world, taken by ordinary versus enlightened beings – the word 'conventional' is understood with this cluster of connotations, all present in Nāgārjuna's treatment. Our primary concern as we get to the heart of this exploration will be, however, with the notion of ultimate truth (reality) (*paramārtha-satya*, literally *truth of the highest meaning*, or *truth of the highest object*). This we can define negatively as the way things are,

---

[8] *Madhyamakāvatāra-bhāṣya* VI: 28–31.

considered independently of convention, or positively as the way things are, when understood by a fully enlightened being who does not mistake what is really conventional for something that belongs to the very nature of things.

What is ultimate truth/reality, according to Nāgārjuna? To understand this, we have to understand the notion of emptiness, which for Nāgārjuna is emphatically *not* non-existence, but, rather, interdependent existence. For something to have an essence (Tibetan, *rang bzhin*; Sanskrit, *svabhāva*) is for it to be what it is, in and of itself, independently of all other things. (This entails, incidentally, that things that are essentially so are eternally so; for if they started to be, or ceased to be, then their so being would depend on other things, such as time.) To be empty is precisely to have no essence, in this sense.

The most important ultimate truth, according to Nāgārjuna, is that everything is empty. Much of the *Mūlamadhyamakakārika* (or *MMK* as we shall refer to it) consists, in fact, of an extended set of arguments to the effect that everything that one might take to be an essence is, in fact, not one – that everything is empty of essence and of independent identity. The arguments are interesting and varied, and we will not go into them here. But just to give the flavour of them, a very general argument is to be found in *MMK* v. Here, Nāgārjuna argues that the spatial properties (and by analogy, all properties) of an object cannot be essential. For it would be absurd to suppose that the spatial location of an object could exist without the object itself – or, conversely, that there could be an object without its location. Hence, location and object are co-dependent.

> From this it follows that there is no characterized
> And no existing characteristic.
>
> (*MMK* v: 4ab)

The existence in question here is, of course, ultimate existence. Nāgārjuna is not denying the conventional existence of objects and their properties.

With arguments such as the preceding one, Nāgārjuna urges that everything is empty, contingently dependent on other things – dependently co-arisen, as it is often put. We must take the 'everything' here very seriously, though. When Nāgārjuna claims that everything is empty, *everything* includes emptiness itself. The emptiness of something is itself a dependently co-arisen property of that thing. The emptiness of emptiness is perhaps one of the most central claims of the *MMK*.[9] Nāgārjuna devotes much of chapter VII to this topic. In that chapter, using some of the more difficult arguments of the *MMK*, he reduces to absurdity the assumption that dependent co-arising is itself an (ultimately) existing property of things. We will not go into the argument here: it is its consequences that will concern us.

---

[9] See, e.g., Garfield (1990), (1994), (1995), (1996), Huntington and Wangchen (1989), Kasulis (1989).

For Western philosophers, it is very tempting to adopt a Kantian understanding of Nāgārjuna (as is offered, e.g., by Murti (1955)). Identify conventional reality with the phenomenal realm, and ultimate reality with the noumenal, and there you have it. But this is not Nāgārjuna's view. The emptiness of emptiness means that ultimate reality cannot be thought of as a Kantian noumenal realm. For *ultimate* reality is just as empty as *conventional* reality. Ultimate reality is hence only conventionally real! The distinct realities are therefore identical. As the *Vimilakīrti-nirde śa-sūtra* puts it:[10]

To say this is conventional and this is ultimate is dualistic. To realize that there is no difference between the conventional and the ultimate is to enter the Dharma-door of nonduality.

Or as the *Heart Sūtra* puts it more famously:[11]

> Form is empty;
> emptiness is form;
> form is not different from emptiness;
> emptiness is not different from form.

The identity of the two truths has profound soteriological implications for Nāgārjuna, such as the identity of *nirvāṇa* and *saṃsāra*.[12] But we will not go into these. We are now nearly in a position to address the first of Nāgārjuna's limit contradictions.

16.4 Nāgārjuna and the law of non-contradiction

Before we do this, there is one more preliminary matter we need to examine: Nāgārjuna's attitude towards the law of non-contradiction in the domain of conventional truth. For to charge Nāgārjuna with irrationalism, or even with an extreme form of dialetheism according to which contradictions are as numerous as blackberries, is, in part, to charge him with thinking that contradictions are true in the standard conventional realm. Though this view is commonly urged (see, e.g., Robinson (1957), Wood (1994)), it is wrong. Though Nāgārjuna does endorse contradictions, they are not of a kind that concern conventional reality, *qua* conventional reality.

We can get at this point in two ways: First, we can observe that Nāgārjuna himself never asserts that there are true contradictions in this realm (or, more cautiously, that every apparent assertion of a contradiction concerning this domain, upon analysis, resolves itself into something else). Second, we can observe that Nāgārjuna takes *reductio* arguments to be decisive in this domain. We confess: Neither of these strategies is hermeneutically unproblematic. The

---

[10]   See Thurman (1976), p. 73.
[11]   For a translation and commentary on the text, see Lopez (1998).
[12]   These are taken up most notably in the Zen tradition. See Kasulis (1989).

first relies on careful and sometimes controversial readings of Nāgārjuna's dialectic. We will argue using a couple of cases that such readings are correct. Moreover, we add, such readings are defended in the canonical tradition by some of the greatest Madhyamaka exegetes.

The second strategy is hard because, typically, Nāgārjuna's arguments are directed as *ad hominem* arguments against specific positions defended by his adversaries, each of whom would endorse the law of non-contradiction. If we argue that Nāgārjuna rejects the positions they defend by appealing to contradictory consequences of opponents' positions he regards as refutatory, it is always open to the irrationalist interpreter of Nāgārjuna to reply that for the argument to be successful one needs to regard these only as refutations *for the opponent*. That is, on this reading, Nāgārjuna could be taken not himself to find contradictory consequences as problematic, but to be presenting a consequence unacceptable to a consistent opponent, thereby forcing his opponent to relinquish the position on the opponent's own terms.   And indeed such a reading is cogent. So if we are to give this line of argument any probative force, we will have to show that in particular cases Nāgārjuna *himself* rejects the contradiction and *endorses* the conventional claim whose negation entails the contradiction. We will present such examples.

Let us first consider the claim that Nāgārjuna himself freely asserts contradictions. One might think, for instance, that when Nāgārjuna says:

> Therefore, space is not an entity.
> It is not a nonentity.
> Not characterized, not without character.
> The same is true of the other five elements.
>
> (*MMK* v: 7)

he is endorsing the claim that space and the other fundamental elements have contradictory properties (existence and non-existence, being characterised and being uncharacterised). But this reading would only be possible if one (as we have just done) lifts this verse out of context. The entire chapter in which it occurs is addressed to the problem of reification – to treating the elements as providing an ontological foundation for all of reality, that is, as essences. After all, he concludes in the very next verse:

> Fools and reificationists who perceive
> The existence and nonexistence
> Of objects
> Do not see the pacification of objectification.
>
> (*MMK* v: 8)

It is then clear that Nāgārjuna is not *asserting* that space and the other elements have contradictory properties. Rather, he is rejecting a certain framework in which they play the role of ultimate foundations, or the role of ultimate property bearers.

Moreover, though Western and non-Buddhist Indian commentators have urged that such claims are contradictory, we also note that they are not even *prima facie* contradictions unless one presupposes both the law of the excluded middle, and that Nāgārjuna himself endorses that law. Otherwise there is no way of getting from a verse that explicitly rejects both members of the pair 'Space is an entity' and 'Space is a non-entity' to the claim that, in virtue of rejecting each, he is accepting its negation, and hence that he is asserting a contradiction. Much better to read Nāgārjuna as rejecting excluded middle for the kind of assertion the opponent in question is making, packed as it is with what Nāgārjuna regards as illicit ontological presupposition (see Garfield (1995)).

Let us consider a second example: In his discussion of the aggregates, another context in which his concern is to dispose of the project of fundamental ontology, Nāgārjuna says:

> The assertion that the effect and cause are similar
> Is not acceptable.
> The assertion that they are not similar
> Is also not acceptable.

> (*MMK* IV: 6)

Again, absent context, and granted the law of the excluded middle, this appears to be a bald contradiction. And again, context makes all the difference. The opponent in this chapter has been arguing that form itself (material substance) can be thought of as the cause of all psychophysical phenomena. In the previous verse Nāgārjuna has just admonished the opponent to 'think about form, but | Do not construct theories about form' (5cd). The point of this verse is just that form, *per se*, is a plausible explanation neither of the material world (this would beg the question) nor of the non-material world (it fails to explain psychophysical relations). We are not concerned here with whether Nāgārjuna is right or wrong in these cases. We want to point out only that in cases like this, where it might appear that Nāgārjuna does assert contradictions, it is invariably the case that a careful reading of the text undermines the straightforwardly contradictory reading. And once again, we note that when read with logical circumspection we have here, in any case, only a rejection in a particular context of the law of the excluded middle, and no warrant for moving from that rejection to any rejection of non-contradiction.

We now turn to the fact that Nāgārjuna employs *reductio* arguments in order to refute positions he rejects, showing that at least with regard to standard conventional situations, the fact that a claim entails contradictions is good reason to reject it. In chapter XV of *MMK*, Nāgārjuna considers the possibility that what it is to exist and what it is to have a particular identity are to be explained by appeal to essence. But he is able to conclude that:

> Those who see essence and essential difference
> And entities and nonentities,
> They do not see
> The truth taught by the Buddha.

> (*MMK* XVI: 6)

precisely on the grounds that:

> If there is no essence,
> What could become other?
> If there is essence,
> What could become other?

> (*MMK* XV: 9)

In this argument, lines c and d – the rest of whose details, and the question of the soundness of which, we leave aside for present purposes – Nāgārjuna notes that an account of existence, change, and difference that appeals to essence leads to a contradiction. Things do 'become other'. That is a central thesis of the Buddhist doctrine of impermanence that Nāgārjuna defends in the text. But if they do, he argues, and if essence were explanatory of their existence, difference, and change, they would need both to have essence, in order to account for their existence, and to lack it, in virtue of the fact that essences are eternal. Since this is contradictory, essence is to be rejected. And of course, as we have already noted, Nāgārjuna does reject essence. That is the central motivation of the text.

In XVII: 23 Nāgārjuna responds to the opponent's suggestion that action may be something uncreated, a desperate ploy to save the idea that actions have essences. He responds that:

> All conventions would then
> Be contradicted, without doubt.
> It would be impossible to draw a distinction
> Between virtue and evil.

> (*MMK* XVII: 24)

Again, neither the details of the argument nor its success concerns us here. Rather, we emphasise the fact that, for Nāgārjuna, contradictory consequences of positions in the standard conventional realm are fatal to those positions.

As a final example, we note that in chapter XVIII Nāgārjuna concludes:

> Whatever comes into being dependent on another
> Is not identical to that thing.
> Nor is it different from it.
> Therefore it is neither nonexistent in time nor permanent.

> (*MMK* XVIII: 10)

Here Nāgārjuna notes that the contradiction (not identical/not different) follows from the disjunction 'an entity is either nonexistent or permanent', and so opts for the claim that existent phenomena are impermanent. We conclude, then, not only that Nāgārjuna does not freely assert contradictions; but that when he employs them, at least when discussing standard conventional truth, he does so as the conclusions of *reductio* arguments, whose point is to defend the negation of the claim he takes to entail those contradictions.

At this stage, then, we draw the following conclusions: Nāgārjuna is not an irrationalist. He is committed to the canons of rational argument and criticism. He is not a mystic. He believes that reasoned argument can lead to the abandonment of error and to knowledge. He is not of the view that the conventional world, however nominal it may be, is riddled with contradictions.[13] If Nāgārjuna is to assert contradictions they will be elsewhere, they will be defended rationally, and asserted in the service of reasoned analysis.

16.5 The ultimate truth is that there is no ultimate truth

We are now in a position to examine Nāgārjuna's first limit contradiction. The centrepiece of Nāgārjuna's Madhyamaka, or 'middle way', philosophy is the thesis that everything is empty. This thesis has a profound consequence. Ultimate truths are those about ultimate reality. But since everything is empty, there is no ultimate reality. There are, therefore, no ultimate truths. We can get at the same conclusion another way. To express anything in language is to express truth that depends on language, and so this cannot be an expression of the way things are ultimately. All truths, then, are merely conventional.

Nāgārjuna enunciates this conclusion in the following passages:

> The Victorious ones have said
> That Emptiness is the relinquishing of all views.
> For whoever emptiness becomes a view
> That one will accomplish nothing.
>
> (*MMK* xiii: 8)

> I prostrate to Gautama
> Who, through compassion
> Taught the true doctrine
> Which leads to the relinquishing of all views.
>
> (*MMK* xxvii: 30)

---

[13] On the other hand, it is no doubt true that on Nāgārjuna's view many of our pretheoretical and philosophical conceptions regarding the world are indeed riddled with incoherence. Getting them coherent is the task of *MMK*.

Nāgārjuna is not saying here that one must be reduced to total silence. He himself certainly was not! The views that one must relinquish are views about the ultimate nature of reality. And there is no such thing as the ultimate nature of reality. That is what it is for all phenomena to be empty.

It might be thought that the rest is simply ineffable. Indeed, Nāgārjuna is sometimes interpreted in this way too. (See Gorampa (1990).) But this, also, would be too simplistic a reading. There *are* ultimate truths. *MMK* is full of them. For example, when Nāgārjuna says (*MMK* xxiv: 19):

> Something that is not dependently arisen
> Such a thing does not exist.
> Therefore a non-empty thing
> Does not exist

he is telling us about the nature of ultimate reality. There are, therefore, ultimate truths. Indeed, that there is no ultimate reality is itself a truth about ultimate reality, and is therefore an ultimate truth! This is Nāgārjuna's first limit contradiction.

There are various objections one might raise at this point in an attempt to save Nāgārjuna from (ultimate) inconsistency. Let us consider two. First, one might say that when Nāgārjuna appears to assert ultimate truths, he is not *really* asserting anything. His utterances have some other function. One might develop this point in at least two different ways. First, one may say that Nāgārjuna's speech acts are to be taken, not as acts of assertion, but as acts of denial. It is as though, whenever someone else makes a claim about ultimate reality, Nāgārjuna simply says 'No!' This is to interpret Nāgārjuna as employing a relentless *via negativa*. Alternatively, one may say that in these utterances Nāgārjuna is not performing a speech act at all: he is merely uttering words with no illocutory force. In the same way, one may interpret Sextus as claiming that he, also, never made assertions: he simply *uttered* words, which, when understood by his opponents, would cause them to give up their views.[14]

Whilst these strategies have some plausibility (and some ways of reading Bhāivaviveka and Candrakirti have them interpreting Nāgārjuna in just this way), in the end the text simply cannot sustain this reading. There are just too many important passages in the *MMK* in which Nāgārjuna is not simply denying what his opponents say, or saying things that will cause his opponents to retract, but where he is stating positive views of his own. Consider, for example, the central verse of the *MMK*:

> Whatever is dependently co-arisen,
> That is explained to be emptiness.

---

[14] See 3.4, though we take no position here on any debates in Sextus interpretation, or on whether Sextus would be correct in characterising his own method in this way.

> That, being a dependent designation,
> Is itself the middle way.

(MMK xxiv: 18)

Or Nāgārjuna's assertion that *nirvāṇa* and *samsāra* are identical:

> Whatever is the limit of *nirvāṇa*,
> That is the limit of cyclic existence.
> There is not even the slightest difference between them,
> Or even the subtlest thing.

(MMK xxv: 20)

These are telling it like it is.

The strategy of claiming that, in the relevant portions of the text, Nāgārjuna is not making assertions gains some exegetical plausibility from the fact that sometimes Nāgārjuna can be interpreted as describing his own utterances in this way. The *locus classicus* is his *Vigrahavyāvartanī* where Nāgārjuna responds to a Nyāya charge that he has undermined his own claim to the emptiness of all things through his own commitment to his assertions. In his autocommentary to verse 29, he says:[15]

If I had even one proposition thereby it would be just as you have said. Though if I had a proposition with the characteristic that you described, I would have that fault, I have no proposition at all. Thus, since all phenomena are empty, at peace, by nature isolated, how could there be a proposition? How can there be a characteristic of a proposition? And how can there be a fault arising from the characteristic of a proposition? Thus, the statement, 'through the characteristic of your proposition you come to acquire the fault' is not true.

But context and attention to the structure of the argument make all the hermeneutic difference here. The Nyāya interlocutor has charged Nāgārjuna not simply with *asserting things* but with a self-refutatory commitment to the existence of convention-independent truth-makers (propositions – *pratijñā*) for the things he says, on pain of abandoning claims to the truth of his own theory. Nāgārjuna's reply does not deny that he is asserting anything. How could he deny *that*? Rather he *asserts* that his use of words does not commit him to the existence of any convention-independent phenomena (such as emptiness) to which those words refer. What he denies is a particular semantic theory, one he regards as incompatible with his doctrine of the emptiness of all things precisely because it is committed to the claim that things have natures. (See Garfield (1996).) Compare, in this context, Wittgenstein's rejection of the theory of meaning of the *Tractatus*, with its language-independent facts and propositions, in favour of the use-theory of the *Investigations*. We conclude

---

[15] For a translation and commentary on the text, see Bhattacarya, Johnston, and Kunst (1978). Their translation is on p. 23.

that even the most promising textual evidence for this route to saving Nāgārjuna from inconsistency fails.

A second way one might interpret Nāgārjuna so as to save him from inconsistency is to suggest that the assertions Nāgārjuna proffers that appear to be statements of ultimate truth state merely conventional, and not ultimate, truths after all. One might defend this claim by pointing out that these truths can indeed be expressed, and inferring that they therefore *must* be conventional, otherwise they would be ineffable. If this were so, then to say that there are no ultimate truths would be simply *true*, and *not* also false. But this reading is also hard to sustain. For something to be an ultimate truth is for it to be the way a thing is found to be at the end of an analysis of its nature. When, for instance, a Mādhyamika says that things are ultimately empty, that claim can be cashed out by saying that when we analyse that thing, looking for its essence, we literally come up empty. The analysis never terminates with anything that can stand as an essence. But another way of saying this is to say that the result of this ultimate analysis is the discovery that all things are empty, and that they can be no other way. This, hence, is an ultimate truth about them. We might point out that the Indo–Tibetan exegetical tradition, despite lots of other internecine disputes, is unanimous on this point.

There is, then, no escape. Nāgārjuna's view is contradictory.[16] The contradiction is clearly a paradox of expressibility. Nāgārjuna succeeds in saying the unsayable, just as much as the Wittgenstein of the *Tractatus*. We can think (and characterise) reality only subject to language, which is conventional, so the ontology of that reality is all conventional. It follows that the conventional objects of reality do not ultimately (non-conventionally) exist. It also follows that nothing we say of them is ultimately true. That is, all things are empty of ultimate existence; and this is their ultimate nature, and is an ultimate truth about them. They hence cannot be thought to have that nature; nor can we say that they do. But we have just done so. As Siderits ((1989), p. 231) has put it, 'the ultimate truth is that there is no ultimate truth'.

16.6 Positive and negative tetralemmas; conventional and ultimate perspectives

It may be useful to approach the contradiction at the limits of expressibility here by a different route: Nāgārjuna's unusual use of both positive and negative forms of the *catuḥskoṭi*, or classical Indian tetralemma. Classical Indian logic and rhetoric regards any proposition as defining a logical space involving four candidate positions, or corners (*koṭi*), in distinction

---

[16] The fact that Nāgārjuna's view is inconsistent does not, of course – on his own view or on ours – mean that it is *incoherent*.

to most Western logical traditions which consider only two – truth and falsity: The proposition may be true (and not false); false (and not true); both true and false; neither true nor false. As a consequence, Indian epistemology and metaphysics, including Buddhist epistemology and metaphysics, typically partitions each problem-space defined by a property into four possibilities, not two.[17] So Nāgārjuna in *Mūlamadhyamakakārikā* considers the possibility that motion, for instance, is in the moving object, not in the moving object, both in and not in the moving object, and neither in nor not in the moving object. Each *prima facie* logical possibility needs analysis before rejection.

Nāgārjuna makes use of both positive and negative tetralemmas, and uses this distinction in mood to mark the difference between the perspectives of the two truths. Positive tetralemmas, such as this, are asserted from the conventional perspective:

> That there is a self has been taught,
> And the doctrine of no-self,
> By the buddhas, as well as the
> Doctrine of neither self nor non-self.
>
> (*MMK* XVIII: 6)

Some, of course, interpret these as evidence for the irrationalist interpretation of Nāgārjuna we defused before. But if we are not on the lookout for contradictory readings of this, we can see Nāgārjuna explaining simply how the policy of two truths works in a particular case. Conventionally, he says, there is a self – the conventional selves we recognise as persisting from day to day, such as Jay and Graham, exist. But selves don't exist ultimately. They both exist conventionally and are empty, and so fail to exist ultimately – indeed, these are exactly the same thing. This verse therefore records neither inconsistency nor incompleteness: rather, it affirms the two truths and demonstrates that we can talk coherently about both, and about their relationship – from the conventional perspective, of course.

The distinctively Nāgārjunian negative tetralemmas are more interesting. Here Nāgārjuna is after the limits of expressibility, and the contradictory situation at that limit when we take the ultimate perspective:

> 'Empty' should not be asserted.
> 'Non-empty' should not be asserted.
> Neither both nor neither should be asserted.
> These are used only nominally.
>
> (*MMK* XXII: 11)

---

[17] See Hayes (1994) and Tillemans (1999) for excellent general discussions of the *catuḥṣkoṭi* and its role in Indian logic and epistemology.

The last line makes it clear (as does context in the text itself) that Nāgārjuna is discussing what can't be said from the ultimate perspective – from a point of view transcendent of the conventional. And it turns out here that *nothing* can be said, even that all phenomena are empty. Nor its negation. We can't even say that nothing can be said. But we just did. And we have thereby characterised the ultimate perspective, which, if we are correct in our characterisation, can't be done.

The relationship between these two kinds of tetralemma generates a higher-order contradiction as well: they say the same thing: each describes completely (though from different directions) the relationship between the two truths. The positive tetralemma asserts that conventional phenomena exist conventionally and can be characterised truly from that perspective, and that ultimately nothing exists or satisfies any description. In saying this, it in no way undermines its own cogency, and in fact affirms and explains its own expressibility. The negative counterpart asserts the same thing: that existence and characterisation make sense at, and only at, the conventional level; and that, at the ultimate level, nothing exists or satisfies any description. But in doing so it contradicts itself: if true, it asserts its own non-assertibility. The identity of the *prima facie* opposite two truths is curiously mirrored in the opposition of the *prima facie* identical two tetralemmas.

16.7 All things have one nature, that is, no nature

We have examined the contradiction concerning the limits of expressibility that arises for Nāgārjuna. But as will probably be clear already, there is another, and more fundamental, contradiction that underlies this. This is the ontological contradiction concerning emptiness itself. All things, including emptiness itself, are, as we have seen, empty. As Nāgārjuna puts it in a verse that is at the heart of the *MMK*:

> Whatever is dependently co-arisen,
> That is explained to be emptiness.
> That, being a dependent designation,
> Is itself the middle way.

> (*MMK* xxiv: 18)

Now, since all things are empty, all things lack any ultimate nature; and this is a characterisation of what things are like from the ultimate perspective. Thus, ultimately, things are empty. But emptiness is, by definition, the lack of any essence or ultimate nature. Nature, or essence, is just what empty things are empty of. Hence, ultimately, things must lack emptiness. To be ultimately empty is, ultimately, to lack emptiness. In other words, emptiness is the nature of all things; in virtue of this, they have no nature, not even emptiness. As

Nāgārjuna puts it in his autocommentary to *Vigrahavyāvartanī*, quoting lines from the *Aṣṭasāhasrikā-prajñāpāramitā-sūtra*:[18]

By their nature, the things are not a determinate entity. Their nature is a non-nature; it is their non-nature that is their nature. For they have only one nature, i.e., no nature ...

Nāgārjuna's enterprise is one of fundamental ontology, and the conclusion he comes to is that fundamental ontology is impossible. But that is a fundamentally ontological conclusion – and that is the paradox. There is no way that things are ultimately, not even that way. The Indo-Tibetan tradition, following the *Vimalakīrti-nirdeśa sūtra*, hence repeatedly advises one to learn to 'tolerate the groundlessness of things'. (See Thurman (1976), p. 73.) The emptiness of emptiness is the fact that not even emptiness exists ultimately, that it is also dependent, conventional, nominal, and in the end, it is just the everydayness of the everyday. Penetrating to the depths of being, we find ourselves back on the surface of things, and so discover that there is nothing, after all, beneath those deceptive surfaces. Moreover, what is deceptive about them is simply the fact that we take there to be ontological depths lurking just beneath.[19]

There are, again, ways that one might attempt to avoid the ontological contradiction. One way is to say that Nāgārjuna's utterances about emptiness are not assertions at all. We have discussed this move in connection with the previous limit-contradiction. Another way, in this context, is to argue that even though Nāgārjuna is asserting that everything is empty, the emptiness in question must be understood as an accident, and not an essence, to use Aristotelian jargon. Again, though this exegetical strategy may have some plausibility, it cannot be sustained. For things do not simply *happen* to be empty, as some things *happen* to be red. The arguments of *MMK* are designed to show that all things cannot but be empty, that there is no other mode of existence of which they are capable. Since emptiness is a necessary characteristic of things, it belongs to them essentially – it is part of the very nature of phenomena *per se*. As Candrakīrti puts it, commenting on *MMK* xiii: 8:[20]

As it is said in the great Ratnakūṭa sūtra, 'Things are not empty because of emptiness; to be a thing is to be empty. Things are not without defining characteristics through characteristiclessness; to be a thing is to be without a defining characteristic ... whoever understands things in this way, Kāśyapa, will understand perfectly how everything has been explained to be in the middle path'.

---

[18] Bhattacharya, Johnston, and Kunst (1978), p. 23. It should be noted that they locate this passage in a footnote. In the original it is part of the text.

[19] Kasulis (1989) appropriately draws attention to the way in which Nāgārjuna's account of this intellectual journey – returning us to the conventional world, but with deeper insight into its conventional character – is taken up by the great Zen philosopher Dōgen in his account of the great death and its consequent reaffirmation of all things.

[20] *Prasannapadā*, ch. xiii; trans. from 83b–84a of the Tibetan Canon. A looser translation is given by Sprung (1979), p. 248.

To be *is* to be empty. That is what it is to be. It is no accidental property; it is something's nature – though, being empty, it has no nature.

This paradox is deeply related to the first one that we discussed. One might fairly ask, as have many on both sides of this planet, just *why* paradoxes of expressibility arise. The most obvious explanations might appear to be semantic in character, adverting only to the nature of language. One enamoured of Tarski's treatment of truth in a formal language might, for instance, take such a route. One might then regard expressibility paradoxes as indicating a limit*ation* of language, an inadequacy to a reality which must itself be consistent, and whose consistency would be mirrored in an *adequate* language. But Nāgārjuna's system provides a very different attitude towards these paradoxes, and hence to language. Each limb of the second (ontological) contradiction entails a limb of the first contradiction (of truth). Reality has no nature. Ultimately, it is not in any way at all. So nothing can be said about it. Essencelessness thus induces non-characterisability. On the other side of the street, emptiness is an ultimate character of things. And this fact grounds the (ultimate) truth of what we have just said. The paradox of language is therefore grounded in the contradictory nature of reality itself.

We think that the ontological insight of Nāgārjuna's is distinctive of the Madhyamaka; it is hard to find a parallel in the West prior to the work of Heidegger.[21] But even Heidegger does not follow Nāgārjuna all the way to the dramatic insistence on the identity of the two realities and the recovery of the authority of the conventional. This extirpation of the myth of the deep may be Nāgārjuna's greatest contribution to Western philosophy.

16.8 Nāgārjuna and inclosure

> Everything is real and is not real,
> Both real and not real,
> Neither real nor not real.
> This is Lord Buddha's teaching.
>
> (*MMK* xvIII: 8)

Central to Nāgārjuna's understanding of emptiness as immanent in the conventional world is his doctrine of the emptiness of emptiness. That, we have seen, is what prevents the two truths from collapsing into an appearance/reality or phenomenon/noumenon distinction. But it is also what generates the contradictions characteristic of philosophy at the limits. We have encountered two of these, and have seen that they are intimately connected. The first is a paradox of expressibility: Linguistic expression and conceptualisation can express only conventional truth; the ultimate truth is that which is inexpres-

---

[21] On the paradoxical nature of being in Heidegger, see ch. 15.

sible and that which transcends these limits. So it cannot be expressed or characterised. But we have just done so. The second is a paradox of ontology: All phenomena, Nāgārjuna argues, are empty, and so ultimately have no nature. But emptiness is, therefore, the ultimate nature of things. So they both have and lack an ultimate nature.

That these paradoxes involve Transcendence should be clear. In the first case, there is an explicit claim that the ultimate truth transcends the limits of language and of thought. In the second case, Nāgārjuna claims that the character of ultimate reality transcends all natures. That they also involve Closure is also evident. In the first case, the truths are expressed and hence are within the limits of expressibility; and in the second case, the nature is given and hence is within the totality of all natures.

Now consider the Inclosure Schema. This concerns properties, φ and ψ, and a function, δ, satisfying the following conditions:

(1) $\Omega = \{x; \varphi(x)\}$ exists, and $\psi(\Omega)$

(2)   For all $x \subseteq \Omega$ such that $\psi(x)$:

   (i) $\delta(x) \notin x$ (Transcendence)

   (ii) $\delta(x) \in \Omega$ (Closure)

Applying δ to Ω then gives: $\delta(\Omega) \in \Omega$ and $\delta(\Omega) \notin \Omega$. (For a visual illustration, see Fig. 1 on p. 156.)

In Nāgārjuna's ontological contradiction, an inclosure is formed by taking:

$\varphi(x)$ as 'x is empty'
$\psi(x)$ as 'x is a set of things with some common nature'
$\delta(x)$ as 'the nature of things in x'

To establish that this is an inclosure, we first note that $\psi(\Omega)$. For Ω is the set of things which have the nature of being empty. Now assume that $x \subseteq \Omega$ and $\psi(x)$, that is, that x is a set of things with some common nature. $\delta(x)$ is that nature, and $\delta(x) \in \Omega$ since all things are empty (Closure). It follows from this that $\delta(x)$ has no nature. Hence, $\delta(x) \notin x$, since x is a set of things with some nature (Transcendence). The limit-contradiction is that the nature of all things (Ω) – viz, emptiness – both is and is not empty. Or to repeat Nāgārjuna quoting the *Prajñāpāramitā*, 'all things have one nature, that is, no nature'.

In Nāgārjuna's expressibility contradiction, an inclosure is formed by taking:

$\varphi(x)$ as 'x is an ultimate truth'
$\psi(x)$ as 'x is definable'
$\delta(x)$ as the sentence 'there is nothing which is in d', where 'd' refers to x.
(If x is definable, there is such a d.)

To establish that this is an inclosure, we first note that $\psi(\Omega)$. For '$\{x; x$ is an ultimate truth$\}$' defines Ω.

Now assume that $x \subseteq \Omega$ and $\psi(x)$, then $\delta(x)$ is a sentence which says that nothing is in x. Call this s. It is an ultimate truth that there are no ultimate truths, i.e., that there is nothing in Ω; and, since $x \subseteq \Omega$ it is an ultimate truth that there is nothing in x. That is, s is ultimately true: $\delta(x) \in \Omega$ (Closure). For Transcendence, suppose that $s \in x$. Then $s \in \Omega$, that is, s is an ultimate truth, and so true, i.e., nothing is in x. Hence, it is not the case that $s \in x$. Thus, $\delta(x) \notin x$ (Transcendence). The limit-contradiction is that $\delta(\Omega)$, the claim that there are no ultimate truths, both is and is not an ultimate truth.

Thus, Nāgārjuna's paradoxes are both, precisely, inclosure contradictions. These contradictions are unavoidable once we see emptiness as Nāgārjuna characterises it – as the lack of any determinate character. But this does not entail that Nāgārjuna is an irrationalist, a simple mystic, or crazy; on the contrary: he is prepared to go exactly where reason takes him: to the trans-consistent.

16.8 Nāgārjuna's paradox and others like and unlike it

Demonstrating that Nāgārjuna's two linked limit paradoxes satisfy a schema common to a number of well-known paradoxes in Western philosophy (the Liar, Mirimanoff's, Burali-Forti's, Russell's, the Knower, to name a few) goes further to normalising Nāgārjuna. We thus encounter him as a philosopher among familiar, respectable, philosophers, as a fellow traveller at the limits of epistemology and metaphysics. The air of irrationalism and *laissez-faire* mysticism is thus dissipated once and for all. If Nāgārjuna is beyond the pale, then so, too, are Kant, Hegel, Wittgenstein, and Heidegger.

This tool also allows us to compare Nāgārjuna's insights to those of his Western colleagues, and to ask what, if anything, is distinctive about his results. We suggest the following: The paradox of expressibility, while interesting and important, and crucial to Nāgārjuna's philosophy of language (as well as to the development of Mahāyāna Buddhist philosophical practice throughout central and East Asia), is not Nāgārjuna's unique contribution (though he may be the first to discover and to mobilise it, which is no mean distinction in the history of philosophy). It recurs in the West in the work of Wittgenstein, Heidegger, and Derrida, to name a few, and shares a structure with such paradoxes as the Liar. Discovering that Nāgārjuna shares this insight with many Western philosophers may help to motivate the study of Nāgārjuna by Westerners, but it does not demonstrate that he has any special value to us.

The ontological paradox, on the other hand – which we hereby name 'Nāgārjuna's Paradox' – though, as we have seen, intimately connected with a paradox of expressibility, is quite distinctive, and to our knowledge is found nowhere else. If Nāgārjuna is correct in his critique of essence, and if it hence turns out that all things lack fundamental natures, it turns out that they all have the same nature, that is, emptiness, and hence both have and lack that very nature. This is a direct consequence of the purely negative character of the property of emptiness, a property Nāgārjuna first fully characterises, and the centrality of which to philosophy he first demonstrates. Most dramatically, Nāgārjuna demonstrates that the emptiness of emptiness permits the 'collapse' of the distinction between the two truths, revealing the empty to be simply the everyday, and so saves his ontology from a simple-minded dualism. Nāgārjuna demonstrates that the profound limit-contradiction he discovers sits harmlessly at the heart of all things. In traversing the limits of the conventional world, there is a twist, like that in a Möbius strip, and we find ourselves to have returned to it, now fully aware of the contradiction on which it rests.[22]

[22] See p. 233. Thanks to Paul Harrison, Megan Howe, and Koji Tanaka for comments on earlier drafts of this essay, and to our audience at the joint meeting of the Australasian Association of Philosophy and the Australasian Society for Asian and Comparative Philosophy, University of Melbourne, 2000, especially Peter Forrest, Tim Oakley, and John Powers.

17 Further reflections

17.1 Dialetheism

The present chapter is provoked largely by reviews and critical notices of the first edition of the book, and responds to some of the points that critics have made.[1] In the last section I will also comment briefly on the two preceding chapters.

Let me start with what, I presume, is the most contentious aspect of the book: dialetheism. Dialetheism, the view that there are true contradictions, is now more popular than it was in 1995: it takes the fingers of two hands to count the number of people who subscribe to it. Unsurprisingly, some reviewers attacked dialetheism. The aim of the book was not to defend this thesis directly. I did that in *In Contradiction* (1987), and the defence has been continued in many papers since then.[2] Neither is it appropriate to mount a full-scale defence of dialetheism here. Let me reply to a couple of specific attacks, however.

Zalta (forthcoming) claims that dialetheism is incompatible with our understanding of predication. He says, in his concluding remarks:

Since dialetheic logicians conceive ... predication to be such that there are objects x and properties F such that $Fx\&\neg Fx$, they force us to abandon our pretheoretic understanding of what it is to instantiate ... a property. Our pretheoretic understanding of ordinary predication is grounded in such basic cases as the exemplification of simple and complex properties. Even if we don't have exact analyses for the simple or complex properties in question, we have a pretheoretic understanding of what it is for something to exemplify being red, being round ... Part of that under-

---

[1] Since most of the articles concerned are relatively short, I shall not normally give page references. Italics in all quotations are original. I am very grateful to the following for their thoughtful comments on material in this chapter: J. C. Beall, Ivor Grattan-Guinness, Fred Kroon, Richard Gaskin, Nick Smith, Neil Tennant, Alan Weir, and Ed Zalta.
[2] To mention some of the less technical ones: Aristotle on the Law of Non-Contradiction is taken apart in Priest (1998a); dialetheic negation is discussed and defended in Priest (1999a); dialetheism is shown to be consistent with standard accounts of truth in Priest (2000a); how it is possible to accept contradictions rationally is analysed in Priest (forthcoming a); the nature of logic in general, and the possibility of revising our beliefs about it is analysed in Priest (forthcoming b). The problem of the general structure of inconsistent models of arithmetic (mentioned on p. 173) is now partially solved in Priest (2000d).

standing is that if an object x exemplifies a property P, then it is not the case that it fails to exemplify P. How are we to understand ordinary predication, or understand the idea of an object exemplifying such properties as having a color, having a shape, etc. if an object *exemplifying* such properties doesn't exclude its failure to exemplify such properties? Of course, a dialetheic logician may counter that they only abandon our ordinary notion of predication in special cases. But my claim is that the ordinary cases ground our understanding of *what it is* to exemplify a property – what exemplification is excludes something's both exemplifying and failing to exemplify a property. If the special cases force us to abandon this, then it is unclear whether we really understand what exemplification is.

This argument fails. Dialetheism cannot interfere with our 'pretheoretic understanding of predication' (whatever this phrase means) for the following reason: dialetheism concerns the simultaneous truth of statements of the form α and $\neg\alpha$; as such, it concerns the behaviour of negation; predication is a quite independent issue. One can even imagine a language which consisted *entirely* of atomic predications. The question of dialetheism would not even arise.

Zalta can tie the issues of predication and negation together only by presupposing a certain theory of negation, namely:

$\neg\alpha$ is true iff α is not (fails to be) true

For then $\neg Px$ is true iff Px is not true; and given that Px is true iff x exemplifies P, it follows that $\neg Px$ is true iff x does not exemplify P. The theory of negation in question may be an orthodox one, but it is not one to which I subscribe (as explained, pp. 171f).[3]

But let us suppose that Zalta is right about dialetheists needing to endorse some things of the form: x both does and not exemplify P. These are contradictions, and Zalta is simply denying them. He therefore begs the question. He might point out that it is not any old contradiction that is at issue here: contradictions concerning exemplification are a special case. But why? Zalta says that the failure of such a contradiction is constitutive of our understanding of predication. All I can say here is that it is not constitutive of mine. Unless there are some independent arguments for this claim, it would seem to be just a statement of dogma.

Since, as I have observed, the notion of negation is central to dialetheism, it is natural to attack dialetheism via negation. This is what Tennant (1998) does. He says (sect. 2.4):

[Denying the law of non-contradiction] is meaning-violating because of what negation means. One proves a negation ¬A by showing that the assumption of (the truth of) A is contrary to (the assumed truth of) whatever other premises X one wishes to hold on to:

---

[3] What is more, making the connection in this way assumes that the biconditional 'Px is true iff x exemplifies P' contraposes. Given the doubts about contraposition and the T-schema (Priest (1987), 4.9), this step is also dubious.

$$\mathrm{X, \bar{A}}^{(i)}$$

$$\vdots$$

$$\frac{\perp}{\neg A} \ (i)$$

Thus I would argue [Footnote: See Tennant (1999).] the notion of negation actually rests on the more fundamental notion of *necessary contrariety*, or *impossibility of joint truth* of at least two different propositions. For the notion of negation to have entered the language, it would have sufficed, on this view, for the language to have had contrary atomic propositions. Such propositions B, C would have admitted a primitive atomic inference of the form:

$$\frac{\mathrm{B \qquad C}}{\perp}$$

Pairs of propositions like this abound: colour exclusions, conflicting location reports . . . These *non-independent* atomic propositions would form the soil in which negation, hence explicit denial, could subsequently flourish: from B one could infer $\neg C$, and from C one could infer $\neg B$. It would then be analytic that it is impossible for both P and $\neg P$ to be true.

The reply to Tennant, *en bref*, is that his account of negation is a theory of its behaviour that the dialetheist may, and does, reject. There are good independent reasons to do so, as well. The logic that Tennant endorses is neither classical nor intuitionist logic. It is, in fact, a paraconsistent logic (though not one that I subscribe to). According to his account, the inference A, $\neg A \vdash B$ is *invalid*. Given this account, there is therefore no *logical* bar to dialetheism. It is a question of extra-systematic interpretation.

Crucial to this matter is Tennant's interpretation of $\perp$. He explains that this is not to be interpreted in the usual way, as an embeddable propositional constant. It would be better simply to leave a blank. We use it 'to register the metaphysical primal badness of simultaneous predication of antonyms, or of conflicting colour or shape attributions, or conflicting spatial locations of one and the same body, or conflicting temporal orderings of distinct events, etc.'. [4]

Now, this tells us what it is to infer $\perp$ from pairs (or more) of sentences. But what of single sentences? The introduction rule for negation when there are no undischarged assumptions is simply:

$$\underline{\qquad}(i)$$

$$\mathrm{A}$$

$$\vdots$$

$$\frac{\perp}{\neg A}(i)$$

[4] Tennant (1999), pp. 217f.

In other words, to say categorically that ¬A holds is to say that A entails some metaphysical absurdity, such as something's being red and green all over.[5] It seems clear that this is far too strong. I am now seated (and so not standing), but my being standed is not a metaphysical absurdity, like (supposedly) something's being red and green all over. (Even if being both standed and seated is a metaphysical absurdity, my being standed does not entail *that*.)

These considerations are bolstered by the following. If ⊥ is treated as a logical constant (though not necessarily an embeddable one), its characteristic inference is:

$$\frac{\bot}{A}$$

This says that, however the notion is interpreted, ⊥ is something that entails everything.[6] Now, to interpret ¬A as a claim that A entails something as strong as this is clearly excessive. I am not standing, but the claim that I am standing does not entail that I am a frog. The absurdity sign makes perfectly good sense from a paraconsistent/dialetheic point of view. It is just that if → records entailment, A →⊥ is a lot *stronger* than the negation of A.[7]

The third sort of objection to dialetheism produced by reviewers concerns its supposed implications on the question of belief-revision. Weir (1999) puts one such objection thus:

The crucial failing [of dialetheism] is in its inability to explain why abandonment of theories is sometimes rationally compelling. Priest's explanation comes down to saying that when a theory entails something with low probability, say a 'malign' zero-probability contradiction, then it should be abandoned ...

He then goes on to object that this cannot work. For in such circumstances one can simply revise the probability of the contradiction upwards, and so continue to accept it.[8]

---

[5] In the proof-theoretic tradition to which Tennant subscribes, the introduction rules of a connective are taken to characterise its meaning. The corresponding elimination rules simply unpack the introduction rules.

[6] One reason Tennant gives for not treating ⊥ as a logical constant is that there is, he claims, no uniform (language invariant) sentence that fills this role. In fact, there is. 'Everything is true' will do nicely. And truth, though it is not a standard part of the vocabulary of first-order logic, is a logical predicate, just as much as identity is.

[7] Tennant also asks why, if we are prepared to consider the possibility that some things are both true and false, we should not also consider the possibility that some things are true only and both true and false, etc. He calls this possibility 'dizzy'. In fact, the possibility makes perfectly good technical sense; the iteration does not have any effect on the notion of validity. See Priest (1984).

[8] He seems to think that this is a possibility only if one subscribes to a subjectivist notion of probability. I think this is false. Even if one subscribes to an objective epistemic account of probabilities, the probability of the contradiction may go up once it is found to be supported by something with higher probability.

But Weir goes wrong at the first step. When we find some belief that we accept entails something that we reject, we have a choice of two possibilities: continue to accept the former, and in consequence the latter; or continue to reject the latter, and consequently the former. The probabilistic scenario Weir describes is just a variant of this. When we discover that something to which we ascribe a high probability entails something to which we ascribe a low probability, the probabilities have to be revised, but we have a choice of two ways in which to do this.

Given the choice, which should be taken? As Priest (1987), 7.5, explains, the rational thing to do is to formulate both possibilities explicitly, and then evaluate the two resultant theories methodologically. That is, we adopt whichever alternative comes out best under the standard criteria of theory evaluation.[9] The original theory may well be abandoned as a result of the process. Just possibly, though, one may come to accept an inconsistent position,[10] though not, perhaps, normally.[11]

It might be thought, as Weir has suggested in conversation, that this solution is methodologically vicious. Non-deductive reasoning of this kind should never be able to trump deductive principles, such as the law of non-contradiction – or all hope of objectivity is lost. It is not: the criteria of theory evaluation may be defeasible and fallible ones, but this does not deprive them of objective force. A fallible seatbelt is objectively better than no seatbelt at all. In any case, where do our beliefs in deductive principles come from? They are just as much a historical product as all other acts of human theorising. And jettisoning such beliefs is well known in the history of logic. To give but one, very clear, example, many early medieval logicians, and arguably Aristotle as well, held that nothing could entail its own negation – a 'connexive' principle. The belief was overturned in the later Middle Ages. It was overturned because the non-connexive logics that were developed then proved to give overall superior accounts of validity.[12] As is always the case in belief-revision, the connexive principles could have been maintained, but only at the cost of making the account much more complex and *ad hoc* than its rivals. Non-deductive criteria trumped deductive. Even if something appears to be *a priori* certain – and how much of this is simply a function of one's educa-

---

[9] See further Priest (2001b).

[10] In particular, it may, *contra* Weir, be rational to accept that dialetheism is both true and false. In a sense, this is what I do accept: not only are some sentences of the form $\alpha \wedge \neg\alpha$ true, but $\neg(\alpha \wedge \neg\alpha)$ is itself a logical truth. See Priest (1987), 4.9. It is no refutation of one's view to hold that it is false, i.e., has a true negation, if one's view is precisely that some contradictions, in particular ones of this kind, may be true.

[11] Evnine (1997) says that I owe 'some explanation of the normality of non-contradiction'. The matter is addressed in Priest (1987), 8.4. More recent and extended discussion can be found in Priest (2001a) and (forthcoming a).

[12] See Sylvan (2000).

tion? – belief in it may yet be overturned. Friends of consistency should remember the fate of many of the principles that Kant held to be *a priori* certain.

Let me finish this section with the following observation. Some reviewers pointed out that arguments for dialetheism often proceed by showing that the law of non-contradiction is incompatible with other things that we are inclined to believe true, e.g., that one can give an account of the semantics of our language (Weir (1999)), that we can always think about the totality of things of a certain kind as a single thing (Moore (1995)), or that certain totalities – or the values of certain functions – exist (Kroon (2001)). They claim that these other things should be rejected before the belief in the law of non-contradiction; but they rarely *argue* that this option is the rationally preferable one.[13] The dialetheic option concerning inclosure paradoxes is simpler, more natural, and does justice to the data better than consistent accounts.[14] Those who think otherwise could at least try to show that this is not so. In particular, their position might be a bit more persuasive if they could provide good reasons for supposing the law of non-contradiction to be true; and thus that their subscribing to it is not simply an attachment to the familiar and the comfortable.

17.2 The inclosure schema

I now turn to the contents of the book proper. The first subject to take up here is its central theoretical structure, the Inclosure Schema:

(1) $\Omega = \{x; \varphi(x)\}$ exists, and $\psi(\Omega)$

(2)   For all $x \subseteq \Omega$ such that $\psi(x)$:

    (i) $\delta(x) \notin x$

    (ii) $\delta(x) \in \Omega$

All the contradictions with which the book concerns itself are inclosure contradictions, that is, contradictions fitting the Inclosure Schema.[15] In par-

---

[13] An honourable exception is Zalta (forthcoming), who recognises very clearly the methodological nature of the choice to be made here.

[14] See Priest (2001a).

[15] Tennant (1998) and Kroon (2001) point out that I am assuming that for all $x \subseteq \Omega$ such that $\psi(x)$, and in particular for $x = \Omega$, $\delta(x)$ exists. This is quite correct. It is implicit in the notation, but could well be made explicit. Doing so has the advantage of making it clear that this point is one that can be challenged. This matter is not ignored in the book, though. The way, if there is one, that the point may challenged will vary from paradox to paradox, and different challenges are considered in different places. For example, in the set-theoretic paradoxes (Table 7, p. 131) $\delta(\Omega)$ is some absolute infinity, such as the set of all ordinals or of all sets. The existence of such sets follows from the Domain Principle (see below). In the definability paradoxes (Table 8, p. 134) such as Berry's, $\delta(\Omega)$ is an (or the least) object of a certain kind. The existence of

ticular, it is shown that all the standard paradoxes of self-reference fit the Schema.[16] I claimed that it is this Scheme which generates the paradoxes. Some commentators have objected. One such is Grattan-Guinness (1998), who argues that satisfying the Schema is neither necessary nor sufficient for a paradox of the family.

Grattan-Guinness' example of a non-paradox that fits the Schema is the well-known Barber Paradox.[17] His argument that there is a version of this paradox that fits the form of the Schema is rather sketchy, and it is not clear to me what he has in mind exactly. But the details are not so important: the Barber certainly can be put into the form of the Schema, as we saw (p. 157 n. 2). But there is more to the Schema than its form. Let me elucidate.

It is clear that the premises of an instance of the Inclosure Schema entail a contradiction: $\delta(\Omega)$ is both in and not in Ω. So an inclosure argument is valid. But one needs more than this for a paradoxical argument: the premises must also be true, at least *prima facie*, or none would suppose the situation paradoxical. It is this fact that rules out the Barber Paradox and its like as inclosure paradoxes. We have no good reason to suppose that there is a barber of the required kind.[18]

There is a possible reply here though. Could there not be good inductive evidence for the existence of such a barber.[19] (We interview the first man in the town, then the second, ...) I do not think that such an argument would be cogent, but if one takes this possibility seriously, one can avoid it by putting a slightly stronger condition on the premises of an inclosure contradiction: not just that the premises are *prima facie* true, but that they are *a priori* so. For exactly this is true of the standard paradoxes of self-reference: Transcendence and Closure would appear to be *a priori* certified. The contradictions to which these give rise seem to be inherent in thought itself, intrinsic to our conceptual structures. This, indeed, is a *leitmotiv* of the book.

---

such an object is a standard part of the paradox argument. In the Bii paradoxes (Table 9, p. 146), $\delta(\Omega)$ is a certain truth-bearer. If truth-bearers are sentences, the existence of the appropriate bearer is manifest. If they are propositions, this is not the case. But attempts to deny the existence of the appropriate propositions founder on the reef of extended paradoxes such as 'this sentence expresses no proposition or a false one'. See Priest (1987), ch. 1.

[16] Another which fits the Schema, not discussed in the book, is Yablo's paradox. See Priest (1997a).

[17] He gestures towards others, but it is unclear to me what these are supposed to be. He also claims that 'the seemingly consistent Gödel's incompletability theorem also fits the Schema'. I do not know what, exactly, he has in mind here. There certainly is a paradox underlying the standard proof of Gödel's first incompleteness theorem. This is the 'Knower paradox', and it fits the Schema, as we saw in 10.2.

[18] Restall (1996) points out that Kant's Antinomies also fit the *form* of an inclosure as well. Despite Kant's view, it is hard to see these arguments – at least, both horns of each one – as having *prima facie* plausibility.

[19] Nick Denyer has pressed this point on me on a couple of occasions.

The premises in the case of the Barber and its kind, were they ever to be true, are only so *a posteriori*.[20]

Grattan-Guinness' examples of paradoxes of self-reference that do not fit the Schema are those of Curry.[21] The existence of Curry paradoxes is discussed in 11.8. As I noted there, whether or not such paradoxes fit the Schema depends on how the conditional involved is interpreted. If it is interpreted as a material conditional, Curry paradoxes are just variants of standard paradoxes, and so fit the Schema. If not, they do not.[22] Such paradoxes are, therefore, of a different kind. They are paradoxes that involve essentially conditionality, and especially the principle of Contraction $((\alpha \rightarrow (\alpha \rightarrow \beta) \vdash \alpha \rightarrow \beta))$. As Curry himself put it: 'the root of the difficulty lies in ... [the axioms for] implication'.[23] Genuine Curry paradoxes are therefore ones that depend on a mistaken theory of the conditional, and are perhaps best thought of as more like the 'paradoxes of material implication'.

It is agreed, then, that there are paradoxes – puzzling arguments that end in contradiction – that involve self-reference and that do not fit the Schema. But this is hardly news. Many paradoxes involve self-reference in one way or another, but no one would suppose that they belong with the Liar and its mates. As an illustration, just consider the person – a fallibilist – who claims that one can never be certain of anything. This, of course, is self-reflexive. It follows that the fallibilist who claims this, if right, cannot be certain of it. What one makes of the matter is another issue. Those who think that to claim anything is to claim certitude can infer that the fallibilist cannot consistently maintain their own views. Fallibilists will prefer to maintain that one can assert things without being certain. But whatever one makes of the matter, the utterance is not an inclosure contradiction. Or consider another example: there are versions of the Surprise Exam paradox that are self-referential. (See, e.g., Halpern and Moses (1986).) The information given to students is that there will be an exam next week, but that they will not be able to infer

---

[20] There are, of course, versions of the standard paradoxes where some of the premises required to establish Transcendence and/or Closure are *a posteriori*; for example, where a premise refers to a sentence by a description such as 'the only sentence on such and such a page' and it is an empirical fact that it, itself, is that sentence. Such *a posteriori* elements, though, are always accidental in a certain sense. They are ways of securing an effect that could be secured by *a priori* means.

[21] He attributes them to Löb (1955). As far as I am aware, paradoxes of this kind were first pointed out by Curry in (1942). Williamson (1996) and Grim (1998) also cite these paradoxes as counter-examples to the Inclosure Schema.

[22] What if the conditional is a strict conditional – as asked by Williamson (1996)? Then, as Williamson observes, the paradox is equivalent to the necessary Liar: this sentence is necessarily false. And it fits the schema: it is a variant of the Knower paradox.

[23] Curry (1942), p. 117. It should also be noted that rejecting Contraction, and so solving the Curry paradoxes in this way, will not also solve all inclosure paradoxes. Some of these, such as Berry's, do not use the principle at all. See Priest (1987), 1.8.

when *from this very information*.) Again, such paradoxes are different from inclosure contradictions: they turn on the use of backwards induction, and the assumptions implicit in this.

Some commentators have argued that even my location of some of the standard paradoxes within the Inclosure Schema is problematic. One reason for this is that the contradiction occurs at, and only at, the limit; the behaviour of the machinery elsewhere is really irrelevant 'noise'.[24] But someone who considers only the limit situation misses, it seems to me, an essential part of the story. The paradoxes are produced by a certain mechanism: it is this which generates the contradiction. When one understands this, one understands *why* contradictions of this kind arise. The mechanism operates below the surface. One can, as it were, just look at the surface (the limit case), but if one does this, one's understanding of the situation will be strongly incomplete, to put it mildly. It is rather like a volcano. The only part of this one can normally see is the eruption, and it is tempting to think of this as the volcano. But it is precisely the geothermal activity, kilometres underground, that causes the eruption. If you don't understand this, you don't understand volcanoes. More of this later.

A different sort of reason (given by Tennant (1998), Kroon (2001)) focuses on the fact that the Inclosure Schema embroils the notion of *set* in all the paradoxes. But one can formulate the Liar paradox, for example, simply using the predicate 'is true'; one does not have to bring in the notion of set at all. As pointed out in 10.2, this point is superficial, since there is a conceptual connection between satisfying a condition – being true – and being a member of a certain totality – being one of the totality of true things. Since many opponents of dialetheism will be inclined to reject this 'naïve' notion of sethood, it may well be thought that this move is question-begging.

If any questions are begged here, they are unbegged elsewhere. (See p. 144 n. 3.) But, in any case, I do not see the matter as question-begging. The reasons for this are three. First, the Inclosure Schema is not intended as an argument for dialetheism. It is intended as an analysis of the nature of limit contradictions. As such, it may be accepted by dialetheists and non-dialetheists alike.[25] Like all analyses, it does have theoretical underpinnings, and the naïve notion of set is certainly one of these, but that is beside the point here.

Secondly, the connection between satisfying a condition and being a member of a collection is about as simple and natural a conceptual connection as there can be. Indeed, when we speak of something as of a certain sort, it is virtually impossible not to hear this something simultaneously as *satisfying a certain condition* and as *being one of a certain group*. Even those who subscribe

[24] Some remarks of Tennant (1998) can be read in this way.
[25] There are certainly set theories that accept naïve comprehension (every condition determines a set), but are consistent. See Brady (1983).

officially to something like Zermelo–Fraenkel set theory, in which some conditions correspond to no totality, recognise this fact: the language of proper classes beckons ineluctably. (Of course, what properties those collections, totalities, groups – whatever one calls them – have is another matter.) No one would ever have doubted this connection, had it not been for the fact that it gives rise to contradictions in certain contexts. Given that the major thesis of the book is exactly an endorsing of those contradictions, it is those who would deny the connection who beg the question in the present case.

Finally, to insist on the connection between conditions and sets – or at least, the contentious half, that every condition determines a set – does not beg the question in the context of the book, since the claim follows from something else that the book endorses and argues for: the Domain Principle. The Domain Principle states that quantifying presupposes a corresponding totality of quantification. As Moore (1995) puts it nicely: there is a unity in this multiplicity. Given any condition, one can clearly talk of all the things satisfying that condition. The result follows.[26]

17.3 The domain principle

The Domain Principle seems patent to me. It would seem to be an obvious and brute semantic fact that whenever there are things of a certain kind, there are *all* of those things. Yet the Principle has drawn flak from some commentators (e.g., Dümont and Mau[27] (1997), Kroon (2001), Weir (1999)). Dümont and Mau refer readers to Cartwright on the matter. Cartwright rejects the Domain Principle, which he calls the 'All-in-One Principle', for reasons that he explains as follows ((1994), p. 8):

There would appear to be every reason to think ... [the All-in-One Principle] false. Consider what it implies: that we cannot speak of the cookies in the jar unless they constitute a set; that we cannot speak of the natural numbers unless there is a set of which they are the members; that we cannot speak of all pure sets unless there is a class having them as members. I do not mean to imply that there is no set the members of which are the cookies in the jar, nor that the natural numbers do not constitute a set, nor even that there is no class comprising the pure sets. The point is rather that the

---

[26] It should be noted, also, that the notion of sethood may be eliminated entirely from the Inclosure Schema, since the Schema may be formulated equivalently in terms of properties. Thus, where φ is a property, it may be stated thus:

    (1) φ exists and $\Psi(\varphi)$

    (2) For all θ such that $\Psi(\theta)$ and $\forall x(\theta x \rightarrow \varphi x)$

        (i) $\neg \theta \delta(\theta)$

        (ii) $\varphi \delta(\theta)$

Fitting the standard paradoxes into the new formulation of the Schema is a routine exercise.

[27] Who say that no reasons are given for the Domain Principle. This is false. Arguments are given in 8.8.

needs of quantification are already served by there being simply the cookies in the jar, the natural numbers, the pure sets; no additional objects are required.

It is one thing for there to *be* certain objects; it is another for there to be a *set*, or set-like object, of which those objects are the members. [The paragraph goes on to discuss Russell's distinction between a set as many and a set as one.]

The passage is rhetorically persuasive, but it achieves this effect by trading on a number of important confusions. The first is between quantification and description. Cartwright says that the Domain Principle entails that 'one cannot speak of the cookies in the jar unless they constitute a set'. It does not. Speaking of *the cookies in the jar* does not quantify over the cookies. It refers to them by means of a definite description. (It is a plural description, but this does not affect the matter.) Clearly, to speak of *the so and so(s)* requires us to presuppose no more than the existence of the so and so(s).[28]

The passage also holds up as implausible the thought that one can speak of all (pure) sets without there being a set of (pure) sets. This *is* a consequence of the Domain Principle. But once one separates it from the case of descriptions, its supposed implausibility is much harder to see. As I noted in 8.8, for any claim of the form 'all sets are so and so' to have determinate sense there must be a determinate totality over which the quantifier ranges. It would clearly be wrong to suppose that this totality is a set satisfying the axioms of Zermelo–Fraenkel set theory, or of some other theory of sets; but that there *is* a well-defined totality seems to me undeniable. Moreover, it is clearly a totality that we can think of as a single thing, since we can legitimately refer to it as *that totality*: the totality of all sets.

The passage continues by saying that 'the needs of quantification are already served by there being simply the cookies in the jar'. This bring us to the second confusion in the passage. Loosely, it is a confusion between sense and reference. What are 'the needs of quantification'? First of all, the variable of the quantifier must have values. These are the cookies in the jar themselves: $cookie_1$, $cookie_2$, $cookie_3$, ... This, indeed, has nothing to do with totalities of any kind. The totality is presupposed as soon as we talk, not of the possible references of the variables, but of the sense of the sentence containing the quantifier. This is not determinate unless the totality of the cookies is determinate. We can put the point in a Quinean fashion. The ontological commitments of the sentence concerned, the entities there must be for the sentence to be true, are precisely $cookie_1$, $cookie_2$, $cookie_3$, ... But it is not the ontological commitment of the sentence that is at issue

[28] Of course, if, after Russell, one takes definite descriptions to be paraphrasable away in terms of quantifiers, this is not the case. But such an account of descriptions cannot be maintained. Descriptions (or at least many uses of them) are referential, as is shown by the fact that that reference may be picked up by subsequent occurrences of pronouns, as in 'I saw the man who crashed the car.' 'Did you? What did he look like?' 'He was pretty shaken when he got out.'

here; it is the sense of the sentence; the determinacy of this does require there to be a determinate totality of cookies.

Of course, if this totality is thought of as something independent of the cookies, this may again sound implausible. If you are talking about certain things, and if all existences are distinct, then invoking the existence of another entity would seem *de trop*. This is the rhetorical strategy employed in the last sentence quoted, 'It is one thing for there to *be* certain objects; it is another for there to be a *set*, or set-like object, of which those objects are the members.' But the set and its members are not distinct existences. There could be no set of cookies if there were no cookies – and vice versa. These are no atomic, independent, existences.

Weir's objection to the Domain Principle is different. He suggests that it may be undercut by an appeal to 'semantic nihilism', a view according to which a systematic account of the functioning of language, and, in particular, of how the quantifiers work, is given up as impossible. The idea here seems to be this. If one gives the standard model-theoretic account of how quantifiers function, one must perforce take the quantifiers to range over a set. However, if one eschews such an account, nothing need commit one to such a view. This observation misses the point, however. The argument from the determinacy of sense just rehearsed does not depend on a model-theoretic account of the quantifiers, or of any other. It simply appeals to the fact, on which all may agree, that 'everything is α' has no determinate sense unless the *everything* in question is a determinate totality. The model-theoretic account of quantification is simply a formal way of recognising this fact. If someone eschews this account, they are not refuted by the words from their own mouth. They are refuted none the less.

17.4　Another solution that reproduces the problem

I now turn to the paradoxes that fit the Inclosure Schema. Many of these are very orthodox. Many reviewers, unsurprisingly, favoured some of the more orthodox solutions that have been proposed. Virtually all of these are addressed explicitly or implicitly in Part 3, as well as in Part 1 of Priest (1987). I have nothing of substance to add to these matters here.

One very novel solution that is not addressed in either of these places is that proposed by Zalta (forthcoming). The main idea here is that there are two distinct notions of predication. The more familiar of these is *exemplification*; Zalta writes 'x exemplifies P' as Px. The other notion, which is typically how objects of thought have those properties that they have in thought, he calls *encoding*; Zalta writes 'x encodes P' as xP. The hope is that this distinction will allow one to show that the paradoxes arise due to a confusion of ambiguity. The general strategy is therefore a familiar one: parameterisation. When a contradiction arises, look for a difference in respects. Though it should be pointed out that the origin of Zalta's distinction has nothing to do with the paradoxes. It arose in connection with his Meinongian account of objects.

The distinction between the two notions of predication has much to be said in its favour.[29] The first thing to note here, though, is that simply drawing a distinction never, in itself, solves a paradox. In a sense, it makes matters worse. For we now have *two* arguments, one employing each of the disambiguated notions. We have to explain what is wrong with both of these. (See 6.7.) And as far as I can see, Zalta does not really address this matter. For example, the notion of predication employed in Berkeley's paradox, as I intended it, is the usual one: exemplification. Zalta does not explain why, for this notion, the argument fails. He simply suggests that the premise that there is something that is not conceivable is true in the sense of encoding: $\exists x \neg x \tau$. But the question is why it is not true in the sense of exemplification: $\exists x \neg \tau x$. After all, 4.7 gives a number of arguments for this conclusion. Similar comments apply to Zalta's discussion of the Inclosure Schema. He suggests that one of Transcendence or Closure should be understood in terms of exemplification, whilst the other should be understood in terms of encoding. I intended it uniformly in terms of exemplification, and I ask: what is wrong with it understood in those terms? A couple of the paradoxes concern objects of thought, notably Berkeley's paradox and the Fifth Antinomy. Conceivably, the notion of encoding might get some purchase here, but most inclosure contradictions are not of this kind.

But worse is in store. Zalta has given us some new machinery to play with, and as is so often the case, the machinery gives inclosure contradictions of a new kind. Let us consider exemplification first. The machinery in use here is the familiar second-order logic. Second-order variables range over properties, which can be specified by λ-terms. Familiar as this machinery is, it is not innocent of problems. The crucial question is how properties are to be thought of. One way of thinking of them is as objects of a certain kind. After all, λ-terms are noun-phrases, and so are naturally thought of as referring to objects. But if we think of properties in this way, then they should be within the range of the first-order variables, in which case, Russell's paradox, a paradigm inclosure contradiction, is forthcoming in the usual way. The requirement that properties not be in the range of first-order variables appears, in this context, as an unprincipled evasion.

The alternative is to think of properties as *sui generis*. This, after all, is how Frege, the inventor of second-order logic, thought of them. In particular, properties are not simple objects, but are unsaturated – else we have no account of the unity of the proposition. But in that case we are back with

---

[29] Though I think that it may well be possible to handle one of the major problems to which Zalta applies the idea without it. This is the problem concerning (possibly non-existent) objects of thought and their properties. See Priest (2000c).

Frege's problem of the concept *horse*, an inclosure contradiction at the limit of the expressible (12.2).[30]

Now let us turn to encoding. Meinongian objects would seem to be able to have any sorts of properties whatever: we can certainly contemplate an object with arbitrary properties. Of course, these objects cannot *exemplify* those properties, or all hell breaks loose. Hence, on Zalta's view, they must encode them. We are therefore led to the characteristic postulate of Zalta's theory: for any condition on properties, $\alpha(F)$, there is an object that encodes exactly the properties satisfying it:

$$\exists z \forall F(zF \leftrightarrow \alpha(F))$$

(For any given $\alpha(F)$, this z turns out to be unique.) Now, take $\alpha(F)$ to be: F is the property of encoding a property that is not exemplified. That is, let $\alpha(F)$ be $F = P$, where

$$P = \lambda x \exists G(xG \wedge \neg Gx)$$

We then get:

$$\exists z \forall F(zF \leftrightarrow F = P)$$

Let this z be a_P. Then since $P = P$, it follows that:

$$a_P P$$

Now suppose that Pa_P. Then $\lambda x \exists G(xG \wedge \neg Gx)a_P$, i.e., $\exists G(a_P G \wedge \neg Ga_P)$. Since a_P encodes only one property, $G = P$; and thus $\neg Pa_P$. If, on the other hand, $\neg Pa_P$, then $a_P P \wedge \neg Pa_P$. Hence, $\exists G(a_P G \wedge \neg Ga_P)$, i.e., Pa_P. In either case, we have a contradiction: $Pa_P \wedge \neg Pa_P$. The paradox is due originally to Clark (1978).

The contradiction can be put into the form of an inclosure contradiction. Let $\varphi(x)$ be Px, so that $x \in \Omega \leftrightarrow Px$. Let $\psi(x)$ be the vacuous condition $x = x$ (so we may ignore it). For any set, x, let [x] be $\lambda y(y \in x)$; and this time, let $\alpha(F)$ be $F = [x]$. Then Zalta's characteristic postulate tells us that:

$$\exists z \forall F(zF \leftrightarrow F = [x])$$

Let this z be $a_{[x]}$, and let $\delta(x)$ be $a_{[x]}$. Then we have $a_{[x]}[x]$.

Now suppose that $x \subseteq \Omega$. For Transcendence: suppose that $a_{[x]} \in x$, i.e., $[x]a_{[x]}$. Since $x \subseteq \Omega$, $Pa_{[x]}$, i.e., $\exists G(a_{[x]}G \wedge \neg Ga_{[x]})$. Then $G = [x]$; so $\neg[x]a_{[x]}$. Thus, $\neg a_{[x]} \in x$, as required. But then $a_{[x]}[x] \wedge \neg[x]a_{[x]}$. Hence, $\exists G(a_{[x]}G \wedge \neg Ga_{[x]})$, i.e., $Pa_{[x]}$, i.e., $a_{[x]} \in \Omega$, which is Closure.

---

[30] Zalta's object theory allows us to talk not only of the property of being a horse, but also of the object that encodes the single property of being a horse. Frege's problem concerns, of course, the former.

The contradiction arises when $x = \Omega$. For then we have $a_{[\Omega]} \in \Omega \wedge \neg a_{[\Omega]} \in \Omega$, i.e., $Pa_{[\Omega]} \wedge \neg Pa_{[\Omega]}$. But $x \in \Omega \leftrightarrow Px$, and so $[\Omega] = P$. Thus, the contradiction is: $Pap \wedge \neg Pap$.

Zalta is well aware of Clark's paradox, of course. His solution[31] is to insist that sentences that contain encoding do not specify properties, so that encoding predications cannot occur inside an occurrence of λ, as in the property, P, required for Clark's paradox. The sadness of this move from a Meinongian point of view is clear. The whole point about thought is that we can think of objects satisfying *arbitrary* conditions. There ought, therefore, to be objects encoding all conditions, even those that concern encoding – or what on earth are we thinking about when we appear to be thinking about such things?[32] An honest theory of encoding should, like an honest theory of exemplification, be a dialetheic one, which endorses arbitrary comprehension principles, and the contradictions to which they lead.

What Zalta gives us, then, as is so often – and tellingly[33] – the case, is a solution to the problem that reinstates the problem – twice in fact: once for exemplification, in the form of Russell's paradox or the concept *horse* (you can choose), and once for encoding, in the form of Clark's paradox.

17.5 Berkeley's paradox

One inclosure paradox that is not orthodox is Berkeley's paradox. Some commentators singled this out for special treatment. The most detailed critique is provided by Kroon (2001), who has a number of objections. The first is that, though it may appear that one can conceive of something that is inconceivable, one may not, in fact, be doing that.[34] Why not? In 4.8 all that is required for something to be conceivable is that a name, or other representation, that refers to the thing in question be brought before the mind. This, says Kroon, is too thin for real conception. More is needed: 'knowing-who or knowing-what properties, properties that at the very least help us to fix the object's place in the larger scheme of things'. As I said in 4.8, there

---

[31] See Zalta (1983), pp. 158 ff.

[32] Zalta has replied (in conversation) that encoding is a merely theoretical notion, and we are therefore free to specify how it behaves, subject only to preserving the phenomena. But if natural language predication is ambiguous between exemplification and encoding, encoding is no mere theoretical construct: it is part of our vernacular expression. Zalta has also replied (in correspondence) that constraining the comprehension scheme for properties is no more *ad hoc* than giving up the law of non-contradiction in connection with predication. As far as I can see, the law was never involved in our understanding of predication. (See 17.1 above.) I am not, therefore, giving it up, in this context – in an *ad hoc* way or otherwise.

[33] See pp. 227f.

[34] Dale (1996) also says the same, but he does not spell out his reasons. He also worries about the Prefixing Principle of 4.6, but his worries appear to be addressed in that very section; and in any case, as 4.9 points out, the core argument, Berkeley's paradox, makes no use of this Principle.

are, no doubt, many different notions of conceivability; and the argument may well fail for such notions. But if the argument works for the notion I explained, that is enough.[35]

Kroon also doubts[36] that indefinite descriptions (or their formal representations, ε-terms) refer in the appropriate sense. I think he is wrong about this. There are uses of indefinite descriptions in English which are clearly referential. Merely consider the sentences 'John saw a man. Mary saw the same man'. 'A man' here is a noun-phrase, whose function is to pick out a certain object. How do we know? Because the phrase 'the same man' functions in such a way as to refer to the same object. And if one worries that the term in question is some sort of covert quantifier, as footnote 20 of page 69 points out, there are situations where this is *demonstrably* false.

The question of how reference is achieved by indefinite descriptions is an important one. I do not have an answer to that question that satisfies me – or even such an answer for the more usual cases of reference; but neither, in the present context, do I need one. *That* the terms refer is sufficient. And in any case, as page 69 points out, the issue of indefinite descriptions is rather a red herring. For there are versions of the argument that use definite descriptions. All we need is to apply the argument to some domain that is appropriately ordered, and we can replace the indefinite description 'a thing such that ... ' with a definite description 'the least thing in the ordering such that ... '.

Finally, Kroon suggests that the contradiction is to be solved by insisting on the context-dependence of conceivability. A thing that is not conceived (in this context) is not conceived (in this context); but it may well be conceived (in another). Indeed, the mentioning of the thing may launch us into this other context. As is clear, this is a familiar parameterisation strategy, with all its attendant problems, which I spelled out in 10.6 and 10.7. In particular we can just run the argument employing the phrase 'conceived in some (actual) context or other', and we are back with the problem. Thus, write this predicate as Cx; then as long as $\exists x \neg Cx$, $\varepsilon x \neg Cx$ is one such thing, $\neg C\varepsilon x \neg Cx$; but I do conceive it in the present context, so $C\varepsilon x \neg Cx$.

One may ask, as Kroon does, how one then knows that there are things that are not conceived in any (actual) context. The answer is essentially as given in 4.7.[37] A necessary (and sufficient) condition for conceiving something (in

---

[35] Regarding the Conception Schema, Zalta (forthcoming) asks why one should suppose that the conceivability of an object *de re* follows from the *de dicto* conceivability of something concerning it. The reason is as explained in 4.8: to conceive that such and such is so and so requires one to bring before the mind a name that refers to such and such; and this is what it takes to conceive of something on the account in question.

[36] As does Tennant (1998), 2.3.

[37] See also p. 154f.

whatever context you like) is to bring a representation of it before the mind. Since this takes some minimum time, any individual can conceive of only a finite number of things. There are a lot left over.[38]

17.6 The principle of uniform solution

A popular solution to some of the inclosure paradoxes is to reject the existence of the limit totality, Ω. This line is endorsed, for example, by Moore (1995) and Tennant (1998). Indeed, Tennant says ((1998), 2.1) that the rejection of the existence of Ω is:

> such a time-honoured response to the paradoxes of the absolute infinite in the early history of set theory that it is remarkable to find no sustained argument from Priest for why this response really will not do.

I am not sure what counts as a sustained argument in this context, but the argument for the existence of Ω in the case of paradoxes of absolute infinity is provided by the Domain Principle, as already discussed.

But if the argument of 11.5 is right, the rejection of absolute infinities, such as the set of all ordinals, cannot possibly provide an adequate solution. This is because, in a number of cases (e.g., Berry's paradox), the limit totalities are 'small' sets, such as the set of natural numbers. It is an act of desperation to reject the existence of such a set; and the inclosure paradoxes, *being of a single kind, require a uniform solution*. The principle invoked here is the Principle of Uniform Solution (PUS): same kind of paradox, same kind of solution.[39] Some commentators have objected to this principle, or at least its application here. Grattan-Guinness (1998), for example, takes the Principle to be contentious. For my part, I regard it as little more than a truism. If two paradoxes have different solutions, this itself would seem to show that they are of different kinds. What is not at all truistic is what constitutes a kind. Let me say more about this.

Let us start with an analogous principle: same kind of illness, same kind of cure – if two people have the same illness, they are to be cured in the same

---

[38] Kroon raises the possibility of a representation (and specifically a name) that changes what it represents at random. Perhaps it could refer to many things in the time that it is before the mind? It would have to refer to an infinitude of things – indeed, a very large infinitude – if the force of this argument is to be avoided. And here I am inclined to say, with Aristotle (*Met.* 1006^{b}5–10), that a word that could represent such an infinity in this way in the short space of time that it is in mental focus would have no determinate content, and so would not be a representation at all.

[39] Conversely, if two paradoxes are of different kinds, there is no reason why one should expect them to have similar solutions. This is why it is no surprise if the Curry paradoxes which do not fit the inclosure schema have a different kind of solution from inclosure paradoxes. One might also note that it is at least *possible* to offer a uniform and consistent solution to the paradoxes. That, after all, is what Russell's ramified theory of types purported to do.

way. In a superficial sense, this is obviously false. For example, the same illness can be treated with two different drugs. But in a more profound, and more important, sense, the principle is clearly correct: if we have one illness in the two people, this must be due to the same cause. So the two people must be cured in the same way, namely, by attacking that cause.[40] In the preceding example, the notion of a kind of illness is relatively unproblematic. The kind in question is a natural kind, to be individuated by its causal structure. When we are talking of kinds of paradox, rather than illness, we are no longer talking about kinds that can be individuated causally; but, it seems to me, we still have an operative notion of kind. The cause explains its illness. In mathematics, there are no causes, but there certainly are explanations: it still makes sense to single out the essential features of the situation that are responsible for something or other. For example, we can explain why the integers have a certain property by pointing out that they form a group under addition, and that all groups have that property. The other properties of the integers, such as how addition interacts with multiplication, are irrelevant to an understanding of why integers possess that property. What constitutes an explanation in mathematics, and how this notion relates to that of proof, for example, is a hard question, and I do not know the answer.[41] Yet it is not necessary to be able to define something in order to be able to recognise it. Mathematicians usually recognise an explanation when they see one; and I see one in the shape of the Inclosure Schema: an inclosure is what explains why the paradoxes arise. This is why such paradoxes are of a kind.

By way of further explanation, consider the following paradoxes of infinity (which we met in 2.6):

(1)   If the world is infinite in time past then the number of days before today is equal to the number of days before yesterday. But there are obviously fewer of these.

(2)   If the world is infinite in time past then the number of months before now must be twelve times the number of years before now, but this is already infinite, and so is as large as can be.

(3)   There are more natural numbers than even natural numbers; yet there must be the same number of each, since they can be put into one-to-one correspondence.

These paradoxes were known to the medievals, but it was not clear in the Middle Ages that they are members of a kind. Certainly, solutions were offered

---

[40]   As medical research develops, it is not uncommon to find that a syndrome that had been given a single name is, in fact, a multiplicity of separate illnesses. They are different illnesses because they have different causes – though ones with similar effects. This appears to be the case with schizophrenia and maybe cancer, for example.

[41]   The matter is discussed in Steiner (1978), Resnik and Kushner (1987).

for some of them, which did not apply to others. For example, John Philoponus suggested that the solution to the first two was that time past was not infinite. (Indeed, he used these as arguments for that claim.) This clearly has no relevance to paradox number 3.

With the wisdom of hindsight, however, we can now see that they are the same kind of paradox. This is because they are all examples of a single phenomenon, namely, that an infinite set can have a proper subset that is the same cardinal size as itself. This fact also provides the solution to all the paradoxes. And for just this reason, Philoponus' solution, even if he is right about the length of time past, is beside the point. (Just as those solutions are beside the point which maintain that in some inclosure paradoxes the totality, Ω, does not exist.) How do we know that this phenomenon is behind each paradox? Simply because it explains each of its manifestations. Once one understands this fact about cardinality, one sees why each of the examples arises.

Now, in exactly the same way, all inclosure contradictions are generated by the same underlying mechanism: an operation that diagonalises out of totalities of certain kinds – subsets of Ω – whilst giving an object that is still in Ω. The contradiction arises when we diagonalise out of Ω itself. This is the mechanism that underlies each of the contradictions, explaining why, essentially, it arises. As I put it in 9.5: once one understands how it is that a diagonaliser manages to 'lever itself out' of a totality and produce a novel object of the same kind, it becomes clear *why* a contradiction must arise at the limit.

That an inclosure is the underlying mechanism of each paradox may not be obvious to the casual observer: one has to examine the details. But the underlying mechanism of the medieval paradoxes of infinity just cited was not obvious at the time either. And once one does grasp the details, it is hard, I think, to resist the conclusion that the existence of an inclosure provides the explanation of the paradoxes. The inclosure paradoxes, then, are of a kind, just as much as illnesses with the same cause, and the paradoxes of infinity just discussed.

Another commentator (Smith (2000)) also objects to my use of the PUS. He suggests that the notion of a kind is relative to a degree of abstraction. That Bill loves Monica, and that Lee shot John, are not the same relative to the level of abstraction *a loves b* and *a shot b*; but they are with respect to the level of abstraction aRb. Moreover, the PUS should read: same kind of paradox *at a given level of abstraction*, same kind of solution *at that level*. Given this, there is nothing problematic about standard paradox solutions. For relative to the level of abstraction of the Inclosure Schema, both sorts of solution are the same: they are of the form 'circumvent the Schema'. Whereas at a lower level of abstraction, the paradoxes are not of the same kind: one mentions sets; the other does not. Moreover, the standard solutions are at this level: solutions to the set-theoretic paradoxes mention sets; solutions to the semantic paradoxes do not. Hence, these solutions are quite appropriate at their level.

Let us grant that kindhood is relative to degree of abstraction. In some sense, this is clearly right. It is not clear to me what counts as a level of abstraction if we are talking of paradox solutions. It is certainly not a matter of simply blanking out symbols of predefined grammatical categories. The Inclosure Schema does that, but it does a lot more than this too. But let this pass.[42] The real problems with Smith's argument lie elsewhere: in the assumption that all levels are equal. Let me explain.

Consider an example. The Liar paradox comes in many varieties. In some of them, self-reference is achieved by means of a demonstrative ('this sentence', etc.); in others, it is obtained by a description ('the first sentence on such and such a page', etc.); in yet others, it is obtained by some diagonal argument employing Gödel-numbers as names. Now, at some level of abstraction, these paradoxes are, presumably, of different kinds. The first, after all, depends on context-dependent features of utterance; the second presupposes some account of the way that descriptions work; the third employs numbers. Suppose that I propose three corresponding kinds of solution. The first kind of paradox is solved by some theory of speech acts; the second is solved by some theory of the semantics of descriptions; the third is solved by an appeal to mathematical nominalism. Even if all the solutions were to work for their own kind, it appears to me undeniable that, collectively, there is still something wrong with them. The exact *mechanisms* of reference are, in a clear sense, accidental to what is going on. The solutions may avoid the paradoxes, but they do so by attacking peripherals, not essentials. In all versions of the Liar paradox, there is a sentence, α, such that:

$$\alpha \text{ iff } \langle\alpha\rangle \text{ is false (or not true)}$$

where $\langle\alpha\rangle$ is some singular term referring to α. Call this the *Fixed-Point Schema*. It is this that needs to be taken on board, not the contingent fact of how the reference is achieved. Nor does it help to point out that, at this level, the level of abstraction of the Fixed-Point Schema, all the solutions *are* the same: they are all 'Fixed-Point Schema circumventers'. This is just a bit of linguistic legerdemain. It is clear that the solutions are not getting to the essence of things. (The paradoxes of the infinite that we have just looked at provide another example of a bunch of paradoxes which are, at some 'level of abstraction', different – some involve time and some do not – but where trying to solve them at that level is clearly incorrect.)

Now, it seems to me, things are exactly the same with the standard paradoxes of self-reference. The existence of an inclosure is what explains these. As I just put it, once one sees that a certain operation on any totality of objects of a

---

[42] Let pass, too, the fact that the PUS shows that the set-theoretic paradoxes on their own are not well solved by standard solutions. See 11.5.

particular kind generates a novel object of that kind, it becomes clear *why* applying the operation to the totality of all such objects must give rise to contradiction. Focusing on how the inclosure is achieved is like focusing on how the self-reference is achieved. It mistakes the symptom for the cause. Moreover, saying that the standard solutions to the semantic and set-theoretic paradoxes *are* the same at the level of the Inclosure Schema, in that they are all 'Schema circumventers', is just throwing linguistic dust in one's eyes. As Smith in effect notes, this is an entirely empty claim. That they circumvent the Schema does not show that they address the essence of the phenomenon, any more than in the case of the Liar paradox just cited. It's not that they are simply different ways of circumventing the Schema. Rather, they entirely miss the essence of the phenomenon.[43]

In other words, and to relate all this to the notion of level of abstraction, the appropriate level at which to analyse a phenomenon is the level which locates underlying causes. Smith himself illustrates this with a biological example. It would be wrong to suppose that certain phenomena in botany and zoology have the same explanation merely because they both concern, in some sense, branching processes. The correct level of abstraction at which to analyse the problems in question is the level of the relevant causal mechanisms. Similarly, just as with the example of the Liar paradox above, the correct level of abstraction for an analysis of inclosure paradoxes is not one which depends on the presence of certain words ('set', 'true', etc.); it is one which isolates the underlying structure that generates and causes the contradictions: the level of the Inclosure Schema.

If all this is right, then even if it were the case that orthodox solutions to the paradoxes of self-reference work at their corresponding level of abstraction – which, whatever this means, they do not, as we saw in chapters 10 and 11 – this would not suffice to protect them from criticism based on the PUS. Some levels are more equal than others.

17.7 Language and its meaning

Let us now turn to some comments on Part 4 of the book. The aim here was to show that many of the standard contemporary theories of language end up with contradictions at the limit of the expressible. I did not endorse any particular theory of language. The point, rather, was that whatever theory one subscribes to one ends up in this situation (p. 224).[44]

---

[43] As in Smith's example (2000), n. 4. Someone who did not understand that weight loss/gain is a matter of calories in minus calories out would have missed the essence of the problem.

[44] One theory of meaning not considered in this chapter, and that is now attaining some popularity, is a deflationary account. See, e.g., Horwich (1998). The precise details of such theories need not concern us here, save to note that they piggyback on a deflationary theory

Tennant (1998) is not impressed by this. He claims, concerning a number of these theories, if I understand him correctly, that the contradictions to which the theories lead can be taken as *reductios* of those theories. Indeed they can – though they will not be interpreted in this way by those who subscribe to the theories in question; but anyway, this is beside the point, which is just that the contradictions seem to arise whichever of the theories one subscribes to (see 13.3).[45]

However, Tennant's major remarks in this context concern theories that endorse the existence of semantic correlates: the meanings of linguistic units that come together to form the meaning of a whole sentence. There must be things that hold the components together in a unity. I called these *gluons*, and argued that these cannot be referred to, though they can be. In the case of Frege, Tennant remarks, there are no gluons. It is the unsaturatedness of concepts that glues the components together. But in Frege, it is precisely the concepts that *are* the gluons. And the Fregean arguments about concepts show that they cannot be referred to (12.2).

More generally, Tennant argues, gluons do not satisfy Transcendence. This is because:[46]

the correct contrast between the components of thought, and whatever gluons might be involved in that thought, is that the components are things *by means of which* we think (or make judgments), whereas gluons are not such things. Rather, gluons are things *by means of which* we can make judgments *by means of* thought components. Their intentional instrumentality, as it were, is at one remove.

I confess that I cannot make much of this distinction. But whatever it is, the upshot is that the gluon of a sentence cannot be a component of the sentence. This must be false (as p. 193 n. 22 points out). Merely consider: 'I am thinking about the gluon of this very sentence'. The gluon in that sentence is certainly a component.

---

of truth. This theory endorses, as conceptually definitive of the nature of truth, the T-schema: ⟨α⟩ is true iff α. Such theories therefore also naturally generate contradictions at the limit of thought in the form of the Liar paradox. (For a further discussion of deflationism about truth, see Priest (2000a).) Horwich and others have also endorsed a deflationary theory of reference, based on the 'R-schema': ⟨n⟩ refers to x iff n = x (where n is any name). Unsurprisingly, schemas of this kind produce further paradoxes of the same family. See Priest (1997b).

[45] Tennant also takes me to task, in connection with Davidson, for not considering semantically closed theories of truth. To a certain extent, these are considered in chapter 10. A more pointed discussion is in Priest (1987), ch. 1. Another commentator, Marconi (1997), criticises my treatment of the later Wittgenstein. I argue (ch. 14) that, according to Wittgenstein, meaning is not determinate. Yet in our language game about meaning, which is definitive, meaning *is* determinate. Marconi points out that the mere fact that these 'moves' are made in the language game does not mean that they are *'universally* authoritative' – i.e., that one is committed to their truth. This may be so, but it is beside the point. My point was that the upshot of Wittgenstein's conclusions cannot be consistently expressed in our language game about meaning. He has argued himself out of the possibility of expressing this – yet he does.

[46] Tennant (1998), 2.5.

Perhaps Tennant's distinction is that which is more clearly articulated by Gaskin (1995).[47] Starting from an essentially Fregean perspective, Gaskin argues, following Wiggins (1984) and *contra* Frege, that concepts are objects of a certain kind. The unity of the proposition is to be accounted for by the behaviour of the copula – the verb 'is' and its cognates, or the finite verb endings of other verbs. Thus, to take a simple example, in 'Marcus is tall', 'Marcus' and 'tall' have as semantic correlates certain things. 'Is' is a word whose function is simply to join by way of predication. There is clearly now no problem about referring to concepts.

But, as Gaskin observes, we are not out of the woods yet. The gluon is now the copula, and it poses the familiar problem. The copula itself has a meaning. After all, it expresses exactly the relationship between an object and a property that it instantiates. We are forced, like it or not, to recognise the meaning that *being* has. As Gaskin puts it (p. 175):

if the copula lacks reference (and indeed, lacks reference on the model of proper name and bearer) it is impossible to see how we should be able, as we are, to talk about predicative being. The copula must, in some way, refer.

Gaskin proposes a solution to the problem, which goes as follows. The copula is meaningful; how is one to explain its meaning? Consider a sentence of the form:

a is b

This means that:

a instantiates b-ness (i.e., is an instantiation of b-ness).

If this is supposed to specify the meaning of the copula, it clearly leaves something to be desired, since the statement itself *uses* the copula. We can, of course, explain the meaning of the copulation in this sentence, in the same way, to obtain:

a instantiates instantiation of b-ness

But we now have the same problem with this. We are clearly off on an infinite regress: Bradley's regress. We can never explain the meaning of a copula without residue.

Gaskin continues (pp. 175f.):

My suggestion is now that ... [the condition:[48] x is y iff x instantiates y-ness], in specifying a referent for the copula, not only shows us how we can talk about instantiation, but also, in virtue of its generation of the regress, captures the sense in which the

[47] This paper contains an excellent discussion of the problem of the unity of the proposition, its history, and its location in Frege and Wittgenstein.
[48] I simplify here a little, but not in a way that affects the point.

copula is unsaturated. For fixing the reference of the copula in terms of the relation of instantiation remains, given the possibility of endlessly rerunning ... [the condition] on the relation of instantiation itself, inevitably inchoate: the final specification of the reference keeps eluding our grasp. The copula does indeed contain a conceptual component – hence our ability to talk about the relation of instantiation – but attempting to specify that component leads to a bifurcation into a further conceptual and a further predicative component; the attempt to capture this further conceptual component leads to another bifurcation; and so on. The unsaturatedness of the copula is, then, underwritten by Bradley's regress. For the copula introduces unsaturatedness into the proposition in just the infinitistic way embodied in the regress. It is not that the copula lacks reference *simpliciter*; it is that the reference it has is endlessly deferred. (If one asks the question 'What does the copula refer to?', it is only the beginning of the answer to reply 'Instantiation'. Better would be to say 'The instantiation of instantiation'; better still 'The instantiation of the instantiation of instantiation'; better still ...)

Now, Gaskin's line here strikes me as not really getting to grips with the issue. If he is right, the meaning of 'is' cannot be expressed by a finite paraphrase. Perhaps so; but this does not really help solve the problem of the unity of meaning consistently. We have a dilemma. 'Is' has a meaning. If this is an object, then a proposition is not a unity, merely a list of meanings (including the meaning of 'is'). If, on the other hand, it is not an object (unsaturated), it cannot be referred to be a noun-phrase; but 'the meaning of "is"' (or *being*, if you like) would seem to do just that. The concept *horse* rides again.

In fact, there is a quite definitive reason as to why the problem cannot be solved by means of an appeal to the nature of predication: the same problem arises where there is no predication. Consider, for example, the description 'the father of Frege'. This does not express a proposition, but it certainly expresses what we might call an idea, a single thing. This idea is not a congeries of its components *father of* and *Frege*, and, moreover, there is no predication in sight. The problem of the unity of thought is much more general than that of the unity of the proposition. For Frege, after all, all functions are unsaturated.

17.8 The ontological turn

Finally, let us return, once more, to the subject of dialetheism. The title of the book makes reference to 'the limits of thought'. One reviewer (Evnine (1997)) pointed out that the contradictions with which the book concerns itself are not contradictions in thought, but contradictions in reality, and wondered if the name was appropriate.[49] I think it is. As page 1 points out, the concern with thought here is not with subjective mental states, but with objective content; and one cannot divorce this content of thought from the reality of which the thought is about.

---

[49] Similar points are made by Restall (1996) and Dümont and Mau (1997).

I claim that reality is, in a certain sense, contradictory. I do not, of course, mean that the objects that constitute reality, like chairs and stars, are contradictory. That would simply be a category mistake. What I mean is that there are certain contradictory statements (propositions, sentences – take your pick) about limits, that are true. I am enough of a realist to hold that there must be something about reality that makes them so (though I take no stand on the matter of whether reality comprises entities of the category *fact*). When I say that reality is contradictory, I mean that it is such as to render those contradictory statements true. If we are to think about that reality in an adequate fashion, it follows that those contradictions must be part of the content of our thought.

The limits of thought that the book deals with are of various kinds – though all satisfying the Inclosure Schema. Some of them may concern human products, like language; the limits discussed in Part 4 of the book are principally of this kind. But some are not. If there were prime matter, in Aristotle's sense, then this would be contradictory (1.5–1.7), whether or not there had ever been people around to think or talk about it.

This fact is underlined by the two previous chapters. In the taxonomy of limit contradictions given in page 11, the paradoxes in these chapters concern the limits of expression. But they concern limits to expression not because of the nature of what is doing the expressing, language, but because of what is being expressed about – to put it clumsily. For both Heidegger and Nāgārjuna, what it is to be, in some most fundamental sense, is contradictory.[50]

Though this is not a novel development in the book, these two new chapters, which put *what is* at centre stage, certainly mark an ontological turn in focus. The philosophy of language took pride of place in twentieth-century philosophy. Certainly there is no going back to how things were before this. But maybe this century will see a return to the mainstreaming of a more traditional philosophical issue, the nature of reality – and if I am right, a nature that is contradictory.

---

[50] It is worth noting that a contradiction at the limits of expressibility occurs in the other great Mahāyāna school of Buddhism, the Yogācāra of Vasubhandu and Sthiramati. (See, e.g., Stcherbatsky (1978).) In this, unlike the Madhyamaka of Nāgārjuna, conventional and ultimate reality are simply distinct. All truth is conventional, and the rest is ineffable. But it is *still* claimed that it is an ultimate truth that everything (except emptiness itself) is empty – though emptiness here is interpreted somewhat differently (essentially, as mind-dependence). Yogācāra is not involved in the ontological contradiction of 16.7, however. In this school, emptiness simply is (consistently) the nature of all things. The contradiction common to Madhyamaka and Yogācāra is generated by two things: (i) a claim that language can characterise only 'ordinary' reality; (ii) claims about what a reality beyond the 'ordinary' is like. It is exactly (i) and (ii) that also generate Kant's contradictory predicament concerning noumena, and the predicament of anyone else who wants to tell us something about a realm beyond the access of language. That what may lie beyond the 'ordinary' is itself contradictory is a further claim.

Bibliography

Aczel P. (1988), *Non-Well-Founded Sets*, CLSI Lecture Notes, no. 14, Stanford.

Al-Azm S. J. (1972), *The Origins of Kant's Arguments in the Antinomies*, Clarendon Press.

Alston W. (1956), 'Ineffability', *Philosophical Review* 65, 506–22.

Anderson A., Belnap N., and Dunn J. M. (1992), *Entailment: the Logic of Relevance and Necessity*, vol. 2, Princeton University Press.

Anscombe G. E. (1959), *An Introduction to Wittgenstein's* Tractatus, Hutchinson and Co.

Armstrong D. M. (1965), *Berkeley's Philosophical Writings*, Collier-Macmillan.

Bacon J. (1996), Review of *Beyond the Limits of Thought*, *Australasian Journal of Philosophy* 74, 542.

Bailey C. (1970), 'Continuity and Infinity in Space', pp. 32–7 of M. Capek (ed.), *The Concepts of Space and Time*, Boston Studies in the Philosophy of Science, vol. 22, Reidel.

Barnes J. (1979), *The Presocratic Philosophers*, Routledge and Kegan Paul.

(ed.) (1984), *The Complete Works of Aristotle*, Princeton University Press.

Barwise J. and Etchemendy J. (1987), *The Liar*, Oxford University Press.

Beck L. W. (trans.) (1950), *Prolegomena to any Future Metaphysics*, Bobbs-Merrill.

(1966), 'The Second Analogy and the Principle of Indeterminacy', *Kant-Studien* 57, 199–205; reprinted in T. Penelhum and J. MacIntosh (eds.), *The First Critique*, Wadsworth, 1969.

Bell J. and Machover M. (1977), *A Course in Mathematical Logic*, North Holland Publishing Co.

Bennett J. (1966), *Kant's Analytic*, Cambridge University Press.

(1974), *Kant's Dialectic*, Cambridge University Press.

Bhattacarya K., Johnston E. H., and Kunst A. (1978), *The Dialectical Method of Nāgārjuna: Vigrahavyāvartanī*, Motilal Banarsidass.

Black M. (1964), *A Companion to Wittgenstein's* Tractatus, Cambridge University Press.

(1968), 'Frege on Functions', in E. Klemke (ed.), *Essays on Frege*, University of Illinois Press.

Boghossian P. (1989), 'The Rule-Following Considerations', *Mind* 98, 507–49.

Bolzano B. (1950), *Paradoxes of the Infinite*, Routledge and Kegan Paul.

Boolos G. and Jeffrey R. (1974), *Computability and Logic*, Cambridge University Press.

Bostock D. (1973–4), 'Aristotle, Zeno and the Potential Infinite', *Proceedings of the Aristotelian Society* 74, 37–53.

(1988), *Plato's* Theaetetus, Clarendon Press.

Brady R. (1983), 'The Simple Consistency of Set Theory Based on the Logic *CSQ*', *Notre Dame Journal of Formal Logic* 24, 431–9.

Brandom R. (1983), 'Asserting', *Noûs* 17, 637–50.

Burali-Forti C. (1897), 'A Question on Transfinite Numbers', reprinted in van Heijenoort (1967).

Burge T. (1979), 'Semantic Paradox', *Journal of Philosophy* 76, 169–98; reprinted in Martin (1984).

Bury R. G. (trans.) (1933), *Sextus Empiricus*, vols. 1–4, Harvard University Press.

Campbell R. (1976), *From Belief to Understanding*, Faculty of Arts, Australian National University.

Candlish S. (1978), Review of Fogelin (1976), *Australasian Journal of Philosophy* 56, 81–6.

Cantor G. (1899), 'Letter to Dedekind', in van Heijenoort (1967).

Carnap R. (1959), 'The Elimination of Metaphysical Language through Logical Analysis of Language', ch. 3 of A. J. Ayer (ed.), *Logical Positivism*, Free Press.

Carroll L. (1895), 'What the Tortoise Said to Achilles', *Mind* 4, 278–80.

Cartwright R. L. (1994), 'Speaking of Everything', *Noûs* 28, 1–20.

Chalmers A. (1976), *What is This Thing Called Science?*, Queensland University Press.

Charlton W. (trans.) (1970), *Aristotle's* Physics; *Books I and II*, Clarendon Press.

Chihara C. (1973), *Ontology and the Vicious Circle Principle*, Cornell University Press.

Clark R. (1978), 'Not every Object of Thought has Being: a Paradox in Naïve Predication Theory', *Noûs* 12, 181–8.

Copleston F. C. (1961), *Aquinas*, Penguin.

Cornford F. M. (1935), *Plato's Theory of Knowledge*, Routledge and Kegan Paul.

Crombie I. M. (1963), *An Examination of Plato's Doctrines*, vol. 2, Routledge and Kegan Paul.

Culler J. (1979), 'Jacques Derrida', pp. 154–79 of J. Sturrock (ed.), *Structuralism and Since: from Lévi-Strauss to Derrida*, Oxford University Press.

Curry H. B. (1942), 'The Inconsistency of Certain Formal Logics', *Journal of Symbolic Logic* 7, 115–17.

Da Costa N. and Bueno O. (1996), Review of *Beyond the Limits of Thought*, *History and Philosophy of Logic* 17, 158–60.

Dale A. J. (1996), Review of *Beyond the Limits of Thought*, *Philosophy* 71, 308–10.

Dancy J. (1987), *Berkeley: an Introduction*, Basil Blackwell.

Dancy R. (1975), *Sense and Contradiction: a Study in Aristotle*, Reidel.

(1978), 'Aristotle's Second Thoughts about Substances: Matter', *Philosophical Review* 87, 372–413.

Dauben J. W. (1979), *Georg Cantor: his Mathematics and Philosophy of the Infinite*, Harvard University Press.

Davidson D. (1967), 'Truth and Meaning', *Synthèse* 17, 304–23; reprinted as ch. 2 of (1984).

(1973), 'Radical Interpretation', *Dialectica* 27, 313–28; reprinted as ch. 9 of (1984).

(1974a), 'Belief and the Basis of Meaning', *Synthèse* 27, 309–23; reprinted as ch. 10 of (1984).

(1974b), 'On the Very Idea of a Conceptual Scheme', *Proceedings and Addresses of the American Philosophical Association* 47, 5–20; reprinted as ch. 13 of (1984).

(1977), 'Reality without Reference', *Dialectica* 31, 247–53; reprinted as ch. 15 of (1984).

(1979), 'The Inscrutability of Reference', *Southwestern Journal of Philosophy* 10, 7–19; reprinted as ch. 16 of (1984).

(1984), *Inquiries into Truth and Interpretation*, Oxford University Press.

Davies P. (1984), *Superforce*, Heinemann.

Dedekind R. (1888), *Was sind und was sollen die Zahlen*, reprinted in English in *Essays on the Theory of Numbers*, Dover Publications, 1963.

Denyer N. (1991), *Language, Thought and Falsehood in Ancient Greek Philosophy*, Routledge.

Derrida J. (1974), *Of Grammatology* (trans. G. C. Spivak), Johns Hopkins University Press.

(1978), 'Structure, Sign and Play in the Discourse of the Human Sciences', ch. 10 of *Writing and Difference*, Routledge and Kegan Paul.

(1981), *Positions* (trans. A. Bass), University of Chicago Press.

(1982), '*Différance*', ch. 1 of *Margins of Philosophy*, Harvester Press.

Dummett M. (1973), *Frege: Philosophy of Language*, Duckworth.

(1977), *Elements of Intuitionism*, Clarendon Press.

(1991), *Frege: Philosophy of Mathematics*, Duckworth.

Dümont J. and Mau F. (1997), 'Are there any True Contradictions?', *Journal for the General Philosophy of Science* 7, 1–11.

Dunn J. M. (1979), 'A Theorem in 3-Valued Model Theory with Connections to Number Theory, Type Theory, and Relevant Logic', *Studia Logica* 38, 149–69.

Edwards P. (ed.) (1967), *Encyclopedia of Philosophy*, Collier-Macmillan.

Evinine S. (1997), Review of *Beyond the Limits of Thought*, *Manuscrito* 20, 103–10.

Ewing A. C. (1938), *A Short Commentary on Kant's* 'Critique of Pure Reason', Methuen.

Feyerabend P. (1975), *Against Method*, New Left Books.

(1977), 'Marxist Fairytales from Australia', *Inquiry* 20, 372–97; reprinted as part 3, ch. 3 of *Science in a Free Society*, New Left Books, 1978.

Findlay J. N. (1958), *Hegel: a Re-examination*, Allen and Unwin.

Fitch F. B. (1946), 'Self-Reference in Philosophy', *Mind* 55, 64–73; a revised version appears as Appendix C of *Symbolic Logic*, Ronald Press Co., 1952.

Fitting M. (1972), 'An ε-Calculus System for First Order S4', pp. 103–10 of W. Hodges (ed.), *Conference in Mathematical Logic, '70*, Springer Verlag.

Fogelin R. J. (1976), *Wittgenstein*, Routledge and Kegan Paul.

Fowler H. N. (trans.) (1970), *Plato*, vol. 4, Loeb Classical Library.

Fraenkel A., Bar-Hillel Y. and Levy A. (1973), *Foundations of Set Theory*, second revised edition, North Holland Publishing Co.

Frege G. (c1892), 'Comments on Sense and Meaning', pp. 118–25 of *Posthumous Writings*, Basil Blackwell, 1979.

Furth M. (trans.) (1967), *The Basic Laws of Arithmetic*, University of California Press.

Garfield J. (1990), 'Epoche and Śūnyatā: Scepticism East and West', *Philosophy East and West* 40, 285–307.

(1994), 'Dependent Co-origination and the Emptiness of Emptiness: Why did Nāgārjuna Start With Causation?', *Philosophy East and West* 44, 219–50.

(1995), *The Fundamental Wisdom of the Middle Way: Nāgārjuna's Mūlamadhyama-kakārikā*, Oxford University Press.

(1996), 'Emptiness and Positionlessness: Do the Madhyamika Relinquish All Views?', *Journal of Indian Philosophy and Religion* 1, 1–34.

Garver N. (1973), preface to J. Derrida, *Speech and Phenomena: and other Essays on Husserl's Theory of Signs*, Northwestern University Press.

Gaskin R. (1995), 'Bradley's Regress, the Copula and the Unity of the Proposition', *Philosophical Quarterly* 45, 161–80.

(2001), *Grammar in Early Twentieth Century Philosophy*, Routledge.

Geach P. (1972), *Logic Matters*, Basil Blackwell.

Geach P. and Black M. (1960), *Translations from the Philosophical Writings of Gottlob Frege* (second revised edition), Basil Blackwell.

Genesereth M. and Nilsson N. (1987), *Logical Foundations of Artificial Intelligence*, Morgan Kaufmann.

Gödel K. (1944), 'Russell's Mathematical Logic', in P. A. Schilpp (ed.), *The Philosophy of Bertrand Russell*, Tudor; reprinted in P. Benacerraf and H. Putnam (eds.), *The Philosophy of Mathematics*, Cambridge University Press, 1964.

Goldfarb W. (1985), 'Kripke on Wittgenstein on Rules', *Journal of Philosophy* 82, 471–88.

Gorampa (1990), *Nges don rab gsal*, Sakya Students' Union.

Grattan-Guinness I. (1998), 'Structural Similarity or Structuralism', *Mind* 107, 823–34.

Grene M. (1976), 'Life, Death and Language', *Partisan Review* 43, 265–79.

Grewe R. (1969), 'Natural Models of Ackermann's Set Theory', *Journal of Symbolic Logic* 34, 281–8.

Grice P. (1957), 'Meaning', *Philosophical Review* 66, 377–88; reprinted in P. Strawson (ed.), *Philosophical Logic*, Oxford University Press, 1967.

Griffin J. (1964), *Wittgenstein's Logical Atomism*, Oxford University Press.

Grim P. (1991), *The Incomplete Universe: Totality, Knowledge and Truth*, Bradford Books, Massachusetts Institute of Technology Press.

    (1998), Review of *Beyond the Limits of Thought*, *Philosophy and Phenomenological Research* 58, 719–23.

Grünbaum A. (1973), *Philosophical Problems of Space and Time*, Boston Studies in the Philosophy of Science, vol. 12, Reidel.

Guthrie W. C. K. (1981), *A History of Greek Philosophy, Vol. 6: Aristotle, an Encounter*, Cambridge University Press.

Hacking I. (1975), *Why does Language Matter to Philosophy?*, Cambridge University Press.

Hallett M. (1984), *Cantorian Set Theory and Limitation of Size*, Clarendon Press.

Halmos P. (1950), *Measure Theory*, Van Nostrand.

Halpern J. Y. and Moses Y. (1986), 'Taken by Surprise: the Paradox of the Surprise Test Revisited', *Journal of Philosophical Logic* 15, 281–304.

Harris R. (1988), *Language, Saussure and Wittgenstein: How to Play Games with Words*, Routledge and Kegan Paul.

Hart K. (1989), *The Trespass of the Sign*, Cambridge University Press.

Hart W. D. (1975–6), 'The Potential Infinite', *Proceedings of the Aristotelian Society* 76, 247–64.

Hawking S. (1988), *A Brief History of Time: from the Big Bang to Black Holes*, Bantam Press.

Hayes R. (1994), 'Nāgārjuna's Appeal', *Journal of Indian Philosophy* 22, 299–378.

Hazen A. (1987), '*Contra Buridanum*', *Canadian Journal of Philosophy* 17, 875–80.

Heidegger M. (1959a), *The Question of Being*, trans. W. Kluback and J. T. Wilde, Vision.

    (1959b), *An Introduction to Metaphysics*, trans. R. Manheim, Yale University Press.

    (1971), *Poetry, Language, Thought*, trans. A. Hofstadter, Harper and Row.

    (1977a), 'The End of Philosophy and the Task of Thinking', in Krell (1977).

    (1977b), 'What is Metaphysics?', in Krell (1977).

    (1977c), 'On the Origins of the Work of Art', in Krell (1977).

    (1991), *The Principle of Reason*, trans. R. Lilly, Indiana University Press.

    (1992), *The Metaphysical Foundations of Logic*, trans. M. Heim, Indiana University Press.

    (1996), *Being and Time*, trans. J. Stambaugh, State University of New York Press.

van Heijenoort J. (ed.) (1967), *From Frege to Goedel*, Harvard University Press.

Heron G. (trans.) (1954), *Of Learned Ignorance*, Routledge and Kegan Paul.

Herzberger H. (1970), 'Paradoxes of Grounding in Semantics', *Journal of Philosophy* 67, 145–67.

    (1980–1), 'New Paradoxes for Old', *Proceedings of the Aristotelian Society* 81, 109–23.

Hick J. (ed.) (1964), *The Existence of God*, Collier-Macmillan.

    (1970), *Arguments for the Existence of God*, Macmillan.

Hopkins J. and Richardson H. (trans.) (1974), *Anselm of Canterbury*, vol. 1, Edwin Mellen Press.

Horwich P. (1998), *Meaning*, Clarendon Press.

Hughes G. E. (1982), *John Buridan on Self-Reference: Chapter Eight of Buridan's 'Sophismata' Translated with an Introduction and Philosophical Commentary*, Cambridge University Press.

Huntington C. and Wangchen N. (1989), *The Emptiness of Emptiness*, University of Hawai'i Press.

Hylton P. (1984), 'The Nature of the Proposition and the Revolt against Idealism', in R. Rorty, J. B. Schneewind and Q. Skinner (eds.), *Philosophy in History: Essays on the Historiography of Philosophy*, Cambridge University Press.

(1990–1), 'Translation, Meaning, and Self-Knowledge', *Proceedings of the Aristotelian Society* 91, 269–90.

Inwood M. J. (1983), *Hegel*, Routledge and Kegan Paul.

Johnson B. (1981), translator's preface to J. Derrida, *Dissemination*, University of Chicago Press.

Joseph G. (1980), 'The Many Sciences and the One World', *Journal of Philosophy* 77, 773–91.

Jowett B. (trans.) (1953), *The Dialogues of Plato*, Clarendon Press.

Kaplan D. and Montague R. (1960), 'A Paradox Regained', *Notre Dame Journal of Formal Logic* 1, 79–90; reprinted as ch. 8 of Montague's *Formal Philosophy*, Yale University Press, 1974.

Kasulis T. (1989), *Zen Action/Zen Person*, University of Hawai'i Press.

Kemp Smith N. (1923), *Commentary to Kant's* Critique of Pure Reason, second edition, Macmillan.

(trans.) (1933), *Immanuel Kant's* Critique of Pure Reason, second edition, Macmillan.

Kenny A. (1969), *The Five Ways*, Routledge and Kegan Paul.

Kerford G. B. (1967), 'Protagoras of Abdera', pp. 505–6 of vol. 6 of Edwards (1967).

King H. R. (1956), 'Aristotle Without *Prima Materia*', *Journal of the History of Ideas* 17, 370–89.

Kneale W. and Kneale M. (1962), *The Development of Logic*, Oxford University Press.

König J. (1905), 'On the Foundations of Set Theory and the Continuum Problem', in van Heijenoort (1967).

Krell D. F. (ed.), *Martin Heidegger: Basic Writings*, Harper and Row.

Kretzmann N. (ed.) (1982), *Infinity and Continuity in Ancient and Medieval Thought*, Cornell University Press.

Kripke S. (1975), 'Outline of a Theory of Truth', *Journal of Philosophy* 72, 690–716; reprinted in Martin (1984).

(1982), *Wittgenstein on Rules and Private Languages*, Basil Blackwell.

Kroon F. (2001), 'Beyond Belief? A Critical Study of Graham Priest's *Beyond the Limits of Thought*', *Theoria* 87, 48–61.

Latta R. (1898), *Leibniz:* The Monadology *and other Philosophical Writings*, Oxford University Press.

Lear J. (1977), 'Sets and Semantics', *Journal of Philosophy* 74, 86–102.

(1979–80), 'Aristotelian Infinity', *Proceedings of the Aristotelian Society* 80, 187–210.

Lehrer K. (1990), *The Theory of Knowledge*, Routledge and Kegan Paul.

Leisenring A. C. (1969), *Mathematical Logic and Hilbert's ε-Symbol*, MacDonald and Co.

Lewis D. (1991), *Parts of Classes*, Basil Blackwell.

Löb M. H. (1955), 'Solution of a Problem of Leon Henkin', *Journal of Symbolic Logic* 20, 115–18.

Lopez D. (1998), *Elaborations on Emptiness*, Princeton University Press.

Łukasiewicz J. (1953), 'The Principle of Individuation', *Proceedings of the Aristotelian Society*, Supplementary Volume 27, 69–82.

—— (1971), 'On the Principle of Contradiction in Aristotle', *Review of Metaphysics* 24, 485–509.

Mackie J. (1982), *The Miracle of Theism*, Clarendon Press.

Maddy P. (1988), 'Proper Classes', *Journal of Symbolic Logic* 48, 113–39.

Marconi D. (1997), Review of *Beyond the Limits of Thought*, *Philosophical Review* 106, 620–2.

Martin G. (1955), *Kant's Metaphysics and Theory of Science*, Manchester University Press.

Martin R. L. (ed.) (1984), *Recent Essays on Truth and the Liar Paradox*, Oxford University Press.

Mayberry J. (1977), 'On the Consistency Problem for Set Theory: an Essay on the Cantorian Foundations of Classical Mathematics (I)', *British Journal for the Philosophy of Science* 28, 1–34.

McDowell J. (1973), *Plato*; Theaetetus, Clarendon Press.

—— (1976), 'Truth Conditions, Bivalence and Verificationism', ch. 3 of G. Evans and J. McDowell (eds.), *Truth and Meaning*, Cambridge University Press.

Mendelson E. (1997), Review of *Beyond the Limits of Thought*, *Mathematical Reviews* 97a:00014.

Meyer R. K. (1973), 'Intuitionism, Entailment, Negation', ch. 10 of H. Leblanc (ed.), *Truth, Syntax and Modality*, North Holland Publishing Co.

—— (1976), 'Relevant Arithmetic', *Bulletin of the Section of Logic, Polish Academy of Sciences* 5, 133–7.

—— (1987), 'God Exists!', *Noûs* 21, 345–61.

Meyer R. K. and Mortensen C. (1984), 'Inconsistent Models of Relevant Arithmetic', *Journal of Symbolic Logic* 49, 917–29.

Miller A. V. (trans.) (1969), *Hegel's Science of Logic*, Allen and Unwin.

Moore A. W. (1985), 'Set Theory, Skolem's Paradox and the *Tractatus*, *Analysis* 45, 13–20.

—— (1990), *The Infinite*, Routledge.

—— (1995), 'Getting above Ourselves', review of *Beyond the Limits of Thought*, *Times Literary Supplement*, 15 December 1995.

Murdoch J. E. (1968), 'On "Equality" of Infinities in the Middle Ages', *Actes du XIe Congrès International d'Histoire des Sciences*, Ossolineum.

—— (1981), 'Henry of Harclay and the Infinite', in A. Maieru and A. Paravicini-Bagliani (eds.), *Studi sul XIV seculo in memoria di Anneliese Maier*, Rome.

—— (1982), 'Infinity and Continuity' in N. Kretzmann, A. Kenny, and J. Pinborg (eds.), *The Cambridge History of Later Medieval Philosophy*, Cambridge University Press.

Murti T. R. V. (1955), *The Central Philosophy of Buddhism*, Allen and Unwin.

Nagel T. (1986), *The View from Nowhere*, Oxford University Press.

Nehamas A. (1985), *Nietzsche: Life as Literature*, Harvard University Press.

von Neumann J. (1925), '*Eine Axiomatisierung der Mengenlehre*', *Journal für die reine und angewandte Mathematik* 154, 219–40; reprinted in van Heijenoort (1967).

Norris C. (1987), *Derrida*, Fontana Press.

Orenstein A. (1977), *Williard van Orman Quine*, Twayne Publishers (G. K. Hall and Co.).

Parkinson G. H. (1973), *Leibniz: Philosophical Writings*, Dent and Sons.

Parsons C. (1971), 'Ontology and Mathematics', *Philosophical Review* 80, 151–76; reprinted as ch. 1 of (1983).

(1974a), 'Informal Axiomatization, Formalization, and the Concept of Truth', *Synthèse* 27, 27–47; reprinted as ch. 3 of (1983).

(1974b), 'Sets and Classes', *Noûs* 8, 1–12; reprinted as ch. 8 of (1983).

(1974c), 'The Liar Paradox', *Journal of Philosophical Logic* 3, 381–412; reprinted with an appendix in (1983) and Martin (1984).

(1977), 'What is the Iterative Conception of Set?' in R. E. Butts and J. Hintikka (eds.), *Logic, Foundations of Mathematics and Computability Theory*, Reidel; reprinted as ch. 10 of (1983).

(1983), *Mathematics in Philosophy*, Cornell University Press.

Passmore J. (1970), *Philosophical Reasoning* (second edition), Duckworth.

Peano G. (1906), 'Addition E', *Rivista di Mathematica* 8, 143–57.

Pears D. F. and McGuinness B. F. (trans.) (1961), *Tractatus Logico-Philosophicus*, Routledge and Kegan Paul.

Pitcher G. (1977), *Berkeley*, Routledge and Kegan Paul.

Platts M. (1979), *Ways of Meaning*, Routledge and Kegan Paul.

Pollock J. (1970), 'On Logicism', ch. 24 of E. D. Klemke (ed.), *Essays on Bertrand Russell*, University of Illinois Press.

(1986), *Contemporary Theories of Knowledge*, Rowman and Littlefield.

Popkin R. (1967), 'Skepticism', pp. 449–61, vol. 7 of Edwards (1967).

Prawitz D. (1965), *Natural Deduction: a Proof-Theoretic Study*, Almqvist and Wiksell.

Priest G. (1979a), 'Logic of Paradox', *Journal of Philosophical Logic* 8, 219–41.

(1979b), 'Indefinite Descriptions', *Logique et Analyse* 22, 5–21.

(1983), 'Logical Paradoxes and the Law of Excluded Middle', *Philosophical Quarterly* 33, 160–5.

(1984), 'Hypercontradictions', *Logique et Analyse* 107, 237–43.

(1987), *In Contradiction*, Kluwer Academic Publishers.

(1989a), 'Primary Properties are Secondary Properties too', *British Journal for the Philosophy of Science* 40, 29–37.

(1989b), 'Dialectic and Dialetheic', *Science and Society* 53, 388–415.

(1989c), 'Reasoning about Truth', *Artificial Intelligence* 39, 231–44.

(1990), 'Boolean Negation and All That', *Journal of Philosophical Logic* 19, 201–15.

(1991a), *The Nature of Philosophy and its Role in a University*, University of Queensland Press.

(1991b), 'Intensional Paradoxes', *Notre Dame Journal of Formal Logic* 32, 193–211.

(1991c), 'Minimally Inconsistent LP', *Studia Logica* 50, 321–31.

(1992), 'Russell's Schema and some Inconsistent Models', a paper read to a meeting of the Australasian Association for Logic in Canberra; abstracted in *Journal of Symbolic Logic* 58 (1993), 1481.

(1993), 'Another Disguise of the Same Fundamental Problems: Barwise and Etchemendy on the Liar', *Australasian Journal of Philosophy* 71, 60–9.

(1994a), 'Some Priorities of Berkeley', in B. J. Copeland (ed.), *Logic and Reality: Essays in Pure and Applied Logic in Memory of Arthur Prior*, Oxford University Press.

(1994b), 'Is Arithmetic Inconsistent?', *Mind 103*, 337–49.

(1994c), Review of V. McGee, *Truth, Vagueness, and Paradox*, *Mind* 103, 387–91.

(1997a), 'Yablo's Paradox', *Analysis* 57, 236–42.

(1997b), 'On a Paradox of Hilbert and Bernays', *Journal of Philosophical Logic* 26, 45–56.

(1998a), 'To Be *and* not To Be—that is the Answer: on Aristotle and the Law of Non-Contradiction', *Philosophiegeschichte und Logische Analyse* 1, 91–130.

(1998b), 'The Import of Inclosure: some Comments on Grattan-Guinness', *Mind* 107, 835–40.

(1999), 'A Defence of a Dialetheic Account of Negation', in D. Gabbay and H. Wansing (eds.), *What is Negation?*, Kluwer Academic Publishers.

(2000a), 'Truth and Contradiction', *Philosophical Quarterly* 50, 305–19.

(2000b), 'On the Principle of Uniform Solution: a Reply to Smith', *Mind* 109, 123–6.

(2000c), 'Objects of Thought', *Australasian Journal of Philosophy* 78, 494–502.

(2000d), 'Inconsistent Models of Arithmetic, Part II: the General Case', *Journal of Symbolic Logic* 65, 1519–29.

(2001a), 'Why it's Irrational to Believe in Consistency', in B. Brogard and B. Smith (eds.), *Rationality and Irrationality: Proceedings of the 23rd International Wittgenstein Conference* öbvahpt.

(2001b), 'Paraconsistent Belief Revision', *Theoria* 67, 214–228.

(forthcoming a), 'Inconsistency and the Empirical Sciences', in J. Meheus (ed.), *Inconsistency and the History of Science*, Kluwer Academic Publishers.

(forthcoming b), 'On Alternative Geometries, Arithmetics and Logics' in the proceedings of the conference *Łukasiewicz in Dublin*, 1995.

(forthcoming c), 'Where is Philosophy at the Start of the Twenty First Century?' *Proceedings of the Aristotelian Society*.

Priest G. and Crosthwaite J. (1989), 'Relevance, Truth and Meaning', ch. 23 of J. Norman and R. Sylvan (eds.), *Directions in Relevant Logic*, Kluwer Academic Publishers.

Priest G., Routley R., and Norman J. (1989), *Paraconsistent Logic*, Philosophia Verlag.

Prior A. N. (1955), 'Berkeley in Logical Form', *Theoria* 21, 117–22; reprinted in Prior's *Papers in Logic and Ethics*, Duckworth, 1976.

(1961), 'On A Family of Paradoxes', *Notre Dame Journal of Formal Logic* 2, 16–32.

Quine W. V. O. (1951), 'Two Dogmas of Empiricism', *Philosophical Review* 60, 20–43; reprinted in *From a Logical Point of View*, Harvard University Press, 1953.

(1959), 'Meaning and Translation', in R. Brower (ed.), *On Translation*, Harvard University Press.

(1960), *Word and Object*, Massachusetts Institute of Technology Press.

(1963), *Set Theory and its Logic*, Harvard University Press.

(1969), *Ontological Relativity and Other Essays*, Columbia University Press.

(1970), *Philosophy of Logic*, Prentice-Hall.

(1975), 'On Empirically Equivalent Systems of the World', *Erkenntnis* 9, 313–28.

(1981), 'On the Very Idea of a Third Dogma', ch. 4 of *Theories and Things*, the Belknap Press of Harvard University Press.

Ramsey F. P. (1925), 'The Foundations of Mathematics', *Proceedings of the London Mathematics Society* 25, 338–84; reprinted in D. H. Mellor (ed.), *Foundations: Essays in Philosophy, Logic, Mathematics and Economics*, Routledge and Kegan Paul, 1978.

Resnik M. (1988), 'Second-order Logic Still Wild', *Journal of Philosophy* 85, 75–87.

Resnik M. and Kushner, D. (1987), 'Explanation, Independence and Realism in Mathematics', *British Journal for the Philosophy of Science* 38, 141–58.

Restall G. (1992), 'A Note on Naive Set Theory in LP', *Notre Dame Journal of Formal Logic* 33, 422–32.

(1996), 'The Inclosure Argument', Review of *Beyond the Limits of Thought, Metascience* 10, 130–4.

Richard J. (1905), 'The Principles of Mathematics and the Problem of Sets', in van Heijenoort (1967).

Robinson A. (1966), *Non-Standard Analysis*, North Holland Publishing Co.

Robinson H. M. (1974), 'Prime Matter in Aristotle', *Phronesis* 19, 168–88.

Robinson R. (1957), 'Some Logical Aspects of Nāgārjuna's System', *Philosophy East and West* 6, 291–308.

(1972), 'Did Nāgārjuna Really Refute all Philosophical Views?', *Philosophy East and West* 22, 325–31.

Ross W. D. (1936), *Aristotle's Physics*, Clarendon Press.

Routley R. (1980), *Meinong's Jungle and Beyond*, Research School of Social Sciences, Australian National University.

Russell B. (1903), *Principles of Mathematics*, Allen and Unwin.

(1905), 'On Some Difficulties in the Theory of Transfinite Numbers and Order Types', *Proceedings of the London Mathematical Society* (series 2) 4, 29–53; reprinted in (1973).

(1906), '*Les Paradoxes de la Logique*', *Revue de Metaphysique et Morale* 14, 627–50; reprinted as 'On "Insolubilia" and their Solution by Symbolic Logic' in (1973).

(1908), 'Mathematical Logic as Based on the Theory of Types', *American Journal of Mathematics* 30, 222–62; reprinted in (1973) and van Heijenoort (1967).

(1913), 'Theory of Knowledge', in E. Eames and K. Blackwell (eds.), *Collected Papers of Bertrand Russell*, vol. 7, Allen and Unwin, 1984.

(1926), *Our Knowledge of the External World*, revised edition, Allen and Unwin.

(1973), *Essays in Analysis* (ed. D. Lackey), Allen and Unwin.

Ryle G. (1990), 'Logical Atomism in Plato's Theaetetus', *Phronesis* 35, 21–46.

Sainsbury R. M. (1988), *Paradoxes*, Cambridge University Press.

Searle J. R. (1987), 'Indeterminacy, Empiricism, and the First Person', *Journal of Philosophy* 84, 123–46.

Siderits M. (1989), 'Thinking on Empty: Madhyamaka Anti-Realism and Canons of Rationality', pp. 231–49 of S. Biderman and B.-A. Scharfstein (eds.), *Rationality in Question: on Eastern and Western Views of Rationality*, Brill.

Slater B. H. (1992), 'Thought Unlimited', *Mind* 101, 347–53.

Slezak P. (1983), 'Descartes's Diagonal Deduction', *Philosophy of Science* 34, 13–16.

Smiley T. J. (1993), 'Can Contradictions be True, I', *Proceedings of the Aristotelian Society*, Supplementary Volume 67, 17–33.

Smith N. (2000), 'The Principle of Uniform Solution (of the Paradoxes of Self-Reference)', *Mind* 109, 117–22.

Solmson F. (1958), 'Aristotle and Prime Matter: a Reply to Hugh R. King', *Journal of the History of Ideas* 19, 243–52.

Sorabji R. (1983), *Time, Creation and the Continuum*, Duckworth.

(1988), *Matter, Space and Motion*, Duckworth.

Sprung M. (1979), *Lucid Exposition of the Middle Way: the Essential Chapters from the Prasannapadā of Candrakīrti*, Routledge and Kegan Paul.

Stace W. T. (1961), *Mysticism and Philosophy*, Macmillan.

Staten H. (1984), *Wittgenstein and Derrida*, University of Nebraska Press.

Stcherbatsky Th. (trans.), (1978) *Madhyānta-Vibhanga: Discourse on Discrimination between Middle and Extremes*, Oriental Books Corporation.

Steiner M. (1978), 'Mathematical Explanation', *Philosophical Studies* 34, 135–51.

Stenius E. (1960), *Wittgenstein's* Tractatus: *a Critical Exposition of its Main Lines of Thought*, Basil Blackwell.

Stough C. L. (1969), *Greek Skepticism: a Study in Epistemology*, University of California Press.

Sylvan R. (2000), 'A Preliminary Western History of Sociative Logics', ch. 5 of D. Hyde and G. Priest (eds.), *Sociative Logics and their Applications: Essays by the Late Richard Sylvan*, Ashgate.

Tait W. W. (1986), 'Wittgenstein on the "Skeptical Paradoxes"', *Journal of Philosophy* 83, 475–88.

Tarski A. (1936), '*Der Wahrheitsbegriff in den formalisierten Sprachen*', *Studia Philosophia* 1, 261–405; reprinted in English in *Logic, Semantics and Metamathematics*, Oxford University Press, 1956.

Taylor C. (1975), *Hegel*, Cambridge University Press.

Taylor R. (1955), 'Spatial and Temporal Analogies and the Concept of Identity', *Journal of Philosophy* 52, 599–612; reprinted in J. J. C. Smart (ed.), *Problems in Space and Time*, Collier-Macmillan, 1964.

Tennant N. (1998), 'Critical Notice of *Beyond the Limits of Thought*', *Philosophical Books* 39, 20–38.

(1999), 'Negation, Absurdity and Contrariety', pp. 199-222 of D. Gabbay and H. Wansing (eds.), *What is Negation?*, Kluwer Academic Publishers.

Thomson J. F. (1956), Review of G. J. Warnock, *Berkeley*, *Mind* 85, 95–101.

Thurman R. A. (1976), The Holy Teachings of *Vimalakīrti: a Mahāyana Scripture*, Pennsylvania State University Press.

Tillemans T. (1999), 'Is Nāgarjuna's Logic Deviant or Non-Classical?', in T. Tillemans, *Language, Logic and Scripture*, Wisdom Publications.

Tipton I. C. (1974), *Berkeley: the Philosophy of Immaterialism*, Methuen.

Todd R. B. (1980), 'Some Concepts in Physical Theory in John Philoponus' Aristotelian Commentaries', *Archiv für Begriffgeschichte* 24, 151–70.

Vlastos G. (1967), 'Zeno of Elea', pp. 369–78, vol. 8 of Edwards (1967).

Wallace W. (trans.) (1975), *Hegel's Logic; being Part One of the Encyclopaedia of the Philosophical Sciences*, Oxford University Press.

Weir A. (1999), Review of *Beyond the Limits of Thought*, *Philosophical Quarterly* 49, 122–5.

Werhane P. (1987), 'Some Paradoxes in Kripke's Interpretation of Wittgenstein', *Synthèse* 73, 253–73.

Whitehead A. and Russell B. (1910), *Principia Mathematica*, vol. 1, Cambridge University Press; second edition, 1927.

Wiggins D. (1984), 'The Sense and Reference of Predicates: a Running Repair to Frege's Doctrine and a Plea for the Copula', *Philosophical Quarterly* 34, 311–28; reprinted as pp. 126–43 of C. Wright (ed.), *Frege: Tradition and Influence*, Basil Blackwell, 1984.

Williamson T. (1996), Review of *Beyond the Limits of Thought*, *British Journal for the Philosophy of Science* 47 (1996), 331–4.

Wisdom J. O. (1953), *The Unconscious Origins of Berkeley's Philosophy*, Hogarth Press.

Wittgenstein L. (1953), *Philosophical Investigations*, Basil Blackwell.

(1975), *Philosophical Remarks*, Basil Blackwell.

Wolff P. R. (1963), *Kant's Theory of Mental Activity*, Harvard University Press.

Wood D. (1980), 'Derrida and the Paradoxes of Reflection', *Journal of the British Society for Phenomenology* 11, 225–38.

Wood T. (1994), *Nāgārjunian Disputations: a Philosophical Journey through an Indian Looking-Glass*, Monographs of the Society for Asian and Comparative Philosophy, no. 11, University of Hawai'i Press.

Zalta E. (1983), *Abstract Objects: an Introduction to Axiomatic Metaphysics*, Kluwer Academic Publishers.

(forthcoming), 'In Defence of the Law of Non-Contradiction'.

Zermelo E. (1908), '*Untersuchungen über die Grundlagen der Mengenlehre* I', *Mathematische Annalen* 59, 261–81; reprinted in van Heijenoort (1967).

Index

Made in the USA
Middletown, DE
16 March 2020